Key Correctional Issues

Roslyn Muraskin

C. W. Post Campus of Long Island University

PEARSON

Prentice
Hall

Upper Saddle River, New Jersey 07458

Library of Congress Cataloging-in-Publication Data

Key correctional issues / [edited by] Roslyn Muraskin.
    p. cm.
Includes bibliographical references.
    ISBN 0-13-035861-4
1. Corrections–United States.   I. Muraskin, Roslyn.

HV9471.K49 2005
365'.973—dc22

2003026377

Publisher: Stephen Helba
Executive Editor: Frank Mortimer, Jr.
Assistant Editor: Sarah Holle
Production Editor: John Shannon, Pine Tree Composition, Inc.
Production Liaison: Barbara Marttine Cappuccio
Director of Manufacturing and Production: Bruce Johnson
Managing Editor: Mary Carnis
Manufacturing Buyer: Cathleen Petersen

Creative Director: Cheryl Asherman
Cover Design Coordinator: Miguel Ortiz
Cover Designer: Ruta Fiorino
Cover Image: Najlan Feanny-Hicks, CORBIS SABA
Editorial Assistant: Barbara Rosenberg
Marketing Manager: Tim Peyton
Formatting and Interior Design: Pine Tree Composition, Inc.
Printing and Binding: Phoenix Color Corp

> Dedicated to the four greatest grandchildren,
> Lindsay, Nickia, Benjamin, & Zachary,
> And to my husband,
> Matthew
> my "lifeline,"
> and to
> all the contributors,
> who were patient and committed to this project

Pearson Education LTD.
Pearson Education Singapore, Pte. Ltd
Pearson Education Canada, Ltd
Pearson Education—Japan

Pearson Education Australia PTY, Limited
Pearson Educaçion de Mexico, S.A. de C.V.
Pearson Education Malaysia, Pte. Ltd

10 9 8 7 6 5 4 3
ISBN 0-13-035861-4

Contents

Preface

This work is not your typical correctional text. It is neither a text written by one author nor primarily a reader, but rather it is a combination. It highlights those issues relevant to the study of corrections and does so in a fashion that is not tedious to read.

Corrections continues to be a relevant part of the American criminal justice system. It is a complex system fragmented by many programs, agencies, and laws that govern both on the federal and local levels. Many of the facilities as they now exist are overcrowded and barbaric to an extent and have varying philosophies depending on who is in charge. Do we have correctional facilities to punish, to rehabilitate, to do both or neither? Is the death penalty fair and just? Are all residents of the correctional facilities treated equally or on a par with each other? Should they be?

If prisons are to rehabilitate, then why do we have continued recidivism? Why are the sentences in this country longer than any other? and for what purpose? The public seems to know little about the correctional facilities other than the fact that this is where we send *bad* people. Yet from a budgetary point of view, corrections is a low-priority item. Are prisoners entitled to rights, and if so, which rights?

Our sentencing process is complex. If we assume that we are to punish *all* who break the law, why then is it not done on an equal basis? Accordingly, "to begin at the elementary beginning, we have an almost entire absence in the United States of legislative determinations—of 'law'—governing the basic questions as to the purposes and justifications of criminal sanctions. Without binding guides on such questions, it is inevitable that individual sentences will strike out on a multiplicity of courses chosen by each decision maker. . . . The result [can] be chaos" (Krantz, 1983, pp. 7–8). This material, written over twenty years ago, has not changed what goes on today.

Historically, the courts held that a prisoner had the status of "slave of the state" with no rights (*Ruffin v. Commonwealth*, 62 Va. (21 Gratt.) 790, 796, [1871], as found in Krantz, *Corrections and Prisoners' Rights: In a Nutshell,* 1983). There existed a philosophy of "hands off." Members of the judiciary believed that once an individual was sentence, it fell to the correctional officers to direct the activities of the inmates and determine the conditions of confinement. That philosophy ended when the courts recognized the atrocities that were present in the correctional facilities.

This text explains relationships that exist in corrections from both a historical and a twenty-first-century point of view. It discusses correctional issues, such as prisoner reentry, changing goals of corrections, suicide, religion, mentally disordered inmates, technocorrections, constitutional rights of prisoners, alternatives to incarceration, as well as the concerns of minority prisoners and the death penalty. *Key Correctional Issues* links important issues that present a reference point and allow for further discussion.

To all those who contributed to this text, my heartfelt thanks. Each has their own area of expertise, and therefore bring to the forefront ideas that are fresh and exciting.

I would like to thank the following reviewers: Prabha Urnithan, Colorado State University; Barbara Belbot, University of Texas—Downtown; Sam Torres, California State University—Long Beach; and Maldine B. Bailey, Charleston Southern University.

Many thanks to all my editors at Prentice Hall, including Sarah Holle, who is very dedicated and works so hard with each of her authors. Special thanks to Frank Mortimer, editor, who has been extremely patient with me while developing this text.

Roslyn Muraskin, Ph.D
Long Island University

About the Editor

Dr. Roslyn Muraskin received her Ph.D. in criminal justice from the Graduate Center of the City University of New York. Her Masters' degree is from New York University, School of Government, and her B.A. degree is from Queens College, where she majored in Political Science—Speech. She is a Full Professor at the C.W. Post of Long Island University, where she teaches criminal justice. She was an Associate Dean in the College of Management for nine years and now directs the activities of the Long Island Women's Institute, College of Management, as well as the activities of the Alumni Chapter, also for the College of Management. She currently holds the position of Trustee of Region One for the Academy of Criminal Justice Sciences. She is a past President of the Northeast Association of Criminal Justice Sciences (NEACJS).

Her works include *Visions for Change: Crime and Justice in the Twenty-First Century* (Prentice Hall, 4th edition, forthcoming); *It's a Crime: Women and Justice* (Prentice Hall, now in its 3rd edition); and *Morality and the Law* (Prentice Hall). She is the Women's Series editor for Prentice Hall as well as the editor of the refereed journal published quarterly, *A Critical Journal of Crime Law and Society*, published by Routledge, Taylor & Francis Group (formerly *The Justice Professional*). She is the author of many published papers and articles and is often quoted in the media as an expert in women's issues and issues of criminal justice.

She is the recipient of many awards, including Woman of the Year, Award for Excellence from the Minorities Section of ACJS, and the Fellow Award from the NEACJS. She has been honored for her work with AIDS education by the Long Island Association for AIDS Care.

This work represents Dr. Muraskin's tenth text in the field of criminal justice.

Contributing Authors

Dale J. Ardovini-Brooker is a doctoral student in the College of Criminal Justice at Sam Houston State University.

Beth Bjerregaard, Ph.D., is an Associate Professor in the Department of Criminal Justice with the University of North Carolina at Charlotte. She received her Ph.D. in Criminal Justice from the State University at Albany.

Scott Blough is an Administrator with the Bureau of Adult Detention at the Ohio Department of Rehabilitation and Corrections, Columbus, Ohio.

Alan S. Bruce received his Ph.D. in sociology from Bowling Green State University, Ohio, and is an Assistant Professor of Criminal Justice and Sociology at Quinnipiac University in Hamden, Connecticut.

Todd R. Clear, Ph.D., is a Distinguished Professor at John Jay College of Criminal Justice, City University of New York. His Ph.D. in criminal justice is from The University at Albany.

Neal A. Elover, M.Ed., received his degree in criminal justice from Coppin State College. He is a freelance criminal justice legal researcher specializing in criminal law, correctional law, juvenile justice, and criminal constitutional law.

Karen Fein, Ph.D., is with The Richard Stockton College of New Jersey, in the School of Behavioral Sciences.

Sondra J. Fogel, Ph.D., is with the School of Social Work at the University of South Florida, Tampa, Florida. She received her M.S.W. from Columbia University and her Ph.D. from the University of Illinois at Urbana–Champaign.

Keith N. Haley, Ph.D., is Dean and Associate Vice-President of the School of Off-Campus Learning, Tiffin University, Tiffin Ohio.

Janice Joseph, Ph.D., is a professor of the Criminal Justice Program at Richard Stockton College of New Jersey. She received her Ph.D. from York University in Toronto, Canada.

Kate King received her Ph.D. in criminal justice from the State University at Albany. She is an Associate Professor of Criminal Justice Administration at Boise State University.

Katrina Miller, Ph.D. is a former corrections professional who has worked extensively with offenders who are deaf. She completed her doctorate degree in deaf education at

Lamar University in Beaumont, Texas. She is currently an assistant research professor at the University of Arkansas Rehabilitation Research and Training Center for Persons Who Are Deaf or Hard of Hearing.

Theresa A. Severance received her Ph.D. in sociology from Bowling Green State University, Ohio, and is an Assistant Professor of Sociology at Eastern Connecticut State University.

Rupendra Simlot, Ph.D., is an Assistant Professor of Criminal Justice at Richard Stockton College of Criminal Justice. He received his Ph.D. in Physical-Organic Chemistry from the University of Rajasthan and an M.B.A. in International Management from the University of Rhode Island.

Kathleen Simon, Ph.D., is a faculty member at the Appalachian State University in the Department of Political Science and Criminal Justice.

M. Dwayne Smith, Ph.D., is Professor and Chair of the Department of Criminology at the University of South Florida, Tampa, Florida. He received his B.S. and M.A. degrees from the University of Houston and a Ph.D. from Duke University.

Ruth Ann Strickland is a faculty member at Appalachian State University, Boone, North Carolina, in the Department of Political Science and Criminal Justice.

Melvina Sumter, Ph.D., is an Assistant Professor at Old Dominion University, College of Arts and Letters, in the Department of Criminal Justice in Norfolk, Virginia. She received her doctorate from Florida State University.

Key Sun, Ph.D., is an assistant professor of Law and Justice at Central Washington University, Lakewood, Washington. He received his Ph.D. in psychology and M.A. in criminal justice from Rutgers University and his M.S.W. from the University of Illinois at Urbana–Champaign.

Christine Tartaro, Ph.D., is a faculty member with the Richard Stockton College of Criminal Justice.

Jeremy Travis, Ph.D., is a Senior Fellow at The Urban Institute, Justice Policy Center.

Donna M. Vandiver, Ph.D., is an assistant professor teaching criminal justice at Illinois State University.

part I

Introductory Remarks

The Correctional Key: In/Out

Lock 'em Up and Throw Away the Key

Roslyn Muraskin

INTRODUCTORY REMARKS: IN OR OUT?

Incarceration punishes those individuals who have violated the law. Depending on the level of the crime committed, the punishment can be lengthy. The legislators dictate the length of sentence or at least its range. *Bad people* are locked up, according to the media as well as Hollywood, which enjoys depicting the "excitement" of crime. What knowledge *John Q. Public* has regarding crime emanates from the media and Hollywood productions. The majority of the population has little understanding of what goes on behind the locked gates; people prefer to think of correctional facilities as places in which to lock up the "bad guys/gals" and throw away the key. Rehabilitation and sentencing alternatives are not uppermost in the mind of the average U.S. citizen. How many "good" people have ever visited a correctional facility?

"You have the right to remain silent. Anything you say may be used against you in a court of law. You have the right to an attorney. If you cannot afford one, one will be appointed for you." Words to that effect are given to all criminal defendants who are arrested, regardless of the charge, and who are in custodial care. After trial/plea they find themselves locked up, usually in a correctional facility. What does it mean to be locked up, and will being locked up do any good? Surely, those individuals who serve time must be bad people, or else why would they be incarcerated?[1] Many of these same individuals will be released ultimately, and then what? We are the only Western civilization to execute our criminals, and we mete out the longest sentences anywhere. Why? What kind of stereotypes do we hold about prisons and their occupants?

What is corrections all about? What purpose does corrections serve, if any? How many citizens have actually been to prison to see what goes on inside? And if they did go in, would they be satisfied with what does occur? How many of us truly understand the environment of a jail/prison facility? Do correctional officers, probation officers, and parole officers work together? When individuals read news stories, view them on television, and hear headlines on the radio, what is their reaction? The individual described in the second of the following news stories (who robbed someone at a gas station and killed him in cold blood) was executed by lethal injection; is this cause for happiness and cheers on the part of the average citizen? Is such punishment acceptable?

There are headlines such as the following:

June 12, 2003
After 17 Years in Prison for Rape, Murder, **Convictions Reversed** *(Newsday, Long Island)*

Three men who spent 17 years in prison for the 1984 rape and murder of a 16 year old Lynbrook girl were freed yesterday after a judge set aside their convictions based on DNA evidence showing that semen inside the victim belonged to none of them.

"I have been in hell for 18 years" [one of those released stated]. . . . he embraced his four children and one grandchild. "Now maybe this will be my heaven . . . I have waited so long for this day." (Toppin and Lam, June 12, 2003, p. A3)

There are so many unanswerable questions. What if capital punishment had been the law in 1985, when [the three defendants were charged in] the rape and murder of the 16 year old girl? What if they had been found guilty of capital murder? How would that girl's death have been vindicated by the execution of three innocent men? (Vitello, June 12, 2003, p. A3)

October 24, 2002
Missouri Inmate Put to Death (Associated Press)

A man convicted of robbing a teenage gas station clerk and shooting him in the back of the head as he lay on the ground was executed early Wednesday.

Stephen K. Johns, 55, was pronounced dead at 12:03 am at the Potosi Correctional Center, two minutes after the first of three lethal doses was administered, state Department of Corrections spokesman John Fougere said. His fate was sealed late Tuesday when the Missouri Supreme Court, the U.S. Supreme Court and Governor, Bob Holden refused to halt the execution. Missouri's seventh this year and the state's 53rd since it resumed capital punishment in 1989.

A jury in St. Louis found Johns guilty of shooting 17 year-old Donald D. Voepel three times in the back of the head at close range after a robbery that netted $248.00. Voepel wasn't even supposed to work the night of February 18, 1982; a co-worker had a date and Voepel agreed to cover his shift.

In an interview Tuesday, Johns continued to maintain his innocence, insisting he has never been to the gas station where Voepel was killed.

"I didn't even know it was there," Johns said. He has been on death row since being sentenced in January 1983. It was the second longest stint on death row in Missouri History. (The Corrections Connection—Today on Corrections 10/24/01, p. 1)

Was justice served in these two cases? In order to comprehend why billions of dollars are spent in the field of corrections, we need to understand what goes on in these facilities and the purposes they serve. The kinds of monies spent in corrections are astronomical as compared with the monies spent on prevention and education. It has been suggested that members of the public should be invited into correctional facilities to better understand what they are about. Viewing correctional facilities on television or in movies does not contribute to the public's understanding of corrections.

A stereotype exists about inmates. Traditionally, corrections is an area closed to the outside world; there is little understanding of such facilities. The feeling of those "in the know" is that these facilities are not for all inmates. There are programs such as probation, alternatives to sentencing, parole, and other community programs that would fit the needs of many inmates today.

The Delaware Department of Corrections Office of Community Relations separated its offices from that of the general media. The reason for this move was that "needs of the community and the needs of the media were so great, it was too much for one person" (Minor, 2001, p. 6). This present office is able to answer all queries about what happens within the Delaware correctional facilities. The public is better informed about the facilities because of the visibility of correctional facilities. As the need for further legislation appears, there exists a better understanding of the needs and missions of correctional facilities, and recommended legislation becomes readily accepted.

In other parts of the country, the field of community corrections, such as in Delaware, makes "partnering with local law enforcement, probation and parole officers . . . more visible, but they also have the ability to witness first-hand the impact they have on the community" (Minor, p. 4). According to Roselyn Powell, Judicial Division Chief for Division Three of the North Carolina Department of Corrections "the importance of [working together] is that ability of the probation officer or community corrections as an agency to actually see the benefit in reducing crime and taking the most violent offenders off the streets" (Minor, p. 5). Accordingly, when violence occurs and door-to-door searches are necessary, the public understanding of the criminal justice system and its various agencies decreases the negativity normally associated with such situations and allows the system to work more smoothly.

According to the Vermont Department of Corrections, it has become committed to the idea of *restorative justice,* whereby in certain low-level crimes and offenses "offenders help restore the community and the victims they have damaged rather than sit behind bars" (Gaseau, 2001a, pp. 1–5). Is restorative justice a "better" form of justice?

In order to get the process of restorative justice rolling, "community members must also be invested in seeing that harm is repaired. A major part of this is training the citizenry on how to work together to achieve the desired result of restoring the damage" (Gaseau, pp. 1–2).

"One way that citizens participate in the process is on reparative probation panels. Citizens from a community volunteer to hear cases, work with the victim, and the offender and create a mutually agreeable way to repair the harm done" (Gaseau, pp. 1–2).

"[Where] the more traditional system looks at the violation, the sanction focuses on the offender, restorative justice looks at the harm done, the damage, how do we fix it, and who is responsible for the various activities that are going to take place" (Gaseau, pp. 1–2).

Restorative justice requires not simply one program but a continuation of programs. Part of the restoration process is a "community-based mediation process" (Gaseau, p. 4).

Under the traditional system of punishment, the perpetrator goes away to serve time; in restorative justice, the damage done, how to correct the damage, and who is responsible for the damage are considered carefully, and this perpetrator is designated to correct the damage. Restorative justice is a process somewhat analogous to a negotiated contract. A proper settlement is negotiated, establishing a "sentence" without having to throw away the key.

The state of Vermont established a program of family group counseling directed at delinquent youth. This is based on a program called *Real Justice*. "This group involves the offenders and his/her support group, the victim and his/her support group and other members of the community such as school officials and others depending on the incident" (Gaseau, 2001a, p. 3). According to Gaseau, "The key difference between conferencing and reparative panels is the members of the group are constantly different. Also, where a reparative board works with cases such as low level property damage and misdemeanors, a community conference is more appropriate for school based incidents that might traditionally have been handled by the local police department" (Gaseau, 2001a, p. 3).

Restorative justice is an approach that incorporates many other models. One other approach is the process of mediation. This becomes an appropriate course of action when the affected parties need a clearer understanding of what occurred and why. This process is in its early stages and is helping communities understand possible alternatives to sentencing into correctional facilities.

In the state of Washington, correctional officials believe that through strengthening ties among corrections staff, a support system will be built thereby solidifying the relationship between the offender and the community. What many citizens forget is that correctional offices are also "locked up" and need to be continually trained as well as supervised in order to perform properly (Gaseau, 2001b, pp. 1–2).

Part of the correctional process in Washington is the need for continual training among staff. The Department of Corrections, through its basic training program, undertakes to improve relationships among its staff. Collegial relationships among staff are an important undertaking in correctional facilities. A built-in peer support system is imperative for new employees as they enter the field of corrections. Training of those entering the field of corrections is more than just being hired to do the job; these individuals must do the job correctly. In essence they are locked up with the inmates for a long period of time, and they must be ready to act and react in all kinds of situations.

Health-Related Problems

Correction officers must be ready to work under all kinds of situations, including working with an inmate population that may have infectious diseases. Improving the health of the correctional population is of prime concern to both those who work inside the correctional facilities and to the community at large. When inmates are released back into the general population, as the majority are, there continue to be concerns regarding health.

A review of cases in Wisconsin found that "Wisconsin's super maximum prison in Boscobel [was] even more inhumane than originally claimed" (June 29, 2001). "The shocking neglect of prisoners in need of medical attention, an increasing bedlam of mentally ill prisoners, and the frequent and repeated use of electroshock weapons on human beings [were] among the violations of rights the plaintiffs [sought] to halt. The class action complaint, which [amended] an earlier filing by individual prisoners, [stated] that medical, mental and dental care at the Super Maximum Correctional Institutions [was] wholly inadequate" (Gaseau, 2001B, p. 1). The citizens of Wisconsin viewed such conditions as subjecting prisoners, "most of whom will be released one day, to a callous, brutal and unnecessary regiment." (pp. 1–2)

An accusation has been made that healthy prisoners develop mental illness while incarcerated due to serious health neglect.

New ACLU Lawsuit Details Horrors at Wisconsin "Supermax" Prison

Wisconsin's super maximum prison in Boscobel is even more inhumane than originally claimed, according to an amended class action lawsuit filed today in Madison by the American Civil Liberties Union of Wisconsin and a group of concerned attorneys.

The shocking neglect of prisoners in need of medical attention, an increasing bedlam of mentally ill prisoners, and the frequent and repeated use of electroshock weapons on human beings are among the violations of rights the plaintiffs seek to halt.

"Today, we hope to shed light on an extraordinary institution. The 'Supermax' is more of an experiment of sensory deprivation than a prison," said E. Garvey, lead counsel of the group of lawyers representing the prisoners at the "Supermax." It is incredible that neither the media or Amnesty International have been allowed access to the "Supermax" to see the conditions there. . . .

. . . [t]he Department of Corrections is ultimately putting the safety of Wisconsin's citizens at risk by subjecting the prisoners, most of whom will be released one day, to a callous, brutal, and unnecessary regimen.

The class action complaint . . . states that the medical, mental health and dental care at the Super Maximum Correctional Institutional (SCMCL) are wholly inadequate.

The "Supermax" in Wisconsin lacks the medical staff and other resources to properly care for the serious medical needs of chronically ill prisoners. . . . the amended complaint [stated] that a prisoner who suffers from terminal stomach cancer [had] lost 56 pounds since his transfer to the facility. The prisoner requires catheterization in order to urinate and must take a strong pain medication, up to once every three hours, to control the pain caused by the disease.

The prisoner often receives his medication at incorrect times, with the result that he suffers severe pain and on one occasion no one came to catheterize him.

Mental illness is endemic at "Supermax" . . .

The conditions in this place make it an incubator of psychosis. Previous healthy prisoners become mentally ill as a result of confinement under these conditions.

According to the complaint, numerous prisoners at the "Supermax" hear voices and are obsessed with suicidal thoughts, smear feces, swallow metal objects, cut their flesh, attempt suicide by drug overdose, attempt to hang themselves, and otherwise attempt to harm or kill themselves.

. . . excessive use of force is an everyday occurrence at the facility. Staff . . . shock prisoners with electroshock weapons that emit a powerful and painful electric shock, often leaving burning marks on their skin.

In one instance, a prisoner with a chronic mental health problem was stunned 10–15 times because he covered his cell's video camera and would not comply with an order to remove the covering from the camera. After being stunned, the prisoner was refused treatment by a nurse for the pain caused by the stun weapon. (ACLU Press Release, June 29, 2001, *www.aclu.org/news/2001/n06290a.html*, 10/24/01)

What rights do prisoners have? The state of Florida has removed all computers and typewriters in prison law libraries, meaning that some prisoners will have to draw up legal appeals in longhand. It appears that whatever can be done in the state of Florida is being done to make it tougher for "inmates to challenge their convictions, sentences and prison conditions" (ACLU 6/22/01 "Florida Inmates Lose Typewriters, Computers," *www.aclu.org/news/2001/w062201a.html*). Many correctional facilities, including the *new generation facilities,* allow inmates the use of computers, with typewriters seemingly a thing of the past. According to the American Civil Liberties Union (ACLU),

With 71,000 inmates, Florida has the fifth-largest prison system in the nation, behind California, Texas, the federal government and New York. Florida has executed 51 inmates since 1979, trailing only Texas and Virginia and have [over] 370 people on death row.

The Institute has received two dozen complaints from inmates who believe their legal motions will be treated less seriously if they are not typed (a reasonable fear).

Law libraries in four Florida prisons do still have computers available to inmates to research legal materials stored on CD-ROMs, but they cannot be used as word processors. (ACLU, 10/24/01)

According to the ACLU, there is a growing dissatisfaction with the current state of the criminal justice system ("New Poll Shows Surprisingly Forgiving Attitude toward Crime and Punishment: Most Americans Don't Want to Throw Away the Key," *www.aclu.org/features/f971901a.html*). There appears to be an emerging feeling that rehabilitation and alternative punishment for nonviolent offenders is the way to go. According to the ACLU,

Contrary to popular belief, punishment and retribution are not foremost in most American minds. . . . our nation [seems] to be far more concerned with rehabilitation and social reintegration than with throwing away the proverbial key.

Of particular interest are the encouraging public attitudes about drugs and drug crimes. . . . a majority of Americans draw sharp distinctions between trafficking in illicit narcotics and other drug offenses. While a majority believes that drug dealers should always be sent to prison, far fewer agree that users . . . , minor possessors . . . , or buyers . . . , should always be locked up.

[According to Nadine Strossen, President of the ACLU,] a majority of Americans have come to realize that we cannot incarcerate our way out of the drug problem. [There is a] glaring spotlight on the misdirection of the drug war over the last two decades.

The public's recognition of the misdirection of the drug war and the race to incarcerate in America . . . is also reflected in the finding that a majority of Americans oppose mandatory sentences that require an automatic sentence for non-violent crimes.

Federal and state policies do not reflect the popular attitude among Americans brought out in the main findings. . . . Specifically . . . lawmakers and prosecutors should start to take into account the fact that a majority of Americans support alternative punishments for non-violent offenders, believe that rehabilitation is an important goal for the courts and prisons, and are strongly dissatisfied with the current state of the criminal justice system. (ACLU, "New Poll")

Organizations such as the ACLU are questioning whether Americans have a lock-'em-up mentality and a desire to throw away the key. Politicians truly believe that placing more and more people behind bars will bring them votes to get elected.

"When inmates are freed, the American public wants to see productive and well-adjusted members of society, not seasoned graduates for Hardened Criminals" (New Polls, etc., p. 2, July 19, 2001).

Prominent in the polling results is surprising support for and emphasis on rehabilitation for non-violent offenders. . . . six in ten Americans believe that it is possible to rehabilitate a non violent offender; four in ten believe the main purpose of prison is rehabilitation, rather than deterrence, punishment, or the protection of society.

[There appears to be] strong public support for changing the current laws so that fewer non-violent offenses are punishable by prison. . . . Americans [show] enthusiasm for alternatives for non-violent offenders such as mandatory education and job training . . . , compensation to victims . . . and community service. . . .

[There is very strong] support for providing inmates with skills training in prison . . .

In many states, more money is spent on locking up non-violent offenders than on higher education. . . . prison cannot be the be-all-and-end-all of American justice.

There is no talk of leniency toward crime, but rather that the punishment should fit the crime. Prison is not the only answer for nonviolent crime. Only a minority of Americans believe that punishment or deterrence is the main role of the prisons and courts. *Rehabilitation* is a word that is tossed back and forth, indicating a dissatisfaction with the current system.

The number of inhabitants in both American jails and prisons has more than tripled in the last fifteen years. Correctional facilities are overcrowded; there is a serious lack of proper medical care; and rehabilitative programs such as work, educational, and treatment programs are inadequate so that idleness and stress lead to greater violence among the inmates. Correctional facilities located through the United States have an incarceration rate higher than that of any other country, and worse, decision makers are unwilling to consider alternatives to incarceration. The argument remains that prisons are for punishment only, and not for incarceration with rehabilitation. Is there a problem with the criminal justice system as we know it? Prisoner bashing is indeed shortsighted as well as counterproductive. According to the ACLU, "The great majority of offenders will return to their home communities; the public interest is ill-served if they return battered in body and spirit, schooled in crime and angry at their treatment by society. Nor is it acceptable for any offender to be sexually assaulted, or beaten, or subjected to medical neglect as part of a criminal sentence" (ACLU).

Jailing adults is something we do quite well, but jailing youngsters as well alongside adult offenders is something that needs to be reconsidered. There are horrors that are faced by adult offenders, but what of those of the young people?

> [Horrors faced by] . . . young people in prison [include] rape, torture, and even murder. . . . three out of four youths admitted to adult courts are children of color, . . . despite the fact that most juvenile crimes are committed by whites.
>
> According to Ira Glasser, executive director of the ACLU "as a result of racial bias, black and Hispanic children are far more likely than whites their age to be prosecuted as adults. 'The entire criminal justice system is riddled with racial prejudice, and the same prejudice applies to young people.' (Newest ACLU Advertisement Deplores Growing Trend Toward Jailing Children in Adult Prisons, July 2, 2000 *www.aclu.org/features/f070700b.html*, pp. 1–2)
>
> Many states and the federal government have adopted laws that permit, encourage, or require youthful offenders to be tried as adults and ultimately transferred into adult prison populations. This ongoing erosion of the juvenile justice system is . . . disastrous for juvenile offenders in general, but minority youths suffer most . . . because they already bear the brunt of socially skewed law enforcement. (ACLU)

The headline "Prisoners' Rights: American Civil Liberties Union" talks of *Policy Priorities for Prison Reform*. There are over 6 million men, women, and juveniles in the United States who are incarcerated. The majority were not convicted of a violent crime. But the political will of lawmakers has these individuals behind bars. " 'Tough on crime' agendas encouraged the development of mandatory minimum sentencing and 'three-strikes-and-you're-out' legislation causing soaring rates of incarceration have overwhelmed an already burdened prison and jail system. Alternatives to incarceration for non-violent offenders are necessary to reduce overcrowding, to constructively and appropriately sentence convicts, to minimize financial costs and to protect offenders from upheaval" (ACLU, p. 1).

Most of our prisons are overcrowded. They are dangerous, and they provide substandard medical and mental health care, thereby not preparing the inmates for the outside world. Prisoner rights are limited. Prisoner access to the courts has become limited, allowing for harsher conditions of confinement. "In Georgia, a senior prison official watched while guards brutally beat handcuffed inmates. Correctional officers in California encouraged combat between prisoners by placing rival gang members together in the prison yard and then shot inmates when they fought" (Ibid.). The practices of overcrowding cells as well as subjecting prisoners to unsafe and unsanitary conditions exist in the twenty-first century, just as they did in centuries gone by. If the Constitution is to protect all of us from cruel and unusual punishment, so then it must protect prisoners; "it is essential that their rights be protected and that inhumane treatment be prevented" (ACLU). According to the ACLU report,

> Educational and vocational training as well as substance abuse treatment services are crucial in order to provide proper rehabilitation to offenders and to reduce recidivism.

NOTE

1. As of this writing, over 111 inmates were released from correctional facilities after being found innocent of all charges due to newly introduced DNA evidence.

REFERENCES

American Civil Liberties Union. 2001. "New Poll Shows Surprisingly Forgiving Attitude toward Crime and Punishment: Most Americans Don't Want to Throw Away the Key." www.aclu.org/features/f971801a.html.

American Civil Liberties Union. 2000. "Newest ACLU Advertisement Deplores Growing Trend Toward Jailing Children in Adult Prisons," pp. 1–2. www.aclus.org/features/f070700b.html.

Associated Press. "Florida Inmates Lose Typewriters, Computer." American Civil Liberties Union, June 22, 2001. www.aclu.org/news/2001/w062201a.html

Associated Press. "Missouri Inmate Put to Death," October 23, 2001. www.corrections.com/news/justin/todayoncc.html.

Gaseau, Michelle. 2001a. "Vt. DOC Involves Community in Restorative Solution." The Corrections Connection News Center—Program Profile. www.corrections.com/news/program/index.html.

Gasseau, Michelle. 2001b. "Washington DOC Creates Community Feeling with Training Program." The Corrections Connections News Center, pp. 1–2. www.corrections.com/news/special/sidebar.html

Minor. 2001. In Keith L. Martin, "Changing the Way the Public Sees Corrections." The Corrections Connection New Center, pp. 1–6.

New ACLU Lawsuit Details Horrors at Wisconsin 'Supermax' Prison, June 29, 2001. www.aclu.org/news/2001/no6290a.html.

Toppin, R. June 12, 2003. Newsday, "Freed after 17 Years," pp. A3, 53.

Vitello, P. June 12, 2003. Newsday, "Untwisting a Trio's Tangled Web," pp. A2, A3.

Correctional Overview

Roslyn Muraskin

Corrections is a large component of the criminal justice process. The process consists of a complex and fragmented blend of many agencies and programs among federal, state, and local jurisdictions. There are jails and prisons; there are diversionary programs, an intricate and fragmented blend of many agencies and programs among federal, state, and local jurisdictions (both pretrial and posttrial); community-based correctional programs; work release and halfway release programs; as well as other sources of programs obtainable through the correctional process.

The most dubious problem faced by correctional officials is the goal of the system: to punish, to punish and rehabilitate, or to rehabilitate. This is where the waters get murky. Herbert Packer (1968, p. 37) claimed that the purpose of criminal sanctions is "generally to be the maintenance of our social order," whereas Robert Dawson (1969) indicates that "the major purpose of the criminal justice system is the identification in a legally acceptable manner of those persons who should be subjected to control and treatment in the correctional process." If corrections fail to perform properly, the entire criminal justice system is likely to suffer. An organization such as corrections that acts ineffectively or unfairly can well render null and void the role of the courts, the prosecutors, and law enforcement. On the other hand, the way in which all other agencies execute their responsibilities plays a major role in the success of the practice. Any individual who is treated unfairly prior to being convicted becomes a difficult subject to rehabilitate.

The traditional objectives of the correctional process have been to rehabilitate, incapacitate, deter, and exact retribution. During the mid-twentieth century (from about the 1940s to the 1980s) the major goal was rehabilitation. In recent years retribution has begun to receive more popular support.

Retribution is a term defined as a means of "getting even." "Retribution is based on the ideology that the criminal is an enemy of society and deserves severe punishment for willfully breaking its rules" (Wallace & Roberson, 2000, p. 6). Often misunderstood as revenge, retribution and revenge are thought to be concerned mainly with the "impact of the punishment on the offender's future behavior or the behavior of others". Unlike revenge, however, retribution attempts to match the severity of the punishment to the seriousness of the crime. Revenge acts on passion, whereas retribution follows specific rules regarding the types and amounts of punishment that may be inflicted. The biblical response of an "eye for an eye" is a retributive response to punishment. Sir James Stephen, an English judge, expressed the retributive view by stating that "the punishment of criminals was simply a desirable expression of the hatred and fear aroused in the community by criminal acts" (Wallace & Roberson, 2000, p. 7).

There is another justification under retribution "only through suffering punishment can the criminal expiate his sin. In one manner, retribution treats all crimes as if they were financial transactions. The criminal got something or did something, therefore the criminal must give equivalent value [suffering]" (Wallace & Roberson, 2000, p. 7).

Just deserts is used to signify retribution. Such a movement

reflects the retribution viewpoint and provides a justifiable rationale for support of the death penalty. This viewpoint has its roots in a societal need for retribution. It can be traced back to the individual need for retaliation and vengeance. The transfer of the vengeance motive from the individual to the state has been justified based on theories involving theological, aesthetic, and expiatory views. According to the theological view, retaliation fulfills the religious need to punish the sinner. Under the aesthetic view, punishment helps reestablish a sense of harmony through requital and thus solves the social discord created by the crime. The expiatory view is that guilt must be washed away (cleansed) through suffering. There is even a utilitarian view that punishment is the means of achieving beneficial and social consequences through the application of a specific form and degree of punishment deemed most appropriate to the particular offender after careful individualized study of the offender (Wallace & Roberson, 2000, p. 7).

According to Wallace and Roberson, the term *deterrence* is a punishment "viewpoint that focuses on future outcomes rather than past misconduct. It is also based on the theory that creating a fear of future punishment will deter crime. It is based on the belief that punishments have a deterrent effect. There is substantial debate as to the validity of the concept. *Specific deterrence* deters specifically the offender, whereas *general deterrence* works generally on others who might consider similar acts. . . . the fear of future suffering motivates individuals to avoid involvement in criminal misconduct. This concept assumes that the criminal is a rational being who will weigh the consequences of his or her criminal actions before deciding to commit them" (2000, p. 8).

A problem with deterrence is the ability to determine the correct "magnitude and nature of punishment to be imposed in order to deter future criminal misconduct" (Wallace & Roberson, 2000, p. 8). As an example, the individual who commits any crime that is considered serious and then regrets his or her actions may necessitate a lesser amount of punishment than the individual who committed a serious crime and has little or no regret. If we buy into the principle of deterrence, then we are making the assumption that the criminal is a rational being who will by strength of character weigh the consequences of his or her criminal actions before deciding to commit them.

"One of the problems with deterrence is determining the appropriate magnitude and nature of punishment to be imposed in order to deter future criminal misconduct. For example, an individual who commits a serious crime and then feels badly about the act may need only slight punishment to achieve deterrent effects, whereas a professional shoplifter may need severe fear-producing punishments to prevent future shoplifting" (Wallace & Roberson, 2000, p. 8).

Through the demonstration of increases in the crime rates as well as high rates of recidivism, there is emitted doubt that the deterrence approach is effective. "Recidivism may cause some doubt regarding the efficacy of special deterrence, but it says nothing about the effect of general deterrence. In addition, unless we know what the crime rate or rates of recidivism would be if we did not attempt to deter criminal misconduct, the assertions are unfounded" (Wallace & Roberson, 2000, p. 8). Can we actually ever know for sure that deterrence will dissuade future criminal acts?

Incapacitation puts the prisoner behind bars. This action prevents him or her from committing prospective crimes. To this extent confinement will reduce criminal behavior, but to what gain? Only those behind bars will not commit crimes, but does it deter these individuals from committing future criminal acts? "Marvin Wolfgang's famous study of crime in Philadelphia indicated that although chronic offenders constituted only 23 percent of the offenders in the study, they committed over 61 percent of all the violent crimes" (Wallace & Roberson, 2000, pp. 8–9). The reasoning used is that by incapacitating 23 percent of the offenders, we have prevented 61 percent of future crimes. "This approach has been labeled the 'nothing else works' approach to corrections. According to this viewpoint, we should make maximum effective use of the scarce prison cells and to protect society from the depredations of such dangerous and repetitive offenders. This approach is expressed in California's 'Three Strikes and You're Out' statute" (Wallace & Roberson, 2000, p. 9).

There exist two points of view about the theory of incapacitation: (1) *Collective incapacitation* refers to those punishments that are given to offenders with no regard to personal characteristics (i.e, being a violent offender); (2) while *selective incapacitation* refers to the process of incapacitating select groups of high risk offenders. Under the punishment referred to as selective incapacitation, these offenders will be the recipient of higher amounts of time to be served than all other offenders (Wallace & Roberson, pp. 8–9).

According to Herbert Packer, "'[I]ncapacitation is a mode of punishment that uses the fact that a person has committed a crime as a basis for predicting that he will commit future crimes.'" Packer continues "that the logic of the incapacitative position is that until the offender stops being a danger, we will continue to restrain him. Accordingly, he contends that pushed to its logical conclusion, offenses that are regarded as relatively trivial may be punished by imprisonment for life" (p. 9).

REHABILITATION

This approach contends "that punishment should be directed toward correcting the offender. This approach is also considered the 'treatment' approach. It considers the criminal misconduct as a manifestation of a pathology that can be handled by some form of therapeutic activity. Although this viewpoint may consider the offender as 'sick', it is not the same as the medical approach. Under the rehabilitation viewpoint, we need to teach offenders to recognize the undesirability of their criminal behavior and make significant efforts to rid themselves of that behavior. The main difference between the rehabilitation approach and the retribution approach is that under the rehabilitation approach, offenders are assigned to programs designed to prepare them for readjustment or reintegration into the community, whereas the latter approach is more concerned with the punishment aspects of the sentence. Packer sees two major objections to making rehabilitation the primary justification for punishment. First, we do not know how to rehabilitate offenders. Second, we know little about who is likely to commit crimes and less about what makes them apt to do so. As long as we are ignorant in these matters, Packard contends that punishment in the name of rehabilitation is gratuitous cruelty" (Wallace & Roberson, pp. 9–10).

In any discussion of punishment we talk from the point of view of the individual being punished, not of society as a whole. According to C. Ray Jeffrey, "punishment serves an important social function in that it creates social solidarity and re-enforces social norms" (p. 10).

The *Violent Control and Law Enforcement Act* (1994) "allocated more than $22 billion to expand prisons, impose longer sentences, hire more police officers, fund prevention programs. However, the following year the money allocated to prevention programs was eliminated" (Jeffrey, p. 10). The feeling among criminal justice experts is that such acts (i.e., allotting more and more monies to corrections) will not solve or decrease the flow of crime. This "enforcement model" is criticized as being racist, costing too much, and failing to prevent the younger generation from entering into a field of crime.

Correctional philosophy is based on three approaches: punishment, treatment, or prevention. During the 1960s we saw the approach of treatment. In the 1970s we saw punishment as the mode. Such a punishment philosophy is costly and overcrowds correctional facilities beyond their ability to operate. During the latter part of the twentieth century, we saw a swing back to treatment and prevention philosophies. There has been a movement afoot to "reduce judicial and correctional imperialism" (Jeffrey, p. 11).

The strategies suggested are as follows:

- *Determinate sentencing.* Establishment of set sentences whereby parole boards are restricted from releasing prisoners before their sentences (minus good time) have expired

- *Mandatory prison terms.* Statutes that require the courts to impose mandatory prison terms for convictions of certain offenses or for convictions of certain offenses or for certain defendants

- *Sentencing guidelines.* Guidelines designed to structure sentences based on the severity of the offense and the criminal history of the defendant

- *Parole guidelines.* Guidelines designed to require parole decisions to be based on measurable offender criteria

- *Good-time guidelines.* Guidelines that allow for reducing prison terms based on an inmate's behavior in prison

- *Emergency overcrowding provisions.* Regulations that allow early release of prisoners based on systematic provisions to relieve overcrowding (pp. 11–12)

In the majority of states, guidelines for correctional facilities are established for judges to follow. In most instances a presentence report is required. This report indicates the kind of person the defendant is and describes his or her criminal background, if any exists, as well as any and all circumstances that might impact on the sentence of the defendant.

These guidelines are used first and foremost to give judges a guide to sentence the defendant to the correct sentence as outlined by the legislators. The only time that the members of the judiciary may depart from those sentences as outlined is when they note circumstances that would change their decisions.

The Federal Sentencing Guidelines enacted in 1984 have governed federal sentencing decisions since 1989. These guidelines, as promulgated by the Sentencing Commission, created 43 offense levels. Each level reflects the increased severity of crime. Offenders were divided into six categories depending on their criminal history. "The net result is a grid containing 258 cells, each of which has a sentencing range expressed in terms of months. The intent was to have the grids serve as an advisory to judicial decision-making on sentencing. While the stated objective of the federal sentencing reform was to encourage alternative sanctions to prison, the guidelines are constructed in such a manner that they discourage judges from imposing alternative sanctions" (Jeffrey, p. 13).

Prior to the use of sentencing guidelines (1984), something like 52 percent of felony federal offenders were sentenced to prison. As of 1991, this percentage had increased to over 70 percent (Jeffrey, 2000, p. 13). There has been much criticism regarding these guidelines: too harsh, too limiting, too heavily relying on prison. An alternative to sentencing guidelines has been the use of presumptive sentencing. Here the state legislature would set minimum, average, and maximum prison terms. Judges opt for the appropriate term based on certain characteristics of the defendant. "The first decision that the judge would have to make is the 'out or in' decision: whether the defendant should be placed on probation (out) or sentenced (in) to prison. If the judge decided that imprisonment is the correct sentence, the judge would award four years, the average sentence, unless there were mitigating or aggravating circumstances. Under aggravating circumstances, the sentence would be six years, and under mitigating circumstances, the sentence would be two years. Examples of mitigating circumstances would be that the defendant is a first-time offender or the crime was committed under strong peer pressure. Examples of aggravating circumstances include a prior criminal record or great harm to the victim" (Jeffrey, p. 14, 2000 in Wallace & Roberson).

The term *misdemeanants* refer to those offenders who are convicted for minor crimes. Their sentences to jails would usually not exceed a year, fines, community service, and/or attendance at some kind of behavior modification track. On any given level on any day it is estimated that there are over 500,000 individuals confined to the local jails. This is often referred to as revolving justice. Felons are those individuals who are committed to the prisons (Jeffrey).

If we look at alternative means of sentencing, then we would turn our attention to diversionary-type programs. One such example is that of *deferred adjudication,* whereby a form of probation is used without the finding of guilt of the defendant. The defendant pleads guilty and defers further proceedings so that he or she may attend programs such as behavior modification. If the defendant completes such programs successfully, charges are dismissed, and there is no record for the defendant. If the defendant fails to follow the requirements as set forth in the program, the court will then sentence the individual to a time that is consistent with his or her original plea (Jeffrey, p. 15).

Under *pretrial diversion* we see the defendant being placed on a program akin to probation with no sentence being given. "Pretrial diversion is used primarily for offenders who need treatment or supervision and for whom criminal sanctions would be excessive" (Jeffrey, 2000, p. 16). The main concern with such a program is that individuals who would have received no jail time at all find themselves involved in these diversionary programs— punishment for individuals where there would have been none!

Those who are confined within the facilities are obliged to obey rules. Those inmates who commit an infraction will face further punishment within the correctional facility. "The inmate receives notice of the report with written notification of the charge and a hearing date. At the hearing, the hearing officer receives the evidence presented by the institutional division and any other factors presented by the inmate. The formal rules of evidence do not apply at the hearings. The hearing officer decides whether the inmate committed the infraction. Possible punishments include loss of time credited for good conduct or participation credit, solitary confinement, extra work, loss of certain privileges (recreation, commissary, television, access to personal property, or contact visits) for stated periods of time. Generally, the inmate may appeal the hearing officer's findings and/or punishment to the unit warden" (Jeffrey, p. 16).

Corrections is a complicated area to understand. The ultimate reason for sending individuals to correctional facilities is to punish and to maintain order in the community. According to Jeffrey, punishment should have as its purpose to have the public disapprove of the criminal act. Through punishment in the correctional facilities, we return life to a somewhat normal pace, following what are considered the mores of society.

Correctional policies are determined more by political institutions that are sensitive to public opinion rather than through an exact science. To inflict punishment means that we may be able to alter behavior of those serving time while at the same time achieving justice. To understand corrections we need to know if its goal is punishment or treatment. No easy solution exists as to the problems within correctional facilities, but an understanding of why and how they work, the goal of this chapter, is necessary.

REFERENCES

Clear, T. R., & Cole, G. F., (2000) *American Corrections,* fifth edition, by West/Wadsworth.

Dawson, R. (1969), Sentencing: The decision as to type, length and conditions of sentence. Boston: Little Brown & Co.

Packer, H. L. (1968) The limits of criminal sanction. Stanford University Press.

Silverman, I. J., (2001) Corrections—A comprehensive review (2nd edition). Wadsworth: Thomason Learning.

Wallace & Roberson, (2000). Legal aspects of corrections. Incline Village, Nevada: Cooperhouse Publishing Co.

Correctional History

Roslyn Muraskin

PUNISHMENT

The year was 1757 and the chief judge rose to announce the sentence on Robert Francois Damiens, convicted of trying to assassinate King Louis XV:

> He is to be taken and conveyed in a cart, wearing nothing but a shift, holding a torch of burning wax weighing two pounds; in the said cart to the Place de Greve, where on a scaffold that will be erected there, the flesh will be torn from his breasts, arms, thighs and calves with red-hot pinchers, his right hand, holding the knife with which he committed the said parricide, burnt with sulphur, and, on those places where the flesh will be torn away, poured molten lead, boiling oil, burning resin, wax and sulphur meted together and then his body drawn and quartered by four horses and his limbs and body consumed by fire, reduced to ashes and his ashes thrown to the wind (Clear & Cole, 2000, p. 23).

According to Clear and Cole, the accounts in the newspapers of the punishment at that time were apparently more horrible than required by the sentence. "Because the horses were not able to pull him 'limb from limb,' the executioner resorted to the hacking of Damien's arms and legs. All this occurred while the man was still alive" (2000, p. 24).

During this time in history all punishments were held out for public view. "Crowds taunted the condemned as the executioner or sheriff conducting whippings, burnings, pilloryings, and hangings on orders of the king or court. Punishment-as-spectacle was used to control crime and to exhibit the sovereign's power" (Clear & Cole, 2000, p. 24).

The Hammurabic Code as developed by the king of Babylon (1750 B.C.) was the first all-inclusive announcement of behavior that was prohibited during this time in history. It was not until the 1200s that forms of legal sanctions appear that are familiar today. Before that time in Europe, re- sponses to crime were viewed as a private affair, with vengeance as a duty to be carried out by the person wronged or by a family member. Wrongs were avenged in accordance with *lex talionis,* or law of retaliation. This principle underlayed the laws of Anglo-Saxon society until the time of the Norman Conquest of England in 1066. During the Middle Ages the *secular law* of England and Europe was organized according to the feudal system. In the absence of a strong central government, crimes among neighbors took on the char- acter of war, and the public peace was endangered as feudal lords sought to avenge one another's transgressions. In response, in England by the year 1022 a system of *wergild,* or payment of money as a compensation for a wrong, had developed as a way of reducing the frequency of violent blood feuds. During this period the custom of treating offenses as personal matters to be settled by individuals gradually gave way to the view that the peace of society required the public to participate in determining guilt or innocence and in ex- acting a penalty (Clear & Cole, 2000, pp. 24–25).

The foremost importance of criminal law therefore was on the maintenance of pub- lic order among people of equal position and riches.

> If, in the heat of the moment, or in a state of intoxication, someone committed an offense against decency, accepted morality, or religion, or severely injured or killed his neighbor . . . a solemn gathering of free men would be held to pronounce judgment and make the culprit pay Wergild or do penance so that the vengeance of the injured parties should not develop into blood feud and anarchy (Clear & Cole, 2000, p. 25).

Thus, the main punishment for criminal acts were penance, fines or restitution. Those lower class offenders who had no money received physical punishment from their masters.

The church as the principal social institution maintained its own form of reprimand During the Inquisition of the 1300s and 1400s, the church "zealously punished those who violated its law. At the same time, it gave refuge from secular prosecution to people who could claim *benefit of clergy.* In time, benefit of clergy was extended to all literate persons" (Clear and Cole, 2000, p. 25).

The criminal law system as we recognize it was further developed during the 1400s and 1500s. "With the rise of trade, the breakdown of the feudal order, and the emergence of a middle class, other forms of sanction were applied. In addition to fines, five punish- ments were common in Europe before the 1800s: galley slavery, imprisonment, trans- portation, corporal punishment, and death" (Clear & Cole, 2000, p. 25). Each punishment described held very definitive purposes. At this time there existed no formal police force as we know it today, nor was there any other "centralized instruments of order, deterrence was the dominant purpose of the criminal sanction. Thus, before the 1800s it was believed that one of the best ways to maintain order was to intimidate the entire population by publicly punishing offenders" (Clear & Cole, 2000, p. 25).

Jails were the means of both detaining and punishing individuals who committed crimes up until the early nineteenth century. According to Clear and Cole, "In ancient times offenders were incarcerated in cages, rock quarries, or even in chambers under the Roman

Forum while they awaited punishment, but for more offenders imprisonment was not *the punishment*" (2000, p. 26). Furthermore, "Conditions in these prisons were appalling. Men, women, and children, healthy and sick, were locked up together; the strong preyed on the weak, sanitation was nonexistent, and disease was epidemic. Furthermore, authorities made no provision for the inmate's upkeep. Often the warden viewed his job as a business proposition, selling food and accommodations to his charges. The poor thus had to rely for survival on alms brought to them by charitable persons and religious groups" (Clear & Cole, 2000, p. 26).

The reform of prisons started in the sixteenth century, when we witness the disintegration of feudalism with political power becoming more centralized. The rural poor started to roam about the countryside or departed for the cities. "The emphasis of the Protestant Reformation on the importance of hard work and the sinfulness of sloth stirred European reformers to urge that some means be found to provide work for the idle poor. Out of these concerns the *house of correction* or 'workshop' was born" (Clear & Cole, 2000, p. 26).

The first house of correction was Bridewell Palace in 1553. "The facility was not merely a place of detention as was the jail, but combined the major elements of a workhouse, poorhouse, and penal institution. Whereas jails were thought to promote idleness among the inmates, the house of correction was expected to instill 'a habit of industry more conducive to an honest livelihood.' The inmates—primarily prostitutes, beggars, minor criminals, and the idle poor—were to be disciplined and set to work. The products made in the house of correction were to be sold on the market, so that the facility would be self-sufficient and not need government subsidy. The term *Bradwell House* came to be used for all versions of the English house of correction" (Clear & Cole, 2000, p. 26).

Similar institutions were established in Holland, France, Germany, and Italy. A motto carved over the doorway "defined the authority of the law with regard to the inmates: 'My hand is severe by my intention benevolent.' This motto influenced the later development of the penitentiary" (Clear & Cole, 2000, p. 26). Moreover, "Conditions in England's Bridewells deteriorated as the facilities increasingly housed criminal rather than the poor, the orphaned, and the sick. In the 1700s the labor power provided by the inmate was no longer economically profitable, and the reformative aim of the institution vanished" (Clear & Cole, 2000, p. 26).

Since ancient times those who have disobeyed the rules of a community have been thrown out or banished. With the collapse of feudalism and the degenerative economic conditions in 1600s, prisons and houses of correction in England and Europe overflowed to the point of "no room at the inn." "The 'New World' represented a convenient place to send French, Spanish, and English offenders from which they would probably not return. For Russians *transportation* to Siberia often meant death. With passage of the Vagrancy Act of 1597, transportation became prescribed. By 1606, with the settlement of Virginia, the transportation of convicts to North America became economically important for the colonial companies for whom they labored for the remainder of their sentences. It also helped relieve the overcrowding of prisons of England" (Clear & Cole, 2000, p. 27).

"Transportation seemed so successful that in 1717 a statute was passed allowing convicts to be given over to private contractors, who then shipped them to the colonies and sold their services. Prisoners who returned to England before their terms expired were executed. The Transportation Act of 1718 made transportation the standard penalty for non-capital offenses. From 1718 to 1776 an estimated fifty thousand British convicts were shipped to the American colonies. In 1772 three-fifths of male convicts were transported" (Clear & Cole, 2000, p. 27).

When the American Revolution began, transporting prisoners was halted. "[I]n 1837 a select committee of Parliament reported that, far from reforming criminals, transportation created thoroughly depraved societies. Critics argued that the Crown was forcing Englishmen to be 'slaves until they were judged to become peasants' " (Clear & Cole, 2000, p. 28).

Corporal punishment as used was punishment that was inflicted on an offender through the use of whips or any other devices that caused severe pain. Though used throughout history, the use of corporal punishment was considered to be extremely brutal. Once again punishments were carried out in the public square. "The punishments themselves were harsh: whipping, mutilation, and branding were used extensively, and death was the common penalty for a host of felonies. For example some 72,000 people were hanged during the reign of Henry VIII (1509–1547), and in the Elizabethan period (1558–1603) vagabonds were strung up in rows of 300–400 at a time. Capital punishment could either be a 'merciful' instant death (beheading, hanging, garroting, and burying alive), or a prolonged death (burning alive on the wheel)" (Clear & Cole, 2000, p. 28). What was known then as now was that the death penalty was not a deterrent.

"Those criminals who were not executed were subjected to various mutilations—removing a hand or finger, slitting the nostrils, severing an ear, or branding—so that the offenders could be publicly identified. Such mutilation usually made it impossible for the marked individual to find honest employment. . . . almost every imaginable torture was used in the name of retribution, deterrence, the sovereignty of the authorities and the public good" (Clear & Cole, 2000, p. 28).

Since ancient times to today, capital punishment has represented the most severe retort to criminal behavior in most societies. "In many cultures, death was the most frequently used means to punish offenders. As communities developed, it seemed to provide the only definite means of ridding the community of troublesome and offensive characters, while at the same time satisfying the desire for vengeance" (Silverman, 2001, p. 73).

"Among the earliest recorded laws in ancient China, beheading was the prescribed method. The oldest recorded death sentence can be found in the Amherst papyri, which included an account of the trial of a state criminal in Egypt in 1500 B.C.: the condemned offender was found guilty of using 'magic' and sentenced to death. In England, capital punishment emerged in about 450 B.C." (Silverman, 2001, p. 73).

Commencing with the Norman Conquest in the eleventh through the seventeenth centuries, the death penalty was normally shared with estate forfeiture, in so doing impoverishing the offender's family. All felonies and high and petty treasons were considered capital crimes. During the years of "1688 to 1820 the number of capital offenses in England soared from 50 to over 200. Many of these were implemented to protect property. Early on, there were two ways to escape the death penalty. First, one could refuse to go to trial and be pressed to death by giant stones. This saved the family's property from forfeiture. Second, one could have the case transferred to an ecclesiastical court (benefit of clergy), which could not impose the death penalty except in cases of heresy. Over time, crimes designated as 'felonies without benefit of clergy' diminished" (Silverman, 2001, p. 73).

It was through this period when the hefty number of capital crimes led England's criminal code to be referred to as the "Bloody Code." Interestingly, the death sentence was not meted out to all offenders convicted of capital crimes. This would have been socially and politically objectionable and could have threatened the public's acceptance of the law. The courts circumvented the harshness of these laws by its use of discretion in implementing the death sentence and *transportation* to distribute sentences in order to realize the appropriate blend of deterrence and retribution.

"Historically, methods of execution have been limited only by human imagination and ingenuity and have included flaying or burying alive, boiling in oil, crushing beneath the wheels of vehicles or feet of elephants, throwing to wild beasts, forcing combat in the arena, blowing from the mouth of a cannon, impaling, piercing with javelins, starving to death, poisoning, strangling, suffocating, drowning, shooting, beheading, and, more recently, electrocuting, using the gas chamber, and giving a lethal injection. The severity of the execution was often based on factors such as the social class of the offender and the degree to which the crime offended the ruling powers." Furthermore, "During the Middle Ages, an offender's death would often be preceded by excruciating *torture*, including drawing and quartering, being dragged to the gallows tied to the tail of a horse, having bellies slit open and entrails cut out, and being burned by the executioner. The most widely used form of execution has been hanging, which has been used from ancient times to the present" (Silverman, 2001, p. 72).

Silverman states that "with the 'progress' of humankind, there has been a demand for more humane methods of execution. The invention of the electric chair in the late 1800s was one such innovation" (2001, p. 74).

BANISHMENT

According to Silverman (2001), "Banishment was an acceptable alternative to the death penalty because it had the same effect of ridding the community of the offender. Among the oldest forms of punishment, *banishment* has historically included both temporary and permanent exclusion from the community and enslavement or exile of offenders to a penal code" (p. 74).

"The practice of outlawry dates back to the fourth century in England. Outlaws were men and women who either fled from justice . . . or had been banished to the wilderness, which became their 'penal colony.' Their property was forfeited to the king, they could be killed by anyone, and their children were also viewed as outlaws. They could only return to the community by securing a royal pardon. During medieval times, outlaws banded together for both camaraderie and to accomplish their criminal objectives. When pursued by sheriffs and bounty hunters, outlaws were allowed by medieval kings to purchase a pardon either by a monetary payment or performance of some service" (Silverman, 2001, p. 74).

"By the 1400s, being declared an outlaw became less of a hardship. Instead of taking to the woods and becoming professional robbers, some hid out with friends until a pardon could be secured, whereas others moved away and continued their trades. Outlawry was not abolished in England until 1938; in the United States, North Carolina had an outlaw statute until 1970" (Silverman, 2001, p. 74).

TRANSPORTATION

"As early as the 15th century, Spain and Portugal shipped convicts to colonies and distant military settlements; however, this practice was abandoned because these men were needed on the galleys. England became the first country during the early modern period that dates from the 16th century onward, to systematically ship offenders to its colonies. France and Russia also used this practice" (Silverman, 2001, p. 74).

England pioneered the organization of workhouses, "but rather than adapt this system to incarcerate felons, it chose to transport them to its new American colonies. Magistrates were given the authority to exile rogues and vagabonds, and by 1615 less serious offenders who were sentenced to death were also eligible. Thus, transportation served as an intermediate punishment between execution and lesser sanctions such as whipping or pillorying" (Silverman, 2001, p. 74).

> The widespread use of this sanction began with the Transportation Act of 1718, which was passed to deal with an alarming increase in crime caused by the disorganizing effects of the transition from the medieval to modern times. The reduced need for farm workers, along with insufficient industrial development and a doubling of the population during a 100-year period, produced high unemployment. These displaced workers were responsible for increased crime. Parliament, pressured to do something about crime, chose transportation rather than expanding their workhouses or increasing their use of capital punishment. Imprisonment did not gain favor because of its high costs and the fear that it might be used by a tyrant to subjugate the nation. Capital punishment also declined in favor. . . .
>
> Transportation was the ideal solution because it had none of the drawbacks of other alternatives: undesirables were not supposed to be able to return; the costs were minimal; it provided a source of labor for the new developing colonies; and it might serve as a means for reforming these offenders (Silverman, 2001, pp. 74–75).

THE INDENTURE SYSTEM

During the eighteenth century, there was a system of white servitude that prevailed in the colonies prior to the Revolution as transported convicts were part of this transportation.

> The system of indentured servitude provided colonists with a needed labor force about one quarter of the cost of a free man. Indentured servants also tended to be more obedient and dependable workers, because the penalties for sassing a boss or running away were

severe. Indentured servants comprised two types of individuals: those who came voluntarily and exchanged their labor for the benefit of being transported to the Americas, and criminals and others (e.g., those who were shanghaied—kidnapped) who were involuntarily sentenced. Regardless of how they came, all were considered "slaves" for the term of their indenture. In total, indentured servants represented half (30,000 to 50,000) of all the colonists coming to this country from the early 1600s to the 1700s.

Convicts awaiting shipment to the colonies were detained in gaols (jails) for up to 6 months or more under notoriously unhealthy conditions. Their voyage to America differed little from that experienced by African slaves. They were chained below deck in damp, cramped quarters with little fresh air or light and disease was rampant.

The sale of convicts and other servants upon their arrival was likened to cattle auctions. Women were considered less valuable because they could not perform heavy labor, however, the colonies had a shortage of females, so they contributed to make life a bit more tolerable by becoming the wives, mistresses, or simply adding an amiable dimension to colonial life.

For the British, the transportation of convicts provided a cheap and easy means of dealing with their criminal population. Despite colonists' fears of the dangers posed by these criminals, life in America provided fewer opportunities for property crime. The outbreak of the American Revolution had a devastating effect on English corrections. It meant that fewer convicts could be shipped to the American colonies, and other methods of dealing with the convict population were not in place. Although more than 200 offenses still carried the death penalty, its implementation was still not tolerated in large numbers (Silverman, 2001, p. 75).

FLOATING PRISONS

"With transportation to the colonies a dwindling option, the Hulks Act of 1776 specified that convicts were to be put to work at hard labor on the Thames River. There were to be housed in **hulks** (broken-down and abandoned war vessels and transport ships) that were transformed into nautical prisons. . . . the English government was forced to use goals and workhouses, which were unsuited for long-term imprisonment. The construction of prisons was too costly, so the government continued to put more hulks into service despite death rates of up to one third of 5,792 inmates aboard these vessels between 1776 and 1795. At their peak in the early 1800s, there were 10 of these vessels holding 5,000 convicts. Conditions aboard these hulks (e.g., poor sanitation and ventilation, a starvation diet, harsh discipline, overcrowding) led convicts to use the phrase 'hell upon earth' to describe them" (Silverman, 2001, p. 76).

A NEW SOCIETY

According to Silverman, "About 24,000 women were transported to Australia between 1788 and 1852. No formal policy prescribed that women were sent for breeding and sexual convenience; however, this was implicit in the governor's first request for more women convicts. He wanted them for purposes of marrying and raising native-born families who would then provide the base for an agricultural society of small farms. Initially, women were assigned as mistresses, which was akin to a 'mail-order bride' system" (2001, p. 78).

"Despite the unfavorable portrait of convict women, many were able to raise children who benefited the community. The population of native-born children grew rapidly, and schools were established to facilitate their development. The first generation of native children were the most law-abiding, morally conservative people in the country. From a population of convicts rose a society of lawyers, magistrates, constables, educators, superintendents, and owners of large enterprises and farms" (Silverman, 2001, p. 78).

EVOLUTION OF IMPRISONMENT

"Corporal and capital punishment were commonly employed for most offenses. During the 1700s, criminal codes specified a variety of punishments including fines and whippings, banishment, and hanging. Branding was also used . . . to identify strangers and community members who had committed crimes. This, along with forms of public ridicule (e.g., stocks, pillory) served as an important social control mechanism in tight-knit communities where people were concerned about their reputations with their neighbors" (Silverman, 2001, p. 76).

Following the American Revolution (1783), according to Silverman (2001, p. 86),"new ideas of penal reform, espoused by Cesar Becarria, founder of the classical school of criminology, were adopted. He asserted that the causes of crime could be traced to the antiquated colonial criminal codes. Beccaria felt that to prevent crimes:

> laws must be clear . . . ; punishment should be based on the extent of harm that the act causes society . . . [and] used only . . . on the supposition that it prevents crime. . . . Punishment for each crime should be inevitable, prompt and public [and it] . . . should be severe enough to override any pleasure that accrues from the criminal acts.

"Many reformers embraced the idea of imprisonment simply because it was more humane than hanging and whipping." Other reformers were instrumental in developing the *Pennsylvania system.* "In 1787, penal reformers formed the Philadelphia Society for Alleviating the Miseries of Public Prisons. This group was instrumental in persuading the legislature to designate the *Walnut Street Jail* as a temporary state prison and change its orientation toward reformation" (Silverman, 2001, p. 86).

The Walnut Street Jail

The reformers who designed the Walnut Street Jail, considered our first correctional facility, faced the same tribulations that we wrestle with today:

> (1) Should prisoners be housed separately or in association? and (2) should it be for the purpose of punishment? The Quakers wanted to develop a program that reformed offenders while also providing humane treatment. To accomplish this, the Walnut Street Jail was remodeled in 1790 to provide for the confinement of two classes of offenders.

More serious offenders, previously subjected to corporal or capital punishment, were confined in a newly built penitentiary house containing 16 solitary cells called *punishment cells*. After a period of time, these inmates could earn the privilege of working while still confined to their cells, and after completing a portion of their sentence, they could be released into the general population of the prison. Less serious offenders were congregately housed in eight large rooms and were permitted to work at occupations basic to the economy of the period.

The prisoner labor system presented authorities with the issue of which incentives are effective in encouraging inmate production. The same two incentives that are typically used today were used then. Inmates were paid wages with deductions made for daily maintenance, tools, court costs, and fines. Most left with money in their pockets. However, the major incentive was not the money but the hope of a pardon, which might be awarded for their good work. Discipline of inmates was humane—prisoners were not shackled and corporal punishment was not used. However, disobedient offenders could be put in solitary cells and charged daily maintenance expenses (Silverman, 2001, pp. 86–87).

Initially the programs at Walnut Street Jail were evidently successful. "Street crime dropped to a point where people felt secure on the streets as well as in their homes and businesses. Despite its great promise, by 1800, a number of factors contributed to its downfall. Discipline at the institution became lax; pardons were issued to placate convicts and achieve order. . . . the primary factor causing Walnut Street's failure was its inability to handle the increasing inmate population. This resulted from (1) Pennsylvania's growing population, and (2) the increased substitution of solitary confinement for capital punishment, which resulted in more commitments and longer prison terms" (Silverman, 2001, p. 87).

"Recognizing that reform was impossible under overcrowded conditions, the Pennsylvania legislature authorized the construction of two penitentiaries, the Western Penitentiary at Pittsburgh and the Eastern Penitentiary at Cherry Hill. The Western Penitentiary was demolished because poor planning and construction made it impossible to utilize its goals of solitary confinement or work. It was replaced with a facility similar in design to the one at Cherry Hill, which could meet these objectives."

The Eastern Penitentiary

Opened in 1829, the Eastern Penitentiary at Cherry Hill was the first facility to put into effect the Pennsylvania system, or "separate system." It was designed so inmates would not have to be removed from their cells except when sick. Inmates ate, slept, read their Bibles, received moral instruction, and worked in their cells. Their only interpersonal contact was with the warden, guards, the chaplain, and members of some Philadelphia organizations interested in inmate care and welfare. Inmates were not permitted to receive or send letters to family or anyone on the outside.

The Cherry Hill facility had seven wings, resembling the spokes of a wheel and extending from a hub-like center with a total of 252 cells. Each cell block had a passage running down the center with 21 spacious cells—each 12 feet wide by 7 feet long by 16 feet high—on either side of the outside wall. All inmates were allowed one hour of exercise per day; those in first floor cells had individual walled exercise yards, whereas those on the second floor were given an extra cell for exercise purposes. The institutional program was based on solitary confinement, work, and penitence and was justified on the grounds that

1. Communication in any [form] contributed to the contamination of the less hardened by the vicious.
2. Solitary confinement without the opportunity of communication with fellow prisoners would stop all such contamination.
3. Living in silence day and night, [the inmate] would inevitably reflect upon his sins and resolve to forever abandon such activity.
4. Labor in the cell would enable him to contribute to his support and at the same time would relieve the dreadful monotony of solitary confinement (Silverman, 2001, p. 88).

In this country this kind of system did not receive great acceptance while in the European countries it was used as a model.

The Auburn System

There being no acceptable prison regimen at this pointing time, a new system was evolving at Auburn, under the supervision of Warden Elam Lynds. Auburn was a compromise between solitary confinement and the congregate confinement of earlier facilities.

By 1823, this new Auburn System was in full operation. It included (1) separate confinement of each inmate at night, (2) work in groups in the prison shops and yards during the day, which paid inmate imprisonment costs, and (3) rigidly enforced silence day and night, which prevented inmates from corrupting each other or plotting escapes and riots. This system met the objectives of imprisonment and provided an economical system of management and strict discipline, allowing for the safe and efficient functioning of the prison.

Inmates received no inducements to comply with the system's rigid requirements. Obedience was obtained by a prompt, severe system of punishment, which inmates dreaded, known as the "stripes"—flogging. Disobedient inmates were taken from the work area and flogged with a rawhide whip in a way that would not endanger their health or ability to work. Thus the key features of the Auburn system were silence, hard congregate labor, and corporal punishment for rule violators (Silverman, 2001, p. 89).

The Auburn-Pennsylvania Controversy

By the 1830s, these two American correctional systems had achieved wide-reaching respect, and concentration was centered on which provided the best model for potential prisons. According to Silverman, "The Pennsylvania camp insisted that the separate design (1) eliminated contamination and plotting by inmates, (2) did not require well-trained guards because contact with inmates was minimal, and (3) allowed convicts, once isolated, to immediately begin the reformation process. There was little need for the whip because isolation provided few chances to violate the rules" (2001, p. 86).

"Pennsylvania supporters criticized the Auburn system on the basis that it was nearly impossible to enforce silence, when inmates worked, ate, and exercised together. Further, inmate contact for long periods without talking was cruel and unenforceable as shown by the frequency with which inmates were punished. Auburn advocates criticized the Pennsylvania system, saying that prolonged isolation was cruel, dangerous, and unnatural, as proved by its trial at Auburn, which bred insanity and suicide" (Silverman, 2001, p. 86).

"The most persuasive argument for the Auburn system were that (1) Auburn-type institutions were less costly to construct because cells could be smaller because inmates only slept in them, and (2) profits were greater due to the greater efficiency resulting from the variety and quantity of products produced when convicts worked together. In fact, in 1828 Auburn's warden announced he no longer needed state funds to run the prison. Indeed, the Auburn system eventually prevailed in the United States due to cost issues" (Silverman, 2001, p. 89–90). After a while the Pennsylvania system model was abandoned, and Cherry Hill became another Auburn.

> The Auburn system became the model for United States prisons primarily because of its economic advantages. Further, doctrines of separation, obedience, labor, and silence were consistent with the values of the time regarding reformation. Maintaining a daily routine of hard work was consistent with views on the causes and results of crime; those not willing to work were seen as prone to commit crime. Idleness also gave inmates opportunities to teach each other the values and techniques of crime. Thus, the tougher the regimen, the greater the possibilities of successful reformation.
>
> To achieve these goals a quasi-military model was adopted. This included a daily schedule that was organized around a military routine. Convicts were matched in striped uniforms from place to place in "close order-single file," each looking over the next man's shoulder with their faces pointed to the right to prevent conversation and their feet moving in unison. This type of formation, known as the *lockstep,* became a hallmark of American prisons well into the 1930s (Silverman, 2001, p. 90).

"Although many states embraced the Auburn model, their institution failed to follow its rigid standards. The degree to which the model was followed depended largely on the varying skills and concerns on those running these prisons. Generally, the farther west the state, the more loosely enforced were the model's rigid rules of discipline. . . . it is important to note that many elements of this system (including the lockstep, silent system, regimented routines and fortress prisons) evolved over time and remained part of our penal system well into [this century]" (Silverman, 2001, pp. 91–92).

ANTECEDENTS OF THE REFORMATORY MOVEMENT

At the end of the Civil War, it became apparent that the inadequacies of both the Pennsylvania and Auburn systems were abundantly clear. The inflexible discipline of both systems had degenerated to more or less fraudulent, slipshod, and cruel routines. Further, excessive numbers of offenders within the facilities along with understaffing made the silence system unenforceable.

In their place, prison industries run by private contractors, who leased inmate labor, became the major focus of institutional operations because they were so profitable. Although benefiting the state, this diminished the authority of prison staff over inmates because during work hours contractors had control of the inmates. Discipline was used to maintain production, and its use for reformative purposes became secondary.

Taken together, these circumstances created turmoil in the prisons. Wardens resorted to a variety of harsh and bizarre punishments to regain control, including flogging and placing inmates in solitary confinement—dungeons—on a bread and water diet. The most horrendous punishment was the Kansas "water crib," where an inmate was placed faced down in the crib with hands cuffed behind his back. As the water rose, the inmate, slowly drowning, fought to keep his head above the rising water. Whereas in solitary it took days to bring a man around, this torture was said to get his cooperation immediately.

Reformers were appalled by these forms of torture and punishment. In searching for programs that could be used to develop a new prison system, reformers were heavily influenced by the works of Captain Alexander Maconochie and Sir Walter Crofton (Silverman, 2001, p. 92).

Alexander Maconochie's Mark System

While serving as a young naval officer in 1810, Alexander Maconochie was captured by the French and became a prisoner of war; this made him sensitive to the brutalities of prisons. Later, he investigated the convict transportation system as the lieutenant governor of a prison colony off the cost of Australia. This led him to develop a revolutionary plan for penal reform.

Maconochie believed that pain and suffering were an essential part of any penal system, because they deterred others from violating the law and reinforced in the offender's mind the wrongfulness of his behavior. However, he felt its major objective should be to reform offenders. This required a prison program that emphasized persuasion, not coercion, and included (1) punishment for past behavior and (2) training to prepare offenders to return to society as useful, honest and trustworthy citizens. He also felt that a system of reformation needed trained personnel. This required the formation of a Prison Service Career Tract, which should have a distinct status for prison administrators and a career ladder with promotion based on their success in reforming offenders.

Maconochie believed that to change an offender, his sentence should be "task oriented"—that is, based on good conduct and performance of a specified quantity of labor rather than on a period of time. This came to be known as the *mark system,* because sentences were to consist of specified number of marks or points based on the seriousness of the offense. Rather than a 10-year term for burglary, an offender's sentence might be 10,000 marks. The offender had to earn enough marks to pay off the debt to be released (Silverman, 2001, p. 93).

According to Silverman, there were four stages in Maconochie's system:

Penal Stage: Upon entering prison, the inmate would be exposed to a short but severe penal stage designed to punish him for his past offenses. This included placement in solitary confinement, on a diet of bread and water, and moral instruction to instill in him a feeling of remorse for his past actions.

Associational Stage: Felons then entered a second stage, which provided more freedom and allowed association between inmates. They were also given the opportunity to earn marks to reduce those assigned by the court. However, they could choose to do nothing and remain in prison indefinitely on a diet of bread and water. Marks were viewed as wages and could be earned by working, participation in educational programs, and good behavior. They could also be used to buy better clothing and food, deposited in a prison bank to be redeemed for cash upon discharge, or used toward obtaining an earlier release.

Finally, punishment for prison violations was imposed by adding marks to an offender's sentence. Maconochie felt this placed offenders' fate in their own hands. This was the first system to employ a form of indeterminate sentencing.

Social Stage: Inmates entered this third stage when the marks they earned had been reduced to those owed by a given percentage. This was labeled the "social stage," because inmates with common interests could organize into groups of six. Daily earning were awarded to the group with each inmate receiving one sixth of the total and conversely, individual fines and expenses were deducted from the group's total. This made each inmate responsible for the conduct of all group members. This taught inmates a sense of social responsibility, which Maconochie felt was required to live in society.

Ticket of Leave: Finally, convicts earning a sufficient number of marks to offset those debited to them at sentencing were entitled to a conditional pardon known as a *ticket of leave.* Maconochie felt that once released, offenders should be able to feel totally free. They should not be subjected to police questioning, summary jurisdiction, (the power to arrest and imprison them), or any other special conditions. Only a new conviction for a crime justified imprisonment. This is in contradiction to those who credit him with contributing to the development of parole, because parole has always involved supervision (Silverman, 2001, p. 93).

Application of the Mark System

In 1840, as the administrator of Norfolk Island penal Colony off the coast of Australia, Maconochie first applied his system. This was one of Britain's worst colonies because it held the "twice condemned" criminals sent from England to penal colonies in Australia, where they committed new offenses. He was only able to implement a modified version of his program; it included an initial penal stage in which progress was made on the acquisition of marks. He was unable to release offenders earning enough marks to offset those owed but did issue an "island ticket of leave" allowing them to live outside the main barracks and use their leisure time to work for themselves.

Despite these limitations, Maconochie was able in four short years to transform Britain's most dreaded penal colony into a modern, open institution. He dismantled the gallows, and almost totally eliminated whipping and confinement in irons. He also established schools, encouraged reading, and allowed convicts to eat with forks and knives instead of their fingers.

Maconochie recognized the importance of being open and available to talk to inmates and of treating them with dignity. He managed by walking, which more than 100 years later came to be viewed as a key element in effective prison management."

Maconochie's Recall

Maconochie found Norfolk Island a turbulent, brutal hell, and left it a peaceful, well-ordered community. However, English society still associated imprisonment with punishment and misery, which made many of his superiors hostile to his views. When word reached London that he had allowed inmates the luxury of celebrating the Queens birthday with games and dinner, he was removed. He also was recalled because under his regime inmate costs increased by 21 percent, which contradicted his claims that his program would be less expensive. What he meant was that, in the long run, if offenders were reformed this system would save the government money. This is a problem that has continually plagued corrections; institutions with good programs will invariably cost more to operate. However, if these programs reduce recidivism rates, their higher short-term costs will be offset by long-term savings. Maconochie's superiors apparently ignored evidence that its program was successful; under 3 percent of 1,450 inmates discharged from the penal colony were convicted of new crimes, and only 20 of the 920 doubly convicted and "allegedly irreclaimable" were reconvicted. This is quite remarkable given the high unemployment rate in the areas where these inmates were released. Any warden today would be pleased with results of this kind, given the 52.3 percent recidivism rates of prison inmates during the late 1990s (Silverman, 2001, pp. 93–94).

"In 1848, Maconochie was appointed governor of the new Birmingham Borough Prison, but again, he was unable to fully implement his system. Maconochie failed in both cases because of the legally entrenched sentencing system, the inability to recruit a staff that subscribed to his principles, and the outward hostility of public officials."

Sir Walter Crofton's Irish System

"The penal philosophy of Alexander Maconochie would have died if Sir Walter Crofton had not been appointed chairman of the board of directors of the Irish convict prisons. In 1854 when he assumed this position, his most pressing problem was overcrowding. He solved this by developing a new system that was labeled the *Irish system*. Like Maconochie's Crofton's system they (1) punished convicts for their past crimes and (2) prepared them for release by giving them the opportunity to earn increased responsibility and privileges while progressing through a four-stage system. Its basic facets:"

Solitary Confinement Stage   Entrance phase

1. Entering offenders were incarcerated in a conventional prison (for about 9 months).
2. Regimen: Silence and solitary confinement, except during school, exercise, chapel, and work.

Associational State   Commenced after successful completion of solitary confinement

1. Convicts were transferred to prisons where they worked on public works projects.
2. Had to progress through three conduct classes, which required the accumulation of 108 marks and took about 12 months. Progress up the class structure brought rewards of better clothes and more privileges.

Intermediate State   Crofton's unique contribution; entered after the accumulation of 108 marks

1. About three quarters of all convicts entered this state.
2. Rationale:
   a. Inmates had to prove to society that they were reformed by showing they had developed sufficient powers of self control to resist temptation under circumstance of relative freedom.
   b. Training under conditions of partial freedom prepared offenders for full freedom on release; thus, inmates were minimally supervised.
3. Uniqueness: Represented an early antecedent of current prerelease centers.
4. Objections:
   a. The requirement that prisons had to be built where the work was performed.
   b. High cost of supervising the inmates.
      (1) Solution: Build two portable huts that housed guards and inmates that could be dismantled and moved to another location when a project was completed.

Conditional Release Stage   Entered upon completion of intermediate stage

1. Inmates granted a conditional pardon (ticket of leave) for the remainder of their sentence; represented first use of parole as the term is applied today.
   a. Inmates were under supervision, and those disobeying regulations could be charged with a misdemeanor, summarily tried, and if convicted, have their tickets of leave revoked (Silverman, 2001, p. 94).

"A variety of measures were used to gauge the success of this system. Among the most reliable was the decline in the prison population from 3,933 in 1854 when Crofton took office to 1,314 by 1862. Equally impressive was the number of convicts who were successfully discharged from conditional release as compared with those returned to prison. Between 1856 and 1861, 1,227 tickets of leave were issued, of which only 5.6 percent were revoked" (Silverman, 2001, pp. 94–95).

THE REFORMATORY SYSTEM

"In the United States, the Irish system was a rallying point for penal reformers. They organized to translate these new principles of reform into practice. From this emerged the reformatory movement. In 1870, reformers developed a model for a new prison system at a conference in Cincinnati—the National Congress on Penitentiary and Reformatory Discipline—at which the **National Prison Association** (NPA) was organized. The leading reform ideas of the era were discussed and incorporated into a **Declaration of Principles** that was adopted by the conference." It advocated a philosophy of reformation as opposed to the adoption of punishment, progressive classification of prisoners based on the mark system, the indeterminate system, and the cultivation of the inmate's self-respect. The adoption of these principles was truly remarkable considering the brutal conditions of prisons during this era.

The Elmira Reformatory

Elmira Reformatory in New York, opened in 1877 and headed by Zebulon T. Brockway, was the first reformatory opened. For the next 20 years Brockway made one of the most ambitions attempts to put the Declaration of Principles into effect at Elmira. According to Silverman (2001),

> Judges sentenced first-time felons, ages 16–30, capable of being reformed to Elmira. These offenders received modified indeterminate sentences, under which they were incarcerated until they were reformed or served their maximum term.
>
> Upon entering the institution, inmates were placed in Grade 2. If they behaved acceptably and successfully completed their work or school assignments, they received 3 marks per month in each of these three areas (for a total of 9 marks per month). They needed 54 marks (which could be earned in as few as 6 months) to be promoted to Grade 1. Six additional months of good behavior in Grade 1, which yielded an additional 54 marks, entitled the inmate to parole. Thus "an obedient inmate could . . . earn release after just one year of confinement irrespective of his minimum sentence." Uncooperative inmates were punished by being demoted to Grade 3. Promotion from Grade 3 to Grade 2 required 3 months of satisfactory behavior (p. 95).

Brockway's Innovative Programs

"Brockway established a school program that enabled inmates to progress from learning basic arithmetic, reading, and writing skills to classes in psychology, ethics, and other studies. He also developed an industrial arts program that transformed Elmira into a truly industrial 'reformatory.' By the late 1880s, inmates could choose from more than 20 trades, and within the next 10 years, 36 were available (e.g., shoemaker, fresco painter, blacksmith, carpenter, tailor). In 1888 when inmate labor was abolished because of business and labor pressure, Brockway established a military system, which included dressing inmates in uniforms, assigning them ranks, and dividing them into companies. This early precursor to *boot camps* involved inmate soldiers marching 5–8 hours per day under military discipline that paralleled that at West Point. This was also one of the first prisons to use recreation (e.g., track, basketball) as a method of treatment" (Silverman, 2001, pp. 95–96).

The first parole system in the United States is credited to Brockway.

> Inmates successfully completing the grade system could request a hearing before the parole board, called the board of managers, who would determine their suitability for release after consulting with the superintendent. To be eligible they had to have a job and a place to live. While under supervision, they were required to (1) remain employed for 6 months, (2) submit monthly reports, consigned by their employers, stating they were maintaining good work habits, (3) keep the same job, and (4) behave—that is, avoid alcohol use and association with undesirables. There were no paid parole officers, so Brockway had to rely on volunteers to supervise parolees during the six month parole period. Inmates violating the conditions of their parole were returned to Elmira and placed in the second or third grade at Brockway's discretion and given another chance at reform.

Basic Tenets of the Declaration of Principles

1. Reformation, not vindictive suffering, should be the purpose of penal treatment of prisoners.
2. Classification should be made on the basis of a mark system, patterned after the Irish system.
3. Chief obstacles to prison reform are the political appointment of prison officials, and the instability of management
4. Rewards should be provided for good conduct.
5. The prisoner should be made to realize that his destiny is in his own hands.
6. The prison officials should be trained for their jobs.
7. Indeterminate sentences should be substituted for fixed sentences, and the gross disparities and inequities in prison sentences should be removed. Also, it should be emphasized that repeated short sentences are futile.
8. Religion and education are the most important agencies of reformation.
9. Prison discipline should be such as to gain the will of the prisoner and conserve his self-respect.
10. The aim of the prison should be to make industrious freemen rather than orderly and obedient prisoners.
11. Industrial training should be fully provided for.
12. The system of contract labor in prisons should be abolished.
13. Prisons should be small, and there should be separate institutions for different types of offenders.
14. The law should strike against the so-called higher-ups in crime, as well as against the lesser organizations.
15. There should be indemnification for prisoners who are later discovered to be innocent.
16. There should be revision of the laws relating to the treatment of insane criminals.
17. There should be a more judicious exercise of the pardoning power.
18. There should be established a system for the collection of uniform penal statistics.
19. A more adequate architecture should be developed, providing sufficiently for air and sunlight, as well as for prison hospitals, school rooms, etc.
20. Within each state, prison management should be centralized.
21. The social training of prisoners should be facilitated through proper association and the abolition of the silence rules.
22. Society at large should be made to realize its responsibility for crime conditions (Silverman, 2001, p. 95).

Finally, despite his progressive ideas for reform, Brockway's disciplinary methods were more severe than those advocated in the Declaration of Principles; however, he considered these punishments therapeutic. This position was consistent with his belief that inmates were disobedient patients and punishment was an interview process. One inmate who worked outside an "interview room" and observed inmates after they left related:

> He not alone paddles, but pounds, stamps, kicks, not alone the kidneys but all over the head and body. To be cut, scarred, marred, and beaten entirely out of shape is a frequent occurrence, and very often with a wide red mark across the face . . . which originated from Brockway's oiled strap.
>
> Brockway also employed other disciplinary methods, including (1) solitary confinement in what he called rest cure cells where inmates were placed on a restrictive diet of bread and water, sometimes put in restraints so they cold not sit for hours; (2) administering a quick slap or punch in the face; and (3) whipping with a rubber hose. Apparently, Brockway considered these types of discipline appropriate because he never denied administering them and, in fact, argued they were for the inmate's own good (Silverman, 2001, pp. 95–96).

Reformatory Models Fell Short

According to Silverman (2001, pp. 96–97),

> Between 1877 and 1913 reformatories were established in 17 states. These institutions failed to socialize their inmates and mold them into obedient citizens-workers. Inmates at all these facilities rejected the authority of their custodians and, responding to the deprivations of prisons life coped by "resorting to . . . violence, revolts, escapes, drugs, arson, homosexuality [and] suicide" [which] forced reformatory [staff] to focus [on] custody and control in the interest of personal and organizational survival. . . . [Thus] American's adult reformatories [including Elmira] were . . . ineffective and brutal prisons [rather than institutions of benevolent reform].

By 1910, the reformatory movement had reached its peak and was on the decline.

Silverman continues, "Although reformatories failed in practice, they crystallized progressive correctional thought. During the Big House Era that spanned the first half of the 20th century, there continued to be sporadic attempts to introduce bits and pieces of the Declaration of Principles into juvenile programs and even into adult institutions. However, it was not until after World War II, that the necessary support became available to create a new type of prison—the "rehabilitative institution—in which these ideas could be tested more fully" (2001, p. 97).

THE RISE OF THE PROGRESSIVES

According to Clear and Cole (2000),

> The first two decades of the 1900s, called the "Age of Reform," set the dominant tone for American social thought and political action until the 1960s. Industrialization, urbanization, technological change, and scientific advancements had revolutionized the American

landscape. A group known as Progressives attacked the excesses of this emergent society, especially those of big business, and placed their faith in state action to deal with the social problems of slums, adulterated food, dangerous occupational conditions, vice, and crime.

   The Progressives, most of whom came from upper-status backgrounds, were optimistic about the possibility of solving the problems of modern society. They were concerned in particular about conditions in cities, with their large immigrant populations. They believed that civic-minded people could apply the findings of science to social problems, including penology, in ways that would benefit all. Specifically they believed that through individualized treatment criminals could be rehabilitated (pp. 44–45).

Individualized Treatment and the Positivist School

According to David Rothman, the Progressive programs can be epitomized in two words: conscience and convenience. "The reforms were promoted by benevolent and philanthropic men and women who sought to understand and cure crime through a case-by-case approach. They believed that the reformers of the penitentiary era were wrong in assuming that all deviants were 'victims of social disorder' and that the deviants 'could all be rehabilitated with a single program, the well-ordered routine,' or the prison" (Clear & Cole, 2000, p. 45). Furthermore,

> The Progressives thought it necessary to know the life history of each offender and then devise a treatment program specific to that individual. However, to diagnose each criminal, prescribe treatment, and schedule release to the community, correctional administrators had to be given discretion. From this orientation the phrase "treatment according to the needs of the offender" came into vogue, in contrast to "punishment according to the severity of the crime," which had been the hallmark of Beccaria and the reformers of the early 1800s.
>
>   Rothman argues that because discretion was required for the day-to-day practice of the new penology, correctional administrators responded favorably to it. The new discretionary authority made it easier for administrators to carry out their daily assignments. He also notes that the Progressives committed to incarceration were instrumental in promoting probation and parole, but supporters of the penitentiary used the requirement of discretion to expand the size of the prison population. The Progressives had faith that the state would carry out their reforms with justice. In the same way they looked to government programs to secure social justice, they assumed the agents of the state would help offenders. Rothman notes:
>
>> In criminal justice, the issue was not how to protect the offender from the arbitrariness of the state, but how to bring the state more effectively to the aid of the offender. The state was not a behemoth to be chained and fettered, but an agent capable of fulfilling an ambitious program. Thus, a policy that called for the state's exercise of discretionary authority in finely tuned responses, was at its core, Progressive.
>
>   As members of the **positivist school,** the Progressives looked to social, economic, biological, and psychological rather than religious or moral explanations for the causes of

crime and they applied modern scientific methods to determine the best treatment thera-pies. Recall that the classical school of Beccaria and Bentham had emphasized a legal ap-proach to the problem, focusing on the act rather than the criminal. In contrast, the scien-tific positivists school shifted the focus from the criminal act to the offender. By the beginning of the twentieth century, advances in the biological and social sciences provided the framework for the reforms proposed by the Progressives. Although several theoretical perspectives can be found within the positivist school most of its practitioners shared three basic assumptions:

1. Criminal behavior is not the result of free will but stems from factors over which the individual had no control: biological characteristics, psychological malad-justments, sociological conditions.
2. Criminal can be treated so that they can lead crime-free lives.
3. Treatment must be focused on the individual and the individual's problem (Clear & Cole, 2000, p. 45).

Progressive Reforms

Armed with their views about the nature of criminal behavior and the need for state action to reform offenders, the Progressives fought for changes in correctional methods. They pur-sued two main strategies: (1) improve conditions in social environments that seemed to be breeding grounds for crime and (2) rehabilitate individual offenders. Because they saw crime as primarily an urban problem, concentrated especially among the immigrant lower class, the Progressives sought through political action to bring about changes that would improve ghetto conditions: better public health, landlord-tenant laws, public housing, play grounds, settlement houses, education. However, because they also believed that criminal behavior varied among individuals, a case-by-case approach was required.

By the 1920s the Progressives had succeeded in getting wide acceptance of four portions of their program: probation, indeterminate sentences, parole, and juvenile courts. These elements had been proposed at the 1870 Cincinnati meeting, but the Pro-gressives and their allies in corrections were instrumental in implementing them through-out the country (Clear & Cole, 2000, p. 46).

Probation

Probation had its origin in the work of John Augustus in the Boston Police Court in 1841. This alternative to incarceration fitted nicely into the Progressive scheme, for it recognized individual differences and allowed offenders to be treated in the community under super-vision. Although Massachusetts passed a probation law in 1878, no other state took the step until 1897, and in 1900 only six states provided for probation. But by 1920 every state per-mitted probation for juveniles and thirty-three states permitted it for adults. By 1930 the federal government and the thirty-six states, including every industrialized state, had state probation laws on their books. However, probation remained primarily an urban strategy; it never took root in rural or small-town America. The reason may have to do with the cost-effectiveness of the approach in areas where populations are scattered, or perhaps it reflects a different mind set among rural people.

In urban areas problems with staffing, caseload size, and the quality of supervision caused probation to fall short of expectations. Almost no jurisdiction met the 50 : 1 ratio of clients to supervisors then advocated by penologists. Perhaps more important, probation officers were given an almost impossible task: With very little scientifically based theory to guide their actions, they were expected to keep their charges crime-free. What passed as ways to reform probationers often turned out to be little more than attempts to indoctrinate them with middle-class injunctions—work, go to church, keep clean, get ahead, be good—attitudes not consistent with real life in city slums. In addition, politicians sometimes attacked probation as "coddling" criminals. Nevertheless the system prevailed, in part because it was useful for inducing the guilty plea, then tough necessary to relieve overcrowded courts (Clear & Cole, 2000, p. 46).

Indeterminate Sentences and Parole

Although the idea of parole release had been developed in Ireland and Australia in the 1850s and Zebulon Brockway had instituted it at Elmira in 1876, not until the mid-1920s did it really catch on in the United States. By then thirty-seven states had indeterminate sentencing laws and forty-four provided for release on parole. Fixed sentences were retained for lesser offenses, but during this period more than three-quarters of convicted offenders whose maximum terms exceeded five years were serving indeterminate sentences.

The sentences were called "indeterminate," but nearly always minimum and maximum terms were set, within which the correctional process of rehabilitation could operate. At no time were state legislatures willing to give correctional officials unbridled authority to decide when (or if) a prisoner could be released. Yet over time legislatures tended to expand the outer limits of sentences. Especially in response to public outcries over crime, politicians often increased the maximum penalties, thus giving wider discretion to parole decision makers (Clear & Cole, 2000, p. 46).

A Medical Approach

Other models were developed during this period. The thought developed that criminals suffered from mental illness. "At the 1870 Cincinnati congress one speaker described a criminal as 'a man who has suffered under a diseased evinced by the perpetration of a crime, and who may reasonably be held to be under the domination of such disease until his conduct has afforded very strong presumption not only that he is free from its immediate influence, but that the chances of its recurrence have become exceedingly remote'" (Clear & Cole, 2000, p. 47).

Though there was the feeling that offenders were capable of being rehabilitated, it was not until the 1930s that urgent endeavors were made to execute what has been known as the *medical model*. This was "a model of corrections based on the assumption that criminal behavior is caused by social, psychological, or biological deficiencies that require treatment" (Clear & Cole, 2000, p. 47). When the Federal Bureau of Prisons was sanctioned by Congress to establish those correctional institutions that would guarantee proper classification, care, and treatment, rehabilitation gained prominence as the primary reason for incarceration (Clear & Cole, 2000, p. 47).

States such as New York, Illinois, California, and New Jersey began to accept programs that had as their aim of reform through treatment. The rhetoric of rehabilitation was there throughout the country. Punishment was looked upon as an outdated concept. "Prisons were thus to become something like mental hospitals that would rehabilitate and test the inmate for readiness to reenter society. In many states, however, the medical model was adopted in name only: departments of prisons became departments of corrections, but the budgets for treatment programs remained about the same" (Clear & Cole, 2000, p. 47).

The fact that corrections moved into a medical model should come as no shocker. It was during the early 1920s that social work came into its own gaining legitimacy and professional status. As casework approaches were being utilized, and as social workers were analyzing cases in order to help those less fortunate, new methods of measuring mental fitness and assessing personality were being addressed. "The theories of Sigmund Freud and Carl Jung dominated American psychiatry, and these approaches began to take their place alongside biological explanations for illness. Advocates of the medical model sought to bring about change through treatment programs, most often with a psychological base" (Clear & Cole, 2000, p. 47). It was observed by Karl Menninger, a psychiatrist that acts deemed criminal "are signals of distress, signals of failure . . . the spasms of struggles and convulsions of a sub-marginal human being trying to make it in our complex society with inadequate equipment and inadequate preparation" (Clear & Cole, 2000, pp. 47–48).

As the tools for parole, probation, and indeterminate sentencing were already in place, "incorporating the medical model only required adding classification systems to diagnose offenders and treatment programs to cure them. Tests were developed to help psychologists, psychiatrists, and social workers in determining the cause of the inmate's problem and indicating appropriate treatment. Recognizing that the prison environment would influence the effectiveness of treatment, supporters of the medical model argued that different types of institutions should be developed for different types of offenders" (Clear & Cole, 2000, p. 48).

Classifications were to differ on a statewide basis. Little effort was made to differentiate inmates who were to benefit from those who would not. Using Wisconsin as an example,

> [I]nmates were put into one of seven exclusively psychiatric groupings:
> 1. Mentally deficient: arrested intellectual development, "feebleminded"
> 2. Mentally defective: inadequate personality, "criminal"
> 3. Mentally diseased: psychotic, "insane"
> 4. Mentally deviate: neurotic, "borderline insane"
> 5. Mentally distorted: inadequate state, "morally aberrant"
> 6. Mentally delayed: (minors)
> 7. Atypical or unclassifiable (Clear & Cole, 2000, p. 48).

The use of psychiatry grew after World War II. "Group therapy, behavior modification, shock therapy, individual counseling, psychotherapy, guided group interaction, and many other approaches all became part of the 'new penology'" (Clear & Cole, 2000, p. 48). The best example given is that of Maryland's Patuxent Institution. It opened in 1955 and was based on the principles of the medical model. It was built on the idea that we treat adult offenders who received indeterminate sentencing and as being judged to be "defective delinquents." Those who administered the program had the authority to "control intake, to experiment with a treatment milieu, and to decide when to release 'patients.'" During this period of time patients were both diagnosed and treated (Clear & Cole, 2000, p. 48).

As criticism rose with the medical model because of its lack of success, the legislature in Maryland reduced its authority. "By 1991 the legislature had also changed the institution's goal from rehabilitation to remediation . . . helping inmates overcome such problems as lack of reading skills, poor behavior controls or substance abuse" (Clear & Cole, 2000, p. 48).

It appears that there has been much criticism thrown at the rehabilitation model, let alone the medical model. Those who criticize these models suggest that the relationships with inmates is hard to achieve, when the overall concern with prisons and its prisoners appears to be custodial care and safety, putting aside much of the treatment needed by these inmates.

During the days of the civil rights movement, it was stated by the President's Commission in 1967 that "crime and delinquency are symptoms of failures and disorganizations of the community. . . . The task of corrections, therefore, includes building or rebuilding social ties, obtaining employment and education, securing in the larger senses a place for the offender in the routine functioning of society" (Clear & Cole, 2000, p. 49). This was the feeling of the advocates of community corrections. Community corrections was to have as it goal the reintegration of prisoners into society.

Prisons were to be avoided. The medical model was to be followed. By placing an inmate into an atmosphere that was human made, we were intruding on his or her ability to become part of society. Psychologically, we want prisoners to be reintegrated into society. "Probation would be the sentence of choice for nonviolent offenders so that they could engage in vocational and educational programs that increased their chances of adjusting to society. For the small portion of offenders who had to be incarcerated, the amount of time in prison would be only a short interval until release on parole. To further the goal of reintegration, correctional workers would serve as advocates for offenders as they dealt with governmental agencies providing employment counseling, medical treatment, and financial assistance" (Clear & Cole, 2000, p. 49).

Such an idea was the dominant theme in corrections until the late 1970s. This model gave way to punishment as well as determinate sentencing. Crime rates were once again on the rise. There was an urging that if there is to be rehabilitative type programs it would be done on a voluntary basis, but punishment was still to be the goal of corrections.

It was stated by James Q. Wilson that this "'new realism' in regard to treatment programs and crime rates has been frustrated by our 'optimistic and unrealistic assumptions about human nature'" (Clear & Cole, 2000, pp. 49–50).

During this time we saw a decline in the rehabilitation model. Researchers at this time, including Robert Martinson for the New York State Governor's Special Committee on Criminal Offenders, demonstrated that recidivism rates were high and that rehabilitation programs were not accomplishing what they set out to do. Too much discretion was given to parole boards and others involved in deciding how to handle inmates.

All of this was followed by the *crime control model*. This was a model founded on the notion that all criminal behavior can be controlled by additional use of incarceration under the strictest of supervision.

"The critique of the rehabilitation model led to changes in the sentencing structures of more than half of the states and to the abolition of parole release in many." The key was determinate sentencing laws that were to incarcerate prisoners for longer periods of time. The thought behind the crime control model was risk containment (Clear & Cole, 2000, p. 50).

"The punitive ethos of the 1980s and 1990s appeared in the emphasis of dealing more strictly with violent offenders and career criminals. It was also reflected in the trend toward intensive supervision of probationers, the detention without bail of the accused persons thought to present a danger to the community, reinstitution of the death penalty in thirty-seven states, and the requirement that judges impose mandatory penalties for persons convicted of certain offenses or having extensive criminal records. By the end of the decade, the effect of these 'get tough' policies was evidenced by the record number of prisoners, the longer sentences being served, and the size of the probation population" (Clear & Cole, 2000, p. 50). Was this the reason crime rates fell, or is this simply a question of a cyclical movement?

Today we see a decrease in murders nationwide yet a rise or same number of rapes. Why?

REFERENCES

Clear, T. R., & Cole, G. F. (2000) *American Corrections* (5th ed.). West/Wadsworth. Belmont, California.

Silverman, I. J. (2001). *Corrections—A Comprehensive Review* (2nd ed.). Wadsworth: Thomason Learning.

part II

Issues in Corrections

Changing Goals of Corrections

Roslyn Muraskin

To understand punishment, we must understand that its rationale is broadly influenced by philosophical, political, and social themes. The causes of crime are very much tied to "questions of responsibility and hence to the rationale for specific sanctions" (Clear & Cole, 2000, p. 55). It is obvious to the student of criminal justice that the classical school of criminology, as founded by Cesare Beccaria, was similar to the concept of the Age of Reason as set forth by Jeremy Bentham's utilitarianism. "Making the punishment fit the crime" became a "humanistic advance as it sought to do away with the brutal punishment often inflicted for trivial offenses. With the rise of science and the development of positivist criminology toward the end of the 1800s, new beliefs emerged about criminal responsibility" (Clear & Cole, 2000, p. 56). Criminal behavior as we understand it from the school of positivists was the consequence "of sociological, psychological, or biological factors and therefore directed correctional work toward rehabilitating the offender through treatment" (Clear & Cole, 2000, p. 56).

When we speak of punishment, what is it that we refer to? It was argued by Herbert Packer that

> punishment is marked by these three elements:
> 1. An offense
> 2. The infliction of pain because of the commission of the offense
> 3. A dominant purpose that is neither to compensate someone injured by the offense nor to better the offender's condition but to prevent further offenses or to inflict what is thought to be deserved pain on the offender (Clear & Cole, 2000, p. 56).

The fact is that Packer emphasized two of the major goals of punishment: that is, "inflicting deserved suffering on evildoers and preventing crime" (Clear & Cole, 2000, p. 56).

The four objectives of criminal sanctions are "retribution (deserved punishment) deterrence, incapacitation, and rehabilitation" (Clear & Cole, 2000, p. 56). A fifth goal that is noted is that of restorative justice.

Retribution or deserved punishment "is punishment inflicted on a person who has infringed on the rights of others and deserves to be punished. The biblical expression 'an eye for an eye, a tooth for a tooth' illustrates the philosophy of underlying retribution. Retribution means that those who commit a particular crime should be punished alike, in proportion to the gravity of the offense or to the extent to which others have been made to suffer. Retribution focuses on the offense. . . . Offenders must be penalized for their wrongful acts, simply because fairness and justice require that they be punished" (Clear & Cole, 2000, p. 56).

However, as time goes by, retribution has lost much of its value. There are those who believe that retribution is needed in a society where you do no want lawlessness. The feeling is that the state must punish in order for others to understand that you break the law, there is punishment. How much punishment is necessary? How far should the state go in punishing the wrong doer? Is respect for law lost if punishment is not meted out properly, but then what constitutes proper punishment? Since the 1970s there has grown a new feeling that rehabilitation does not work, and therefore punishment is the way to go. "Using the concept of 'just deserts or deserved punishment,' to define retribution, some theorists argue that a person who infringes on the rights of others deserve to be punished. This approach is based on the philosophical view that punishment is a moral response to harm inflicted on society" (Clear & Cole, 2000, pp. 56–57).

According to Andrew von Hirsch, "the sanctioning authority is entitled to choose a response that expresses moral disapproval: namely punishment." According to him and others such as Norval Morris, "punishment should be applied only to exact retribution for the wrong inflicted and not primarily to achieve other goals such as deterrence, incapacitation, or rehabilitation" (Clear & Cole, 2000, p. 56–57).

Deterrence is viewed as sending a message to the would be criminal. We find the roots of deterrence in eighteenth-century England with Jeremy Bentham, who "argued that retribution was pointless and unjustified except when pain inflicted was demonstrably more beneficial to society than pain withheld. The presumed benefit of punishment was the prevention of crime. The basic objective of punishment . . . was to deter potential criminals by the examples of the sanctions laid on the guilty" (Clear & Cole, 2000, p. 57). Deterrence does not work that way. The feeling that average citizens will be deterred by seeing the kind of punishment meted out if they commit crimes does not appear to deter many, if any, from committing crimes. Even in the days when hanging for the crime of pick pocketing in England was held in a public square, while the hanging took place, pockets were being picked. A specific deterrence is supposed to discourage any individual from committing any kind of crime, but that is not the case. For someone to say that he or she is dissuaded from committing crimes because of the nature of the punishment is to assume that all individuals act in a rational manner and that is not the case, especially those prone to commit any type of crime.

Then there is the theory of **incapacitation.** Here the assumption is that "society can remove an offender's capacity to commit further crimes by detention in prison or by execution. Many people express such sentiments when urging that we should 'lock 'em up and throw away the key!' " (Clear & Cole, 2000, p. 58). Perhaps in primitive societies this method worked, but not in modern times. The ultimate method of incapacitation is the use of the death penalty, but here again, we know of no statistical proof that indicates that the death penalty deters, though it obviously prevents one from committing further crimes.

The fact is that the factor of incapacitation focuses on the offender rather than the offense. Using Clear and Cole's examples, "[u]nder the incapacitation theory, . . . a woman who kills her abusive husband as an emotional reaction to his verbal insults and physical assaults could receive a light sentence. As a one-time killer who felt driven to kill by unique circumstances, she is not likely to commit additional crimes. By contrast someone who lifts merchandise from a store and has been convicted of the offense on ten previous occasions may receive a severe sentence. The criminal record and type of crime indicate that he or she will commit additional crimes if released" (2000, p. 59).

What is the proper sentence to be given? How can society let alone jurists and legislators determine whether a person will commit further crimes? You cannot punish for crimes not yet committed.

"In recent years, greater attention has been paid to the concept of *selective incapacitation* whereby offenders who repeat certain kinds of crime are sentenced to long prison terms. Research suggests that a relatively small number of offenders commit a large number of violent and property crimes" (Clear & Cole, 2000, p. 59). There are those who believe that "career criminals" should be locked away for a long time. This becomes very costly, not only in terms of building more correctional facilities, but more time spent in court, on trials, and less time on plea bargaining.

Again according to Clear and Cole (2000), "[t]he idea of confining or closely supervising repeat offenders is appealing, yet it involves costs to the criminal justice system. . . . selective incapacitation raises disturbing moral and ethical questions. Because the theory looks at aggregates—the total harm of a certain type of crime versus the total suffering to be inflicted to reduce its incidence—policymakers may tend to focus on 'cost benefit' comparisons, disregarding serious issues of justice, individual freedom and civil liberties" (p. 59).

The one way to bring a convicted offender back into the fold of society is by **rehabilitation.** There are those who truly believe that by rehabilitating offenders they can be resocialized to live productive lives. "If the offender's criminal behavior is assumed to result from some social, psychological or biological imperfection, then treating the disorder becomes the primary goal of corrections. The goal of rehabilitation is oriented solely toward the offender. . . . People who commit lesser offenses may receive long prison sentences if experts believe that a long period of time is required to successfully rehabilitate them. By contrast, a murderer may win early release by showing signs that the psychological or emotional problems that led to the killing have been corrected" (Clear & Cole, 2000, p. 60). Under the guise of rehabilitation, offenders are to be treated and then returned to society when deemed cured. "Consequently, judges should not set a fixed sentence but one with maximum and minimum terms so that parole boards may release inmates when they have been rehabilitated" (Clear & Cole, 2000, p. 60). This is referred to as the indeterminate sentence. Such a sentence has been simplified by the feeling that if the inmate knows the date of release, no effort will be made to participate in a rehabilitation program of any type. On the other hand, if they will be released only if deemed cured, then the likelihood of their going for treatment exists. This is theory.

"From the 1940s until the 1970s the rehabilitative goal was so widely held that treatment and reform of the offender were generally regarded as the only issues worthy of serious attention. During the past twenty-five years . . . the assumptions of the rehabilitation model has been questioned. . . . people no longer take for granted that crime is caused by identifiable, curable problems such as poverty, lack of job skills, low self-esteem, and hostility toward authority" (Clear & Cole, 2000, p. 60). The argument is set forth that we do not know how to solve the problems related to criminal behavior. "Morris has argued that coerced in-prison treatment programs not only waste resources but are morally wrong on human rights grounds, even if they might be effective in changing behavior" (Clear & Cole, 2000, p. 60).

There are new approaches to punishment. As Gordon Bazemore and Mark Umbreit note, "crime has traditionally been viewed as violating the state, but people now recognize that a criminal act also violates the victim and the community. In keeping with the focus on *community justice*—by the police, courts and corrections—advocates are calling for *restoration* (restorative justice) to be added to the goals of the criminal sanction" (Clear & Cole, 2000, p. 60).

Under restorative justice, crime is viewed as "a violation of penal law. The criminal law also practically and symbolically denies community. It breaks trusts among citizens and requires community members to determine how 'to contradict the moral message of the crime that the offender is above the law and the victim beneath its reach.' Crime victims suffer losses involving damage to property and self that results from the act" (Clear & Cole, 2000, p. 60). By changing the focus to restorative justice, we are able to provide methods for the offender to patch up the damage done to both victim and the community. Under these circumstances the offender attempts to "undo" what he or she has done while promising to obey the law at all times in the future. "The victim must specify the harm of the offense and the resources necessary to restore the losses suffered, and the victim must lay out the conditions necessary to diminish any process, . . . "he/she must provide also support to restore the victim, while providing opportunities for the offender to perform reparative tasks" (Clear & Cole, 2000, pp. 60–61).

How do we punish? The following terms are easily defined for the types of punishment available depending on the offense and the offender's record:

Probation: Offender reports to probation officer periodically, depending on the offense, sometimes as frequently as several times a month or as infrequently as once a year.

Intensive supervision probation: Offender sees probation officer three to five times a week. Probation officer also makes unscheduled visits to offender's home or workplace.

Restitution and fines: Used alone or in conjunction with probation or intensive supervision and requires regular payments to crime victims or to the courts.

Community service: Used alone or in conjunction with probation or intensive supervision and requires completion of set number of hours of work in and for the community.

Substance abuse treatment: Evaluation and referral services provided by private outside agencies and used alone or in conjunction with either simple probation or intensive supervision.

Day reporting: Clients report to a central location every day where they file a daily schedule with their supervision officer showing how each hour will be spent at work, in class, at support group meetings, and so on.

House arrest and electronic monitoring: Used in conjunction with intensive supervision and restricts offender to home except when at work, school, or treatment.

Halfway house: Residential settings for selected inmates as a supplement to probation for those completing prison programs and for some probation or parole violators. Usually coupled with community service work and/or substance abuse treatment.

Boot camp: Rigorous military-style regiment for younger offenders, designed to accelerate punishment while instilling discipline, often with an educational component.

Prisons and jails: More serious offenders serve their terms at state or federal prisons, while county jails are usually designed to hold inmates for shorter periods.[1]

Kinds of Sentencing

Indeterminate sentencing: A period of incarceration with minimum and maximum terms stipulated so that parole eligibility depends on the time necessary for treatment; closely associated with the rehabilitation concept.

Determinate sentencing: A fixed period of incarceration imposed by a court; associated with the concept of retribution or deserved punishment.

Presumptive sentence: A sentence for which the legislature or a commission sets a minimum and maximum range of months or years. Judges are to fix the length of the sentence within that range allowing for special circumstances.

Mandatory sentence: A sentence stipulating that some minimum period of incarceration must be served by people convicted of selected crimes, regardless of background or circumstances.[2]

The Punishment of Offenders[3]

Form of Sanction	Description	Purposes
Incarceration	Imprisonment	
Indeterminate sentence	Specifies a maximum and minimum length of time to be served	Incapacitation, deterrence, rehabilitation
Determinate sentence	Specifies a certain length of time to be served	Retribution, deterrence, incapacitation
Mandatory sentence	Specifies a minimum amount of time for given crimes that must be served	Incapacitation, deterrence
Good time	Subtracts days from an inmate's sentence because of good behavior or participation in prison programs	Rewards behavior, relieves prison crowding, helps maintain prison discipline
Intermediate sanctions	Punishment for those requiring sanctions more restrictive than probation but less restrictive than prison	Retribution, deterrence
Administered by the judiciary		
Fine	Money paid to state by Offender	Retribution, deterrence
Restitution	Money paid to victim by offender	Retribution, deterrence
Administered in the community		
Community service	Requires offender to perform work for the community	Retribution, deterrence
Home confinement	Requires offender to stay in home during certain times	Retribution, deterrence, incapacitation
Intensive probation, supervision	Requires strict and frequent reporting to probation officer	Retribution, deterrence, incapacitation
Administered institutionally		
Boot camp/shock incarceration	Short-term institutional sentence emphasizing physical development and discipline followed by probation	Retribution, incapacitation, rehabilitation
Probation	Allows offender to serve a sentence in the community under supervision	Retribution, deterrence, rehabilitation
Death	Execution	Incapacitation, deterrence retribution[4]

Clear and Cole (2000) *American Corrections,* Belmont, CA: West/Wadsworth.

NOTES

1. This material was taken from *Seeking Justice: Crime and Punishment in America* (1997). New York: Edna McConnell Clark Foundation, pp. 32–33.
2. The material regarding definitions of sentences was taken from Clear and Cole, *American Corrections* (2000). Belmont, CA: West/Wadsworth, pp. 64–65.
3. Ibid., p. 71.
4. Ibid.

REFERENCE

Clear, T. R., & Cole, G. F. (2000). *Introduction to Corrections.* West/Wadsworth: Belmont, California.

Introduction to "Prisoner Reentry: The Iron Law of Imprisonment"

Roslyn Muraskin

According to James P. Lynch and William J. Sabol, in their *Crime Policy Report* (2001) published by the Urban Institute, the following is to be considered: "[t]he number of prisoners released each year has increased, but the rate of increase has declined. The number of prison releases has increased more slowly than the prison population has increased. The proportion of released prisoners who are violent offenders has remained stable, while drug offenders account for a larger proportion of released prisoners. The released prisoners pool consists of more 'churners.' The expansion of incarceration has increased the number of persons released from prison for the first time in their lives. Recently released prisoners are less likely to have participated in prison programs than they were in the past. The size of the parole population has increased, but the growth of the population is slowing. Unconditional releases have contributed to the slowing of the growth of the parole population. The decrease in overall time served on parole has contributed to the slowing of the growth of the parole population. 'Churners' on parole are being created at a faster rate than they have successfully completing prison (p. 1).

With a massive increase in the correctional population, attention is being diverted to the growing number of prisoners returning to the community. Concerns about public safety have been raised. "Yet, throughout the 1990s, as the annual number of offenders released from prison increased, the aggregate crime rate actually decreased" (Lynch & Sabol, 2001, p. 2). What the public is concerned about is that with the "increasing number of offenders released from prison with no conditions of supervision, or 'unconditionally,' . . . the absence of a parole officer can be a detriment to reentry, as parole officers can offer minimal help to ex-prisoners in locating resources" (Lynch & Sabol, 2001, p. 3). Though there is a large number of individuals being incarcerated today, most of them do not recidivate. It may well be that there is a larger reentry of prisoners into the community today, but what of the limited supervision? What are the problems?

There appears not to be a single type of reintegration problem. "There are more violent offenders returning to communities, more offenders coming back from their first experience with incarceration, and more offenders returning after a churning[1] experience. Offenders have been out of the community for longer periods, and they are less likely to have participated in education and training programs. Communities, therefore, face a complicated set of problems related to reintegrating offenders" (Lynch & Sabol, 2001, p. 14). The assumption is that communities are willing to accept back into their communities those incarcerated, but public safety still remains a concern. There is to be considered the "Weed and Seed" model—that "the 'weeding' out of offenders must occur prior to 'seeding' prevention efforts—then the return of violent offenders may be like 'sowing weeds' back into the communities" (Lynch & Sabol, 2001, p. 15).

There are about 600,000 individuals being released each day from both state and federal prisons. "Ever since prisons were built, individuals have faced the challenges of moving from confinement in correctional institutions to liberty on the street" (Travis et al., 2001, p. 1). Since the days when the first correctional institutions were built, the challenge has remained the same, returning to the community. "Yet from a number of policy perspectives, the age-old issue of prisoner reintegration is taking on new importance. More prisoners are returning home, having spent longer terms behind bars, less prepared for life on the outside, with less assistance in their reintegration. Often they will have difficulties reconnecting with jobs, housing, and perhaps their families. . . . Most will be rearrested, and many will be returned to prison for new crimes or parole violations. . . . this cycle of removal and return of large numbers of individuals, mostly men, is increasingly concentrated in a relatively small number of communities that already encounter enormous social and economic disadvantages" (Travis et al., 2001, p. 1).

The cost of this cycle with regard to both incarceration and reentry are high. "First and foremost is the public safety dimension. Nearly two-thirds of released prisoners are expected to be rearrested for a felony or serious misdemeanor within three years of their release. Such high recidivism rates translate into thousands of new victimizations each year. Second, there are fiscal implications. Significant portions of state budgets are now invested in the criminal justice system. Expenditures on corrections alone increased from $9 billion in 1982 to $44 billion in 1997 (accessed 2001). These figures do not include the cost of arrest and sentencing processes, nor do they take into account the cost to victims. Third there are far-reaching social costs. Prisoner reentry carries the potential for profound collateral consequences, including public health risks, disenfranchisement, homelessness, and weakened ties among families and communities" (Travis et al., 2001, p. 1).

With costs being great so are opportunities. To manage reentry[2] would mean a reduction in fewer crimes and fewer returns to correctional facilities.

SENTENCING[3] AND SUPERVISION

According to Travis, Solomon, and Waul (2001), "Over the past generation, sentencing policy in the United States has been characterized by three major developments. The first is a remarkable increase in U.S. imprisonment rates. There are now more than a million people in state and federal prisons—a fourfold increase since 1973. The second is a shift in sentencing and supervision policy away from indeterminate sentencing and earned release to greater (but not universal) reliance on determinate sentencing and mandatory release. Third, the system of parole supervision has undergone significant changes, with increasing caseloads, new monitoring capacities, and an increase focus on surveillance over rehabilitation. Taken together, these trends place an increased burden on the formal and informal processes that should work together to support successful reintegration" (p. 4).

According to Travis and colleagues, the "per capita rate of imprisonment in America hovered at about 110 per 100,000 from 1925 to 1973, with little variation. Starting in 1973, however, the rate of imprisonment has grown steadily, so that in 1999 there were 476 incarcerated individuals for every 100,000 residents—more than four times the 1973 level. . . . state prisons now house 1,200,000 individuals and federal prisons house 135,000. Another 605,000 persons are held in local jails" (2001, p. 4). The conclusion? The more that go in, the more that go out. As of 2000 the number of prisoners released annually has grown to an estimated 585,000 almost fourfold from 1977.

"Over the same period, the overarching jurisprudential and penal philosophy that once guided the reentry process, namely the process of rehabilitation and earned reintegration within a framework of indeterminate sentencing, lost its intellectual and policy dominance" (Travis et al., 2001, pp. 4–5). The indeterminate approach provided broader ranges of sentences allowing for the release of prisoners by parole boards while embracing the idea of rehabilitation.

Equating staples of correctional management "as good-time credits earned through compliance with requirements and successful completion of in-prison programming and discretionary release through review by a parole board [has] been abolished or curtailed in many states" (Travis et al., 2001, p. 5). Surveys of parole officers indicate that priority is given to parole officers as law enforcement officers as opposed to rehabilitation functions.

There has been a recent increase in parole violations: "the burden on the systems that manage reentry has increased substantially and the operational capacity to manage these increases has not kept pace" (Travis et al., 2001, p. 5).

Just who is coming home? (see Table 5–1) "Of the nearly 600,000 inmates returning to communities across the country each year, most have not completed high school, have limited employment skills, and have histories of substance abuse and health problems. . . . there are substantially more individuals released from prison having served a term for a drug-related or violent offense. The large majority of returning prisoners are male (88 percent), although the percentage of women in the parole population has risen from 8 to 12 percent over the past decade. The median age is 34 and the median education level is 11th grade. In 1998, more than half of returning prisoners were white (55 percent) and 44 percent were African American. Twenty-one percent of parolees were Hispanic (and may be of any race)" (Travis et al., 2001, p. 9).

It is interesting to note the change in crimes for which individuals have been convicted: "the number of released prisoners convicted of violent crimes has nearly doubled from 1985 to 1998—from about 75,000 in 1985 to more than 140,000 in 1998—and presumably will continue to increase. Over the same period, both the number of released pris-

Table 5–1   PROFILE OF PAROLEES

Gender	
Male	88%
Female	12%

Race	
White	55%
Black/African American	44%
Other	1%

Hispanic Origin	
Hispanic	21%
Non-Hispanic	79%

Age (median)	*34 years*
Education level (median)	*11th grade*

Sources: T. P. Bonczar and L. E. Glaze, "Probation and Parole in the United States, 1998," Bureau of Justice Statistics, NCJ 160092, August 1999; and J. Petersilia, "Parole and Prisoner Reentry in the United States." In M. Tonry and J. Petersilia (Eds.), *Prisons.* Chicago: University of Chicago Press, 1999.

oners who had been convicted of drug offenses (sales and possession) and their share of the returning population increased significantly. The number of released drug offenders rose from about 25,000 in 1985 to 182,000 in 1998. The proportion of released prisoners who were drug offenders rose from 11 percent in 1985 to 26 percent in 1990 and to 32 percent in 1998" (Travis et al., 2001, pp. 9–10).[4]

Due to the sentencing reforms during the last two decades, which include compulsory minimums and truth-in-sentencing laws, those prisoners released have, "on average, served longer sentences than prisoners in the past. The amount of time prisoners serve prior to release has increased 27 percent since 1990, from an average of 22 months spent in prison for those released in 1990 to 28 months for those released in 1998" (Travis et al., 2001, p. 11).

Prisoners who are released return to their communities with a host of health problems. Substance abuse and mental illness are among those health problems that were rarely treated while the individuals were incarcerated.

"A disproportionate share of the prison population also live with chronic health problems or infectious diseases. In 1997, about one-quarter of the individuals living with HIV or AIDS in the United States had been released from a correctional facility (prison or jail) that year. Approximately one-third of those infected with hepatitis C and tuberculosis were released from a prison or jail in 1999" (Travis et al., 2001, p. 11). About 2 to 3 percent in prison are HIV positive or have AIDS; about 18 percent are infected with hepatitis C; while 7 percent are found to suffer from TB. This number is at least five to ten times greater than the general population of the United States. (Travis et al., 2001, p. 11). Presenting challenges to the United States are the factors of employment, health, education, substance abuse, as well as housing. How do we reintegrate all these individuals back into society?[5]

Female prisoners who return to the community, though composing a small number of the corrections population, present risks and challenges sometimes more serious and widespread than their male counterparts.[6]

What is the profile of female prisoners? The majority are minorities.

Nearly two-thirds (63 percent) of these confined to state prisons are black, Hispanic, or other non-white ethnicity. Minorities make up only 26 percent of the general female population. Female prisoners are more likely to come from lesser economic circumstances than male prisoners. Thirty-seven percent of females and 28 percent of males had incomes of less than $600 per month prior to arrest. Thirty percent of females and 8 percent of males were receiving welfare assistance prior to arrest. Female prisoners are less likely to be married than the general population. Nearly half of all women in state prisons have never been married and another 20 percent are divorced. Among the general population, only 21 percent of females and 8 percent of males were receiving welfare assistance prior to arrest. Female prisoners are less likely to be married than the general population. Nearly half of all women in state prisons have never been married another 20 percent are divorced. Among the general population, only 21 percent of women 18 or over have never been married. Female prisoners are likely to be parents. Sixty-five percent of female prisoners have a child below the age of 18. More than 1.2 million children have a mother who is either in prison or under probation or parole supervision (Travis et al., 2001, p. 13).

What are the challenges that face females who reenter their communities? According to Travis and colleagues (2001, p. 13),

- *Many women are released with serious health problems.* Three-and-a-half percent of the female inmate population are HIV positive, a slightly higher percentage than for males. Nearly one-quarter (23 percent) of women in prison receive medication for emotional disorders. More than half of the females (60 percent) in state prisons report a history of physical or sexual abuse.

- *Many women have serious, long-term substance abuse problems.* Increasingly more women are being incarcerated for nonviolent drug offenses (possession and distribution). Forty percent of incarcerated women report that they were under the influence of drugs and 29 percent report they were under the influence of alcohol at the time of their offense. Sixty percent of women in state prison were using drugs in the month before the offense. One-third of women in prison said they committed the offense to obtain money for drugs.

- *Reestablishing relations with children after incarceration is difficult.* Research shows that incarceration of a mother results in emotional, financial, and social suffering for children and that often mother-child relationships are beyond repair after a period of incarceration. It may be more difficult for mothers to have personal visits with their children while incarcerated because they are typically located in distant facilities—an average of 160 miles farther from their children than are incarcerated fathers.

RELEASE DECISIONS

Historically, prisoners were returned to their communities after the parole boards made the determination that they were ready. Prisoners served a portion of their sentences in the correctional facilities and the rest was to be served out in the community. This method was to give prisoners the incentive to behave well behind the walls of the prison facility while going through some rehabilitation process. By the late 1970s and into the early 1980s, the use of indeterminate sentencing and parole were no longer the clear choice. We saw the passage of "truth in sentencing laws" that were passed, in essence eliminating the parole boards for some prisoners. Fewer prisoners are released on parole today.[7]

In Table 5.2 we see more prisoners serving their full times with no early release, and no parole supervision.

"Under indeterminate sentencing practices, prisoners were released from prison to parole only after a parole board had deemed them 'ready'—meaning at least theoretically, they had been rehabilitated and/or had productive connections to the community, such as a job, a housing arrangement, and ties to family. Release to parole was positioned as a privilege to be earned. . . . this system was increasingly criticized over the years as arbitrary, racially biased, and a politically expedient way to relieve prison overcrowding" (Travis et al., 2001, p. 14). Sentence reforms were passed.

Table 2   DEFINITIONS

- **Determinate sentencing**—A prison sentence with a fixed term of imprisonment that can be reduced by good-time or earned-time credits.
- **Indeterminate sentencing**—A prison sentence whose maximum or minimum term is established at the time of sentencing—but not a fixed term. Parole boards determine when to release individuals from prison.
- **Mandatory release**—The release of an inmate from prison to supervision that is decided by a board or other authority.
- **Discretionary release**—The release of an inmate from prison to supervision that is decided by a board or other authority.
- **Conditional release**—The release of an inmate from prison to community supervision with a set of conditions for remaining on parole. Conditions can include regular reporting to a parole officer, drug testing, curfews, and other conditions. If the conditions are violated, the individual can be returned to prison or face another sanction in the community.
- **Unconditional release**—The release of an inmate from prison where he or she is not under supervision of a community corrections agency and is not required to abide by special conditions (and therefore cannot be returned to prison without conviction for the commission of a new offense).

Source: From Prison to Home—The Dimensions and Consequences of Prisoner Reentry, by Jeremy Travis, Amy L. Solomon, and Michelle Waul. Washington, DC: The Urban Institute, 2001.

Thus, the reason for truth-in-sentencing laws passed in the early 1980s and 1990s: These laws were passed with the intent to "reduce the discrepancy between the sentence imposed and the actual time individuals serve in prison" (Travis et al., 2001, p. 14). This has resulted in fewer parole decisions.

Such legislation has impacted the management of corrections facilities. Has the incentive for good behavior been removed? "Does an automatic release process diminish the prisoner's incentive to find a stable residence or employment on the outside—the factors that traditionally influenced parole board decisions? Does a mandatory release policy decrease a correctional agency's commitment to developing links between an inmate's life in prison and his or her life outside prison? Does mandatory release remove the ability of a parole board to reconsider the risk posed by the individual, once his or her prison behavior has been observed? And, for states with policies granting victims' rights to participate in parole board hearings, what role do victims have in the release process?" (Travis et al., 2001, pp. 14–15).

Those prisoners who are released without supervision include (1) those convicted of a violent crime and who are unlikely to be released on parole; (2) those who demonstrated poor behavior in the correctional facility; as well as those (3) who were sentenced to short terms (Travis et al., 2001, p. 16).

Are prisoners prepared to return to society? There are certain treatment interventions that work, including "cognitive skills, drug treatments, vocational treatment, educational, and other prison-based programs" working to reduce recidivism. Understanding that idle prisoners are more likely to cause problems than those occupied, proper correctional management is necessary to keep "quiet" within the facilities. Idle hands cause problems, particularly in correctional facilities. However, the majority of prisoners do not participate in prison programs: "about one-third of soon-to-be released inmates reported they participated in vocational programs (27 percent) or educational programs (35 percent), down from 31 percent and 43 percent, respectively, in 1991" (Travis et al., 2001, p. 17). These numbers mean that a major number of inmates are being released without any kind of vocational and/or educational preparation.

Worse is the factor that fewer prison inmates who suffer from substance abuse problems are receiving professional help: "the profile of the prison population reveals significant deficiencies in human capital that reduce an individual's capacity to function and contribute to society" (Travis et al., 2001, p. 18).

Prisoners go from a well-controlled environment to sometimes low levels of supervision to absolute freedom. This places many released prisoners at high-risk places that lead to recidivism. Few resources are open to those released.[8]

There exist more parole violators than ever before. The violators account for about one-third of prisons admissions throughout the country. Of the parole violators returned to prison, nearly one-third were returned for a new conviction and two-thirds for a technical violation. "In 1998 nearly half of all parolees (42 percent) were returned to prison, translating to some 206,000 parole violators who were returned that year." The high figures may be attributed to "a function of better monitoring techniques and technologies that make it easier to detect violations such as drug use and missed curfews. Parole revocation may be an expression of tough-on-crime sentiment in some jurisdictions, or perhaps more individuals are actually committing crimes while on parole. This failure rate may also reflect cutbacks in preparation for reentry, such as in-prison and community-based treatment, job training, and education" (Travis et al., 2001, p. 22).

A minority of states still turn to intermediate sanctions for violations, including residential treatment, electronic monitoring, curfew, community service, increased supervision levels, counseling, as well as drug and alcohol testing (Travis et al., 2001, p. 22).

POST-RELEASE ISSUES

When prisoners reenter society, where do they live? The issue of housing has been ignored, leaving many prisoners homeless. "Most individuals leave prison without enough money for a security deposit on an apartment" (Travis et al., 2001, p. 35). Section 8 providers as well as other federally assisted housing programs deny housing to those with criminal records. Homeless shelter usually require that a person be homeless for at least 24 hours.

There is also a loss of some civil liberties. "In addition to the substance abuse, health, housing, and employment issues facing returning prisoners, released inmates as a group experience a series of collateral consequences, most often as a result of a felony conviction. . . . in many states, convicted felons are precluded from voting, holding political office, serving on jury duty, owning a firearm, or holding certain jobs. In addition, they may temporarily or permanently lose eligibility for certain public benefit programs."

Voting Rights

"Denial of the right to vote has significant implications for individual offenders and, increasingly, for certain communities in the United States. Nearly all states restrict the voting rights of convicted felons in some way. The laws of 46 states and the District of Columbia stipulate that convicted offenders cannot vote while in prison, and 32 states prohibit offenders on probation or parole from voting. In more than a dozen states, a convicted felon loses the right to vote for life. According to one estimate, nearly 4 million Americans—one in fifty adults—are either currently or permanently prohibited from voting because of a felony conviction. Of these, 1.4 million are African American, accounting for 13 percent of the adult black male population. In states that impose lifetime voting bans on convicted felons, the aggregate consequences in African American communities are profound. One in every four African American men have lost the right to vote for life in Alabama, Florida, Iowa, Mississippi, New Mexico, Virginia, and Wyoming.

Criminal Registration Requirements

"Over the last 15 years the trend has been to extend the period of punishment beyond an individual's probation, prison, and parole sentence, particularly for sex offenders. In 1986, only eight states required released offenders to registers with a police department in their area. A series of high-profile, violent crimes committed by released offenders resulted in legislative initiatives requiring offenders to register with law enforcement agencies upon their release. By 1998, convicted sex offenders in every state were subject to a registration requirement following release from prison. As of 1998, there were nearly 280,000 sex offenders listed in state sex offender registries across the country" (Travis et al., 2001, p. 36).

There remains a tremendous impact on families of prisoners returning. By 1999 more than half of all states' inmates had children under the age of 18 for a total of about 1.5 million children. "The substantial increase in the number of female offenders sentenced to prison in recent years . . . contributes significantly to the number of inmates who have children" (Travis et al., 2001, p. 36). This becomes significant because of the relationships between parents, particularly mothers, and their children.

"Incarcerated males are fathers to 1.2 million children. "Only 40 percent of incarcerated fathers report having weekly contact with their children. Although women represent a much smaller proportion of the prison population, the female prison population is growing faster than the male population. . . . mothers are more likely to be the primary caregivers, [thus] a child's placement after a mother is more uncertain than when the father is imprisoned. Fewer than one-third of all children with an incarcerated mother remain with their fathers. Most are cared for by extended family—53 percent of children with an incarcerated mother live with a grandparent and 26 percent with other relatives. Some children . . . become part of the foster care system. Ten percent of incarcerated mothers and 2 percent of incarcerated fathers report they have a child place in foster care" (Travis et al., 2001, p. 38).

Two percent of all minor children residing in the United States have a parent who is incarcerated, with about 7 percent of African American children finding themselves with a parent either in state or federal prison. Studies have demonstrated that many of these children will have problems (i.e., low self-esteem, depression, withdrawal from friends and/or family, and behavior problems at school). Attempting to maintain relationships between parent and child are hard. Obstacles include inadequate information about visiting procedures, the time that it takes to visit a facility, uncomfortable visiting procedures, as well as reactions to having to visit a parent who is incarcerated (Travis et al., 2001, p. 38).

"Although children may be better off without a neglectful and abusive parent in their lives, there are many caring and committed incarcerated mothers and fathers who expect to resume their parenting. . . . Recent legislative initiatives . . . have made it more difficult for incarcerated parents—particularly mothers. . . . the 1997 Adoption and Safe Families Act . . . mandates termination of parental rights once a child has been in foster care for 15 or more of the past 22 months. Welfare reform legislation . . . also makes it very difficult for parents to rebuild a life with their children. Individuals in violation of a condition of their parole or probation can be barred from receiving federal welfare benefits (TANF), food stamps, Supplemental Security Income, and access to public housing. . . . individuals convicted of a drug felony are permanently banned from receiving TANF or food stamps. This could have profound implications for incarcerated mothers, because 35 percent are incarcerated for a drug charge" (Travis et al., 2001, p. 40).

The research has demonstrated that a great many of the prisoners happen to be from a small number of neighborhoods. As an example, in Brooklyn, New York, "one out of eight parenting-age males is admitted to jail or prison in a single year. . . . the six police precincts with the highest number of residents on parole account for only 25 percent of the total population of Brooklyn, but the same six precincts are home to 55 percent of all the parolees in Brooklyn. . . . 11 percent of the block groups account for 20 percent of the population in Brooklyn, yet are home to 50 percent of the parolees" (Travis et al., 2001, p. 41).

With ever so many being incarcerated, yet being reintegrated into society, there must be efforts to understand what it is these individuals need and what is necessary for the communities. Attention must be paid to ever-changing correctional policies. Communities have to work with ways to deal with reentry. Some of the ways mentioned in the study by Travis and colleagues include the following:

- Begin working with prisoners and the department of corrections before prisoners are released to arrange for job, housing, treatment, and health care upon release.

- Meet prisoners upon release, helping navigate the first hours or days in the community.

- Create or build on neighborhood-based networks of workforce development partners and local businesses who will target the preparation and employment of parolees.

- Engage local community-based organizations that can learn how to help family members support the parolee to overcome substance abuse problems, stay employed, and meet the overall requirements of his or her supervision and reintegration plans.

- Involve local faith institutions that can facilitate mentoring support in the neighborhood to parolees and their family members.

- Provide parolees opportunities to participate in community service and demonstrate that they can be community assets rather than simply neighborhood liabilities.

- Develop coalitions of resident leaders who will oversee the reentry efforts and provide accountability for community obligations (Travis et al., 2001, p. 43).

The problem of reentry is not new. Since the days that the first prisons were built, we have been confronted with the same problem: what to do when the prisoner comes home. What mutual obligations exist for the co-offender and his or her family? "How is failure defined . . . ? One cannot escape the conclusion that the attention focused on prison expansion and the frenetic pace of sentencing reform over the past generation have been at the expense of systematic thinking about the goals and processes of prisoner reentry. The reductions in per capita funding for parole supervision . . . present a clear example of the policy tradeoff. If the prisoner walks out the prison door having completed his sentence, is there no societal interest in his/her reintegration?" (Travis et al., 2001, pp. 46–47).

We still worry about the safety of the public. We worry about public health and substance abuse. New policies should reflect the age old questions of what constitutes the goals and objects of the criminal law.

NOTES

1. Churners are being created at a faster rate than they are successfully completing parole.

2. Reentry is defined as the process of leaving prison and returning to society. All prisoners experience reentry irrespective of their method of release or form of supervision. So both prisoners who are released on parole and those who are released when their prison term expires experience reentry (Travis et al., p. 1).

3. In 1999, 476 persons per 100,000 residents were sentenced to at least a year's confinement—equivalent to 1 in every 110 men and 1 in every 1695 women. These rates vary dramatically by race. In 1999, 1 in every 29 African-American males was sentenced to at least a year's confinement, compared with 1 in every 75 Hispanic males, and 1 in every 240 white males. One in every 472 African-American females was sentenced to at least a year's confinement, compared with 1 in every 1149 Hispanic females, and 1 in every 3704 white females (Travis et al., 2001, p. 1).

4. Most prisoners have a criminal history: Nearly half have been convicted of a violent offense at some point in the past. Three-fourths of state prisoners have been sentenced to probation or incarcerated at least once; 43 percent have been sentenced to probation or incarcerated at least three times.

5. Impact of Incarceration and Reentry on African American Families and Communities

   Young, poor, black males are incarcerated at higher rates than any other group, and therefore they are most affected by reentry. The Bureau of Justice Statistics calculated that, in 1991, an African American male had a 29 percent lifetime chance of serving at least one year in prison, six times higher than that for white males. Hispanic males, who may be of any race, have a lifetime chance of imprisonment of 16 percent. Nine percent of African American males age 25 to 29 were in prison in 1999, compared with 3 percent of Hispanic males and 1 percent of white males of the same age group. . . . according to one estimate, more than one-third of young, black, male high school dropouts were in prison or jail in the late 1990s—more than were employed.

   The disproportionate representation of African Americans in the criminal justice system has been exacerbated by changes in sentencing policy. Sentencing policy changes throughout the 1980s and early 1990s requiring mandatory minimum sentences for a variety of drug-related offenses resulted in a significant increase in drug offenders sentenced to prison and in longer prison terms. This had a significant impact on the African American state prison population. Overall, the number of black drug offenders sentenced to prison increased by 707 percent between 1985 and 1995, while the number of white drug offenders increased by 306 percent. Drug offenders accounted for 42 percent of the rise in the black state prison population during that same 10 year period.

   Concentrations in removal and reentry of African American men also have implications for family formation and stability. In some communities, high rates of incarceration, homicide, and limited employment prospects among African American males have resulted in an imbalance of marriageable African Americans to females" (Travis et al., 2001, pp. 11–12).

6. According to Travis and colleagues (2001, p. 13),

   Females represent a small share of the corrections population. Females accounted for 6 percent of the prison population and 12 percent of the parole population in 1998. *Incarceration rates of females are rapidly increasing.* The number of females per capita in corrections institutions have grown 48 percent since 1990, compared with a 27 percent per capita increase for men.

7. According to Travis and colleagues (2001), The term "parole" refers to two different matters:

   - the decision made by a parole board to release a prisoner onto parole supervision, and
   - the period of conditional supervision following a prison term.

   The movement to abolish parole release resulted in significant reductions in the percentage of prison release decisions made by parole boards. The "truth-in-sentencing" movement also capped the portion of a sentence served in the community, typically to 15 percent of the original sentence. As a result, more prisoners are not returned to the community with less or no time under supervision, and with less consideration of "readiness" for release. A system of parole *supervision* is still operational in some form in nearly all states" (p. 14).

8. The First Month Out: Post-Incarceration in New York City

   In 1999, the Vera Institute of Justice followed a group of 49 adults released from New York State prisons and city jails for 30 days, interviewing them on seven separate occasions to learn about the major challenges facing returning prisoners during this period. The study sought to gain insight into returning prisoners' expectations, the release experience, reunions with family and friends, attempts to find work, and parole supervision experience. . . . the initial period following release from prison is critical.

   This study documented a few key hurdles to successful reintegration—namely, finding a job, finding housing, and getting access to needed health care services. Most returning prisoners who found a job within the first month following their release were either re-hired by former employers or had help from family or friends. Relatively few found new jobs on their own, often because they lacked the skills to conduct an effective job search or could not find employers who would hire ex-offenders. Few parolees reported receiving help from their parole officers. . . . strong family involvement or support was an important indicator of successful reintegration across the board. Returning prisoners who indicated that their families or friends were supportive of their efforts to rebuild their lives had lower levels of drug use, greater likelihood of finding a job, and less continued criminal activity. Most people lived with their families following their release, indicating some level of support. Those who went to homeless shelters were seven times as likely to abscond from parole (Travis et al., 2001, p. 20).

REFERENCES

Lynch, James, P. and William J. Sabol (September 2001). Prisoner Reentry in Perspective. *Crime Policy Report,* Vol. 3. Washington, DC: Urban Institute, Justice Policy Center.

Travis, Jeremy, Solomon, Amy L. & Waul, Michelle (June 2001). *From Prison to Home: The Dimensions and Consequences of Prisoner Reentry.* Washington, DC: The Urban Institute.

chapter 6

Prisoner Reentry: The Iron Law of Imprisonment

Jeremy Travis

THE IRON LAW OF IMPRISONMENT

It could be called the iron law of imprisonment: Except for those few who die in custody, all prisoners come back to live in the free society.

Ever since prisons were built, prisoners have made the journey from prison to community. Some have been well prepared for that journey, having gathered their personal resolve and strengthened their skills so that they could return to family, neighborhoods, peer groups, and civic life without again violating society's laws. Some have found the journey full of challenges and risks, testing their resolve and causing them to stray from the pathways of law-abiding life. For some, the idea of returning to a crime-free life was never a realistic prospect, and they quickly resumed the antisocial behavior that landed them in prison in the first place.

The steady growth of imprisonment in America over the past generation has given the iron law of imprisonment new meaning. At the beginning of the twenty-first century, the flow of prisoners making the journey back into the community had increased fourfold compared to a generation ago. In 2001, more than 600,000 individuals left state and federal prison per year, about 1600 a day. In 1977, by contrast, about 150,000 prisoners were released from the state and federal prison systems. This increase in the reentry population tracks the increase in the number of prison admissions (see Figure 6–1). As the iron law of imprisonment would predict, as more people are sentenced to prison, more are released.

The iron law of imprisonment can also be captured by the concept of prisoner reentry. Reentry is not a form of supervision, like parole. Reentry is not a goal, like rehabilitation or reintegration. Reentry is not an option—it is a fact of imprisonment. With rare exceptions, everyone who is sent to prison returns to live in the community. This chapter explores the reentry concept as a way of unpacking a number of pressing social issues related to the increase in imprisonment in America.

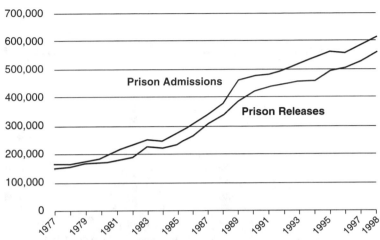

Figure 6–1 Sentenced Prisoners Admitted and Released from Federal and State Prison, 1977–1998
Source: The Urban Institute, 2001. Based on Bureau of Justice Statistics National Prisoner Statistics.

TODAY'S REENTRY POPULATION IS DIFFERENT IN CRITICAL WAYS

The population leaving prison today is in many ways similar to the population that has moved through America's prisons over the past few decades. They are mostly men, often with histories of substance abuse, poorly educated, coming mostly from poor, inner-city communities facing significant disadvantages. Yet there are critical differences in the profile of the reentry population at the turn of the century. These differences raise profound questions about the long-term impact of our increased rates of incarceration upon the goal of reintegrating large numbers of returning prisoners.[1]

First, the prisoners coming home today have been in prison for longer periods of time. The average amount of time in prison increased from 22 months in 1990 to 28 months in 1998, reflecting the impact of truth-in-sentencing legislation and other sentencing reforms that have aimed to increase the length of prison sentences for violent offenders. These longer prison sentences mean that the ties among prisoners, their families, and the networks of support in their communities have been attenuated. To the extent that these familial and community supports enhance a prisoner's chances of making it on the outside, these longer sentences pose new hurdles in the path of successful reintegration.

Second, the prisoners returning today are less prepared for life on the outside (see Figure 6–2). In 1991, 31% of the prisoners scheduled to leave prison in the next year had participated in a vocational program in prison. By 1997, that participation rate had dropped to 27%. In 1991, 43% had participated in an education program; by 1997, that rate had dropped to 35%. In 1991, 25% had participated in a drug treatment program; by 1997,

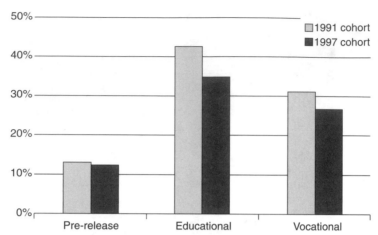

Figure 6–2 Prisoners to be Released in the Next 12 Months: Percent
Participating in Prison Programs, 1991 and 1997
Source: J. P. Lynch and W. J. Sabol (September 2001). *Prisoner Reentry in
Perspective.* Washington, DC: Urban Institute Crime Policy Report.

that rate had dropped to 10%. In both years, only 10-12% of the prisoners scheduled to be released in the next year had participated in formal pre-release programs designed to convey practical information about the transition from life in prison to life in the community. So, to the extent that these programs are successful at increasing the odds that prisoners will be successful in their efforts to join the world of work, maintain their sobriety in the face of high risk of relapse into substance abuse, and navigate the pathways of reentry, then the failure to focus resources on these programs has significant negative effects.

Third, the prisoners returning home today are returning to a relatively small number of communities. In these neighborhoods, the significant increases in arrests, removals, imprisonment, and return of large numbers of individuals have placed severe burdens on the capacity of those communities to do what communities should do—namely, be places where individuals, families, and civic institutions can thrive. For example, according to one study, there are blocks in Brooklyn, New York, where approximately one in every eight parenting-age males is sent to prison or jail each year.

This is, in essence, a new reality, the reality of mass imprisonment in America. This reality poses a number of profound questions for research and policy development. Unfortunately, these questions have not received much attention. For example, little is known about the consequences of mass incarceration for the parenting arrangements for the children left behind. There has been scant research on effects of high rates of incarceration on marriage patterns in these communities or the long-term impact on participation in the workforce.

From a reentry perspective, the geographic concentration of large numbers of returning prisoners raises another set of questions. How should the community be engaged as partner in the reintegration effort? What assistance should community organizations be given to help make these transitions more successful? How should the traditional agencies that have supervised prisoner reentry (e.g., parole supervision agencies) be reorganized to reflect the reality that large numbers of prisoners are returning to small numbers of communities?

In short, the population of individuals leaving prison today is different in several critical respects. There are significantly more of them. They have been in prison longer. They are less prepared for the inevitable journey home. And they are returning in larger numbers to a smaller number of communities in America.

VIEWING FOUR SOCIAL POLICY DOMAINS THROUGH A REENTRY LENS

Scholars and practitioners have recently been adopting a "reentry perspective" to unpack the effects of the growth in incarceration rates in America.[2] In essence, this framework views sentencing and corrections policies from the perspective of the individuals who pass through America's prisons, their families, their communities, and the social processes of prisoner reintegration. This perspective recasts some age-old debates about the role of prisons in our society. The reentry perspective holds the potential for creating new partnerships between criminal justice practitioners, criminologists, and their counterparts in other policy arenas. This section will explore three noncriminal justice policy domains—family, workforce development, public health—to illustrate the power of the reentry perspective. Finally, the reentry perspective raises profound questions about the current relationship between the agencies of the criminal justice system and the communities most directly affected by criminal justice policies.

Family Policy

A static portrait of the impact of mass imprisonment on children and families is quite sobering. More than half of state inmates are parents of children below the age of 18. As prison populations have grown, the number of children with a parent in prison has grown as well. According to the Bureau of Justice Statistics, in 1999 there were 1.5 million minor children with a parent in prison, up from 1 million in 1990. Stated differently, two percent of the minor children in America had a mother or father in prison in 1999. Seen through a racial lens, the impact of imprisonment is even more striking: According to the Bureau of Justice Statistics (BJS), one of every fourteen minor African American children in America had a parent in prison in 1999.[3]

A reentry perspective adds new richness to some of these analyses of the impact of imprisonment on families and children. For example, a more dynamic view of the consequences of our criminal justice policies would focus on the effects of incarceration on the prisoner's family life over the period of incarceration. The impact of the moment of arrest and imprisonment may be quite different for different families and children of the offender. For some, the removal of a disruptive or even violent parent might be beneficial to family functioning and childhood development. For others, the forced departure of a breadwinner might force the family into poverty or dependency on others. A reentry perspective would also inquire into the impact of imprisonment and reentry on parenting arrangements for the children left behind. This inquiry would examine the effects on foster care and kinship care systems. It would document the extent of parenting by grandparents or other next of kin. It would ask whether these temporary arrangements are cast aside when the parent returns from prison or whether they have become a more permanent structural arrangement to which the former prisoner must now adapt.

These avenues for new research inquiries are paralleled by new opportunities for policy collaboration. An awareness of the impact of incarceration and reentry on children and families could give rise to new partnerships between departments of corrections and child and family welfare agencies. Corrections professionals, recognizing the importance of family influences in increasing the likelihood of success of returning prisoners, could create new alliances with community organizations that would attend to the needs of a prisoner's family while he or she is in prison. They could develop new ways for the prisoner to stay in touch with his or her children during incarceration. They could pay attention to the difficult dynamics of reunification and find ways to work through the issues that are likely to arise. When there has been a history of domestic violence in a family or relationship, corrections professionals could work with victim service organizations and law enforcement officials to make sure that the violence does not recur upon release, and to provide for victim safety should the need arise.

Workforce Development

Most prisoners have jobs when they are arrested. Three-quarters were working and, of those, just over half had full-time jobs. So one impact of incarceration is clear: The families of these prisoners are left without the benefit of that income during the period of incarceration. Yet little is known about the job-seeking and job-retention activities of prisoners when they leave prison. According to one small study by the Vera Institute of Justice documenting the experiences of 50 individuals leaving New York State prisons, most returning prisoners who did find jobs were either rehired by former employers or had help from family or friends. Relatively few found jobs on their own.

Labor market economists have examined the relationship between incarceration and employment to determine prison's effects on life-time earnings of former prisoners. According to this body of literature, as the time in prison increases, the likelihood of finding legitimate employment after release from prison decreases. One researcher has calculated a "wage penalty" of incarceration and found that individuals who have been in prison experience a lifetime reduction in earnings of between 10 and 20 percent.

From a reentry perspective, one would ask whether the period of imprisonment could be viewed as an opportunity to reverse these negative effects. An obvious focal point for policy development would be the expansion of the level and quality of in-prison job training programs. Historically, research on the effectiveness of these programs at increasing postprison employment rates (and reducing recidivism) has shown mixed results. Yet more recent reviews of the research literature have provided a more optimistic assessment of this policy opportunity. Perhaps the most promising policy innovation would focus on the linkages between the prison experience and the job opportunities in the community. Over the past several years, the country has witnessed a remarkable shift in policy and practice under the banner of welfare reform where the reformers' rallying cry was "from welfare to work." A number of programs around the country, some involving the private business sector in new partnerships, are embracing a similar mission: "from prison to work."

Health Policy

Individuals in prison have very serious health problems. Eighty percent of the state prison population reports a history of drug and/or alcohol use. More than half of them report that they were using drugs or alcohol at the time they committed the offense for which they were imprisoned. One-quarter report that they have histories of injection drug use. Sixteen percent report a mental condition or an overnight stay in a psychiatric hospital.

Those who pass through correctional facilities also suffer from a number of communicable diseases. During 1997, between 20 and 26 percent of the national population infected with HIV or AIDS, 29 to 32 percent of those with hepatitis C, and 38 percent of those with tuberculosis were released from a correctional facility (including both prisons and jails) that year.

The health profile of the prison population reveals that prisoners experience these health problems at much higher rates than the general population. For example, the overall rate of confirmed AIDS cases among prisoners is five times the rate found in the general population. For HIV, the prison rate is five to seven times higher, for hepatitis C nine to ten times higher than the prevalence of those health problems in the general population.

From one perspective, the high rate of health problems poses a critical challenge to administrators of correctional institutions. They must provide a level of health care that meets applicable constitutional, statutory, and professional standards. From a reentry perspective, the health profile presents a different challenge: How can we develop policies that link in-prison health care with community-based health care in a way that improves overall health outcomes for returning prisoners, their families, and their communities? Given the iron law of imprisonment, the moment of release, for hundreds of thousands of returning prisoners, presents an opportunity to develop a health-specific discharge plan that creates a continuity of health care across the prison walls.

Criminal Justice Policy

Finally, the reentry perspective raises profound questions about the way our society views the process of reintegration of returning prisoners. Most released prisoners will not succeed on the outside. According to the Bureau of Justice Statistics, nearly two-thirds of them will be rearrested within three years of their release at least once. About 40 percent will be reincarcerated during that time. In fact, the first year after getting out of prison is a period of highest risk: 40 percent are rearrested within that time. So the public safety risks posed by the release cohort are high. Yet these data should be kept in perspective: Viewed in terms of all arrests, parolees do not account for a large share. According to BJS, only 6 percent of felony arrests were on parole at the time of their arrest.

The growth in the nation's prison population, the high recidivism rate of the release population, and the adoption of stringent supervision policies by parole agencies have combined to create another important dimension to correctional policy—namely, the high rate of return to prison for parole violations. In 1980, 18 percent of all prison admissions were admitted as parole violators. Parole violators now account for over a third of prison admissions, or more than 200,000 individuals a year. Nearly two-thirds of them are returned to prison for a "technical violation," meaning that the parolee failed to meet a condition of his or her supervision. The remaining third were convicted of a new offense. The net result is the de facto creation of a second pathway to prison, much larger than in times past, with unknown consequences for public safety, prison management, and offender reintegration.

The reentry perspective poses a number of fundamental questions about the role of criminal justice supervision in the postrelease process. For example, research shows that nearly a quarter of released prisoners across the nation are released unconditionally, meaning that they have no legal status, report to no parole officer, and have no special conditions governing their postprison life. Is this sound public policy? Are there some prisoners whose prison terms constitute the entire extent of the criminal sanction? If so, what is the obligation of corrections management for assisting them with a smooth reentry into the world outside the prison?

Viewing these issues from a community perspective adds a rich dimension to the policy challenge. The combination of high rates of incarceration, high concentrations of prisoner reentry to a small number of neighborhoods, and high rates of return to prison has resulted in a phenomenon within those communities unprecedented in American history: Imprisonment has become a common experience. According to an analysis of imprisonment in Brooklyn, New York, there are some city blocks where one in eight parenting-age males goes to jail or prison each year.

Just as incarceration effects are concentrated in some neighborhoods, supervision effects are also concentrated. Eleven percent of the block groups in Brooklyn account for 20 percent of the population yet are home to 50 percent of the parolees. From the community vantage point, these concentrations of criminal justice supervision raise important questions about the organization and nature of criminal justice supervision. For example, one might ask whether parole caseloads should be based on geography, so that a single parole officer is responsible for a caseload consisting of all parolees in a particular neighborhood. Once organized geographically, the parole function might also take on a different mission, one drawing more on community resources as partners in the supervision effort and more attuned to the situational risks present in the community.

CONCLUSION

Mass incarceration is now an important attribute of American criminal justice policy. So, too, high levels of prisoner reentry have redefined the landscape of American society. As we move into the new century, reformers will certainly continue to advocate for policies designed to reduce the high levels of incarceration in America. A focus on the issue of prisoner reentry—a recognition of the iron law of corrections—creates another set of reform opportunities. This focus can bring new perspectives and disciplines to the table, including those interested in workforce development, public health, and family and community well-being. Researchers in these fields of inquiry can contribute shed new light on some classic criminal justice questions, such as the pathways of prisoner reintegration. Policymakers can contribute new models for thinking about the relationship between prisoners and the communities to which they return. These new models may then inform a broader discussion about the response to crime and the pursuit of justice in America.

NOTES

1. For discussion of prisoner reentry, see J. Travis, A. L. Solomon, and M. Waul, *From Prison to Home: The Dimensions and Consequences of Prisoner Reentry,* available at *www.urban.org/pdfs/from_prison_to_home.pdf.*

2. See *Crime and Delinquency,* Vol. 47, Issue 3 (2001) and *Corrections Management Quarterly,* Vol. 5, Issue 3 (2001).

3. See C. J. Mumola, *Incarcerated Parents and Their Children.* Bureau of Justice Statistics, Special Report. Washington, DC: U.S. Department of Justice, Bureau of Justice Statistics, NCJ 182335, August 2000.

REFERENCES

1. This study came from the Anaylsis by E. Cardora and C. Swartz for the Community Justice Project at the Center for Alternative Sentencing and Employment Services (CASES), 2001. Based on data from the New York State Division of Parole. For more information see *http://www.communityjusticeproject.org/.*

2. J. Kling, D.F. Weiman and B. Western, "The Labor Market Consequences of 'Mass Incarceration.'" Paper prepared for the Reenetry Roundtable, Washington, D.C., October 12 and 13, 2000.

3. T.M. Hammett, "Health-Related Issues in Prisoner Reentry to the Community." Paper prepared for the Reentry Roundtable, Washington, D.C., October 12 and 13, 2000.

chapter 7

Suicide in Prisons and Jails

Christine Tartaro

INTRODUCTION

To say that prisons, jails, and police holding facilities house people whose lives are in disarray would be an understatement. The United States Bureau of Justice Statistics (BJS) (1999) reported that 7 percent of the federal correctional population, 16 percent of state prison inmates, and 16 percent of jail detainees reported either a mental condition or an overnight stay in a mental hospital. In 1998, 70 percent (estimated 417,000) of inmates in jail had committed a drug offense or used drugs regularly, and over half of jail (55%) and state (57%) inmates reported using drugs in the month leading up to their offense (BJS, 2000).

Even for offenders who have been incarcerated previously, the placement in custody may cause feelings of frustration and despair (Hayes & Rowan, 1988). This situation is exacerbated by the fact that many who are in the lockups and jails are put there while under the influence of drugs and alcohol (Davis & Muscat, 1993; Farmer et al., 1996; Hayes, 1989; Hayes & Rowan, 1988). These inmates must come to terms with a possible lengthy incarceration, loss of contact with family and friends, the possible loss of a job if legally employed prior to arrest, and an overall feeling of loss of control over their lives. Sykes (1972), in his study of long-term imprisonment, noted that these "pains of imprisonment" are something that inmates must face throughout their entire incarceration. For some, this burden is too much to bear. Some inmates will react to their incarceration by attempting to commit suicide. While it is true that a portion of these attempts are merely efforts aimed at manipulating custodial staff, all acts of self-harm need to be properly addressed by correctional administrators. Failure to do so may result in costly civil suits by the victim's family.

This chapter will discuss factors pertaining to suicide while in custody. Issues such as time, place, victim characteristics, and methods for suicide will be presented. Ideas for prevention are also mentioned. It is important to note that many suicide prevention strategies have come to rely on "hard" prevention techniques that include stripping down an inmate and placing him or her in a bare cell. Many researchers and practitioners have criticized this approach for being inhumane and counterproductive. Alternatives to this method will be discussed. Finally, there will be a review of civil liability issues pertaining to suicide in correctional institutions.

FACTS ABOUT SUICIDE

How Often Correctional Suicides Occur

There have been numerous attempts at calculating the rate of suicide in prisons and jails. Data collected by the Bureau of Justice Statistics' *Correctional Populations in the United States* from 1978 through 1996 (BJS, 1981–1999) reveal that the mean suicide rate for the state prison population was 18.86 per 100,000 inmates. The prison suicide rate during this time peaked in 1979, with 26.67 per 100,000 inmates, and was at its lowest in 1995, with 16.18 per 100,000 inmates. Suicide rates on death row in the United States, however, are much higher. According to BJS statistics, the median suicide rate from 1977 through 1999 was 113 per 100,000, with a mean of 146 (BJS, 1978–2000).[1] Compared to a mean suicide rate of 25 per 100,000 for American men over the age of fifteen in the general population (World Health Organization, 2000), these figures are surprising for inmates who are expected to be closely supervised.

Hayes (1989) reported that the rate of suicide in jails is nine times that of the general population and far higher than the rate of prison suicides. This figure was obtained by dividing the number of suicides that occurred in a jail during a given year by the average daily population of the facilities and multiplying by 100,000. O'Toole (1997) discussed measurement issues that are frequently encountered by researchers attempting to discuss the rate of suicide in jails. O'Toole noted that although the average daily population of United States jails was approximately 500,000 in 1995, admissions to jails for that year were between ten and thirteen million. Due to the differences in admissions in prisons and jails, O'Toole demonstrates that while it takes two years for a prison population to turn over, a jail's population turns over twenty to twenty-five times a year. In other words, even if a prison and a jail have the same average daily population and the same number of suicides, O'Toole cautions against declaring that the suicide rates in the two institutions are equal.

While the difference in suicide rates for prisons and jails may not be as drastic as previously reported, the raw numbers of those who commit suicide behind bars indicate that more jail inmates end their lives than those in prison. For example, BJS (1988; 1989) statistics show that 113 state and federal prison inmates committed suicide in 1985 and 97 died in this manner in 1986, compared with the National Center on Institutions and Alternatives' (NCIA) findings of 453 jail inmates in 1985 and 401 in 1986 (Hayes, 1989).

The statistics just presented should be considered with caution, since they likely present an underestimation of the problem. Welch and Gunther (1997) recommended that readers question the validity of official corrections reports, since they may have been altered to place correctional staff in a more favorable light. The threat of litigation may cause administrators to hesitate to release records. Differences of opinion about the location of a suicide (incidents often are inappropriately listed as occurring in hospitals) (Hayes, 1989) and the absence of a national, state, or local registry to document such incidents contribute to the problem (Davis & Muscat, 1993).

Victims

Males are more likely to commit suicide than females both inside and outside of correctional facilities (Hayes, 1989). Lester (1987) reported a suicide rate for all American prisons from 1980 through 1983 of 24.3 for men and 4.7 per for women. Juveniles are also at a higher risk than adults (Atlas, 1987). Offenders who have a history of drug and alcohol problems or who are incarcerated while under the influence of one of these substances are also more likely to attempt suicide (Davis & Muscat, 1993; Farmer et al., 1996; Liebling, 1992; Loucks, 1997). After reviewing the prison and jail suicide literature, Lester and Danto (1993) reported that most studies agree that the typical victim is a male in his twenties who dies by hanging. Consensus has not been reached on other issues, such as the victims' marital status and psychiatric history.

Attempts have been made to construct a profile of the "typical" suicidal detainee. Based on the 1979 NCIA jail suicide survey, Hayes (1989) reported that the typical jail suicide victim is a twenty-two-year-old white, single male. This person was likely arrested for public intoxication and has no significant history of prior arrests. The victim is placed in isolation for his own protection or for surveillance purposes. Less than three hours into his incarceration period, the victim is dead by hanging. Hayes reported that some jail administrators accepted this information wholeheartedly and began to assume that only inmates meeting this description were at risk. This is clearly a dangerous practice, since the findings of the 1979 NCIA study did state that nonwhites, older, and violent offenders did commit suicide as well. Overreliance on such data has the potential to result in overidentification of those who are not suicidal (false positives) and underprediction of those who are truly at risk (false negatives) (Liebling, 1992; Lloyd, 1990). Furthermore, Lloyd (1990) found that many variables that are associated with suicidal behavior are also characteristics of the entire correctional population. As will be discussed in the prevention section of this chapter, corrections personnel would be more likely than attempting to construct a profile based on demographic data.

How Inmates Commit Suicide

The method by which offenders *attempt* suicide varies depending on whether the inmates are residing in a prison, jail, or police lockup. The explanation for this is simple: Offenders in jails and lockups have relatively few available tools to utilize in a suicide attempt, whereas prison inmates have more personal hygiene and luxury items. Prison inmates are expected to reside at that facility for a long period of time, possibly several years. Although crowding at state prisons has forced some inmates to do long stretches of time in the county jails, the primary function of a jail is to house inmates temporarily. Consequently, they are permitted to obtain and keep fewer belongings in their cells.

Since many victims of suicide in jail commit suicide within the first twenty-four to forty-eight hours of incarceration (Hayes, 1989), they are in a situation where they have few belongings, such as razors or other sharp objects, in their cells. Given this situation, cutting is not a viable option. For obvious reasons, neither is the use of a gun, heavy dose of medication, or lethal gas, all of which are available in the general population. Jumping is clearly not an option for someone who is locked in a cell. The only commonly accepted form of self-harm left is hanging (a generic term for hanging/suffocation/self-suspension/strangulation) (Ingram et al., 1997), which is used by over ninety percent of jail inmates who commit suicide (Hayes, 1989; Ingram et al., 1997; Marcus & Alcabes, 1993). The exact tools for hanging vary, even between jail and police lockup detainees. Hayes (1989) noted that those in police lockups tended to use their clothing to form a noose, while those in the jail were more likely to use their bedding for this purpose. The reason for this is that, unlike the police station detainees, jail inmates have the additional option of bedding, which is not usually provided in police lockups.

Inmates in prison, however, tend to favor cutting as a frequently used method for suicide *attempts* (Inch et al., 1995; Liebling, 1992; Liebling & Krarup, 1993). Prison inmates do have the option of hanging themselves, since all that is required to attempt that is a sheet, a pair of pants, or even socks. The presence of personal belongings in their cells, however, provides them with an additional option. It is interesting to note that although Liebling found that prison inmates frequently resort to cutting as a suicide attempt, most successful suicides in prisons are by hanging. There are two possible explanations for this. One is that the behavior of cutters is more of an attention-seeking mechanism than an actual attempt to die. The second is that hanging is a more dangerous method in that the victim loses consciousness faster than does a cutter. Stone (1999) reports that death from hanging or strangulation occurs within about five to ten minutes after cutoff of oxygen or blockage of blood flow to the brain, and the mortality rate for those who choose this method is near 80 percent. The author further notes that "These [hanging and strangulation] are highly lethal methods and cannot be done safely as a suicidal gesture" (p. 322). For cutting and stabbing, Stone reports a mortality rate near 5 percent. This is a method that is used by both attention seekers and those who are truly attempting suicide, since it is possible to predict the degree of injury with this method.

When Suicide Occurs

The National Commission on Correctional Health Care's (NCCHC) standards (cited in Hayes, 1996) identified the following high-risk periods for inmates: immediately after admission to the facility, immediately after adjudication, following an inmate's return to the facility from court, following the receipt of bad news regarding family or him/herself, and after suffering humiliation or rejection. White and Schimmel (1995) cautioned that the receipt of new charges or additional sentences might also bring about a suicide attempt. Hayes (2000) added that the holidays might also be a particularly stressful and upsetting time.

Past research has supported the NCCHC's statement that most suicides among jail and lockup detainees occur during these crisis periods. The National Center on Institutions and Alternatives reported that over 50 percent of the victims in their 1979 national study of suicide in jails and lockups were dead within the first twenty-four hours of incarceration. Twenty-seven percent of all jail suicide victims were dead within the first three hours of their detention (Hayes, 1989). Marcus and Alcabes (1993) reported that 50 percent of suicides in their study of an urban jail occurred within three days of a court appearance. At that time, the alleged offender must think about having to face the victim and victim's family, see his or her own family, and hear of the court outcome.

Jails typically receive most of the attention when the issue of suicide is discussed, and this is most likely because more suicides occur in jails. White and Schimmel (1995) conducted a study of suicides in United States federal prisons between 1983 and 1992. The researchers found that the average time between initial incarceration and suicide was approximately five years. With regard to particularly dangerous times for inmates, marital or relationship problems tended to precede 23 percent of the suicides. Inmates serving long sentences were especially prone to concerns about their safety in the prison. These inmate-related conflicts often emerged years into the inmates' sentence and prompted suicide attempts.

It is true that stressful events, such as the first few hours of incarceration, court appearances, receipt of bad news, and conflict with other inmates, may precede a suicide attempt. Correctional staff should be vigilant when inmates are experiencing these traumas. Hayes (1996), however, noted that suicides can occur at any time. Staff members, particularly officers, need to be aware of the warning signs of an impending suicide attempt. These signs will be presented later in this chapter.

Where Suicide Occurs

Suicide presents correctional administrators with a unique problem in that its risk factors are unlike those for other acts of violence and security problems in these institutions. A common way of dealing with interpersonal violence and disciplinary issues in a correctional setting is to isolate the inmates to prevent them from being able to commit an assault, participate in an exchange of contraband, or work on an escape. Gang members are routinely segregated, thereby denying them the ability to carry out attacks against staff members or other inmates (Ralph & Marquart, 1991). Potential victims can also be segregated for their own protection. However, segregating inmates either to protect them from violence or prevent them from committing an offense could increase their opportunity and motivation for suicide.

A study conducted by the National Center on Institutions and Alternatives (Hayes, 1989) found that two-thirds of inmates who commit suicide in jails and police lockups do so while in isolation. Inch and colleagues (1995) noted that while isolating inmates "for their own protection" may prevent them from being assaulted, being isolated might increase inmates' sense of despair, thus providing extra motivation for suicide. The move may also increase the inmates' chances of making a successful attempt, since detection and intervention may not occur until it is too late.

Crowding in prisons and jails has been blamed as a factor in nearly every correctional dilemma that administrators face, but rarely is it blamed for suicides. Gaes (1985) (cited in Liebling, 1992), stated that overcrowding and the unpleasant aspects of institutional life that are associated with it may produce the 'onset of a suicidal crisis.' Despite the fact that overcrowding may increase anxiety and feelings of hopelessness, Liebling (1992) argued that overcrowded conditions might actually prevent suicide. Since suicide is most often committed while inmates are in isolation, the lack of privacy may reduce the opportunity to make an attempt. On the other hand, Wooldredge and Winfree (1992) found that suicide is positively related to increases in the inmate to staff ratio, so as institutions become more crowded, officer supervision of inmates may become more difficult, thereby increasing the opportunity for suicide. This problem would likely have more of an adverse affect on inmates who are put in isolation, whether it is disciplinary or a protective custody arrangement, since inmates in general population would lack privacy in an overcrowded institution. If the strains of crowding result in less supervision of those who are housed alone, those inmates will be free to commit acts of self-harm.

SUICIDE PREVENTION

Now that we have discussed where, when, and how suicide in jails is likely to occur, we can explore different suicide prevention methods that are currently in use. The review of suicide prevention will include the following categories: screening, housing and supervision, and standards and training

Screening

One significant problem that researchers have found is that inmates may be placed in cells without being screened for suicidal ideation, psychiatric problems, or intoxication. The NCIA survey for 1985 and 1986 found that 89 percent of victims in jails and 97 percent of victims in police lockups had not been screened for suicidal ideas or behavior before being placed into a cell (Hayes, 1989). Welch and Gunther (1997) found that 22 percent of complainants cited a lack of policies and procedures for screening and monitoring potential suicidal inmates as a contributing factor to the deceased's opportunity to kill him/herself. The Bureau of Justice Statistics (1996) reported that as of midyear 1993, 75 percent of jails responding to their survey indicated that they do have prevention policies that involve screening inmates at the time of intake. Readers should note, however, that this survey only included large jails and did not include any policed lockups. Additionally, the fact that a facility has a written policy does not always mean that it is being implemented.

Several researchers have recommended that booking officers or intake workers interview those entering the institutions (Ingram et al., 1997; Manning, 1989; Marcus & Alcabes, 1993; Rowan, 1989). In addition to questioning inmates about past suicide attempts and their current emotional condition, officers should be trained to detect signs of drug and alcohol influence (Manning, 1989). Checking the detainees' arms for slash marks as evidence of past suicide attempts is also recommended (Ingram et al., 1997).

It must be emphasized to intake workers that screening must be completed *before* an offender is placed in a cell. A report by Ingram and associates (1997) included an account of an inmate who was placed in a cell before the officer had an opportunity to conduct a background check into the offender's psychiatric history. The inmate committed suicide while the officer checked his records and found a report of a previous attempt. Screening inmates also needs to occur continuously and not simply during admission. Screening should occur at the aforementioned high-risk periods, such as after an inmate is returned to jail from court, following the receipt of bad news regarding family or him/herself, and after suffering humiliation or rejection.

A vital component to successful inmate screening is communication between staff members in the facilities. This may seem like an obvious point, but inmates have died when officers neglected to provide the medical staff with the necessary information (Power, 1997). Hayes (1999) summarized the communication process that must occur in a prison or jail with regard to suicide. This is a three-stage process involving (1) communication between the arresting or transporting officer and correctional staff; (2) communication among facility staff (including line officers, supervisors, medical, and mental health personnel); and (3) communication between facility staff and the suicidal inmate.

As was mentioned earlier, profiles of suicidal inmates have been adopted by some administrators as a tool for identifying suicidal inmates. This is problematic, due to the presence of false positives and false negatives in the institutions. Liebling (1992) recommended an alternative approach of working to identify "suicide-prone" inmates and the onset of a particularly stressful situation, arguing that many become suicidal due to particular circumstances and events. Hayes (2000) identified symptoms exhibited by people who are severely depressed and might be contemplating suicide. Officers should look for the following signs: change in appetite, lethargy, expression of strong guilt over the offense, severe agitation or aggressiveness, noticeable mood or behavior changes, speaking unrealistically about getting out of jail, having increased difficulty relating to others, preoccupation with the past, and packing belongings or giving away possessions when release is not imminent. The presence of any of these signs should be communicated to the mental health staff of the facility. Inmates might become depressed at any time, and not just at the high-risk periods that were mentioned earlier. Officers need to constantly be aware of the warning signs of inmates' depression and contemplation of suicide.

Housing and Supervision

While the importance of screening can never be overemphasized, research has indicated that some screened inmates will deny having suicidal ideation (Farmer et al., 1996: Marcus & Alcabes, 1993). Policies of dealing with suicidal and mentally ill inmates have at times motivated offenders to conceal their problems from staff. Admission of either of the aforementioned problems can result in special clothing, placement in isolation, restricted privileges, and ostracism from other inmates. Hayes (1989) has been particularly critical of the use of isolation to deal with suicidal inmates, given that the majority of successful suicides occur while inmates are in isolation. Hayes concluded, "In most instances, the use of isolation is for the convenience of the staff, and usually to the detriment of the inmate because it unconsciously causes reduced staff supervision/observation" (p. 20).

It is recommended that jail and lockup supervisors work to reduce the perceived "penalties" associated with admitting suicidal ideation. Hayes (1999) recommended that corrections staff should also try to avoid canceling privileges, such as telephone access, visits, and recreation time, since elimination of these has the potential to add to inmates' feelings of isolation and distress. When at all possible, staff members should avoid placing inmates in isolation cells, especially offenders who are under the influence of substances or experiencing psychological problems. Given the predominance of suicide during the initial hours of incarceration, it may be better to refrain from placing newcomers into isolation during the first forty-eight hours. This may allow the offender to adjust to the new setting as well as detoxify. In a situation where the inmate is not only a danger to himself but to his roommate, isolation rooms may be used provided that the staff is able to maintain constant supervision (Hayes, 1996).

Hayes (1999) identified two types of supervision that are used with potentially suicidal inmates. Close observation may be used for inmates who have expressed suicidal ideation or have a recent prior history of self-harm. These are inmates who are not actively suicidal, and they may be monitored at staggering intervals that do not exceed fifteen minutes. Constant observation should be used for inmates who are threatening suicide or engaging in the act. It is important to note that constant supervision means continuous observation of an inmate by a corrections officer, a member of the facility's treatment staff, or a trained inmate. Some correctional facilities attempt to accomplish constant supervision by using security cameras and monitors for the "suicide" or "quiet" wing. This author, however, has witnessed officers ignoring the monitors in one jail. The author was in the medical wing of a county jail and watched the officer who was responsible for "constant supervision" of the suicidal inmates move away from the monitor and talk with officers for approximately fifteen minutes. Rowan (1990) noted that an inmate could lose consciousness due to strangulation within thirty seconds. Brain damage and death may follow minutes later. It is unlikely that this was a rare instance, since we have all likely walked past officers or security guards in buildings outside of correctional facilities that were not watching the monitors. Fortunately, no inmates attempted suicide while the author was in the facility. The opportunity was there, however, since the officer left his post. If possible, correctional facilities should implement constant supervision by means of a staff member or trained inmate being physically present outside an inmate's cell.

Supervision of inmates can be difficult for officers faced with more inmates than the facilities were designed to house. Wooldredge and Winfree (1992) found that a change in the ratio of staff to inmates is a significant predictor of shifts in the prevalence of inmates' suicides in that more inmates per staff member in jails might lead to increased suicides. One way to prevent these deaths would be to have more staff members on duty during the night shift. Since quickly solving staff shortages in corrections departments difficult, Manning (1989) proposed a creative way of improving supervision for suicidal inmates. Manning recommended the use of buddies (highly trusted and trained inmates) for watching at-risk inmates. The buddies are placed in cells with suicidal inmates as a form of surveillance, but also to make the troubled inmate feel less isolated. Buddies have assisted corrections officers with one of the most difficult aspects of suicide prevention programs—many inmate victims kill or attempt to kill themselves between midnight and six in the morning (Hardie, 1998), at which time there are fewer corrections officers and possibly little medical personnel. Since inmates are in the facility day and night, they act as an effective form of additional supervision. Buddies are instructed not to intervene or give advice, but to report destructive behavior to a corrections officer. An advantage to this method of dealing with suicidal inmates is that it reduces the need for the use of stripped-down isolation cells, since at-risk inmates are permitted to keep their belongings as long as the buddy is there to watch them.

The Bureau of Parole (BOP) has adopted a similar system of using inmates to watch those at risk for suicide. Inmates are selected by the suicide prevention program coordinator in each participating facility. The inmates are trained to summon staff if those being supervised attempt suicide, but they are also given training in understanding suicidal behavior, empathetic listening, and general communication techniques. White and Schimmel (1995) reported that 65 percent of federal institutions use inmate companions, and of the 75,363 hours of suicide watch in federal institutions in 1992, 72 percent of those hours were handled by inmates.

Another obstacle to effective surveillance is the belief of many staff members that suicidal behavior is exhibited for the purpose of gaining attention and manipulating the officers (Liebling & Krarup, 1993; Power, 1997). This is certainly true in some instances, but Dear, Thompson, and Hills (2001) reported that manipulators and suicide attempters are not always mutually exclusive groups. The researchers interviewed eighty-one prison inmates who had recently committed some act of self-harm. Using a suicidal intent scale, the researchers reported that two-thirds of respondents with manipulative motives indicated at least a moderate suicidal intent. One in six respondents with manipulative motives committed an act of self-harm that resulted in at least some risk to life. Power and Spencer (1987) found that 92 percent of incidents of self-harm in their study involved minimal harm in terms of medical lethality, but they warned that inmates with a lack of available suicide options might utilize a more lethal method of self harm. For example, jail inmates who want to be manipulative or just harm themselves for any reason may not be able to perform a less lethal cutting action and would have to attempt hanging instead. Officers as well as the rest of the correctional staff need to understand that even acts of self-harm committed by manipulative inmates have the potential to be dangerous.

Standards and Training

Several organizations, such as the American Medical Association, the National Commission on Accreditation for Law Enforcement, the American Correctional Association (ACA), and the National Commission on Correctional Health Care have formulated national standards relating to emergency response to suicide attempts in correctional institutions (Kappeler,

1993). The ACA calls for written policy detailing responses to potentially suicidal inmates that includes recognizing symptoms of inmates who might harm themselves, first aid, and procedures for transferring inmates to medical facilities. The NCCHC developed similar standards, with both the NCCHC and ACA emphasizing the need for continuous training (Hayes, 2001). The ACA and NCCHC recommendations, however, are just that. Suicide prevention policies for correctional facilities are not mandated by law.

The NCCHC recommend that a prevention program address, at minimum, the following elements: staff training, intake screening/assessment, housing, levels of supervision, intervention, and administrative review (Hayes, 1996). In a survey of state departments of correction, the District of Columbia correctional system, and the Federal Bureau of Prisons, Hayes (1996) found that forty-one departments (79 percent) had a suicide prevention policy, eight (15 percent) had no policy but had varying numbers of protocols contained in other agency directives, and three systems did not address suicide prevention in writing. Only three departments had prevention policies that addressed all six of the recommended components, and five had policies that included all but one component.

As was stated earlier, the presence of a suicide prevention program on paper does not guarantee that it will be implemented. Liebling (1992), in her study of a British prison, found that although the institution had a suicide prevention program, less than half of the uniformed officers could explain it when asked. Hayes (1999) emphasized the importance of corrections officers' understanding of the prevention procedures, since "very few suicides are prevented by mental health, medical or other professional staff because suicide incidents are usually attempted in inmate housing units, and often during late evening hours or on weekends when inmates are generally outside the purview of program staff" (p. 62). Hayes (1999) recommends that all correctional staff members get eight hours of initial suicide prevention training, followed by a two-hour refresher course each year.

CIVIL LIABILITY ISSUES

When federal, state, or local government takes custody of a person, the government becomes responsible for that person's safety and general well-being. Officers are responsible for not only keeping inmates safe from each other, but they are obligated to keep inmates safe from themselves. The courts have been active in cases involving custodial suicide, and most action has been in the form of wrongful death or negligence suits based on state tort law (Kappeler, 1993). To establish negligence, the court needs to determine whether the officer's act or failure to act created an unreasonable risk to the detainee. Four elements must be considered for this determination: legal duty, breach of duty, proximate cause of injury, and actual injury (Kappeler et al., 1991).

Legal Duty

State courts have commonly recognized an officer's responsibility to provide a general duty of care. To meet this requirement, officers are expected to keep detainees free from harm, treat them humanely, and provide medical assistance whenever necessary (Thomas v.

Williams 1962) (cited in Kappeler, 1993; Kappeler et al., 1991). However, certain circumstances may arise when a special duty of care is necessary. Special duties arise when an officer has reason to believe that the person under supervision poses a risk to him/herself. Kappeler and associates identified two types of detainees whose incarceration results in officers having to perform a special duty of care: those who suffer from a disturbed state of mind and therefore have a diminished ability to protect themselves, and those who are under the influence of drugs and alcohol. Courts have noted that a special duty of care is warranted when officers can reasonably anticipate that a detainee may cause injury or damage. Several factors have been determined by courts to be indicators of the need of a special duty: previous suicide attempts while in custody; detainee's statement of intent to harm him/herself; detainee's history of mental illness; health care professional's determination of suicidal tendencies; emotional state and behavior of the detainee; circumstances surrounding the detainee's arrest; and the detainee's level of intoxication or drug dependence (Kappeler, 1993). The presence of any of these factors can be viewed by a court as a foreseeable indicator of an inmate's plan to commit an act of deliberate self-harm, provided that the information (e.g., knowledge of previous attempts) was accessible to the officers (Kappeler et al., 1991).

Breach of Duty

Courts may find that an officer has committed a breach of duty when there has been a failure to follow agency rules and regulations, properly supervise a suicidal or incapacitated detainee, provide a safe facility, or provide or call for medical assistance (Kappeler et al., 1991). In determining a breach of duty, courts are not always able to refer to the institution's guidelines and make a judgment based on the officer's adherence to it, since not every correctional institution has written policies (Hayes, 1996, 1989; BJS, 1996). Some courts have used the standards developed by the ACA, NCCHC, and other organizations to guide their determination of "duty of care" in deciding whether the correctional staff members were negligent (Bell v. Wolfish, 1979; Rhodes v. Chapman, 1981) (cited in Kappeler, 1993).

Proximate Cause of Injury

This legal requirement establishes the relationship between the detainee's injury and the action or inaction of law enforcement officers. For negligence to be determined, the officer's action or inaction must be proven to be the proximate cause of the inmate's death. When establishing proximate cause, Kappeler (1993) recommended asking the question, "But for the officer's conduct, would the detainee have sustained the injury?" (p. 157). An example of officers' action being ruled the proximate cause of death can be found in Hake v. Manchester Township (1985). Despite knowledge of suicidal ideation, officers neglected to remove an inmate's belt before he was placed in a holding cell. He later used the belt to hang himself. Upon finding the victim, officers neglected to call for medical assistance or attempt first aid. The New Jersey Supreme Court ruled that the victim might have lived if the officers would have taken action (Kappeler, 1993).

CONCLUSION

Inmate suicide is a problem that all federal, state, and local corrections agencies must address. Failure to recognize the danger that inmates sometimes pose to themselves has the potential to be a costly error for corrections agencies, since the courts have proven willing to find in favor of inmates' families in negligence lawsuits. Correctional agencies that have not already adopted the ACA or NCCHC's standards should clearly do so, but formulating a written policy for suicide prevention is not enough. Perhaps the most important element of a jail and lockup suicide prevention strategy is the training of the supervision staff. Poor communication among staff members (e.g., failure to pass on information to mental health workers) and refusals to take threats seriously can doom a program to failure. It must be made clear to staff members that increased supervision and support can help an inmate pass through a suicidal crisis and possibly prevent an attempt altogether. This needs to be made especially clear to officers who are closest to the inmates at all times. The entire administrative and mental health staff can be fully aware and trained in the institution's prevention and intervention policies, but if officers in the cellblocks and pods do not know this information, the program will fail.

NOTE

1. Data were also supplemented by Tracy Snell of the Bureau of Justice. The author would like to thank her for her assistance.

BIBLIOGRAPHY

Atlas, R. (1987). *Guidelines for Reducing the Liability for Inmate Suicide.* Miami, FL: Atlas and Associates.

Davis, M. S., & Muscat, J. E. (1993). An Epidemiologic Study of Alcohol and Suicide Risk in Ohio Jails and Lockups, 1975–1984. *Journal of Criminal Justice.* 21(3):277–283.

Dear, G. E., Thomson, D. M., & Hills, A. M. (2000) Self-Harm in Prison: Manipulators Can Also Be Suicide Attempters. *Criminal Justice & Behavior.* 27(2):160–175.

Farmer, K. A., Felthous, A. R., & Holzer, C. E. III (1996). Medically Serious Suicide Attempts in a Jail with a Suicide Prevention Program. *Journal of Forensic Sciences.* 41(2):240–246.

Hardie, T. J. (1998). Self-Harm Shows Diurnal Variation. *Criminal Behavior and Mental Health.* 8:17–18.

Hayes, L. M. (1989). National Study of Jail Suicides: Seven Years Later. *Psychiatric Quarterly.* 60(1):7–29.

Hayes, L. M. (1995). National and State Standards for Prison Suicide Prevention. In *Prison Suicide: An Overview and Guide to Prevention.* L. M. Hayes (ed)., pp. 1–26. Washington, DC: United States Department of Justice.

Hayes, L. M. (1996). National and State Standards for Prison Suicide Prevention: A Report Card. *Journal of Correctional Health Care.* 3(1):5–38.

Hayes, L. M. (1999). Suicide in Adult Correctional Facilities: Key Ingredients to Prevention and Overcoming the Obstacles. *Journal of Law, Medicine & Ethics.* 27(3):260–269.

Hayes, L. M. (2000). *Jail Suicide/Mental Health Update.* 10(3). Mansfield, MA: National Center on Institutions and Alternatives.

Hayes, L. M. (2001). *Jail Suicide/Mental Health Update.* 10(3). Mansfield, MA: National Center on Institutions and Alternatives.

Hayes, L. M., & Rowan, J. R. (1988). *National Study of Jail Suicides: Seven Years Later.* Alexandria, VA: National Center on Institutions and Alternatives.

Inch, H., Rowlands, P., & Soliman, A. (1995). Deliberate Self-Harm in a Young Offenders' Institution. *Journal of Forensic Psychiatry.* 6(1):161–171.

Ingram, A., Johnson, G., & Hayes, I. (1997). *Self Harm and Suicide by Detained Persons: A Study.* London: Home Office Police Research Group.

Kappeler, V. E. (1993). *Critical Issues in Police Civil Liability.* Prospect Heights, IL: Waveland Press, Inc.

Kappeler, V. E., Vaughn, M. S., & Del Carmen, R. V. (1991). Death in Detention: An Analysis of Police Liability for Negligent Failure to Prevent Suicide. *Journal of Criminal Justice.* 19(4):381–393.

Lester, D. (1987). Suicide and Homicide in USA Prisons. *Psychological Reports,* 61:126.

Lester, D., & Danto, B. L. (1993). *Suicide Behind Bars.* Philadelphia: Charles Press.

Liebling, A. (1992). *Suicides in Prison.* London and New York: Routledge.

Liebling, A., & Krarup, H. (1993). *Suicide Attempts and Self-Injury in Male Prisons.* Cambridge, MA: Institute of Criminology.

Lloyd, C. (1990). *Suicide and Self-Injury in Prison: A Literature Review.* London: Home Office.

Loucks, N. (1997). *Research into Drugs and Alcohol, Violence and Bullying, Suicides and Self-Injury and Backgrounds of Abuse.* Edinburgh, Scotland: Scottish Prison Service.

Manning, R. (1989). A Suicide Prevention Program that Really Works. *American Jails.* 3(1):18–22.

Marcus, P., & Alcabes, P. (1993). Characteristics of Suicides by Inmates in an Urban Jail. *Hospital and Community Psychiatry.* 44(3):256–261.

O'Toole M. (1997). Jails and Prisons: The Numbers Say that They Are More Different than Generally Assumed. *American Jails.* 11(2):32–39.

Power, K. G. (1997). *Evaluation of the Scottish Prison Service Suicide Prevention Strategy.* Edinburgh, Scotland: Scottish Prison Service.

Power, K. G., & Spencer, A. P. (1987) Parasuicidal Behavior of Detained Scottish Young Offenders. *International Journal of Offender Therapy and Comparative Criminology.* 31(3):227–235.

Ralph, P. H., & Marquart, J. W. (1991). Gang Violence in Texas Prisons. *Prison Journal.* 71(2):38–50.

Rowan, J. R. (1989). Suicide detection and prevention: a must for juvenile facilities. *Corrections Today.* 51(5):218–226.

Rowan, J. R. (1990). Design, equipment, construction, and other blunders in detention and correctional facilities. *American Jails.* 4(2) 12–20.

Stone, G. (1999). *Suicide and Attempted Suicide.* New York: Carroll and Graf Publishers, Inc.

Sykes, G. (1972). *Society of Captives: A Study of a Maximum Security Prison.* Princeton, NJ: Princeton University Press.

United States Bureau of Justice Statistics (1978–2000). *Capital Punishment.* Washington, DC: U.S. Department of Justice.

United States Bureau of Justice Statistics (1981–1999). *Correctional Populations in the United States.* Washington, DC: U.S. Department of Justice.

United States Bureau of Justice Statistics (1996). *Mental Health and Treatment of Inmates and Probationers.* Washington, DC: U.S. Department of Justice.

United States Bureau of Justice Statistics (2000). *Drug Use, Testing and Treatment in Jails.* Washington, DC: U.S. Department of Justice.

Welch, M., & Gunther, D. (1997). Jail Suicide and Prevention: Lessons from Litigation. *Crisis Intervention.* 3:229–244.

White, T. W., & Schimmel, D. J. (1995). Suicide prevention in federal prisons: A successful five-step program. In *Prison Suicide: An Overview and Guide to Prevention.* L. M. Hayes (ed)., pp. 48–59. Washington, DC: United States Department of Justice.

World Health Organization. (2000). *Suicide Rates and Absolute Numbers of Suicide by Country.* Geneva: Switzerland. Available at *www.who.int.*

chapter 8

Religion in the Correctional Setting

Melvina T. Sumter & Todd R. Clear

Since the demise of rehabilitation and emergence of the conservative crime control model during the 1970s, based on studies popularly thought to prove that "nothing works," there has been a sharp decline on emphasis and funding for rehabilitative programs for offenders in U.S. prisons. While this is the case, primarily as a result of constitutional guarantees, religious activities are one of the few programming efforts that survived this devolution of treatment intact. Even though this is the case, a growing body of research suggests that religion decreases the risk of deviant behavior (Ellis, 1985; Johnson, 1984; Sumter & Clear, 1998; Title & Welch, 1983). This relationship is of special concern to public policy officials who continue to search for ways to deal with the enormous problem of recidivism among former inmates. The expectation is that the reform of the offender requires a change in the spirit, and the religious experience is the doorway to that change. While this is a popular conception of the role of religion in prison, the question is, "How much do we really know about the effectiveness of religion in helping prisoners return to the community to live crime-free lives?"

This chapter provides a systemic evaluation of the significance of religion and the religious experience in the prison setting. The chapter opens with a brief review of the social history of religion within the development of the U.S. penal system. It then introduces the reader to a discussion of the complexities involved in defining religion; it moves on to discuss core dimensions of religion that are vital to construct operational definitions to measure religion in order to develop a theoretical model to understand the relationship between religiousness and behavior. Afterward, there is then a discussion of the religious orientation and experience in prison. This chapter ends with a discussion of the work examining the relationship between religion and prisoners.

SOCIAL HISTORY OF RELIGION AND THE DEVELOPMENT OF THE U.S. PENAL INSTITUTION

Religion has long been an integral part of the criminal law, influencing law and punishments since ancient times (Woods & Waite, 1941). While it is not known exactly when incarceration was first used as a method of punishment, historical records indicate that during the middle ages, "punitive imprisonment appears to have been introduced into Europe. . . . by the Christian Church in the incarceration of certain offenders against canon law" (Woods & Waite, 1941, p. 488).

The influence of the Christian Church is also present in the U.S. penal process. Ever since the first penitentiary was built in the United States, religion has played a principle role in the efforts of correctional professionals to reform offenders (Clear, 1991). The name *penitentiary* is derived from *penitence,* meaning "regret for wrongdoing or sinning." Thus, penitentiaries were originally seen as places where offenders could go to atone for their sins. Prior to the development of the penal institutions in the United States, religion pervaded all sects of life and colonial settlers believed that God caused crime and that He predetermined some people to become criminals (Newman, 1985). As a result, the role of religion in sanctioning was influential and punitive; the majority of punishments were found in the scriptures. Individuals who committed crimes were viewed as sinners who had made a pact with supernatural forces such as the devil, demons, or evil spirits (Newman, 1985). Thus, crime was equated with sin, and the response to it was revealed in the word of God, according to the dogma of Roman Catholicism (Woods & Waite, 1941). During this time, a major guiding principle of punishment was the notion of an eye for an eye, which is traced as far back as the fourth century A.D. and reached its peak during the period of the Holy Inquisition, which took place in most European countries in the thirteenth century (Newman, 1985). In fact, the law of retaliation known as *lex talionis* is reflected in the Old Testament of the Holy Bible:

> *Leviticus 24:20*
>
> —Breach for breach, eye for eye, tooth for tooth, as he has caused a blemish in a man, so shall it be done to him again.

However, the New Testament of the Holy Bible spoke directly against retribution and called for the forgiveness of any man who lashed out against oneself. For example, Jesus is reported to have said the following:

> *Matthew 5:38*
>
> —Ye have heard that it had been said, An eye for an eye, and a tooth for a tooth: But I say unto you, That Ye resist not evil: but whosoever shall smite thee on thy right cheek, turn to him the other also.

Despite this contrast in the New Testament, retribution remained the most dominant means of social control through the use of brutal punishments. These included branding, various forms of mutilation, public humiliation through the ducking stock (submergence in water until near drowning), whippings, and other means of torture (American Correctional Association, 1983; Newman 1985). During this time, there were no correctional institutions or penitentiaries as we know them today. Instead, the prisons that were built were designed as temporary housing units, until the accused either confessed or appeared before a judge. These gruesome early practices eventually served as the catalyst for a powerful reform movement in the handling of crime and the administration of justice (Newman, 1985).

In response to these early methods of punishment, the penitentiary system in the United States originated under two distinct philosophies: a system of enforced solitude known as the Pennsylvania system and a system of congregate prison discipline known as the Auburn system. The Pennsylvania system was derived from Quaker philosophy, which set out to implement humanistic and religious ideas in the prison. The Quakers did not believe that public punishment could reform the individual. Rather, they felt that it only served to facilitate the spirit of revenge and to increase criminal behavior (O'Connor & Parikh, 1996). The Quakers also believed that all people could obtain God's grace and that institutions should be built where offenders might spend uninterrupted time contemplating their sins in pursuit of that grace. Thus, under the Quaker philosophy, the major goal of confinement was penance through required Bible reading and the reflection on one's sin (Clear & Cole, 1997; O'Connor & Parikh, 1996). As a result, the Quakers emphasized the importance of silent worship in allowing the spirit of God to develop and manifest itself in everyone (O'Connor & Parikh, 1996). Under the Quakers, the establishment of the penitentiary emphasized punishment as well as the rehabilitation of the offender through solitary confinement between intervals of work, the inculcation of good habits, and religious instructions so that the inmates could reflect on their moral obligations to society (Clear & Cole, 1997). For that reason, the early reformers viewed the move toward incarceration as an opportunity to rehabilitate the criminal, as well as to punish (Wright, 1987), and that only by removing the offender from the evils of society and enforcing a steady and regular regimen could society turn the offender into a productive citizen (Clear & Cole, 1997; O'Connor & Parikh, 1996). This provided him with the opportunity to repent from his sins. Accordingly, the Pennsylvania system was a prison with complete solitude, "with labor in the cells and recreation in a private yard adjacent to each cell" (Morse, 1973, p. 23). While this notion of complete solitude seems somewhat simplistic, the concept of separate confinement was guided by the following principles outlined by Sellin (1970):

1. Prisoners should be treated not vengefully but in ways designed to convince them that through hard work and selective forms of suffering, they could change their lives.

2. Solitary confinement of all inmates would prevent the prison from becoming a corrupting influence. Presumably, when prisoners were isolated from each other, they could not conspire and create plans that would bring trouble to the institution.

3. In their seclusion, offenders would have opportunities to reflect on their transgressions so that they might repent.

4. Because humans are by nature social beings, solitary confinement should also provide punishing discipline.

5. Solitary confinement would be more economical because prisoners would not need long periods of time to benefit from the penitential experience and fewer keepers would be required.

Because the Pennsylvania system proved to be very expensive and instead of rehabilitating offenders, in many cases, reports indicate that continued solitary confinement led to the prisoners, as well as other social and behavioral problems, the Auburn system in New York later became the preferred penal model (Sullivan, 1990). The Auburn system was often called "the congregate system," because prisoners were held in isolation at night but silently congregate in workshops during the day, forbidden to talk or even exchange glances while on the job or at meals (Clear & Cole, 1997). In this system, prisoners worked and ate in common areas although they were prohibited from any type of communication, including looking at each other (Clear & Cole, 1997). Strict discipline, such as corporal punishment and solitary confinement, was used to enforce the rule of silence as well as other rules. It is ironic that in order to enforce discipline in the Auburn system, prison officials returned to some of the cruel and harsh punishments the penal system was designed to eliminate. Even so, the Auburn model became the most dominant model of the U.S. prison systems since the prisoners were employed in workshops both as therapy and as a way to finance the institution; therefore, this system also proved to be more financially practical than the Pennsylvania system.

While the Pennsylvania system was an overly religious regime, the Auburn system also emphasized the importance of a Christian spiritual experience. Prisoners attended church, met with chaplains, and were expected to study the Bible. The economical feasibility of the Auburn system was based on congregate work, but the reform of the prisoners was seen as deriving from a similar combination of productive labor, self-conscious contemplation, and succumbing to the imperatives of spiritual truth as the Pennsylvania system.

Religion has remained an important theme in the history of the American prison system. During the late 1950s, with the growth of the Black Muslim religion in prison and the courts' abandonment of the traditional hands-off policy and willingness to hear civil rights claims from prisoners regarding violations of their First Amendment guarantee to freedom of religious practice as well as violations of other constitutional rights, the issue of religious rights gained national attention (Clear & Cole, 1997). The beginning of this movement was spurred by the Black Muslim prisoners, who under protection of the First Amendment guarantee of freedom of religious expression, demanded that they be given the same religious rights as Christian inmates. This group of inmates was initially denied recognition as a bona fide religion. However, in 1962, in *Fulwood v. Clemmer,* the courts ruled that Muslims have the same constitutional rights to practice their religion and to hold services as inmates of other faiths unless prison officials could demonstrate that such activities would pose a threat to institutional security (Krantz, 1976; Selke, 1993). The resolution of the Black Muslim constitutional religious rights meant the standards applied to them could also be applied to any duly recognized religion. Consequently, this landmark decision paved the way for further court proceedings and clarification of religious rights of prisoners. One such example is that in 1972, in *Curz v. Beto,* the Supreme Court ruled Buddhist prisoners have the rights to observe their religion in a manner comparable to that of other religious groups (Krantz, 1976; Selke, 1993). Another example is the case of *Kahane v. Carlson,* where the courts ruled in 1975 that Orthodox Jewish inmates may not be denied a special diet unless prison officials can show cause why such a diet cannot be provided. As such, under protection of the First Amendment guarantee of freedom of religious expression, prison administrators are required to allow equal protection of all prisoners practicing their religious beliefs. These guarantees have resulted in the courts ruling that prisoners practicing their religious beliefs have the right to (1) be served meals consistent with religious dietary laws; (2) be served meals at special feeding times; (3) correspond with religious leaders and possess religious literature; (4) wear emblems and a beard if their religious belief requires it; and (5) assemble for religious services as long as their religion can be established as a bona fide religion and its practice does not present a security threat to the institution (Clear & Cole, 1997; Krantz, 1976; Selke, 1993).

In the more recent history of the American penal system, the importance of religion in the prison setting continues to be demonstrated as prisons provide routine weekly religious programs such as chaplaincy services, spiritual counseling, Bible study, Sunday services, and visitation ministry. In addition, correctional agencies have opened their doors to such nonprofit prison ministries as the Kairos, Jaycees, and Bible Believers Fellowship. These organizations provide services such as prison evangelism, biblical instruction, spiritual growth program, prerelease counseling and support, aftercare and family assistance, and inmate correspondence programs.

A more widely known nonprofit prison ministry is Prison Fellowship (PF), which attracts attention across the country and around the world, encompassing organizations in more than 83 countries, and was founded in 1976 by Charles W. Colson, following his release from prison after serving sentence for a "Watergate"-related crime. Prison Fellowship is a nonprofit volunteer organization that assists the Church in its ministry to prisoners, ex-prisoners, victims, and those affected by crime. The continued importance of religion in the prison setting was demonstrated in 1997, when PF implemented a faith-based prerelease program, called "Inner Change" Pre-Release Program, in the Texas Department of Criminal Justice. This initiative resulted from a mandate by the Senate Committee of Criminal Justice Interim Report, which directed the Texas Department of Criminal Justice to develop a rehabilitation tier of programs that would be evaluated based on its success in reducing recidivism. This faith-based prerelease program, "Inner Change," emphasizes restorative justice, in which offenders work to restore themselves, the community, the victims, and the offender's family. Thus, the history of the prison is very much a history of religious activity in the correctional setting.

WHAT IS RELIGIOUSNESS AND HOW DOES IT WORK?

What is religion? What does it mean to be a religious person? Does religious programming in prison help inmates stay out of trouble during incarceration and after release from prison? If so, how does religion work in a person's life? In order to answer these questions, we must first have an understanding of what religion is. As such, this section will discuss the meaning of religion.

We as individuals, in our attempts to conceptualize a definition of religion, often develop a simplistic, unidimensional definition based on our socialization, familiar culture, and/or spiritual affiliation. Moreover, Westerners limit their definitions of religion to Western theology and rarely include other world affiliations. Although a definition of religion can reflect on one particular viewpoint, academics define it in several ways to emphasize distinctive dimensions.

The English word *religion* is derived from the Latin word *religio,* which refers to the fear or awe one feels in the presence of a spirit or God (Hopfe & Woodard, 1998). Hopfe and Woodard (1998, p. 4) write that "in western culture religion is defined in terms of a set of beliefs having to do with the gods through which one is taught a moral system." The authors state that this definition contains elements found within many of the world religions, although it does not adequately define religion for all of them. For example, some religions, and particularly Eastern religions (i.e., Confucianism), recognize the existence of gods, but they have very little to do with them and then there are others that do not recognize gods at all. Cunningham, Kelsay, Barineau, and McVoy (1995) state that the definitional question regarding what constitutes a religion is controversial because the phenomenon is complex and related to a variety of aspects of existence. Religion is not an isolated aspect of human experience but relates closely to thought, feelings, and actions; to the concerns of the individual and social existence; and to the expression and recognition of values (Cunningham et al., 1995). As a result, "definitions of religion must therefore not only refer to the ways religion helps human beings but also respond to difficult problems" (Cunningham et al., 1995, p. 18). Thus, Cunningham et al. (1995) maintain that an adequate definition of religion should always deal with substance and identify what it is that makes certain responses to suffering and death religious and others not.

Houf (1935) argues that there is no definition of religion that is generally accepted as authoritative. In the "*Varieties of Religious Experience*" William James (1936) proposed that because there are so many definitions of the word religion, we should learn that the whole concept is too large for any one definition to fit all. He says, "the word 'religion' cannot stand for any single principle or essence, but is rather a collective name. . . . Let us rather admit freely at the outset that we may very likely find no one essence, but many characters which may alternately be equally important to religion" (James, 1936, p. 27).

From the point of view of these religious scholars, it is apparent, then, that it is difficult to develop a definition that is representative of all traditions. Despite the variability in these definitions, Yinger (1946) argues that they share some common elements and that our concern should be with all religions. Moreover, while there is not a consensus of a suitable definition of religion, there is a general agreement that the different religions have many common elements. Religions in general teach that this physical and material world is not the only reality and that there is something greater than the here and now, a purpose more profound than mere just survival (Breuilly et al., 1997; Yinger, 1946). According to Yinger (1946), each religion (1) has a set of general beliefs or principles concerning the meaning of life; (2) emphasizes the type of behavior that is acceptable and provides guidelines for its adherents to live by; (3) encourages rituals and practices associated with general beliefs;

(4) has a set of writings or sacred scriptures to guide its adherents; (5) has a group of leaders to teach and guide its adherents; and (6) encourages a growth pattern among its adherents to improve themselves in this life.

And so there are six major world religions: Hinduism, Buddhism, Confucianism, Judaism, Christianity, and Islam. Whereas these distinct religions each reflect a particular image of the culture in which they first arose, they also have common dimensions that are vital to construct operational definitions that measure religion in order to develop a theoretical model to understand the relationship between religiousness and behavior. The next subsection will provide an overview of the core dimensions of religion.

Religion Dimensions

Scholars who study religion have defined it in several different ways. They have tried to assess intrinsic feelings about religion, and they have measured behavior such as church attendance and participation in various religious activities. It is also the case that few studies of religion measure religion as a dummy variable, "yes" or "no." Contemporary views on religion, however, emphasize the complexity of the phenomenon, generally referring to it as a multidimensional ordinal construct by the use of "levels" of various "dimensions" of religiousness. Most scholars believe that a single indicator may be a poor predictor of religion (Ellis, 1985; Johnson, 1984; Knudten & Knudten, 1971; Tittle & Welch, 1983). Therefore, "a multiple dimensional measure of religiousness is generally considered preferable to unidimensional measures because they tap a variety of aspects of religiousness beyond mere participation" (Clear et al., 1992, p. 10).

Just as there is a difficulty in attempting to trace the development of spiritual traditions, there is just as much complexity as well as diversity in identifying the universal dimensions of religion. According to Glock (1973, p. 10), "investigators have tended to focus upon one or another of the diverse manifestations of religiosity and to ignore others." He contends that in one study, attention is confined to studying religious beliefs, whereas in another study the focus may be on studying different religious practices. W. Richard Comstock refers to five methodological perspectives on religion: the psychological, the sociological, the historical, the phenomenological, and the hermeneutical (Carmody & Carmody, 1984). Niniam Smart (1983) identifies six dimensions of religion: the experiential, the mythic, the doctrinal, the ethical, the ritual, and the social. Robert S. Ellwood (1978) divides religion into the self, history, psychology, symbol and rite, sociology, truth, and conceptual expression. Likewise, from a sociological perspective, Charles Glock (1973) identifies five dimensions of religion: the experiential, the ritualistic, the ideological, the intellectual, and the consequential.

An examination of the major religions of the world shows that doctrines of religious expression are extremely varied; moreover, the different religions expect quite different things of their adherents (Gaer, 1952; Hopfe & Woodard, 1998; Yinger, 1946). Despite this great variation of detail, there exists among the world religions considerable consensus regarding the more general areas in which religion ought to be manifested (Comstock, 1995;

Cunningham et al., 1995, Yinger, 1946). According to Comstock (1995), these general areas may be thought of as the core dimensions of religion. After reviewing religious research and scholarly literature on religions, Comstock (1995) identified seven distinct dimensions of religion (e.g., transcendence, history, belief, ritual, morality, community/society, and personal identity) that are recognized and considered by most scholars of religion to be representative of the dominant world religions. In this review, we rely on an analysis by Comstock (1995) of seven distinct dimensions of religion: transcendence, history, belief, ritual, morality, community/society, and personal identity. These multiple dimensions are recognized by scholars of religion to portray the underlying aspects of the dominant world religions, and so they may be thought of as a good general model of religion.

Transcendence or Supernatural

Transcendence is the dimension of religion that differentiates religious and nonreligious rituals and beliefs while distinguishing the sacred from the profane (Comstock, 1995; Cunningham et al., 1995; Durkheim, 1915; Hopfe & Woodard, 1998). For some scholars, the transcendence is also a characteristic of religion that, in one way or another, includes the concept of the supernatural, "the extraordinary," "the infinite," or the power manifesting itself in the universe (Comstock, 1995). Titiev (1954, pp. 395–396) advises that labeling something supernatural suggests that "it can never be made manifest to human taste, touch, smell, sight, or hearing, even with the aid of devices like powerful telescopes or sound amplifiers." He goes on to state that the very core of religion entails believing wholeheartedly in the existence of something that cannot and may never be grasped by one's senses. Humans are not able to determine scientifically the characteristics of the supernatural or to determine whether or not the supernatural exists independent of his definitions (Titiev, 1954). Therefore, Titiev (1954) contends that a great multiplicity of concepts about the supernatural are observable in various cultures throughout the world. For example, the religions of Judaism, Christianity, and Islam are characterized by the present notion of sacred reality as "going beyond" our "ordinary existence" (Comstock, 1995; Cunningham et al., 1995). These authors write that it is difficult to think of these religions without the notion of an all-wise, all-powerful God, who reigns eternally and surpasses human understanding. Cunningham and colleagues (1995, p. 30) illustrate an example from the Holy Bible in the Chapter of Isaiah 55:8–9 that expresses this sentiment well:

> For my thoughts are not your thoughts. Neither are your ways my ways, declared the Lord. For all heavens are higher than earth, so are my ways higher than your ways and my thoughts than your thoughts.

Another example provided by the authors is from the Islamic tradition and is found in the Qur'an:

> Say. He is Allah, the one! Allah, the eternally besought. He begetteth nor was begotten. And there is none comparable to him.

History

According to Comstock (1995), religions, like our lives, follow a course, a trajectory, or path through history from one point to another. Religious traditions develop over time and come to constitute traditions that may be identified with the history of a particular community (Comstock, 1995). Prior to birth, the group has already established the languages the members will speak, the type of clothing they will wear, the ways available for them to make a living, the types of foods they will eat, the type of supernatural being or beings to worship, and how that worship will take place (O'Dea, 1966). The family, society, and culture have already developed the blueprint members are expected to follow in their religious behavior. The religious social heritage and behavior of humans is thus acquired and learned from their culture. Individuals are taught certain religious patterns, such as how to participate in religious activities, how to communicate with the divine being(s), or how to go through the prescribed rituals and ceremonies (O'Dea, 1966). This foundation serves as the trajectory the youth passes through to adulthood. While it is true that some adults adopt religions different from their upbringing, it is also true that most individuals remain with the same religion throughout their life course.

Belief

According to Comstock (1995), it is not enough to believe that the supernatural exists in order to have religion. He (1995) notes that the members of society must also believe in the doctrine of the religion. Upon awareness of this existence, the individual's life is influenced and he or she eventually accepts the beliefs and ideas that are passed down through tradition. Likewise, bodies of belief concerning the sacred and the supernatural are transmitted to new individuals as a part of their culture. Thus, religious beliefs are ideas that adherents hold to be true that sanctify norms of conduct and supply their ultimate justification (O'Dea, 1966). Moreover, religion is characterized by a body of beliefs that provide supernatural and sacred definitions for its followers (Comstock, 1995).

Ritual

Rituals are activities that people perform in accordance with formal or informal rules or customs that reinforce a commitment to their religious values (Cunningham et al., 1995). Likewise, according to Comstock (1995) and Cunningham and colleagues (1995), rituals are regularly patterned acts that are imbued with sacred meanings that express the beliefs of their religious doctrine. These rituals, the authors argue, are the most visible dimension of religion because the activities often include public and group activities. For many religious followers, rituals are an attempt to influence the sacred, as well as express and reinforce a commitment of their beliefs (Comstock, 1995; Cunningham et al., 1995). Moreover, a rite transcends the bonds of the individual private religious experience into a collective experience of individuals with shared values and beliefs (Paden, 1992). For Durkheim (1915), the most important function of the ritual is to renew the foundation of society itself; the ritual serves to reinforce the "life" of religious beliefs. Also, religious rites elicit the acting out of sentiments, which in turn strengthens the fundamental norms and values of society, thereby reinforcing them in the consciousness of its adherents (O'Dea, 1966). For example, the Islamic law requires prayer; an observant Muslim faces toward Mecca five times daily and prays to express commitment to his religious doctrine (Cunningham et al., 1995; Hopfe & Woodard, 1998). Another example is the Christian practice of receiving Holy Communion (Breuilly et al., 1997; Hopfe & Woodard, 1998; Rosten, 1975). This sacrament represents the central beliefs regarding Jesus' mission, death, and resurrection. During Jesus' time a shared meal signified peace, trust, and community solidarity (Hopfe & Woodard, 1998). According to Hopfe and Woodard (1998), today the term *communion* denotes a very similar meaning: a sharing of thoughts and emotions, often simply conceived as fellowship or community.

Morality

Religious doctrine provides life prescriptions that adherents are expected to abide by in this world, as well as those things a person must do or avoid in order to attain salvation (Comstock, 1995). Followers of religious traditions are taught to accept certain behavioral patterns as being in harmony with their religion, whereas others are not (O'Dea, 1966). Those who share common religious beliefs and practices also share common values and come to accept common definitions as to what is good and what is bad (O'Dea, 1996). Through religious teaching, societal members are apprised as to what is good or correct by referring to religious sources, such as the Vedas (for Hindus), the Torah (for Jews), the Holy Bible (for Christians), or the Qur'an (for Muslims). Moreover, religion sancarnazies the norms and values established by society, thus maintaining the dominance of group goals and disciplines over individual impulses and wishes (O'Dea 1966). Thus, Cunningham and colleagues (1995) maintain that the greatest strength of religion is its ability to provide sanctions for moral behavior.

Community or Society

Religion shared by a group of people in every aspect is systematically shown to be an expression of the collective life (Paden, 1992). Central to Durkheim's (1915) functionalist analysis of religion is that religious beliefs and practices operate jointly to bond members into an integrated community. For Durkheim (1915), religion is society; therefore, he maintains that each society constructs religion around its horizon. In other words, all that we know about obligations, loyalty, respect, and moral behavior is learned from society, and our relationship to religious symbols simply mirror these societal relations (Cunningham et al., 1998; Paden, 1992). Durkheim argued that for many societies, religion is a collective expression of what they believe society is, how it is governed, how they relate to it, and what its sanctions are. Only society can evoke religious attitudes and the sort of moral sentiments societal members are expected to uphold. For that reason, the functionalists view religion as a sort of "glue" that holds society together (Glock, 1973). Therefore, the explicit content of religious ideas is not important, because religion expresses sociological, not theological, reality. As a result, only religion is considered to be the ultimate source of human action and social stability while providing answers to the ultimate questions that motivate men (Davis, 1948; Parsons, 1958). According to Durkheim (1915), failure to achieve religious solidarity threatens the entire society, leading to social disorganization and collapse. Notthingham (1954) contends that the very process of sharing "beliefs" and "rituals" tends to strengthen the group's sense of identity, thus accentuating the group's "we" feeling.

Personal Identity

According to Cunningham and colleagues (1995), most of the major religions make a place for individual decisions and encourage adherents to search for unity with their supreme being. Some religious scholars and sociologists (Comstock, 1995; Cunningham et al., 1995; Glock, 1972; Hopfe & Woodard, 1998; Houf, 1935; Parsons, 1958) claim that religion provides answers to our questions concerning the meaning of our relations to others, existence, happiness and suffering, and good and evil. Thus, religion provides the individual with a sense of purpose and meaning in life, since it alone has the means of grasping what is beyond the natural world. Religion also provides adequate responses to questions about suffering, injustice, and evil in human experiences (Durkheim, 1915; Glock, 1973; O'Dea, 1966; Parsons, 1958). Therefore, religion provides people with a sense of security, a feeling of acceptance and belonging, and a source of psychological support during the most trying times of a person's life (O'Dea, 1966). Although Durkheim (1915, p. 387) emphasizes the social phenomenon of religion, he recognizes that religion "gives the believer impressions of comfort and dependence," moreover, "the believer who has communicated with his god. . . . is a man who is stronger." He feels within him more force, either to endure the trials of existence, or to conquer them (Durkheim, 1915, p. 416), thereby leading to the growth and maturation of the individual and his passage through various age grading processes identified by his society (O'Dea, 1966). Thus, "religion provides through its sanctification and renewal of basic norms, a strategic basis for social control in the face of deviant tendencies and the expression of impulses dangerous to the stability of society" (O'Dea, 1966, p. 13). Moreover, religious beliefs and practices facilitate the spiritual development of individuals, which, in turn, increases their self-awareness, providing them with a sense of inner peace and the purpose and existence for their life. In like manner, religion convinces people that they need salvation and prescribes a path to achieve this salvation by sustaining good relations with the supernatural or inner spirit.

Thus, while we have distinct world religions whose doctrines are extremely varied, the religions do have many common elements and a consensus regarding the general areas in which religion should be manifested. The next subsection provides a discussion of the various faith-based groups that shape the reasons for religious practice and the change process within the prison walls.

Prison and Religious Orientation

Religious orientation in the correctional setting mirrors that of general society. Moreover, like mainstream America, Christianity and Islam are the dominant religions in the prison setting. However, faith-based groups, such as Native Americans and Buddhists, and some extreme groups, such as the Aryan Brotherhood, that operate under the auspices of religion also exist in the prison setting (Clear et al., 1992). Although this is the case, very little research has been done on religious groups other than Christianity and Islam. This is not because these two religions are the only legitimate vehicles of religious teaching in the prison, but possibly because they are the most dominant forms of religion in the prison setting. In this subsection, the religious overtones of these two prison religions and a synopsis of two other religious groups in the prisons setting is discussed.

Christianity

Christianity is one of the dominant prison religions studied by Clear and colleagues (1992). Adherents of Christianity are typically identified as being Catholic or Protestant. Catholicism is based on the premise that the Church is empowered to define doctrines for all believers that are moral obligations necessary for salvation. Moreover, through the affirmation of an individual priesthood, adherents are expected to confess their sins to a special ordained priest to obtain salvation. Catholicism also embraces seven sacraments: baptism, the Lord's Supper, confirmation, penance, marriage, ordination of priests, and anointing of the sick (Breuilly et al., 1997; Rosten, 1975). Although Catholics have a strong reliance on the Bible, final interpretation of any specific passage is left up to the priest who heads the church and is appointed custodian of the Bible. Furthermore, Catholicism encourages strict adherence to the moral perspectives delineated by the Bible and does not allow diverse opinions on subjects such as birth control, divorce, or homosexuality, since these issues are believed to be settled by the teaching of the Bible (Rosten, 1975).

Protestants are Christians who accept the basic early Christian creeds (statement of belief) while viewing the Bible as the supreme authority in all matters of faith and practice. Protestants believe in salvation by faith alone and only accept two sacraments (Breuilly et al., 1997; Rosten, 1975). These two sacraments, baptism and the Lord's Supper, are, according to the Gospels, the only two to have the direct touch of Jesus (Breuilly et al., 1997). Breuilly and colleagues (1997) state that unlike the Catholics, the Protestants believe in the individual priesthood of all believers and that God is accessible to each of his children. Protestantism embraces a variety of doctrines with different beliefs, which include Anglican Communion, Adventists, Baptists, Brethren, The Church of God, Disciplines of Christ, Friends (or Quakers), Lutherans, Methodists, Mennonites, Moravians, Pentecostals, Presbyterians, Reformed groups, Shakers, United Church of Christ, and all Christian Fundamentalists, to name a few (Breuilly et al., 1997; Rosten, 1975). Protestants are also divided along liberal, conservative, and fundamentalist lines. The liberal stream is open to critical studies of the Bible, is keen to modernization of the church, and engages in dialogue with other religions. The conservatives adhere mainly to Reformation teaching developed by Luther and Calvin and see other religions as essentially misguided, seeking to convert them to Christianity (Rosten, 1975). These groups tend to read the Bible in a literal manner, rejecting modern biblical criticism and theories such as evolution, which contradicts the biblical account of creation (Breuilly et al., 1997; Rosten, 1975). The fundamentalists also tend to reject historic creeds and forms of worship and emphasize a more literal and individualistic interpretation of the Bible than do conservative Protestants. They also attempt to enforce strict legal and moral codes (Breuilly et al., 1997). Additionally, fundamentalists see God as a lawgiver. They believe salvation results entirely from discipline and strict adherence to the established moral principles found in the Bible, such as the Ten Commandments (Rosten, 1975). For the fundamentalists, everything centers around the church; members are required to attend and participate in social and religious activities, in addition to one or two services on Sunday (Breuilly et al., 1997; Rosten, 1975). Members who do not act in accordance with the established guidelines are often ostracized, which is considered to be a silent invitation to conform or worship elsewhere (Rosten, 1975).

The study findings by Clear and colleagues (1992) indicate that inmates who identi-fied themselves as Protestants tend to adjust better in prison than inmates of other affilia-tions. This may be indicative that conservative or Pentecostal religious orientations that we encounter (especially in the Southern prisons) in the free world also tend to ameliorate the prison environment (Clear et al., 1992). Clear and colleagues (1992) noted that the char-acter of Christian practice depends a great deal on the religious orientation of the chaplain. While this is the case, the researchers noted that there was little influence of liberal theol-ogy in the prison settings. Moreover, the religious orientations of Christians appeared to be more orthodox and doctrinaire. Hence, the religious doctrine in the prison setting was typ-ically socially and theologically conservative (Clear et al., 1992). Religious inmates attend church service, prayer meetings, evening Bible study, and musical performances and adopt religious sacraments as prescribed by their religious teaching. Thus, according to the re-searchers, the prison religion is a discipline within a disciplined world.

Islam

The other dominant religion in the prison system is Islam, which is practiced by African American inmates. The literature suggests that most African Americans who become Mus-lims while being incarcerated do so as an act of rebellion against the perceived oppression they have encountered from a system of rules and politics dominated by white Americans. According to Clear and colleagues (1992), the history of Islam in the U.S. prison system is one of protest by African American inmates. Thus, for the African American prisoner, affil-iation with Islam is a way to repudiate white, Western society (Clear et al., 1992). The re-searchers documented that the history of Islam in the prison setting also includes a tradition of ganglike protection by fellow Muslims. Moreover, joining the ranks of Islam provides a source of protection from other violent, stronger inmates. This obligation to protect fellow Muslims from attack is based on the teaching of the Qur'an, which the Muslim inmates take very seriously (Clear et al., 1992). This source of protection is especially desired by newly admitted young African American inmates. For the Muslim inmates belief alone is mean-ingless; therefore, they are required to express and uphold their faith in their daily lives by practicing the Five Pillars of Islam. Therefore, because Islam is a total way of life, not just a religion or concern with spiritual matters, the newly admitted or young Muslim inmate may not have completely understood or accepted the religious doctrine of Islam. This may ex-plain why the Muslim inmates scored lower on the adjustment scale in the Clear study than other religious groups. In essence, for the African American Muslim inmate, "Islam provides a total lifestyle of discipline to its laws, while also providing social support, a legitimate way to reject the conventions of Western society" (Clear et al., 1992, pp. 29 and 30).

The religion of Islam often runs counter to the administration of prison operations and the requirements of security, which makes it difficult for Muslims to practice their re-ligion faithfully. For example, the requirement of *SALAH* at midday on Friday is often not possible since the institution is either conducting count or the inmates are required to be working, often in different locations, and sometimes outside of the prison compound. It is also difficult to follow the required dietary practice of no pork, since much of the prison menu consists of pork, and many food products include pork ingredients. Another problem documented by Clear and colleagues (1992) is that the prison administrators are often skeptical of Muslim inmates and see them as troublemakers, which can result in prison administrators only reluctantly offering the required as well as requested Islamic services to assist Muslims in their spiritual development. Finally, in most prisons, the chaplains are Christians, which often dictates the types of religious programs offered by the institution and volunteers recruited to assist in the delivery of religious programs. Thus, in many instances, it was often difficult for Muslim inmates to locate an Imam to lead their religious services. As a result of these barriers, Muslim inmates have to rely on one another, which, in turn, strengthens their bonds to each other. Ironically, obstacles placed before the Muslim inmates actually assist them meeting one main requirement of the Qur'an, the strengthening bonds among each other. But it also starts the growth of their religious maturity.

Other Religions in the Prison Setting

In addition to Christians and Islam followers, Clear and his associates also interviewed Native Americans and members of the Aryan Brotherhood. When talking with the researchers, the Native Americans spoke of the need to identify with a particular culture and how religion provides them with a sense of oneness. A final group frequency encountered by the researchers was the Aryan Brotherhood. Their conversation centered on the desire to solicit followers, to promote white supremacy, and to support various forms of satanic worship. For both of these groups, in addition to speaking of their spirituality, religious affiliation is a method for inmates to protest subtly that the cultural order that placed them in prison is morally incorrect (Clear et al., 1992).

In order to make sense of the myriad versions of religious experience in the prison setting, Clear and his associates (1) drew from the vast literature on "orientations" toward religiousness, and (2) based their descriptions of prison life on the substantial literature on prison society (1992). Thus, the most comprehensive body of information documenting why inmates seek religion in prison was completed by Clear and his associates. The next subsection describes the reasons why inmates seek religion within the prison setting.

The Religious Experience in Prison

Johnson's review of the literature (1984) revealed that most writings on the topic of religion and prison have been merely anecdotal descriptions by former chaplains and inmates. Although both religion and the prison have each been topics of considerable writing, we know very little about the way religion works in prison. Clear and colleagues (1992) studied 20 prisons from 12 states located throughout the United States. The researchers gathered data on individual prisoners from all 20 prisons, administered surveys to large sample of prisoners in 3 of the prisons, and interviewed groups and individuals in 6 of the prisons. In all, the researchers conducted over 1000 interviews with prisoners, officials, and professionals involved in prison and religious activity.

The researchers adopted Gordon Allport's well-known concepts of "intrinsic" and "extrinsic" religious orientations to explain why some inmates seek religious experience while incarcerated. The intrinsic orientations result from the prisoner whose main purpose is to express his or her religious sincerity; moreover, they apply to the prisoner whose main purpose is to experience his or her religious conviction personally. Intrinsically motivated prisoners value religion because it improves their understanding and acceptance of their place in life, particularly their current incarceration, and it helps them derive a sense of meaning and purpose for life. The extrinsic orientations apply to prisoners whose main purpose is to seek religion for its instrumental or utilitarian benefits. For them, religion is a means of social gain, acquiring comfort, security, or protection. Both the intrinsic and extrinsic orientations offer plausible explanations as to why religion provides comfort from the deprivations of being imprisoned. Inmates seek religion for both intrinsic and extrinsic reasons; however, one of the orientations is usually more dominant than the other with the inmate. Clear and colleagues (1992) noted that while many of the characteristics are present in all of the institutions, they could not establish a universal "prison religion." Thus, they were careful to caution the reader that the degree of religious practice varied from one prison to the next. This subsection focuses on the intrinsic and extrinsic orientations identified by the researchers to explain religion in the prison setting.

Intrinsic Orientations and Motives for Prison Religion

The results of the Clear study indicated that religion serves as a mechanism to confront the reality of imprisonment while alleviating the dissatisfaction one experiences with life. Three intrinsic reasons were identified as to why inmates seek religion in prison: (1) to deal with guilt; (2) to find a new way of life; and (3) to deal with loss, especially that of freedom.

Dealing with guilt.   The first intrinsic orientation identified in the study was that religion helps prisoners to deal with the guilt of being imprisoned. According to the researchers, incarceration is used in modern society as a means of shaming the offender for the criminal act committed. Thus, the intent is not only to incapacitate the inmates but to ensure also that they feel remorse for their wrongdoing, by experiencing guilt and shame. The prisoner turns to religion to relieve guilt either by exculpatory acceptance of the work of evil in the world or through atonement and forgiveness.

For some prisoners, especially nonreligious inmates, evil was used to explain how they ended up in prison. An example provided by the researchers was "the simple belief that the person's previous rejection of religious obligations put him into circumstances where crime was possible" (Clear et al., 1992, p. 35). Moreover, because he avoided religious fidelity and desired drugs, thrills, sex, and other excitement, he was allowed free reign, which eventually led to his criminal behavior (Clear et al., 1992). A comment made by one of the inmates was

> beware of the tricks of the devil. He has a lot of tricks. He uses the things of the world. He will use people to get in your face. . . . He uses different ways, but you have to be wise. You have to avoid it (Clear et al., 1992, p. 36).

While some inmates adopted an exculpatory view of their guilt, many others began to accept profound personal responsibility for their crimes and misbehavior. One inmate stated,

> If you talk to everyone here, they'll tell you they're in prison because of a mistake. Most of them, it was a bad attorney, a judge, a stupid mistake in the way they did the crime. The religious inmate, he realizes the mistake was doing the crime in the first place (Clear et al., 1992, p. 36).

For these inmates, religion served as a way to atone for their past behavior and seek forgiveness from a higher power while beginning the journey to a more fulfilling, law-abiding life. As a result, "by adopting a religious identity, the inmate aligns with a logic that allows guilt, but surpasses it, with a stronger self-image intact" (Clear et al., 1992, p. 36).

Finding a new way of life.   The second intrinsic orientation for seeking religion in prison was that religion provided an opportunity for the prisoners to search for a new beginning in life. The researchers noted that a central theme among the inmates was the discussion of how their faith had "changed" them. Several statements from the inmates include the following:

> My faith has made me excited about when I go home. This person has never been on the streets before (Clear et al., 1992, p. 37).

> Religion is a guide not to get out of hand; it gives you a straight path (Clear et al., 1992, p. 37).

The inmates who adopted religion as a new way of life not only stated that religion changed them but also commented on how religion forced them to understand how their behavior and actions contributed to their current circumstances. One of the inmates commented,

> Before I became a Muslim I would not even think of what the consequences were. But religion teaches you these things, it makes you more conscious to every act you do (Clear et al., 1992, p. 37).

The inmates also drew meaning from their religious orientation with regard to how they felt God was playing an active role their lives. These inmates reported a sense of empowerment and a change in their sense of personal power, enabling them to contend with the difficulties, pressure, and pain of being imprisoned. Note the statement from another inmate:

> We ain't did nothing. Anything that's happened in our lives. He [God] has done. . . . The Father wants you to be completely empty so he can fill you (Clear et al., 1992, p. 37)

Dealing with loss, especially of freedom.   The third and final intrinsic orientation identified in the study was that prisoners seek religion while in prison to search for and develop a sense of personal peace. Whereas this motive was also identified by nonreligious prisoners, it was typically discussed more often among the religious prisoners. For these inmates, religion provided a sense of harmony and freedom within the prison walls. Psychologically, the inmate no longer had a sense of being locked up. A couple of the inmates commented,

It is not the prison that incarcerates us, it is a man's mind (Clear et al., 1992, p. 38).

I am able to live a normal life and uphold my character with dignity. The first objective of prisons is to strip you of your dignity. It takes your self-esteem, your dignity, and everything about you. Religion has helped me to regain this (Clear et al., 1992, p. 38).

Clear et al. (1992, p. 38) noted that "freedom is an essential doctrine of the major religions, in which a sharp distinction is made between things of 'the world' and that which is spiritual or 'belongs' to God, in which adherents are taught to value the latter." For that reason, religion offered the prisoners a mental escape from the deprivation of being removed from society and being confined. Moreover, these inmates revealed that their "new life," was God's work and will, and it was something they could handle. A few of the inmates commented,

[My faith] was not as strong until after being incarcerated. Suddenly I found myself alone and with no one. That is when religion and belief in God became stronger. It kept me sane (Clear et al., 1992, p. 39).

The only thing that is lacking in here is freedom of movement and women, but that is only a state of mind. I've sees some guys who don't really realize that they are in prison because it is not the prison that they see, it is the walk with God. Prison doesn't bother them anymore (Clear et al., 1992, p. 39).

Extrinsic Orientations toward Religion in Prison

To alleviate the deprivations imposed by prison life and the negativistic culture of the prison environment, prisoners also seek religion for extrinsic reasons such as social or personal gains. The extrinsic reasons for seeking religion varied by prison and were contingent on the inmate and the social setting of the prison. The researchers identified four extrinsic reasons why prisoners turned to religion while being confined in the correctional setting. Below are the extrinsic reasons identified by the researchers.

Safety.   A major concern for both violent and nonviolent offenders entering prison is their personal safety. In fact, the threat of being harmed while in prison is believed to be a major deterrent for many individuals who opt not to commit criminal offenses. Society and public policy makers rely on this mechanism, which are evident in their investment in programs such as "Scared Straight." However, there are particular types of inmates (sex offenders, for example) who legitimately fear for their safety while incarcerated. If their heinous offenses became known, they were more likely to face possibilities of physical or sexual abuse by other inmates at the institution. Often these inmates were excluded from limited social activities offered at the institution (Clear et al., 1992). For them, religion provided a safe haven from their peers. Religious groups practiced and encouraged forgiveness based on their religious doctrine, and so otherwise ostracized inmates were accepted among the religious regardless of how violent and/or malicious their past deeds may have been. A couple of the inmates commented,

The sex offenders who show up in the Christian group so they won't get hurt. They need to get protected (Clear et al., 1992, p. 40).

A person with a nasty crime is accepted into the group. Whether you did the crime or not, they are going to protect you (Clear et al., 1992, p. 40).

The researchers also noted that the chapel was a safe haven for prisoners, because it was off limits to the general population and provided a place to avoid the negative culture associated with prison life. The inmates emphasized that it was important to interact with and be surrounded by fellow inmates who also wanted to avoid the trouble and hassles often associated with incarceration. One of the inmates commented,

When I am talking about protection, I am talking about it as protection against myself. I can protect myself from the things that I would do that would cause me to violate and get me more time (Clear et al., 1992, p. 41).

Another important reason expressed for being a part of certain religious groups was the protection from physical aggression and manipulative tactics provided by members of the religious group, especially the designated leader speaking on one's behalf. This protection was not automatic and was only offered "so long as, (1) the threatened inmate's religious involvement is generally perceived as 'sincere', (2) the authority of the inmate intervening in his behalf is respected, and (3) the aggression was not a result of failure to pay debts or some other legitimate prison economic transaction" (Clear et al., 1992, p. 41). The intervention of a religious leader on behalf of another inmate was most often not an aggressive act, since religions in prison adhere to the same doctrine as nonprison religions which emphasize nonviolence or nonaggressive acts. One of the inmates commented,

Being a Muslim will benefit you spiritually, your soul, and then there are some other aspects, like protection. Muslims are obligated to protect another Muslim if they aren't doing anything wrong. If the guy is weak, and we know that he is weak, we are obligated to protect him and help him grow spiritually, because we don't know what is in his heart (Clear et al., 1992, p. 41).

Material comforts.   The second extrinsic factor identified in the study was the relief from material deprivations the prisoner encountered as a result of being incarcerated. Being involved with prison religious programs helped to alleviate the pain of material deprivation. In some of the prisons "church services were often followed by informal gatherings, in which punch and various cookies and cakes were served, and the leftovers could be taken back to cells for later or to be sold or traded for other goods" (Clear et al., 1992, p. 43). One of the inmates commented,

The big thing is that everyone knew that the Father was bringing in cookies and cakes and doughnuts and so forth. So naturally, everyone wanted to come (Clear et al., 1992, p. 43).

Access to outsiders.   The third extrinsic orientation identified in the study by the researchers was that religious activities in the prison provided access to outsiders, especially females. For an offender, "having an outsider to talk with can play an enormous role in reducing the excruciating sense of the inmate that he is forgotten by society" (Clear et al.,

1992, p. 44). However, more important for the offender was when the outsider is a female. According to Clear et al. (1992, p. 44), "the self-confirming nature of these contacts takes on a different meaning, for the inmate is able to experience a prison rarity—to meet a woman who is a stranger." A couple of the inmates commented,

> Because a lot of women come from the outside. There are a couple of cuties coming in, the word gets around. They have been in jail so they want to see women (Clear et al., 1992, p. 43).
>
> Sometimes there will be some good looking ladies [volunteers] in the chapel on a Sunday. Then you're likely to see this place filled, with all the guys coming here to stare and laugh and say rude stuff to each other (Clear et al., 1992, p. 44).

Inmate Relations.   The final extrinsic orientation identified in the study was the social support system experienced by participating in religious programming inside the prison. Religious participation provided inmates with the opportunity to interact with their peers and receive companionship, friendship, and the intimacy of a family and community that free citizens receive. For the inmate assigned a housing partner, who is a stranger he had nothing in common with, the opportunity to seek out familiar faces and people from his neighborhood was often afforded by the chapel. A couple of the inmates commented,

> I wanted to see a friend of mine that was in another unit. . . . It was the only place we could meet (Clear et al., 1992, p. 45).
>
> A lot of people attend services just to get out of their . . . 6×9 cell. It's just the opportunity to get out of your cell and socialize with somebody else (Clear et al., 1992, p. 45).

According to Clear and colleagues (1992, p. 45), "in prison 'friendship' is not merely an emotional relationship; it is a reciprocal one, involving trade-offs and obligations." Thus, there were reasons some prisoners did not want the traditional prison "friendship" since often times it carried the commitment to share many aspects of the prison environment the inmate wanted to avoid. The researchers noted that this was especially true for inmates who were alarmed by and wanted to avoid the power machinations within prison. This was also true for the inmate who felt alienated or weary from the street culture that defined much of prison life. One of the inmates commented,

> What these people need now is a friend. A confidant. Someone to talk to . . . someone you can share your last candy bar with (Clear et al., 1992, p. 46).

In addition to seeking familiar peers, religious group interactions provided inmates the opportunity to socialize and affiliate with others ascribing to similar values, beliefs, and conduct standards within the general prison population. Thus, the religious inmates were not forced to socialize all the time with others who adhered to the traditional prison culture and supported the "inmate code." Association with inmates "who subscribe to religious values helps the inmate avoid the difficulties of traditional inmate life" (Clear et al., 1992, p. 46). According to an inmate,

> It has helped me to change and to hang with people who don't get into nothing. . . . They don't fight, they don't steal. . . . If you are somewhere else [than the chapel], you are apt to be stealing, then you get into trouble, then you get more time. . . . There's all kinds of things going on in prison (Clear et al., 1992, p. 46).

Clear and colleagues (1992) noted that religious groups were the only ones who would accept certain inmates, especially those who had committed heinous crimes. One of the inmates commented,

> Anybody with a sex beef [conviction] or child beef will find himself in Christian programs. Anybody who is looking for something in prison one step away from protective custody. It's sad, because that is what happens. Most cases, they are not sincere. They got to have some friends who are going to hang out with them, and only other Christians will do that (Clear et al., 1992, p. 46).

This adaptation varied somewhat for different religious groups. Muslims demonstrated their commitment to their faith by adhering to the "laws" of their faith, particularly the individual and group prayers. For Muslims, the discipline of daily devotions was not only a public symbol of obedience to Allah, but also a personal reminder of their commitment to Qur'an requirements. For Christians who "talk the talk," there was continual scrutiny to see if they could "walk the walk." Inmates were interested in determining if they lived by standards different from the Christian religion. Thus, Christians inmates felt like nonbelievers were watching to observe abnormal conduct or lifestyle. One of the inmates commented,

> Sincere people are judged harder. If you are with them, you are judged harder . . . It's what has helped me to change [because] I got to do things right (Clear et al, 1992, p. 47).

According to Clear and colleagues (1992), the social needs of the religious inmates stem in part from their desire to be different from the remaining population. Inmates who embraced religion to challenge their peers, symbolically argued that their way was better and more righteous. It is therefore understandable why some inmates were suspicious and resented the religious prisoners. Their reaction commonly takes the form of "testing," "baiting," "provocation," and "taunting," which often had the mark of hostility. For support, the religious inmates turned to each other, in which the social support often had the flavor of a community within a community. In some of the prisons in the sample, gatherings of religious inmates were occasions where discussions of the travails of their "walk" was openly encouraged. Whether this was a formal agenda was not obvious in most discussions. However, discussions with religious inmates included the ways they tried to help each other keep their vows of faith and avoid the temptations of prison life within the "code." One of the inmates commented,

> In Islam, we don't separate the "secular" from the "religious." In Islam, anything could be addressed. We open with a prayer; we close with a prayer. But we talk about just about anything in between. That's how we help each other to see things. To understand about doing our time, here (Clear et al., 1992, p. 47).

According to Clear and colleagues (1992, p. 47), "the religious inmate has the same social needs that are not materially different than anyone else's, but he seeks to meet them without the normal asset of traditional inmate collegiality." Thus, the religious inmates assisted in making this possible by being available and supportive. The researchers noted that this was one of the reasons many religious inmates emphasize the importance of "hanging together." One of the inmates commented,

> The [religious] group makes me feel like a hypocrite when I don't keep staying with my religion. I know I hurt my family; I see so much of myself in everyone's testimonies. I do this [come to fellowship] in order to be around positive people, and to strengthen my faith (Clear et al., 1992, p. 48).

Clear and colleagues (1992) concluded that inmates embrace religion in prison as a public way of claiming to be different from the person who was initially sentenced to prison. Religious inmates were attracted to religious affiliations to avoid trouble and negative aspects of the prison culture which was achieved through constructive behavior. For example, visiting the chapel helps a religious inmate avoid always being in his living area, thus avoiding the possibility of violating prison conduct rules. Hence, inmates in prison seek religion for the same reasons that free citizens do. Moreover, inmates, like free citizens, seek religion because of a deep commitment to their faith. After fully internalizing their religious beliefs, inmates find a new way of life and answers to questions such as the purpose of existence and death. In addition, inmates seek religion for utilitarian purposes, such as the gain of material comforts and protection from the threat of harm. The final section of this chapter will discuss the process by which religion might change an offender.

The Dimensions of Religion in the Prison Setting

The fact that religion is multidimensional in this way suggests that religion in the prison context may "work" in one or more of several ways, each having to do with the multiple dimensions. There are three primary mechanisms by which religion might be useful in changing offenders: (1) Religion might socialize a person, bringing to that person a sense of morality and identity that eschews old criminal ways and adopts new prosocial ways; (2) religion might put a person in contact with forces of social control, prosocial people, and conventional associations that replace previously antisocial associations; and (3) religion might transform the individual spiritually from a worldly person concerned with self to a devout person concerned with inward, sacred matters. We call these, respectively, *socialization processes, association patterns,* and *transcendence effects.* Each is a mechanism by which religion might change people who have past criminal involvement.

In the following discussion, we explore these three mechanisms of religious change and ask two questions. First, we ask how the change process works. Then we ask what is known about each of these processes as they relate to the religious experience in the correctional setting.

Socialization processes

Belief: The dimension of belief concerns the idea that God or Allah exists and the doctrines inmates hold true about their religion. Clear and colleagues (1992) stated that when inmates spoke in reference to their religious views, they often took a literal interpretation of their faith. Moreover, both Christian and Muslim inmates provided direct quotations from the Bible or the Qur'an when referring to their religious doctrine and religious beliefs. According to Clear and colleagues (1992), for some inmates, religion in its substance provided some possible routes out of their dilemma. Thus, religion not only explained the cause of their failure, but it also prescribed the solution.

Morality: The dimension of morality in religion provides moral prescriptions that inmates are expected to follow in order to obtain salvation. This dimension defines acceptable behavior patterns with regard to what is accepted as being good or bad. It also establishes conduct codes that are accepted by the inmate's religious doctrine. Some inmates stated that because of their new religious commitment, they now accept moral responsibility for their past misbehavior. According to one of the inmates,

> Religion is a guide not to get out of hand; it gives you a straight path (Clear et al., 1992, p. 37).

The inmates who adopted religion wanted to appear deeply committed to their religious doctrine. This commitment was expressed by their knowledge and reading of the Bible and Qur'an and other religious writings.

History: The dimension of history represents the heritage of religious beliefs and behavior of the inmate. It is the religious foundation established by the inmate's community and/or family members prior to entering the prison. While some of the inmates converted to other religions, such as Islam or the Aryan Brotherhood (at least they identified themselves as being a religion), many adopted a more conservative Christian religious ideology. It appeared that many of the inmates continued to uphold the religious doctrine of their community. For instance, in many Southern prisons, the religious orientation of inmates was often conservative and fundamentalist, even though the fundamentalist advocates strict adherence to religious doctrine, speaks strongly against committing sins or crimes, and encourages the application of strong and punitive penalties for such law violation.

Association patterns

Personal Identity: The dimension of personal identity provides inmates with a sense of purpose and meaning in life, which leads to growth and maturation through various aging processes. Many inmates stated that religion provided them with the opportunity to search for a new beginning in life, which resulted in a change in their sense of personal power and ability to deal with the pressures of being imprisoned. They argued that religion is a way to atone for the wrong they have done and to receive forgiveness needed to establish their personal self-worth. Hence, religion provided the inmate with a sense of personal peace while incarcerated, which in turn alleviated the sense of being confined. Thus, the inmates were provided a mental escape from the deprivation of being removed from society. Moreover, through enhanced self-esteem and increased self-awareness, the inmates were able to mask the deprivation of being confined mentally while developing a sense of personal freedom. For these inmates, religion facilitated their spiritual development, which increased their self-worth, self-awareness, and sense of inner peace. According to these inmates, these changes resulted in their development of a new identity, a totally different person from the "inmate" who was originally incarcerated.

Community or Society: The dimension of community serves as a group aspect of religious commitment, strengthening the group's sense of identity and providing inmates with social networks of inmates who held similar beliefs. Given that both Christianity and Islamic doctrines call for ritual group worship as a normative standard, fellowship in these rituals provides inmates the opportunity to participate in group ceremonies, worship, and devotion. Religion also offered interpersonal and spiritual support for inmates. For religious inmates, social companions deal with concerns about personal safety and the daily struggles of being in a prison environment through group support and providing protection. While this was the case for all religious groups, it was particularly the case for Muslims. In addition, affiliations among religious inmates provided an alternative to traditional inmate relationships. That is, inmates were provided the opportunity to interact with other inmates who claimed to be religious and subscribed to standards than differed from the "inmate code."

Transcendence effects
Transcendence or Supernatural: The transcendence dimension of religion is described as the belief in the concept of the supernatural or an extraordinary, all-powerful being, who lives and reigns eternally over all creation. In the prison study, many inmates talked about being "born again," within the context of their religiosity. For these inmates, there was a consistent theme that God was playing an active role in their lives and was instrumental in changing them. Similarly, there were numerous reports from evangelical Christians about their religious "conversion." They reported that their religion provided the opportunity to atone for past misdeeds and seek forgiveness from God, who was now in control of their lives. This, in turn, they said, facilitated their spiritual development.

Ritual: The dimension of ritual reinforces the inmate's commitment to their religious doctrine. This dimension, according to Comstock (1995) and Cunningham and colleagues (1995), is probably the most visible dimension of religion, since inmates have the opportunity to demonstrate their religious commitment publicly, a process that often separates the "sincere" from the "insincere" religious inmate. A common theme among prisoners who were interviewed was that some of the inmates who professed religious commitment failed to demonstrate that in terms of their actions. As a result, the religious inmate was under constant scrutiny from the nonbeliever and expected to demonstrate his or her religious sincerity. For Muslim inmates, demonstrating their sincerity took the form of adopting a religious lifestyle, which was easy to observe. Adherence to the "laws" was an obvious manifestations of this commitment, particularly individual and group prayer. However, for Christian inmates, this was not the case, because they were constantly scrutinized by nonbelievers to "talk the talk" and "walk the walk." Inmates who professed to be religious felt they were being watched and challenged all the time by nonbelievers. Although these inmates regularly attended chapel services, church attendance was not by itself sufficient to remove the skepticism and doubt of the nonbeliever.

The dimension of ritual also links with other dimensions of religion. For example, participation in religious activities, especially attending services at the chapel, provided inmates with a sort of safe haven, especially for an inmate who had committed violent or heinous offenses. Religious practice also provided inmates with the opportunity to accept moral responsibility for their past behaviors and to search for a new beginning in life, which represents the personal identity dimension. In addition, religious participation provided inmates the opportunity to interact with peers who hold similar convictions and beliefs. That is, religious participation provided inmates with the opportunity to network and experience fellowship with like-minded others, who shared the same religious beliefs and goals that represent the transcendence, belief, and community dimensions of religion. Finally, ritual participation provided inmates with the opportunity to continue religious traditions and rituals practiced by their community that represent the dimension of history.

So now that we know religion is important to inmates, the question becomes, Does religion influence behavior, specifically, deviant behavior? To address this question, the next section provides an overview of the empirical research published since 1985, which explored the relationship between religion and deviance.

LITERATURE

Speculation about the role religion has played in different societies as a means of social control has a rich history. The social control model assumes that the stability of society is assured by teaching and reinforcing an approved set of values, beliefs, and norms for all citizens. The modern sociological perspective views religion as a crucial, integrative mechanism for maintaining social order and fostering a common set of values and beliefs. Hence, religious beliefs are viewed as providing the foundation for moral behavior (Chadwick & Top, 1993). It follows that the more religious a person is, the less likely it is that he or she will deviate from societal norms; conversely, as Pettersson (1991, p. 279) states, "for centuries criminal behavior has been explained by the erosion of religion."

Thus, religion is viewed as a form of social control that strengthens an individual's ties to society by strengthening their religious belief through participation in religious services and sacraments. Therefore, functionalists contend that people who engage in religious activities will be less likely to commit deviant acts than those who do not engage in religious activities.

The postulate that religion inhibits deviance also has an extensive history in the United States, dating back to the early 1900s, grounded in theoretical perspectives such as anomie, social disorganization, differential association, and social control explanations of deviance. Despite this legacy of belief in religion as a social control mechanism, many scholars remain skeptical about the potential of religiosity to inhibit deviant behavior. Their critical views received support from the landmark study by Hirschi and Stark (1969), which questioned the efficacy of religion as a social control mechanism. Hirschi and Stark (1969) administered a self-report survey to 4,077 adolescents in Western Contra Costa County, California. These researchers found that children who attended church were as likely as nonattendees to report involvement in deviant and criminal acts. They also found that "children who attend church are no more likely than non-attenders to accept ethical principles, they are only slightly more likely than non-attenders to respect conventional authority, and they are much more likely to believe in the literal existence of the Devil and a life after death" (Hirschi & Stark, 1969, p. 202). Considering these findings, Hirschi and Stark (1969) concluded that religion was not an inhibitor of deviance. These findings pleased many critical social scientists and stunned others, but eventually they "became, for many observers, the accepted conclusion to a long debated issue in the literature" (Benda, 1995, p. 446).

In spite of the scholarly consensus spawned by Hirschi and Stark (1969), subsequent empirical research examining religion as a preventative mechanism of deviance consistently provided evidence of a significant, inverse relationship between religion and deviance, although the strength of this relationship is typically modest or weak (Cochran et al., 1994; Cochran, 1988, 1989; Ellis, 1985; Johnson, 1984; Tittle & Welch, 1983). In 1983, Tittle and Welch examined 65 previously published studies that reported evidence concerning the nature of the relationship between religion and deviance. Out of the 65 studies, only 10 (15 percent) failed to report a significant negative relationship between religion and deviance. In 1985, a review of thirty-one studies that investigated the link between religion and deviance concluded that "people who attend church most frequently are significantly less involved in crime than those who attended less often" (Ellis, 1995, p. 26). The evidence of an inverse relationship among studies was so consistent that in 1988, Cochran (p. 294) stated that "virtually every research effort subsequent to the Hirschi and Stark study published in 1969 has consistently found evidence of a statistically inverse relationship between some measures of religion and various indicators of deviance." Cochran and colleagues (1994) stated that with the exception of the Elifson, Peterson, and Hadway study in 1983, every published work since Tittle and Welch's (1983) review of the literature also reported that religion has a statistically significant and inverse association to deviance. In essence, since the 1970s, empirical results have consistently demonstrated a significant inverse association between religion and deviance.

Despite these positive reviews, some social scientists continue to doubt that this relationship actually exists. They claim that the observed associations between religion and deviance are either coincidental or spurious (Albrecht et al., 1977; Knudten & Knudten, 1971) or contend that the findings have produced mixed results and are therefore inconclusive (Burkett, 1977; Higgins & Albrecht, 1977; Jenson & Erickson, 1979). For example, in a bivariate analysis, Albrecht and colleagues (1977) found support for Burkett and White's antiascetic thesis, which states that victimless offenses are more likely than victim offenses to produce a statistically significant and inverse association between religion and deviance. However, in a multivariate analysis, when peer expectations and family relationships were added to the model, church participation became less pronounced than in the bivariate model.

Since 1985, twenty-five studies explored the relationship between religion and deviance, to determine if religion deters deviance (for a review, see Sumter and Clear, 1998). Most of this research (twenty of twenty-five studies) produced evidence of a statistically significant inverse relationship between some measures of religion and various indicators of deviance, while five studies did not provide any evidence of a relationship. These results are consistent with the extensive body of earlier empirical studies, which examined this relationship (see Burkett & White, 1974; Cochran & Akers, 1989; Ellis, 1985; Grasmick et al., & 1991; Tittle & Welch, 1983).

Most of this research investigates the way religion affects criminality, generally. From this research, it is fair to conclude that the vast majority of evidence tends to confirm that religious interests are associated positively with conformity, including law-abiding behavior. A specific concern is the way religion "works" in the context of correctional programming. Next, we focus on the empirical research, which examined the relationship between religion and change as it relates to prisoners and religion.

What We Know about Prisoners and Religion

During the twentieth century there had been much speculation by scholars in the United States about the impact of religion on prisoners. Despite this interest, to date, only three studies (Clear et al., 1992; Johnson, 1984; Sumter et al., 2002) have examined the effect of religious participation on institutional adjustment and the commitment of infractions within the prison, and two (Sumter, 1999; Johnson et al., 1997) have examined the effect of participation in prison religious programs on prison or postrelease rearrest rates. In 1984, Johnson collected data on 782 inmates released from Apalachee Correctional Institution in Chattahoochee, Florida from 1978 to 1982, to determine if (1) a greater degree of religion is likely to reduce the amount of disciplinary confinement and (2) the frequency of attendance at institutional church services (and related activities) is related to the likelihood of disciplinary confinement. The results indicated no differences in disciplinary confinement for religious and nonreligious inmates on all these measures. Moreover, Johnson concluded that the religiosity indexes were not statistically related to institutional adjustment.

However, in 1992, Clear and colleagues administered a self-report questionnaire to a nonrandom sample of 769 inmates in 20 prisons from 12 states, in order to determine if inmates' religiousness is related to prison adjustment and the number of disciplinary infractions they received. Unlike Johnson's study, the study by Clear and colleagues (1992) found that a prisoner's religious participation had a significant and positive relationship to prison adjustment. They also found that age interacts with religious participation, which may explain Johnson's earlier failure to find such an impact. Namely, younger prisoners seem to use religion to adjust better psychologically to prison, whereas older inmates who are religious seem to have fewer infractions.

Johnson and colleagues (1997) studied a nonrandom sample of two matched groups of inmates released from four adult male prisons in New York, to determine the impact of religious programs on institutional adjustment and recidivism rates. One group partici-pated in Prison Fellowship (PF) programs and the other group did not. The two groups were matched on key characteristics such as age, race, religious denomination, county of residence, military discharge, minimum sentence, and initial security classification. John-son and his associates found that the level of participation in prison fellowship influenced institutional adjustment. Moreover, high participation Prison Fellowship inmates were less likely to commit infractions than either low or medium participants and less likely than nonreligious inmates to commit serious infractions. In addition, high Prison Fellowship participants were significantly less likely than their non–Prison Fellowship matches to be arrested during the follow-up period.

Subsequently, Sumter (1999) added official criminal history information to an exist-ing data base that had been collected by Clear and colleagues (1992) to determine if an in-mate's religiousness influenced postrelease community adjustment. The inmates were then interviewed by telephone 90 days after their release from prison and followed up for more than six years (80 months) after their release, checking for new arrests. The results did not indicate any difference in the recidivism rates of "religious" and "nonreligious" inmates. They did, however, indicate a statistically significant relationship between belief in the su-pernatural and participation in religious programs and postrelease community adjustment for the combined groups. That is, regardless of how frequently they attended chapel, in-mates who had a greater religious orientation in terms of their values at the time of release were less likely to recidivate, and those attending some religious programming were also less likely to recidivate, consistent with Johnson and colleagues (1997). Moreover, accord-ing to Sumter, increasing participation in religious programs upon prison release, as mea-sured by a self-report questionnaire, was associated with lower levels of rearrest rates, as measured by official FBI criminal history reports. (The irony was that offenders who were heavy chapel attenders prior to release were no more likely to attend religious services af-ter release than nonchapel attenders in prison). As a result, Sumter concluded that higher levels of religious participation and belief in the supernatural were associated with fewer postrelease arrests for inmates regardless of their religious orientation in prison.

Finally, in a more recent study, Sumter and colleagues (2002), as a part of a larger re-search project to explore whether meditation practice is associated with positive adjustment to the community, utilized a before–after study design to explore whether meditation prac-tice was associated with a reduction in medical symptoms, emotions, and behaviors for 34 female detainees in Southeastern Virginia. The researchers looked at differences between fe-male detainees who were randomly assigned to an experimental and control group before and after a structured meditation program intervention. The meditation program was a two-and-a-half-hour session, once a week, and lasted for seven weeks. Sumter and col-leagues found significant differences between the experimental and control group for three variables. Specifically, detainees in the experimental group, who participated in the medi-tation program, had fewer sleeping difficulties, less desire to throw things or hit people, and less nail and cuticle biting at the posttest period compared to the control group. The initial findings suggest that meditation practice, which is deeply rooted in all major religious and spiritual traditions, is an effective mechanism to enhance sleep, reduce stress, and alleviate negative emotions. Moreover, the meditation practice resulted in the detainees in the experimental group being more manageable at the detention facility as they learned to have power over their temperament and were therefore less likely to act out and cause problems at the detention center.

These prison studies are consistent with the empirical studies assessed since 1985 (Sumter & Clear, 1998), which provide evidence of a relationship between religion and deviance. Like these other studies, the findings indicate that religious participation (ritual) and personal religiosity (belief in God—transcendence) are associated with reducing deviant and/or criminal behavior. And, like the empirical studies assessed since 1985, these findings indicate that religious participation is a significant determinant of institutional adjustment and rearrest.

SUMMARY

Religion has played an important role in the way Western society has responded to offenders since the earliest of times. From the fourth century A.D. through the Middle Ages, no major distinction was made between civil and criminal offenses. Accordingly, sanctions for misconduct were derived from Roman Catholic teaching, arranged to accord with the biblical command of an eye for an eye. In the Colonial United States, religion pervaded all aspects of life, and settlers believed that God predetermined some people to become criminals (Newman, 1985). Even for the leaders of The Enlightenment, religious doctrine was a powerful theme in penal arrangements. When reformers of these later eras invented the penitentiary, probation, and parole, they structured their inventions as vehicles where offenders could go to atone for their sinful ways and embrace a spiritually right life.

Today, the importance of religion in the prison setting continues to be demonstrated as prisons provide routine weekly religious programs such as chaplaincy services, spiritual counseling, Bible study, Sunday services, and visitation ministry. In addition, correctional agencies have opened their doors to such nonprofit prison ministries as the Kairos, Jaycees, and Bible Believers Fellowship. These organizations provide services such as prison evangelism, biblical instruction, spiritual growth programming, prerelease counseling and support, aftercare and family assistance, and inmate correspondence programs. Religious significance in the prison setting reached a new eminence when, on January 29, 2001, President Bush issued an executive order directing the Secretary of Health and Human Services (HHS), as well as the heads of the departments of Justice, Education, Labor, and Housing and Urban Development, to establish within each department a Center for Faith-Based and Community Initiatives. A part of this initiative is designed to encourage the faith-based groups to reach out and assist prisoners who are reentering the community.

This review reveals three main conclusions about religious programming in corrections:

1. Despite a very long history of religious correctional programming, very few studies have been conducted on the matter of their effectiveness;
2. Inconsistencies in studies suggest that religion operates at multiple levels and "works" as a multidimensional experience; and
3. Consistent evidence exists that religious programming may play a role in reducing recidivism of offenders who take advantage of those programs.

From the currently available data and studies to date, we cannot say without equivocation that "religion works." There are simply too few studies of the question, and the results pose too many inconsistencies to enable us to make such a claim. Nonetheless, we think there is sufficient evidence to say that religious programming is at least an optimistic strategy for correctional rehabilitation, and may even be very promising indeed. While we would be foolish to jump on a bandwagon and proclaim prison religion as a certain technique of crime prevention (after all, in the Sumter study, 66 percent of the so-called religious prisoners experienced one or more arrests in the follow-up period), we would be equally unwise to reject religious programming as a major need of prisoners and as a method of promoting pubic safety. Religion may work, at least some of the time, and with at least some of the people.

Caveats about this conclusion are as important as the conclusion itself. Religion, as a correctional program, is complicated in two ways. The first is basic: Religious sentiment is multifaceted, as personal as it is social, and of complicated significance in the prison setting. Inmates embrace religious programs in prison for a wide array of reasons, some heartening and some cynical. Religious programs occupy ambivalent space in the correctional environment: Prison chapels are not simply spiritual places but are also physical resources for prisoners to meet one another, meet outsiders, and even get desirable snacks and time out of the cell. Inmates who get involved in religious activity in prison do so for any number of reasons, not all of which would be brought to mind in contemplation of the accustomed spiritual basis of religious practice in other settings. Advocates for religious activity in prison would do well to remember that prison, as a social setting, distorts everything. What might seem like a quest for spiritual awakening on the surface can devolve, in the upside-down world of the institution, into a simple technique to get around the strictures of confinement. Distorted in this way, religious programming can become a sad caricature of itself. Prudence suggests that it would be unwise in the extreme, for example, to take religious program involvement into account in making release decisions, to reward prison religion program participation with internal incentives, or to require attendance in such programs. It is hard to imagine a better way to distort an already fragile intervention.

Related to this multifaceted nature of religion is the fact that we have little understanding of precisely *how* religion works, to the extent it does work in the first place. That is, we can imagine that religion teaches moral reasoning, surrounds one with prosocial supports, and offers spiritual change. But which of these is the most important part? We do not know, and because we do not know, there is no social science basis for preferring one potential strategy of religious programming over another; there is *certainly* no basis for choosing one particular religious tradition, say evangelical Christianity, over another, say Islam or Buddhism. We know enough about the effects of religious programming to say that they are promising and deserve exploration; we know too little to be more prescriptive than that.

Whether religious programs work or not, the question is in some senses moot. This is the second complicated aspect of religious programming in corrections. Most of us would agree that the pursuit of religious understanding is a basic human right; it is certainly codified in law as a Constitutional right. That is, if 1000 evaluations found that religious programming failed, it would not necessarily suggest anything to change policy of religious activity in prison. Prisoners have a right to express their religious views and may refuse to be involved, regardless of social science findings. By the same token, our cautious suggestion that religious programs may work merely supports a policy that already deserves prominent emphasis: Prisoners who wish to develop their spiritual self-understanding ought to be encouraged to do so. But this statement was true without a single social science study to support or question the value of religion as a treatment program. Religion, as a fundamental human desire, must be allowed full expression as the circumstances of prison permit. Our work suggests only that whatever benefits the free expression of religious desire may have for the prisoner, they may also be accompanied by benefits for the rest of us.

REFERENCES

Albrecht, S. L., Chadwick, B. A., & Alcorn, D. S. (1977). Religiosity and Deviance: Application of an Attitude-Behavior Contingent Consistency Model. *Journal for the Scientific Study of Religion.* 16:263–274.

American Correctional Association. (1983). *The American Prison: From the Beginning—a Pictorial History.* College Park, MD: American Correctional Association.

Ashby, P. H. (1963). *History and Future of Religious Thought.* Englewood Cliffs, NJ: Prentice Hall.

Bainbridge, W. S. (1989). The Religious Ecology of Deviance. *American Sociological Review.* 54(2):288–295.

Bailey, W. C. (1966). Correctional Outcome: An Evaluation of 100 Reports. *Journal of Criminal Law, Criminology, and Police Science.* 57:153–160.

Bancroft, A. (1974). *Religions of the East.* New York: St. Martin's Press.

Beckford, J. A. (Ed.). (1986). *New Religious Movements and Rapid Social Change.* Beverly Hills, CA: Sage Publications.

Benda, B. (1995). The Effect of Religion on Adolescent Delinquency Revisited. *Journal of Research in Crime and Delinquency.* 32(4):446–466.

Benda, B. (1997). An Examination of a Reciprocal Relationship between Religiosity and Different Forms of Delinquency within a Theoretical Model. *Journal of Research in Crime and Delinquency.* 34(2):163–186.

Berger, P., & Luckmann, T. (1963). Sociology of Religion and Sociology of Knowledge. *Sociology and Social Research.* 47:417–427.

Blumstein, A., & Larson, R. C. (1971). Problems in Modeling and Measuring Recidivism. *Journal of Research in Crime and Delinquency.* 8:124–132.

Breuilly, E., O'Brien, J., & Palmer, M. (1997). *Religions of the World: An Illustrated Guide to Origins, Beliefs, Traditions & Festivals*. New York: Tansedition Limited and Fernleigh Books.

Brownfield, D., & Sorenson, A. M. (1991). Religion and Drug Use among Adolescents: A Social Support Conceptualization and Interpretation. *Deviant Behavior*. 12(3):259–276.

Burkett, S. R., & White, M. (1977). Hellfire and Delinquency: Another Look. *Journal for the Scientific Study of Religion*. 13:455–462.

Carmody, D. L., & Carmody, J. T. (1984). *Ways to the Center: An Introduction to World Religions* (2nd ed.). Belmont, CA: Wadsworth Publishing Company.

Chadwick, B. A., & Top, B. L. (1993). Religiosity and Delinquency among LSD Adolescents. *Journal for the Scientific Study of Religion*. 32(1):51–67.

Clear, T. (1991). *Prisoners and Religion*. Interim Report, Executive Summary. New Jersey: School of Criminal Justice, Rutgers University. Newark, N.J.

Clear, T., Stout, B., Dammer, H., Kelly, L., Hardyman, P., & Shapiro, C. (1992). *Prisoners, Prisons and Religion: Final Report*. New Jersey: School of Criminal Justice, Rutgers University.

Clear, T., & Cole, G. (1997). *American Corrections* (4th ed.). Belmont, CA: Wadsworth Publishing Company.

Cochran, J. K. (1988). The Effect of Religiosity on Secular and Ascetic Deviance. *Sociological Focus*. 21:293–306.

Cochran, J. K. (1989). Another Look at Delinquency and Religiosity. *Sociological Spectrum*. 26(3):147–162.

Cochran, J. K., & Akers, R. (1989). Beyond Hellfire: An Exploration of the Variable Effects of Religiosity on Adolescent Marijuana and Alcohol Use. *Journal of Research in Crime and Delinquency*. 26(3):198–225.

Cochran, J. K., Wood, P. B., & Arneklev, B. J. (1994). Is the Religiosity-Delinquency Relationship Spurious? A Test of Arousal and Social Control Theories. *Journal of Research in Crime and Delinquency*. 31:92–123.

Comstock, G. L. (1995). *Religious Autobiographies*. Belmont, CA: Wadsworth Publishing Company.

Cornwall, M. (1989). The Determinants of Religious Behavior: A Theoretical Model and Empirical Test. *Social Forces*. 68(2):572–592.

Cunningham, L. S., Kelsay, J., Barineau, R. M., & McVoy, H. J. (1995). *The Sacred Quest: An Invitation to the Study of Religion* (2nd ed.). Englewood Cliffs, NJ: Prentice Hall.

Davis, K. (1948). *Human Society*. New York: Macmillian Company.

Day, J. M., & Laufer, W. S. (Eds.) (1987). *Crime, Values and Religion*. Norwood, NJ: Ablex Publishing.

Durkheim, E. (1915). *The Elementary Forms of the Religious Life: A Study of Religious Sociology*. New York: Macmillian Company.

Elifson, K. W., Peterson, D. M., & Hadaway, C. K. (1983). Religiosity and Delinquency: A Contextual Analysis. *Criminology*. 21:505–527.

Ellis, L. (1985). Religiosity and Criminality: Evidence and Explanations of Complex Relationships. *Sociological Perspectives*. 28(4):501–520.

Ellis, L. (1987). Religiosity and Criminality from the Perspective of Arousal Theory. *Journal of Research in Crime and Delinquency*. 24:215–232.

Ellis, L., & Peterson, J. (1996). Crime and Religion: An International Comparison among Thirteen Industrial Nations. *Personality and Individual Differences*. 20(6):761–768.

Ellis, L., & Thompson, R. (1989). Relating Religion, Crime and Arousal and Boredom. *Sociology and Social Research*. 73(3):132–139.

Ellwood, R. S. (1978). *Introducing Religion: From Inside and Outside*. Englewood Cliffs, NJ: Prentice Hall.

Evans, T. D., Cullen, F. T., Burton, V. S., & Dunway, R. G. (1996). Religion, Social Bonds, and Delinquency. *Deviant Behavior.* 17(1):43–70.

Evans, T. D., Cullen, F. T., Dunaway, R. G., & Burton, V. S. (1995). Religion and Crime Re-Examined: The Impact of Religion, Secular Controls, and Social Ecology on Adult Criminality. *Criminology.* 33:195–224.

Evans-Pritchard, E. E. (1965). *Theories of Primitive Religion.* Oxford: The Clarendon Press.

Fenton, S. (1984). *Durkheim and Modern Society.* New York: Cambridge University Press.

Fernquist, R. M. (1995). A Research Note on the Association between Religion and Delinquency. *Deviant Behavior.* 16(2):169–175.

Free, M. D. (1994). Religious Affiliation, Religiosity and Impulsive and Intentional Deviance. *Sociological Focus.* 25 (1):77–91.

Gaer, J. (1929). *How the Great Religions Began.* Scranton, PA: The Haddon Craftsmen.

Gartner, J. T., O'Conner, T., Larson, D. B., Young, M. C., Wright, K., & Rosen, B. (1990). *Religion and Criminal Recidivism: A Systematic Literature Review.* Paper presented at the meeting of the American Psychological Association, Boston, MA.

Glazier, S. D. (1997). *Anthropology of Religion: A Handbook.* Westport, CT: Greenwood Press.

Glock, C. Y. (1973). *Religion in Sociological Perspective: Essays in the Empirical Study of Religion.* Belmont, CA: Wadsworth Publishing Company.

Grasmick, H. G., Cochran, J. K., Bursik, R. J., & Kimpel, M. (1993). Religion, Punitive Justice and Support for the Death Penalty. *Justice Quarterly.* 10 (2):289–314.

Grasmick, H. G., Davenport, E., Chamlin, M., & Dursik, R. (1992). Protestant Fundamentalism and the Retributivist Doctrine of Punishment. *Criminology.* 30:21–45.

Grasmick, H. G., Kinsey, K., & Cochran, J. K. (1991). Denomination, Religiosity and Compliance with the Law: A Study of Adults. *Journal for the Scientific Study of Religion.* 30(1):99–107.

Grasmick, H. G., & McGill, A. L. (1994). Religion, Attribution Style, and Punitiveness toward Juvenile Offenders. *Criminology.* 32(1):23–46.

Greek, Cecil F. (1992). *The Religious Roots of American Sociology.* New York: Garland Publishing, Inc.

Gerth, H. H., & Mills, C. W. (1946). *Max Weber: Major Features of Religion.* Oxford, NY: Oxford University Press.

Hair, J. F., Anderson, R. E., Tatham, R. L., & Black, W. C. (1998). *Multivariate Data Analysis* (5th ed.). Upper Saddle River, NJ: Prentice Hall.

Hall, W. T. (Ed.) (1978). *Introduction to the Study of Religion.* New York: Harper & Row.

Hepburn, J. R., & Albonetti, C. (1994). Recidivism among Drug Offenders: A Survival Analysis of the Effects of Offender Characteristics, Types of Offenses, and Two Types of Intervention. *Journal of Quantitative Criminology.* 10 (2):159–179.

Hick, J. (1989). *An Interpretation of Religion: Human Responses to the Transcendent.* New Haven: Yale University Press.

Higgins, P. C., & Albrecht, S. L. (1977). Hellfire and Delinquency Revisited. *Social Forces.* 55:952–958.

Hirschi, T., & Stark, R. (1969). Hellfire and Delinquency. *Social Problems.* 17:202–213.

Hopfe, L. M., & Woodard, M. R. (1998). *Religions of the World* (7th ed.). Upper Saddle River, NJ: Prentice Hall.

Houf, H. T. (1935). *What Religion Is and Does: An Introduction to the Study of Its Problems and Values.* New York: Harper and Brothers.

James, W. (1936). *The Varieties of Religious Experience: A Study in Human Nature.* Toronto, Canada: Random House, Inc.

Jenson, G. F., & Erickson, J. (1979). The Religious Factor and Delinquency: Another Look at the Hell-fire Hypothesis. In *The Religious Dimension: New Directions in Quantitative Research*. New York: Academic Press.

Johnson, B. R. (1984). *Hellfire and Corrections: A Quantitative Study of Florida Prison Inmates*. Doctoral dissertation. Tallahassee, FL: Florida State University.

Johnson, B. R. (1987). Religiosity and Institutional Deviance: The Impact of Religious Variables upon Inmate Adjustment. *Criminal Justice Review*. 12:21–30.

Johnson, B. R., Larson, D. B., & Pitts, T. C. (1997). Religious Programs, Institutional Adjustment, and Recidivism among Former Inmates in Prison Fellowship Programs. *Justice Quarterly*. 14:501–521.

Johnson, R. A., Wallwork, E., Green, C., Vanderpool, H. Y., & Santmire, H. P. (1990). *Critical Issues in Modern Religion* (2nd ed.). Englewood Cliffs, NJ: Prentice Hall.

Junger, M., & Polder, W. (1993). Religiosity, Religious Climate, and Delinquency among Ethnic Groups in the Netherlands. *British Journal of Criminology*. 33(3):416–435.

King, W. L. (1954). *Introduction to Religion*. New York: Harper and Row.

Knudten, R. D., & Knudten, M. S. (1971). Juvenile Delinquency, Crime, and Religion. *Review of Religious Research*. 12:130–152.

Krantz, S. (1976). *Corrections and Prisoner's Rights*. St. Paul, MN: West Publishing Co.

Martinson, R. (1974). What Works? Questions and Answers about Prison Reform. *Public Interests*. 10:22–54.

Marx, K. (1969). Religious Illusion and the Task of History. In Normal Birnbaum and Gertrud Lenzer (eds.), *Sociology and Religion: A Book of Readings*. Englewood Cliffs, NJ: Prentice Hall.

Middleton, R., & Putney, S. (1962). Religion, Normative Standards, and Behavior. *Sociometry*. 25:141–152.

Morse, W. (1973). The Attorney General's Survey of Release Procedures. In *Penology*, edited by George Killinger and Paul Cromwell, Jr. St. Paul, MN: West Publishing Co.

Newman, G. (1985). *The Punishment Response*. New York: Harrow and Heston Publishing.

Nottingham, E. (1954). *Religion and Society*. New York: Doubleday and Company, Inc.

O'Connor, T., (1995). The Impact of Religious Programming on Recidivism, the Community and Prisons. *IARCA Journal*. 6(6):13–19.

O'Connor, T., & Parikh, C. (1996). Religious Anthropologies and the U.S. Penal System. *Mentor*. 8–9.

O'Dea, T. F. (1966). *Sociology of Religion*. Englewood Cliffs, NJ: Prentice Hall.

Paden, W. E. (1992). *Interpreting the Sacred: Ways of Viewing Religion*. Boston, MA: Beacon Press.

Parsons, T. (1958). *Essays in Sociological Theory*. Glencoe, IL: The Free Press, Inc.

Petterrson, T. (1991). Religion and Criminality: Structural Relationships between Church Involvement and Crime Rates in Contemporary Sweden. *Journal for the Scientific Study of Religion*. 30(3):279–291.

Robertson, R. (1969). *Sociology of Religion*. Baltimore, MD: Penguin Books Inc.

Robertson, R. (1970). *The Sociological Interpretation of Religion*. New York: Schocken Books, Inc.

Ross, L. E. (1994). Religion and Deviance—Exploring the Impact of Social Control Elements. *Sociological Spectrum*. 14(1):65–86.

Rosten, L. (Eds.). (1975). *Religions of America: Ferment and Faith in an Age of Crisis*. New York: Simon and Schuster.

Ryan, T. A. (1995). *The Female Offender: A Challenge to Corrections*. Columbia, SC: Ryan & Associates. Unpublished document.

Selke, W. L. (1993). *Prisons in Crisis*. Bloomington, IN: Indiana University Press.

Sellin, T. (1970). The Origins of the Pennsylvania System of Prison Discipline. *Prison Journal.* 50:13–21.

Sloane, D., & Potvin, R. (1986). Religion and Delinquency: Cutting through the Maze. *Social Forces.* 65:87–105.

Smart, N. (1983). *Worldviews: Cross-Cultural Exploration of Human Beliefs.* Upper Saddle River, NJ: Prentice Hall.

Stark, R. (1984). Religion and Conformity: Reaffirming a Sociology of Religion. *Sociological Analysis.* 45(4):273–282.

Stark, R., Kent, L., & Doyle, D. P. (1982). Religion and Delinquency: The Ecology of a "Lost" Relationship. *Journal of Research in Crime and Delinquency.* 14:4–23.

Sullivan, L. (1990). *The Prison Reform Movement: Forlon Hope.* Boston: Twayne Publishers.

Sumter, M. T. (1999). *Religiousness and Post-Release Community Adjustment.* Doctoral Dissertation. Tallahassee, FL: Florida State University.

Sumter, M. T., & Clear, T. R. (1998). *An Empirical Analysis of Literature Examining the Relationship between Religiosity and Deviance Since 1985.* Paper presented at the Academy of Criminal Justice Sciences Annual Meeting. Albuquerque, NM, March 1998.

Sumter, M. T., Monk-Turner, E., & Turner, C. (2002). *Benefits of Participation In A Structured Meditation Program: Initial Findings.* Unpublished manuscript. Norfolk, VA: Old Dominion University.

Thomas, E. J. (1975). *The Life of Buddha as Legend and History.* London: Routledge and Kegan Paul.

Thompson, K. (Ed.). (1985). *Readings from Emile Durkheim.* Milton Keynes: The Open University.

Thompson, K. (1986). *Beliefs and Ideology.* London: Travistock Publications.

Tittle, C. R., & Welch, M. R. (1983). Religiosity and Deviance: Toward a Contingency Theory of Constraining Effects. *Social Forces.* 61:653–682.

Titiev, M. (1954). *The Sciences of Man.* New York: Henry Holt and Company.

Voss, C. H. (1968). *In Search of Meaning: Living Religions of the World.* Cleveland and New York: The World Publishing Company.

Wallace, M. I., & Smith, T. H. (Eds.). (1994). *Curing Violence.* Sonoma, CA: Polebridge Press.

Welch, M. R., & Tittle, C. R. (1991). Religion and Deviance among Adult Catholics: A Test of the "Moral Communities" Hypothesis. *Journal for the Scientific Study of Religion.* 30(2):159–172.

Whitehead, A. N. (1926). *Religion in the Making.* New York: Macmillian Company.

Woods, A. E., & Waite, J. B. (1941). *Crime and Its Treatment: Social and Legal Aspects of Criminology.* New York: American Book Company.

Wright, K. (1987). *The Great American Crime Myth.* New York: Praeger.

Yinger, J. M. (1946). *Religion in the Struggle for Power.* Durham, NC: Duke University Press.

Young, M. C., Gartner, J. O., O'Connor, T., Larson, D., & Wright, K. (1995). Long-Term Recidivism among Federal Inmates Trained as Volunteer Prison Ministers. *Journal of Offender Rehabilitation.* 22(1/2):97–118.

Wulff, D. M. (1991). *Psychology of Religion: Classic and Contemporary Views.* New York: John Wiley & Sons.

Mentally Disordered Offenders in Corrections

Key Sun

Abstract

This chapter focuses on the issue of mentally disordered offenders in corrections. The issues examined include the prevalence of offenders with mental disorders in corrections, the definition of the offender population, assessment and treatment for the population, the dual status of mentally disordered offenders, the evolving legal context for the population, ethical and professional conflicts for mental health professionals in corrections, and how the issue of mentally disordered offenders is shaped by the interaction of multiple systems.

THE PREVALENCE OF OFFENDERS WITH MENTAL DISORDERS

The recent surveys completed by the Bureau of Justice Statistics (BJS) (1999) show a growing population of mentally disordered offenders in the correctional field. For example, at midyear 1998, a quarter million of mentally disordered offenders were incarcerated in the nation's prisons and jails. About 547,800 probationers said they had had a mental condition or had stayed overnight in a mental hospital at some point in their lives. The same trend continued in the year 2000 (Bureau of Justice Statistics, 2001b). At midyear of 2000, on average, 1 in 10 state inmates were receiving psychotropic medications. In five states (Hawaii, Maine, Montana, Nebraska, and Oregon), nearly 20% of inmates received psychotropic medications. At least one in eight state inmates were involved in mental health therapy or counseling.

WHO ARE THE MENTALLY DISORDERED OFFENDERS IN CORRECTIONS?

The phrase *mentally disordered offenders* has been used to describe four categories of individuals in the criminal justice system (Dvoskin & Patterson, 1998; Heilbrun & Griffin, 1998): (1) not guilty by reason of insanity (NGRI); namely, the person's mental disorder at the time of his or her offense renders him or her criminally not responsible for the offense; (2) incompetent to stand trial (IST); (3) mentally disordered sex offender; and (4) mentally disordered inmate. In this chapter, mentally disordered offenders in corrections mainly refer to the sentenced offenders serving time in prison or community.

HOW OFFENDERS WITH MENTAL DISORDERS END UP IN CORRECTIONS

The issue of mental disorder for an offender may arise at any point in the criminal process, from arrest, trial, to sentencing, during incarceration, and in community corrections (Cohen, 1996). The movement of offenders with mental disorders through the criminal justice system may start when a person is arrested for a crime and is charged and arraigned. If the defendant seems mentally disordered, the court orders an evaluation of competence to stand trial. If the defendant is found to be incompetent to stand trial, such as being unable to understand the legal process or unable to assist a lawyer in the preparation of a defense, he or she will then be ordered to be treated as competent and the trial begins. If the defendant is found not guilty by reason of insanity, he or she is committed to a secure hospital administered by the State Department of Health and Social Services. If the defendant is found guilty, he or she is sent to corrections (Maier & Fulton, 1998). The state prison systems typically screen inmates for mental disorders at a reception/diagnostic center prior to placement in a state facility (BJS, 2001b).

ASSESSMENT AND TREATMENT

Dvoskin and Patterson (1998) pointed out that mental health services for offenders either in custody or in the community can be placed largely into the following categories: screening, evaluation, psychiatric treatment, rehabilitation, case management, medical treatments, and special treatment (e.g., substance abuse treatment, sex offender treatment programs). When offenders with mental disorders serve their times in the community, however, additional issues, such as housing, public assistance, education and employment, may arise.

The typical assessment tool used by the mental health professionals in corrections involves *The Diagnostic and Statistical Manual of Mental Disorders IV,* or DSM-IV, compiled by the American Psychiatric Association. It is a guidebook for the mental health professional (MHP) to measure major clinical disorders, such as schizophrenia, anxiety, mood disorders, and personality disorders. It also helps the MHP to record a client's functions in other areas, including his or her general medical conditions, psychosocial problems, education, employment, housing, economic problems, problems with access to health care services, interaction with the legal system, and global assessment of functioning.

Because this population includes a diverse group with a wide range of treatment needs, in addition to active psychotic symptoms, their clinical problems include aggression and problems of institutional management, criminal predilection, skill deficits, substance abuse, estrangement from family and friends, and other serious health conditions, such as

HIV/AIDS, tuberculosis, and hepatitis (Conly, 1999; Rice & Harris, 1997). Incarceration conditions, such as crowding-produced stress, also cause mental disorders in corrections by aggravating the existing mental disorders or developing new ones (Sowers et al., 1999). Therefore, the function of treatment includes both the reduction of risk of violence as well as the alleviation of the mental disorders by employing psychotropic medication, individual psychotherapy, group psychotherapy, acute hospitalization, substance abuse treatment, and case management addressing other needs areas (Rice & Harris, 1997).

THE DUAL STATUS OF MENTALLY DISORDERED OFFENDERS

Because mentally disordered offenders overlap with both offender and mentally disordered populations (Rice & Harris, 1997), how to interpret the relations between the two aspects of the offender population exemplifies major issues and conflicts in legal decisions, staff interactions, and treatment models.

History of the Law

The evolving legal milieu related to mentally disordered offenders can be categorized into three stages: pre–civil rights movement, the civil rights movement, and 1980s to the present (Hafemeister, 1998; La Fond, 1996).

At the stage of pre–civil rights movement, individuals with mental disorders could be taken into custody on the arresting officer's judgment. The mental health system had a comparable ability to cast a wide net, with broad civil commitment criteria and few procedural protections. Treatment staff had great control over admission and release decisions. Offenders with mental disorders had virtually no voice of their own.

During the civil rights movement (the early 1960s to about the 1980s), a series of landmark legal cases reaffirmed individual constitutional rights that limited governmental authority, placing restrictions on using the mental health system to remove offenders with mental disorders involuntarily from the community.

These legal cases at this stage were based on the premises that under the equal protection of the law, a prison inmate should be given the same procedural protections as any other individual being civilly committed. Additionally, the judges or juries, rather than clinicians, should be primarily responsible for determining whether offenders should enter the mental health system. Furthermore, the least restrictive treatment alternative should be employed (Hafemeister, 1998; La Fond, 1996).

From the 1980s to 1990s, however, judicial attitudes toward offenders with mental disorders changed. Courts abandoned rehabilitation as the primary purpose of criminal incarceration, adopted a just desserts theory, and became more reluctant to interfere with the administration of large state institutions, including mental hospitals (La Fond, 1996). The courts retreated from earlier assertions that all psychiatric patients have the same rights, permitting greater restrictions on the release of offenders with mental disorders, with the need to protect the community taking priority over the liberty interests of the offender. Offenders with mental disorders may be denied the least restrictive alternative, with the burden placed on them to show an absence of dangerousness (Hafemeister, 1998)[1].

The Current Law

The federal constitutional obligation to provide mental health care to inmates suffering serious medical or mental health conditions results from a combination of judicial interpretation of the Eighth Amendment and the due process clause of the Fourth Amendment (Metzner et al., 1998). In spite of many changes in the legal circumstances, the premises of the 1960s and 1970s do not appear to have been totally abandoned (Hafemeister, 1998). The current legal context reflects an attempt to balance two type of interest: community protection and the constitutional rights of mentally disordered offenders.

For example, the Deshaney principle (*Deshaney v. Winnebago County Department of Social Services,* 1989) maintained the government's obligation to provide health care. A state has a duty to provide necessary services to and to protect from injury, certain classes of persons in custody once they enter into a "special relationship" with the state.

In *Estelle v. Gamble* (1976), the Supreme Court held that responsible correctional staff must be deliberately indifferent to the serious medical needs of inmates before Eighth Amendment liability may apply.

The Supreme Court, in *Washington v. Harper* (1990), ruled that although inmates have a protected constitutional interest in avoiding forced dispensation of psychotropic drugs, this interest must be balanced against the state's interests in prison safety and security. In a recent decision (*Kansas v. Crane,* 2002), the Supreme Court ruled that for states to incarcerate sex offenders after they have served their prison time, the states must show that these inmates have both a mental disorder and "serious difficulty" in controlling their behavior.

ETHICAL AND PROFESSIONAL CONFLICTS FOR THE MENTAL HEALTH PROFESSIONAL IN CORRECTIONS

There are unique ethical and professional conflicts and dilemmas for the MHP (e.g., psychologists, social workers, psychiatrists, correctional mental health counselors, and other therapists) in corrections (Kupers, 1999; Sales & Shuman, 1996; Schultz-Ross, 1993; Weinberger & Sreenivasan, 1994).

First, MHPs have dual roles (both as a treatment staff and as an enforcer of Department of Corrections [DOC] policies). They are compelled to address the needs of the institution as primary and are considered correctional officers first and foremost, and expected to engage in custody-oriented activities (e.g., assisting an evening count, search for contraband of inmates' property, pat search of all inmates). This requirement undermines the traditional therapeutic goals and relationship between the therapist and the individual inmate, compromising the therapist's credibility and efficacy.

Second, the issue of informed consent and confidentiality, which is crucial, is not an issue for correctional administrators.

Third, the conflicts involve how to interpret inmate disruptive behavior. While the custody staff tends to ignore, dismiss, misidentify, or punish problematic behavior, the health professionals tend to see such behavior as a product of mental illness or a reflection of a psychotic episode.

According to Weinberger and Sreenivasan (1994), these conflicts reflect the prevailing ideology of the correctional administration that deemphasizes treatment and emphasizes security and custodial concerns.

Some (e.g., Sales & Shuman, 1996; Schultz-Ross, 1993) maintain that the conflicts involve the interface of mental health (e.g., psychiatry), law, and corrections. The law is based on a strict definition of right and wrong and on absolute judgments of guilt, with an emphasis on incapacitation and social control goals. On the other hand, the goal of mental health is based on medicine and the view that proper treatment will restore the patient to a basic, good adaptation state. The medical position or treatment model is concerned with the offender as an individual and the ability to treat that individual.

MENTALLY DISORDERED OFFENDERS INTERACT WITH MULTIPLE SYSTEMS

Considerable research has been conducted to evaluate the correlation between mental disorder and violence, which has been the subject of political and scientific controversy for decades (Perlin, 2001). Although there appeared to be a greater-than-chance relationship between mental disorder and violence behavior, mental disorders make only a trivial contribution to the overall level of violence in society (Clear & Dammer, 2000; Perlin, 2001; Rice & Harris, 1997). It can be argued, however, that in order to understand the issue of mentally disordered offenders in corrections, make effective interventions, and develop appropriate policies, we need to go beyond the mental disorder–violence theme by understanding the four following issues:

First, the changing legal context has contributed to the growing problems of mentally disordered offenders. Recent changes in the law and courtroom proceedings make it more difficult to divert offenders with mental disorders into noncorrectional treatment programs. Many of the patients formerly taken care of in hospitals are now housed in prisons, because there is an increase in arrests related to drug offenses, and punishments for these offenses are harsher and less flexible (Kupers, 1999; Sowers et al., 1999).

Second, social policies, such as that of deinstitutionalization, which caused the release of thousands of mentally ill people from psychiatric facilities to the community, have contributed to the high prevalence of mental disorders within correctional facilities (Conly, 1999; Kupers, 1999). This otherwise well-intended policy has exacerbated conditions for the mentally disordered and contributed to their increased involvement in the criminal justice system, because it coincides with a lack of adequate social services, including cuts in public assistance, declines in the availability of low-income housing, and limited availability of mental health care in the community.

Third, the issue of mentally disordered offenders in corrections should be examined in the cultural and gender contexts of the offender population.

According to the Bureau of Justice Statistics (2001a, 2001c), the general offender population in correctional facilities is represented by a disproportionate number of African Americans. More than a third of probationers, two out of five parolees (i.e., 9.7 percent) are African Americans between the ages of 25 and 29 years. By the end of the year 2000, we saw a 6.6 percent of women incarcerated with 22 percent of these women on probation and 12 percent parolees.

Although the plight of mentally disordered female prisoners is no better than that of their male counterparts, harsher sentences, especially related to drugs, cause overcrowding in women's prisons (Kupers, 1999). Studies have shown that females in corrections have psychological needs and mental health problems that are different from those of men (e.g., Manhal-Baugus, 1998; Morash et al., 1998). Female offenders not only were more likely to suffer physical and sexual abuse as children but also are more concerned with interpersonal relationships than male offenders. Human connections are extremely important in the psychological development and functioning of women. Women's involvements with crimes and abuse of illegal drugs are often initiated or aggravated by their failed attempts to connect with others (Kupers, 1999).

Fourth, understanding the interpersonal cognitions of mentally disordered offenders is necessary for effective treatment.

Mental disorders are not just biological issues. Although biological therapies such as medication may eliminate or alleviate symptoms, they do not address psychosocial problems or the mental issues of a client (Maxmen & Ward, 1995). The psychosocial problems of the offender population entail counseling interventions to focus on changing offenders' interpersonal cognitions or understandings about relationships between the self and others, rather than on changing a negative concept of the self.

Focusing on the client's interpersonal cognition is important because it has been well documented that dysfunctional social relationships, which prevent individuals from achieving positively valued goals or avoiding negative or adverse stimuli or situations, can lead to crime (see Agnew, 1999; Mazerolle & Maahs, 2000). In addition, clinical observations reveal that offenders use invalid methods to understand or deal with conflicts, such as applying violence or intimidation to get what they want, imposing their desires or commands on others or situations without consideration of reactions of the others or of the circumstances, not because they have misconceptions about their selves but because they misunderstand others (Sun, 2001). On the other hand, building, rebuilding, and strengthening social relationships serve as a buffer against recidivism (Bazemore et al., 2000). All negative social environments and dysfunctional social relations are mediated by offenders' misunderstanding of their interpersonal experience (Fiske & Taylor, 1991).

Studies show that offenders with mental disorders often engage in criminal activities as a way to cope with their interpersonal conflicts and abusive experiences (e.g., Falshaw & Browne, 1997; Gladwell, 1998). Clinical observations reveal that when clients cannot understand or make sense of their frustrations in interpersonal relationships, they often engage in criminal activities (e.g., abusing drugs and alcohol, engaging in gang activities, shoplifting, and running away) as a way to alleviate their emotional pains (Kupers, 1999; Sun, 2001). Their criminal activities, in turn, aggravated their mental conditions by putting themselves in dysfunctional environments (Sun, 2001).

NOTE

1. The concept of just deserts as developed is the idea that anyone who interferes with the rights of others does wrong thereby deserving blame for their conduct. The argument put forward is that criminals should be penalized because they deserve punishment, not by treatment and not to deter further crime, but rather because sanction is demanded by justice.

REFERENCES

Agnew, R. (1999). Foundation for a General Strain Theory of Crime and Delinquency. In F. R. Scarpitti & A. L. Nielsen (eds.), *Crime and Criminals: Contemporary and Classic Readings in Criminology* (pp. 258–273). Los Angeles, CA: Roxbury.

Bazemore, G., Nissen, L. B., & Dooley, M. (2000). Mobilizing Social Support and Building Relationships: Broadening Correctional and Rehabilitative Agendas. *Correctional Management Quarterly,* 4(4):10–21.

Bureau of Justice Statistics, U.S. Department of Justice. (1999). *Mental Health and Treatment of Inmates and Probationers.* Washington, DC: Bureau of Justice Statistics.

Bureau of Justice Statistics, U.S. Department of Justice. (2001a). *Advance for Release: National Correctional Population Reaches New High—Grows by 126,400 during 2000 to Total 6.5 Million Adults.* Washington, DC: Bureau of Justice Statistics.

Bureau of Justice Statistics, U.S. Department of Justice. (2001b). *Mental health treatment in State Prisons, 2000.* Washington, DC: Bureau of Justice Statistics.

Bureau of Justice Statistics, U.S. Department of Justice. (2001c). *Prisoners in 2000.* Washington, DC: Bureau of Justice Statistics.

Clear, T. R., & Dammer, H. R. (2000). *The Offender in the Community.* Belmont, CA: Wadsworth.

Cohen, F. (1996). Offenders with Mental Disorders in the Criminal Justice–Correctional Process. In B. D. Sales & D. W. Shuman (eds.), *Law, Mental Health, and Mental Disorder* (pp. 397–413). Pacific Grove, CA: Brooks/Cole.

Conly, C. (1999). Coordinating Community Services for Mentally Ill Offenders: Maryland's Community Criminal Justice Treatment Program. Washington, DC: National Institute of Justice.

DeShaney v. Winnebago Department of Social Services, 489 U.S. 18 (1989).

Dvoskin, J. A., & Patterson, R. F. (1998). Administration of Treatment Programs for Offenders with Mental Disorders. In R. M. Wettstein (ed.), *Treatment of Offenders with Mental Disorders* (pp. 1–43). New York: The Guilford Press.

Estelle v. Gamble, 429 U.S. 97 (1976).

Falshaw, L., & Browne, K. (1997). Adverse Childhood Experience and Violent Acts of Young People in Secure Accommodation. *Journal of Mental Health (UK),* 6:443–455.

Fiske, S. T., & Taylor, S. (1991). *Social Cognition* (2nd ed.). New York: McGraw-Hill.

Gladwell, M. (1998). Why Some People Turn into Violent Criminals. In P. L. Reichel (ed.), *Selected Readings in Criminal Justice* (pp. 33–53). San Diego: Greenhaven Press.

Hafemeister, T. I. (1998). Legal Aspects of the Treatment of Offenders with Mental Disorders. In R. M. Wettstein (ed.), *Treatment of Offenders with Mental Disorders* (pp. 44–125). New York: The Guilford Press.

Heilbrun, K., & Griffin, P. A. (1998). Community-Based Forensic Treatment. In R. M. Wettstein (ed.), *Treatment of Offenders with Mental Disorders* (pp. 168–210). New York: The Guilford Press.

Kansas v. Crane, 534 U.S.(2002).

Kupers, T. (1999). *Prison Madness.* San Francisco, CA: Jossey-Bass Publishers.

La Fond, J. Q. (1996). The Impact of Law on the Delivery of Involuntary Mental Health Services. In B. D. Sales & D. W. Shuman (eds.), *Law, Mental Health, and Mental Disorder* (pp. 219–239). Pacific Grove, CA: Brooks/Cole.

Maier, G. J., & Fulton, L. (1998). Inpatient Treatment of Offenders with Mental Disorders. In R. M. Wettstein (ed.), *Treatment of Offenders with Mental Disorders* (pp. 126–167). New York: The Guilford Press.

Manhal-Baugus, M. (1998). The Self-in-Relation Theory and Women for Sobriety: Female-Specific Theory and Mutual Help Group for Chemically Dependent Women. *Journal of Addictions & Offender Counseling,* 18(2):78–85.

Maxmen, J. S., & Ward, N. G. (1995). *Essential Psychopathology and Its Treatment* (2nd ed.). New York: W. W. Norton & Company.

Mazerolle, P., & Maahs, J. (2000). General Strain and Delinquency: An Alternative Examination of Conditioning Influences. *Justice Quarterly,* 17(4):753–778.

Metzner, J. L., Cohen, F., Grossman, L. S., & Wettstein, R. M. (1998). Treatment in Jails and Prisons. In R. M. Wettstein (ed.), *Treatment of Offenders with Mental Disorders* (pp. 211–264). New York: The Guilford Press.

Morash, M., Bynum, T. S., & Koons, B. A. (1998). *Women Offenders: Programming Needs and Promising Approaches.* Washington, DC: U.S. Department of Justice, Office of Justice Programs, National Institute of Justice.

Perlin, M. L. (2001). Hidden Agendas and Ripple Effects: Implications of Four Recent Supreme Court Decisions for Forensic Mental Health Professionals. *Journal of Forensic Psychology Practice,* 1:33–64.

Rice, M. E., & Harris, G. T. (1997). The Treatment of Mentally Disordered Offenders. *Psychology, Public Policy and Law,* 3:126–183.

Sales, B. D., & Shuman, D. W. (1996). The Newly Emerging Mental Health Law. In B. D. Sales & D. W. Shuman (eds.), *Law, Mental Health, and Mental Disorder* (pp. 2–14). Pacific Grove, CA: Brooks/Cole.

Schultz-Ross, R. A. (1993). Theoretical Difficulties in the Treatment of Mentally Ill Prisoners. *Journal of Forensic Sciences,* 38(2):426–431.

Sowers, W., Thompson, K., & Mullins, S. (1999). *Mental Health in Corrections: An Overview for Correctional Staff.* Lanham, MD: American Correctional Association.

Sun, K. (2001). *The Implications of Understanding the Interpersonal and Mental Disconnections for Correctional Counseling.* Paper presented at 2001 Annual Conference of Academy of Criminal Justice Sciences, Washington, DC.

Washington v. Harper, 494 U.S. 210 (1990).

Weinberger, L. E., & Sreenivasan, S. (1994). Ethical and Professional Conflicts in Correctional Psychology. *Professional Psychology: Research and Practice,* 25:161–167.

chapter 10

Technocorrections: Biometric Scanning and Corrections

Janice Joseph & Rupendra Simlot

It is the year 2003. An inmate enters a correctional facility escorted by two correctional officers. The officers lead him to a station where he places his finger into a device. He is directed to look into another device. In a flash, the inmate is positively identified 100 percent without question. How is this possible? Biometrics make it possible (Kelley & Oien, 2000, p. 1).

In 2000, 6.5 million adults were under the supervision of state and federal correctional agencies. On December 2000, there were 3,839,532 men and women on probation, 725,527 on parole, 1,312,354 in prison, and 621,149 in jails (U.S. Department of Justice, 2001). With so many persons under its supervision, corrections is sometimes faced with the problem of correctly identifying individuals. Nearly half of all escapees from prisons, for example, leave through the front door posing as someone else. They often leave on visiting day with the other visitors (Page, 1998). For years, correctional personnel had no effective way of identifying the offenders under their supervision. Existing methods of electronic identification—identification cards, card keys, and personal identification numbers—are inadequate. These can be stolen or exchanged for fraudulent purposes. Now, various parts of the body can be used (biometric recognition) instead of a password or a personal identification number. Biometrics is more secure because it measures a physical characteristic or personal trait of an individual and compares that characteristic or trait to a database for purposes of recognizing that individual. It is not surprising, therefore, that today correctional agencies are using biometric techniques. The chapter examines the nature and extent of biometric scanning used in corrections. These include finger scanning, eye scanning, hand scanning/geometry, facial recognition, and voice recognition. The use of biometrics raises several concerns. The chapter, therefore, discusses the legal, policy, and practical issues associated with its use and offers recommendations to address legal, policy, and practical concerns about biometric encryption technology.

INTRODUCTION

Biometrics, which means "life measurement," is based on the principle that everyone has unique physical attributes that, in theory, a computer can be programmed to recognize. It is a science of using a particular biological aspect of the human body to recognize a person for security, attendance, or any other purposes for which proof is required (National Law Enforcement and Corrections Technology Center, 2000). It uses mathematical representations of those unique physical characteristics to identify an individual (Desmarais, 2000; Wood, 2000).

Biometrics is used for two major purposes: identification and verification. Identification is defined as the ability to recognize a person from among all those enrolled (all those whose biometric measurements have been collected in the database) and seeks to answer the question, "Do I know who you are?" It involves a one-compared-to-many match (or what is referred to as a "cold search"). Biometrics is also used for verification, which involves the authentication of a person's claimed identity from his or her previously enrolled pattern. Verification seeks to answer the question, "Are you who you claim to be?" and involves a one-to-one match (see Campbell et al., 1996; Clarke, 2001; Miller, 1996). In order to accomplish this, the system has to (1) receive biometric samples from a candidate/user; (2) extract biometric features from the sample; (3) compare the sample from the candidate with stored template(s) from known individual(s); and (4) indicate identification or verification results (Idex, 2000).

Biometrics can be categorized in several ways: high biometrics, low biometrics, and esoteric biometrics. The first category, high biometrics, refers to biometric technologies distinguished by high accuracy. At present, there are three types of high biometrics that are considered truly consistent and unique: the retina, the iris, and fingerprints (Richards, 1996). The second category, lesser biometrics, requires reasonable accuracy and is not based on truly unique physical characteristics. Examples include hand geometry, face recognition, voice recognition, and signature recognition. The third category, esoteric biometrics, is still in the early experimental and developmental stages and includes vein measurement and the analysis of the chemical composition of body odor (McManus, 1996). Biometrics can also be categorized as either physiological and behavioral. Common physiological biometrics include finger characteristics (fingertip [fingerprint], thumb, finger length or pattern), palm (print or topography), hand geometry, wrist vein, face, and eye (retina or iris). Behavioral biometrics include voiceprints, keystroke dynamics, and handwritten signatures (Desmarais, 2000).

The biometric measure itself may be stored. Alternatively, the data may be subjected to some processing of kind and the results of that processing stored instead. The kinds of processing include (1) compression, which reduces transmission time and costs and/or requires less storage space; (2) encryption, in order to make the data inaccessible to someone who intercepts the data in transmission or accesses them in storage (unless they can gain access to the decryption key or can discover it); and (3) hashing, which is a mathematical conversion that protects the measure from being meaningful to someone who intercepts it in transit. The biometric data storage may be in a central location or may be local to the place where the data are used (for example, in a particular building where the person works), or it may be on a device carried by the person (such as a smartcard, a watch, or a ring), or in two of the above, or even all three. The data may be stored in such a manner that they are only usable for a single purpose by a single organization, or for multiple purposes by a single organization, or for multiple purposes by multiple organizations. Most biometrics technologies do not seek exact equality between the new and the stored measures. Instead they have a preset tolerance range within which the two are deemed to be sufficiently close (Clarke, 2001).

TYPES OF BIOMETRIC SCANNING USED IN CORRECTIONS

Biometric scanning is the process whereby biometric measurements are collected and integrated into a computer system, which can then be used to recognize a person. The application of biometrics in corrections is of major interest to correctional administrators since identification and authentication are fundamental requirements for security in corrections. The use of biometrics in corrections varies greatly, partly because it involves such new technologies and few correctional administrators may not be aware of what they are or how they can be utilized. Jails and state and federal correctional systems use biometrics to monitor, identify, and verify inmates, employees, and visitors.

Finger Scanning

Finger-scan technology is the oldest and most prominent biometric authentication technology used by millions of people worldwide. Finger scanning is considered to be highly accurate. It involves physically placing a finger on a small optical scanner roughly similar to the glass plates seen on many supermarket checkout counters (Chandrasekaran, 1997). This "live" fingerprint is electronically read and converted into a unique byte code stored in a database that can then be compared to other finger images for identification purposes. Finger scanning extracts certain characteristics of the image into templates, known as minutiae, that are unique to each finger. Optical, silicon, and ultrasound are mechanisms that are currently used to capture the fingerprint image with sufficient detail and resolution (Finger-Scan.com, 1999). After the fingerprints are scanned by the reader, templates are recorded and compared with the templates that are stored on the databases (ZDNet, 1999).

The county of Los Angeles is implementing a computer system for all criminal justice agencies in the county that will positively and accurately identify a suspect, defendant, or offender based on a live-scanned fingerprint. The county's database will eventually contain seven million records and be used by 10,000 users, including police, court, and probation officers (Esser, 2000). Middlesex County in Massachusetts has also installed a $1.3 million finger-scan identification and tracking system procedure for prisoners and detainees that will use a database of text information, fingerprint images, and mug shot photographs to help personnel accurately identify prisoners (Newcombe, 1997).

Eye Scanning

Eye scanning is probably the fastest-growing area of biometric research because of its promise for high scan accuracy and great difficulty to fool. There are two types of eye scanning: retinal scanning and iris scanning.

Retinal scans are performed by directing a low-intensity infrared light through the pupil to the blood vessel pattern on the back of the eye. Retinal scanning involves an electronic scan of the retina—the innermost layer of the wall of the eyeball. By emitting a beam of incandescent light that bounces off the person's retina and returns to the scanner, a retinal scanning system quickly maps the eye's blood vessel pattern and records it into an easily retrievable digitized database. The eye's natural reflective and absorption properties are used to map a specific portion of the retinal vascular structure. Once the data are collected, they are digitized and stored as a 96-byte template. Retinal scanning relies on the unique characteristics of each person's retina as well as the fact that the retina generally remains fairly stable through life (Ritter, 1995; Tierney, 1995). Most uses of retinal scanners involve high-security access control, since they offer one of the lowest false rejection rates (FRR) and a nearly 0 percent false acceptance rate (FAR) (IOSoftware, 2000).

The word *iris* comes from the Greek word for rainbow. There is so much variation in the patterns around the pupil that the iris is unique from person to person. The iris is chock full of randomly distributed immutable structures, which means that, like snowflakes, no two irises are ever the same (see Wildes, 1997). Moreover, the iris does not change over time, and the unique patterns in the human iris stabilize within one year of birth and remain constant throughout one's lifetime. In fact, the iris is said to be more unique than the fingerprint (Desmarais, 2000; Woodward, 1997).

While retinal scanning uses lasers that focus on the back of the eye, iris scanning zooms in on the front. Likewise, the iris is the most feature-rich part of the human anatomy that is constantly on view. Iris scans digitally process, record, and compare the light and dark patterns in the iris's flecks and rings, something akin to a human bar code. Software captures the identifying information from the iris and stores it in a 256-byte code (McManus, 1996). A standard video technology can quickly record the features of the iris from about nine inches away, thus obviating the need for invasive physical contact (see Harby, 1996). Iris recognition stands out as perhaps the most "hygienic" of the biometric technologies in that no part of the user's body has to touch anything to operate the system (Woodward, 1997).

In March 1990, the Cook County (Illinois) Sheriff's Department began using Eye-Dent, a device that scans the retina of every inmate. The captured information is then used to identify and keep track of inmates. Upward of 300 inmates are scanned daily, and the sheriff's database includes more than 300,000 retinal patterns (Ritter, 1995). A few other county jails from Florida to Utah rely on retina scanners sold by Eyedentify, Incorporated (National Law Enforcement and Corrections Technology Center, 2000).

In the Sarasota County Detention Center in Florida, there is a biometric identification system now in place where iris scans are used to prevent former prisoners from visiting former inmate friends. In place less than 2 years, the system has more than 40,000 iris scans in its database and has logged 8 hits on former inmates trying to enter the prison under false identities (National Law Enforcement and Corrections Technology Center, 2000). The system made by Iriscan Incorporated proved that three people bought in on arrest warrants and who insisted that they were not the "wanted" persons were really the "wanted" men. It also caught two prisoners trying to escape by posing as prisoners up for parole (Beiser, 1999).

The Lancaster County (Pennsylvania) Prison began using iris scanning in 1996. There are currently 30 county prisons and 10 state prison using iris scanning. Inmates at York County Prison in Pennsylvania are verified by iris recognition before they are released from prison at the end of their sentences and for routine events such as court appearances and medical visits. Iris recognition gives prison officials absolute assurance that the right inmate is being released and eliminates the risk of human error in matching a face with photograph identification. In addition, this iris recognition system lets the prison administration determine if a new inmate was previously incarcerated there under a different name (Center for Criminal Justice Technology Newsletter, 2001).

Hand Scanning/Hand Geometry

The hand scanning/geometry approach uses the geometric shape of the hand for authenticating a user's identity. The system consists of a light source, a camera, a single mirror, and a flat surface with five pegs on it. The user places his or her hand on the flat surface of the device. The five pegs are the control points for an appropriate placement of the right hand of the user and take a three-dimensional record of the length, width, and height of the hand and/or fingers. The results are converted into a less-than-10-byte code. In effect, a digital map of the outline of a person's hand is created. The mirror projects the side view of the user's hand onto the camera. This device is hooked to a personal computer, which provides a live visual feedback of the top view and the side view of the hand. The system is noninvasive, and since the memory requirements are limited, hand geometry requires very little computer storage space (Chandrasekaran, 1997; Zunkel, 1998).

Hand scanning/geometry has been used to identify inmates, employees, and visitors to correctional facilities. The Federal Bureau of Prisons, for example, uses hand geometry to verify the identity of visitors and staff members to avoid mistakenly identifying them as inmates. Inmates use it for access to the cafeteria, recreation, lounge, and hospital. Under Justice Department guidelines, the staff, inmates, and all visitors are required to enroll in the system to control prison security. They have to put their hand biometric on a photo identification card. By the end of 1995, around 30 federal prisons were to have the hand-geometry monitoring system installed (National Law Enforcement and Corrections Technology Center, 2000).

The Minnesota Department of Corrections has hand-geometry systems in the state's three medium-security prisons. People leaving the institution swipe their identification cards into the system while placing their hands on a reader. The system compares the biometric on the card with the person's hand before allowing him or her to leave. Staff members also have photos on their identification cards to supplement hand-geometry verification and make false identification a remote possibility (Coleman, 2000). In San

Antonio, Texas, hand geometry helps to prevent escape attempts. The system scans visitors' hands as they enter and again as they leave to be sure prisoners are not posing as visitors or staff (Bratcher, 1999). Florida Department of Corrections currently also utilizes the Automate Visitor Registration System II (AVRII) in 19 facilities. Officials say the technology will decrease security breaches and speed up the visitor registration process. The program will involve the inclusion of departmental staff in the system. Although an exact date has not been finalized, the target date is early 2002 (The Corrections Connection, 2001).

Hand scanning/geometry is also used in probation and parole. The system features kiosks with video touch screens that allow probationers and parolees to check in electronically with the probation or parole officers on their reporting date. New probationers or parolees are enrolled during a face-to-face meeting, in which their name, identification number, and other pertinent information are collected, together with a photograph and their hand geometry. This information is stored in the kiosk's database. Subsequently, at each reporting date, probationers and parolees register at any kiosk. The system identifies probationers/parolees by reading their hand geometry or fingerprints and then prompts them to answer a series of predetermined questions. In 1997, New York City contracted for an electronic probation monitoring system, for a cost of $925,000. The hand geometry system uses kiosks with video touchscreens that allow probationers and parolees to check in electronically with probation officers on reporting dates. The city expected to use the system to monitor about 35,000 low-risk probationers, allowing probation officers to spend more time supervising high-risk probationers (Coleman, 2000). These kiosks have also been installed in Texas, California, Florida, New York, Georgia, Michigan, Indiana, Washington, Tennessee, Oregon, Maryland, Minnesota, New Mexico, Alabama, Colorado, and Nevada (AutoMon, 2001).

Facial Recognition

The term *facial recognition* covers several different techniques, including video or photo imaging or thermography, which reads the heat pattern around the eyes and cheeks; and the ability to scan the dimensions of an individual's head (National Law Enforcement and Corrections Technology Center, 2000). The facial recognition technique is one of the fastest-growing areas. It measures such characteristics as the distance between facial features (from pupil to pupil, for instance) or the dimensions of the features themselves (such as the width of the mouth). Facial recognition software uses a camera attached to a personal computer to capture and map key identifying features (ZDNet, 1999). The advantage of the facial recognition system is that it can work with people still at a distance. As one approaches, the system could recognize the face and activate the system, such as turning on a computer or unlocking a door. Some applications are focusing on a person's smile as a replacement for a security password. Other techniques based on ear or lip shape and knuckle creases are in the conceptual stages (Desmarais, 2000).

In 1998, the Wisconsin department of corrections awarded Visage Technology, Incorporated a $1.4 million contract to develop a biometric facial identification system for the state's prison system. The Wisconsin biometric identification system has established a database of information on all inmates and offenders who pass through the system. In addition to photographs, the system records other identifying attributes, such as scars, tattoos, and gang insignias. Identification cards are produced for department employees, inmates, and offenders, and face-recognition technology is utilized for positive identification. The system is used in more than 44 locations throughout the state (Colatosti, 1998). Ohio Department of Rehabilitation and Corrections also uses facial recognition to identify inmates (Security Information Management Online Network, 1999).

Voice Recognition

A person's voice, like other biometrics, cannot be forgotten or misplaced. Voice recognition involves taking the acoustic signal of a person's voice and converting it to a unique digital code, which can then be stored in a template. Voice-authentication products create voice-prints based on the inflection points of a person's speech, emphasizing the highs and lows specific to the way that person speaks. Of all the biometric technologies, voice is perhaps the easiest to implement but is also potentially the least secure. Voice, in fact, is considered a hybrid behavioral and physiological biometric because a person can alter his or her voice (Speir, 2000). The user enrolls in the program by first speaking an agreed-on phrase into the voice recognition system. For future recognition, he or she would speak the exact same phrase, the signal would be analyzed by the voice recognition system, and he or she would either be accepted, rejected or, if there were insufficient confidence as to the person's signal, the system could request additional information from him or her (Campbell, 1996). Voice recognition systems are extremely well suited for verifying user access over a telephone (Woodward, 1996). A voice recognition device is a low-cost and easy-to-use system that provides a verifiable record of an offender's location at multiple points every day he or she is being supervised (BI Incorporated, 2000).

Voice recognition is commonly used in community-based corrections, such as probation, parole, and electronic monitoring. One such biometric system is the Contain(SM) voice verification monitoring system, which is a caseload management tool that combines T-NETIX's SpeakEZ Voice Print(SM) technology. The system calls the offender's home, or other agency-approved locations, and prompts the subject, via automated speech, to say a password. Contain(SM) then verifies the speaker's identity by comparing the voiceprints of the speaker with that of the offender. If the speaker is not voiceprint verified, Contain(SM) notifies the corrections officer via beeper, voice (telephone), fax, or e-mail (Internet) depending on the subject's failure parameters. The Contain(SM) system allows the officer to confirm failed verification sessions and compare them to enrolled voiceprints over the Internet and also allows the officer to send a voicemail to the offender. The Contain(SM) system serves more than 1600 facilities and justice departments nationwide (Business Wire, 2001).

Several states use voice recognition for parolees on home detention. Community-based corrections in Colorado and Tennessee use VoiceID, which is a sophisticated yet simple-to-administer voice verification system that allows probation and parole officers, through ordinary telephone service, to verify the location of offenders who have been released into communities. VoiceID monitors offenders with random, scheduled, inbound, and/or outbound verification calls over digital telephones. During a verification call, this system compares the offender's voiceprint to a voiceprint taken during enrollment. VoiceID recognizes the offender's identity and location, and subsequently, the offender's compliance to curfew and schedule restrictions. Alerts are communicated to officers by e-mail, fax, or pager. When an alert is e-mailed, it actually contains an embedded sound file so that with a click of a mouse, an officer can hear the verification session. Immediate and accurate reports about offender compliance are available by Internet, e-mail, or fax (BI Incorporated, 2000). This system is also used by the New York City Department of Probation to monitor juveniles and young adults in community release programs (Markowitz, 2000). Voice verification is also used in Tennessee (BI Incorporated, 2000).

ISSUES REGARDING BIOMETRICS SCANNING

Biometric technology is relatively inexpensive and fast; this makes it attractive to correctional agencies. Although biometrics holds substantial promise for corrections, there are a number of problems associated with its use. Biometrics scanning raises the constitutional issues of privacy and reasonable search, and their accuracy, reliability, and safety are questionable.

Constitutional Issues

Privacy Concerns
One of the most controversial legal issues regarding biometrics is that of privacy. Biometric technologies collect both extrinsic and intrinsic information about a person. While most of the lesser biometrics (face recognition, voice recognition, and signature recognition) are essentially noninvasive and nonthreatening; other biometrics, such as retina, iris, and hand geometry, can provide additional information about individuals. The scanning of the iris and the retina, for example, may capture information about a person's health and medical history. Recent scientific research suggests that finger imaging might also disclose sensitive medical information about a person. There is a relationship between an uncommon fingerprint pattern, known as a digital arch, and a medical disorder called chronic, intestinal pseudo-obstruction (CIP) that affects 50,000 people nationwide. In addition, certain chromosomal disorders are known to be associated with characteristic dermatoglyphic abnormalities. Turner syndrome and Klinefelter syndrome, for example, are chromosomal disorders, and certain nonchromosomal disorders, such as leukemia, breast cancer, and Rubella syndrome, may cause certain unusual fingerprint patterns (see Chen, 1988). Although the findings remain controversial within the scientific and gay communities, several researchers report a link between fingerprints and homosexuality (see LeVay, 1996). Hall and Kimura (1994), at the University of Western Ontario at London, Ontario, Canada, for example, compared the number of ridges (fingerprints) on the index finger and thumb of the left hand with corresponding digits on the right hand. They found that 30 percent of

homosexuals had excess ridges on the left-hand digits, while only 14 percent of heterosexuals showed the same characteristic.

The availability of medical and other types of information on individuals subjected to biometrics, whether they are inmates, employees, or visitors, raises concern about the right to privacy when this information is shared with other agencies. It is quite possible that personal information on individuals stored in correctional databases for the purposes of identification and verification could be disseminated to other sources, since a biometric system in a correctional facility may be connected with other databases in the correctional system. In 1995, for example, the Pennsylvania General Assembly passed welfare reform legislation authorizing the Pennsylvania Department of Public Welfare (DPW) to establish a biometrics-based pilot program known as the Assistance Recipient Identification Program (ARIP). The state allowed the Pennsylvania State Police and the Pennsylvania Board of Probation and Parole, as well as local and county law enforcement authorities in Pennsylvania, to have access to this biometric system (see Weaver & Beitzel, 1996). In addition, many state agencies may have access to each other's databases or they may share information with other states. For example, Connecticut and Massachusetts are discussing the possibility of an interstate cross-matching pilot of facial images. Massachusetts uses facial imaging while Connecticut uses finger imaging, but both collect digital photographs that will be the basis for the pilot (Mintie, 1999). In addition, states may attempt to sell information collected on individuals through biometric technology. In fact, state officials in Florida and South Carolina attempted to sell their databases of digitalized drivers' license photos to the private sector, but public outcry prevented the sale from taking place (Moskowitz, 1999). But without regulation from federal governments, other states may attempt to sell this information. Once in use, therefore, a biometric system in a correctional agency may not be confined to its original purpose. The more people have access to a database, the less likely that this information will remain private.

Privacy becomes a bigger issue when biometrics is used in conjunction with smart cards. Smartcards, which may contain data such as medical, financial, health history, and criminal record, can be stolen or lost. Unauthorized individuals who possess lost or stolen smartcards and have means to decrypt the biometric data could reveal information that is very personal to the card owners (Esser, 2000).

Proponents who support the use of biometrics claim that biometric technology does not violate one's privacy but instead protects one's privacy by safeguarding one's identity. They argue that biometric scanning does not invade privacy, since most agencies (except law enforcement) disregard and remove the actual copy of the biometric images/pattern and store the extracted file created from the user's biometric algorithm. Most of these algorithms are also encrypted to increase data protection. They contend that this information can be restricted based on the "need to know" principle, and if an audit trail is kept detailing who accessed which records, fewer people will have access to the database. Finally, the proponents praised biometrics as a privacy-enhancing technology because it allows users to be anonymous. Since most of the biometric devices digitalize, encode, and encrypt biometric data, the identity of the individual is eliminated, and thus anonymity is preserved (Esser, 2000).

In sum, by requiring citizens to submit to biometrics for official identification and verification, individuals may be providing physical and private information to the correctional agencies for storage, use, and dissemination in other databases. Such correctional-mandated use of biometrics, therefore, directly raises privacy concerns since this information can be disseminated without the individuals' consent or knowledge.

Search

An issue related to that of privacy is whether the use of biometrics by correctional agencies constitutes a search. The question is: Is a biometric scan a search and, if it is, is it reasonable? The Fourth Amendment to the United States Constitution, which governs searches and seizures conducted by government agents, provides that individuals have the right to be secure in their persons, houses, papers, and effects, against unreasonable searches and seizures.

To evaluate whether correctional-mandated biometric scanning constitutes a search, the courts will have to focus on the nature of the intrusion and the scope of the intrusiveness with attention paid to the nature of the private information revealed during the scan (see *Skinner v. Railway Labor Executives' Association,* 1989). If biometric scanning is found to constitute a search, the ultimate measure of the constitutionality of a correctional search is "reasonableness," which is determined by probable cause (see *Vernonia School District 475 v. Acton,* 1995). The court would have to balance the intrusion on the individual's Fourth Amendment interests against the legitimate interests of the correctional systems (see *Skinner v. Railway Labor Executives' Association,* 1989). Given the fact that retina, iris, and finger scanning used in correctional facilities can be considered intrusive and can yield medical information about individuals raises the issue of an illegal search. However, in the long run, the courts may give corrections the same latitude that it has given the federal government for drug testing. The courts have allowed drug testing on large groups of federal employees, even if none were suspected of drug use. This is called "suspicionless search" (Nuger, 2000). In addition, as this technology is used more extensively, the courts may view it as commonplace and, therefore, nonintrusive (see *Breithraupt v. Abram,* 1957; *Perkey v. Department of Motor Vehicles,* 1986; *Schmerber v. California,* 1966). As biometrics continue to develop and be used, their "intrusiveness" may cease to be an issue.

Issues of Accuracy and Reliability

One of the major issues regarding biometric scans is their accuracy. Automated biometric systems are not 100 percent foolproof. Although fingerprints, face, and voice remain constant from day to day, small fluctuations, such as cold or moist hands, different degree of lighting for face recognition, and background noise for voice authentication, can confuse the devices. Setting the sensitivity low increases the odds of an imposter's logon being accepted (false positive). High sensitivity setting means greater security, but it also means that an authorized user may be erroneously rejected (false negative) (Gunnerson, 1999).

There are problems with finger scanning that can produce poor images due to residues, such as dirt and body oils (which can build up on the glass plate), on the finger (see Hansell, 1997; Ritter, 1995). In addition, some people have fingerprints that are harder to image. About 2 percent of the general population's fingerprints baffle computers. It is often difficult to image very small hands and fingers as well as the hands of people who work with their hands or those who have injuries or scars as well as eroded fingerprints from scrapes or years of heavy labor. Also, as people age, they often lose the lipid (fat) layer in their skin and their fingerprints become worn and difficult (Desmarais, 2000). An injury to the hand can cause the measurements to change, resulting in recognition problems (Chandrasekaran, 1997; Clarke, 2001; Miller, 1996).

Although eye scanning is relatively accurate, it can produce incorrect results. Researchers testing one system, for example, discovered that university students who wore patterned "designer" contacts were wrongly rejected because the contacts were in a different position every time the students' eyes were scanned (National Law Enforcement and Corrections Technology Center, 2000). In addition, contact lens wearers or people with optical diseases like glaucoma may not easily pass an eyeball scan (Desmarais, 2000).

Facial scanning has problems similar to those of photographs—people who look alike can fool the scanners. Facial recognition software is terrible at handling changes in lighting or camera angle or images with busy backgrounds. Also, a similar face or a change in appearance can confuse the system (National Law Enforcement and Corrections Technology Center, 2000). In addition, people can significantly alter their appearance, and facial hair may be able to fool the device. Moreover, questions have been raised about how well the software works on dark-skinned people, whose features may not appear clearly on lenses optimized for light-skinned people (American Civil Liberty Union, 2001). Finally, some systems have difficulty maintaining high levels of performance as the database grows in size (Chandrasekaran, 1997; Miller, 1996).

A study conducted by the government's National Institute of Standards and Technology (NIST) found false-negative (not catching people even when their photo is in the database) rates for face-recognition verification of 43 percent using photos of subjects taken just 18 months earlier, and those photos were taken in perfect conditions. The NIST study also found that a change of 45 degrees in the camera angle rendered the software useless. Although the technology works best under tightly controlled conditions when the subject is staring directly into the camera under bright lights, a study by the Department of Defense found high error rates even in those ideal conditions. Other government studies of face-recognition software have found high rates of both false positives (wrongly matching innocent people with photos in the database) and false negatives. Consequently, several government agencies, such as the Immigration and Naturalization Service, which experimented with using the technology to identify people in cars at the Mexico–U.S. border, have abandoned facial-recognition systems after finding they did not work as advertised (American Civil Liberty Union, 2002).

There are also accuracy problems with voice recognition. Some voice and speaker recognition techniques are highly susceptible to background noise and may not provide accurate verification if speakers have a cold or their voices change (for example, when they are sick or in extreme emotional states) (Campbell, 1997; National Law Enforcement and Corrections Technology Center, 2000; Woodward, 1996).

There are already techniques for breaking these biometric devices. Voice and facial recognition technologies are still very immature, and therefore twins or look-alike people might sneak past the security measures at the default setting. Duplicated fingers on thin pieces of rubber have already been experimented with to trick a fingerprint scanner. There is also the possibility that a whole rubber hand, and possibly a rubber face, can also fool biometric systems. According to antibiometric groups, breaking biometric systems is not an impossible mission (Gaudin, 2000). Biometrics, according to the opponents, does not handle failures well. Once an individual's biometric data are stolen, they remain stolen for life; there is no getting back to a secure situation (Schneier, 1999).

Young (1999), in testing several biometric devices to determine their security, found that while fingerprint recognition devices are difficult to fool, face and voice recognition devices were easily fooled. In addition, many biometric systems may not be able to live up to expectations because of the enormous variation among large populations of people.

Because of the problems of individual biometric systems, a few companies are combining multiple biometric systems into an integrated system. Identification based on multiple biometrics represents an emerging trend. The multimodal biometric system, which integrates face recognition, fingerprint verification, and speaker verification in making a personal identification, takes advantage of the capabilities of each individual biometric. It can be used to overcome some of the limitations of a single biometric. Preliminary experimental results demonstrate that the identity established by such an integrated system is more reliable than the identity established by a face recognition system, a fingerprint verification system, and a speaker verification system (Jain et al., 1998).

Safety Issues

Finally, there are rising concerns about the safety of biometrics. Biometric vendors claim that their devices are nonintrusive and present no health or safety risks to either users or operators. They state that these devices do not leave marks nor do they take physical samples and require minimal or no contact by the user. But biometrics is such a new technology and its health impact on its users has not been fully evaluated. Opponents fear that long-term exposure to infrared scanning could be hazardous to the human body (Esser, 2000). Biometrics might have hidden effects on humans that can only be discovered in the future.

Abuse of Biometric Information

Personal data collected by biometric technology can be subjected to abuse. Given the fact that there is a disproportionate number of minorities in the correctional system, the use of biometrics in correctional systems may lead to profiling. Biometric technology could be a new tool for racial and ethnic profiling. In fact, some opponents to biometric technology argue that it is a form of racial profiling (see Trone, 2001). The biometric information collected by correctional agencies could be used to harass, threaten, or stigmatize minorities.

For example, police throughout Michigan, entrusted with the personal and confidential information in a state law enforcement database, have used it to stalk women, threaten motorists, and settle scores (Elrick, 2001). In addition, this information, collected by corrections, can be sold to various government agencies and private companies, which then could use the information to further discriminate against former inmates and their relatives and friends (who used a biometric system while visiting the offender in prison) by subjecting them to more identity checks.

Freedom and Ethics

Biometrics, as a surveillance technology, create an environment in which organizations have enormous power over individuals. The use of biometric technology threatens the freedom of individuals and undermines democracy. There is also the issue of ethics. The use of biometrics tend to dehumanize individuals, who are viewed in terms of specific biological or physical features. The question then becomes whether or not it is ethical to treat human beings in this manner (Clarke, 2001).

THE FUTURE OF BIOMETRICS

Until recently, legislative bodies and organizations were not overly concerned with biometric proposals. However, during the last several years legislative perspectives have become more cautious about biometric applications due to the privacy issues. As a result, a few bills have been introduced/proposed to regulate biometric systems (Esser, 2000).

California, for example, now prohibits any selling or sharing of biometric ID with other people or institution except law enforcement and public services. California's bill also prohibits collecting biometric information without the individual's purposes or consent, or using it to discriminate on any unlawful basis (IOSoftware, 2000; Pavis, 1998). In Missouri legislation was introduced to prevent any business from requesting biometrics from any customer, even if the customer consents. In Colorado, the Department of Revenue is now specifically prohibited from selling biometric and other personal information. Approximately fifteen states introduced antibiometric bills during 1998 and 1999; most of these bills, nevertheless, were defeated by law enforcement and banking/financial institutions (Mintie, 1999). Congress has introduced 38 bills that could affect the biometrics industry and the privacy of individuals (Jacobson, 1999).

The National Security Agency, in an attempt to learn more about biometrics, established an intergovernmental working group, the Biometric Consortium (BC), in 1992, which serves as the U.S. government's focal point for research, development, test, evaluation, and application of biometric-based personal identification/verification technology. BC membership is comprised of representatives of six executive departments and each of the armed forces. Among its responsibilities, the BC addresses legal and ethical issues surrounding biometrics as well as advises and assists member agencies concerning the selection and application of biometric devices. In addition to its regular meetings, the BC can also establish ad hoc bodies to address specific areas of need (Biometric Consortium, 2002).

In 1997, the Biometric Consortium established the National Biometric Test Center at San Jose State University. The primary tasks of the Test Center are to (1) serve the Biometric Consortium as a technical and administrative resource and information clearinghouse; (2) advise the Biometric Consortium on issues related to biometric security; (3) evaluate methodologies; (4) facilitate dialogue between industry users and international groups; (5) collect, catalog, and disseminate database materials and biometric research results; and (6) research biometric issues as directed by the Consortium. The U.S. National Biometric Test Center has also developed a one-semester, three-unit graduate-level course in Biometric Identification Science and Technology (National Biometrics Test Center, 2000).

On February 21, 1999, the Information Technology Laboratory of the National Institute of Standards and Technology (NIST) and the U.S. Biometric Consortium sponsored a workshop to discuss the potential for reaching industry consensus in a common fingerprint template format. As a result of the workshop, the participants agreed to develop a "technology-blind" biometric file format that will facilitate handling different biometric types, versions, and biometric data structures in a common way. Three additional workshops have been held, and a Common Biometric Exchange File Format (CBEFF) document (NISTIR 6529) was published on January 3, 2000. The BC will hold another conference, which was postponed from September 13–15, 2001, on February 13–15, 2002 (Biometric Consortium, 2002).

The federal government has been managing two projects that demonstrate and evaluate biometric technologies in a correctional environment. The first project is a multiphase effort to identify and develop biometric technology to control inmate movement and enhance inmate accountability within a correctional facility. The first phase of this project will develop the necessary software and systems integration to utilize biometric technology and establish a prototype inmate control and accountability system at the Naval Correctional Facility in Charleston, South Carolina. Biometrics will be installed, demonstrated, and evaluated in several key sites inside the Correctional Facility and the results published. Subsequent phases will expand biometrics to the entire Correctional Facility, and the results would be utilized to develop a biometrics demonstration in a civilian jail or prison (National Law Enforcement and Corrections Technology Center, 2000).

The second project is a joint effort between the National Institute of Justice and the Department of Defense Counterdrug Technology Development Program Office to define a facial recognition program plan that will have immediate benefits for corrections. Repeated inquiries from numerous government agencies on the current state of facial recognition technology prompted the Counterdrug Technology Development Program Office to establish a new set of evaluations. The Facial Recognition Vendor Test 2000 (FRVT 2000) was cosponsored by the Department of Defense Counterdrug Technology Development Program Office, the National Institute of Justice (NIJ), and the Defense Advanced Research Projects Agency and was administered in spring 2000. The Facial Recognition Vendor Test (FRVT) 2000 was divided into two evaluation steps: the Recognition Performance Test and the Product Usability Test. The FRVT 2000 Recognition Performance Test is a technology evaluation of commercially available facial recognition systems. For the Recognition Performance Test in FRVT 2000, vendors were given 13,872 images and were asked to compare each image to all the other images (more than 192 million comparisons). These data were used to develop experiments that show how well the systems respond to numerous variables, such as pose, lighting, and image compression levels. The FRVT 2000 Product Usability Test is an example of a scenario evaluation, albeit a limited one. The Product Usability Tests consisted of two timed tests, which were used to measure the response time of the overall system for two different access control scenarios: the Old Image Database Timed Test, which was tested using existing gallery images (the images/templates in the database to which a new image is being compared), and the Enrollment Timed Test, which allowed vendors to enroll subjects at the testing location. Each of the timed tests was performed for both verification and identification and was performed once with overhead fluorescent lighting and again with the addition of backlighting (Bone & Crumbacker, 2001).

Results from FRVT 2000 show mixed conclusions regarding the viability of facial recognition for the correctional environment. In all cases, the facial recognition systems were quicker and more accurate when performing verification experiments than in identification experiments. The Recognition Performance Test within FRVT 2000 indicated that changes in media types, compression, and resolution did not significantly affect performance. The Product Usability Test within FRVT 2000 showed that systems perform quite well when subjects are enrolled at the same location and using the same equipment where they eventually will be subjects for recognition, but perform considerably worse when the location and equipment vary. The findings also suggest that facial recognition systems will not show significant changes in performance if a subject is cooperative versus indifferent as long as the indifferent subject is facing toward the camera. When a moderate, nonvarying backlighting is introduced, there is a small degree of difficulty for the facial recognition vendors, but in most cases it was negligible. Further experimentation with higher-intensity backlighting, lighting from various angles, and varying lighting intensity is necessary to understand the impact of lighting in this scenario. In addition, varying subject–camera distances, poses, illumination, and temporal factors (time difference between enrollment and recognition) are areas that require additional research (Bone & Crumbacker, 2001).

Based on results from the technology evaluation and limited scenario evaluation from FRVT 2000, an operational evaluation is being developed at a correctional facility in Prince George's County, Maryland. The method through which facial recognition is being used at the facility could change throughout the evaluation as more about the system capabilities are learned as well as the interaction between the system and Prince George's County personnel. The initial phase of this operational evaluation and demonstration uses proximity card readers and facial recognition technology to assist correctional officers in their decision to unlock an electronically controlled door providing access to the facility. Employees enter the facility via a 20-foot hallway with an electronically controlled door on the far end and an open-wall office for access control personnel along the side of the hallway. A proximity card reader will be placed at the entry to the hallway for employees entering the facility and another inside the secured area of the facility for exiting employees. Correctional officers will unlock the electronically controlled door leading into the facility based on information from the proximity readers (Bone & Crumbacker, 2001). If this system proves successful, it will be used to monitor visitors as well (National Law Enforcement and Corrections Technology Center, 2000).

RECOMMENDATIONS

Despite the aforementioned efforts, more needs to be done with regard to the use of biometrics in corrections and society in general. The following are some recommendations designed to improve the use of biometrics and prevent abuses:

1. State and federal governments should establish working groups to study in greater detail the legal and policy implications of biometric technologies when used by correctional agencies. The groups should also address any medical information concerns raised by the use of biometrics. The findings of the working groups should be publicly disseminated, in the form of a conference, seminar, or newsletter.

2. To curtail the unauthorized use of biometrics by correctional personnel, Congress should pass legislation regulating the use of the technology. The legislation should clearly stipulate that the use of biometric identification should be limited to its original purpose and additional information, such as medical information, should remain private. Violation of the legislation should result in criminal sanctions.

3. State and federal government should make biometric databases physically secured. Any physical documents pertaining to the database should be kept in a secured area that could be protected by security personnel, alarm systems, video surveillance, and other related security devices to prevent unauthorized access to the information. In addition, databases should be protected so that they may not become targets of hackers (Woodward, 1997).

4. Correctional agencies should investigate the viability of adopting newly developed biometric technologies, which use the individual's physical characteristics to construct a digital code for identification without storing the actual physical characteristics in a database. This will protect individuals' privacy, especially their personal information.

5. Correctional agencies should properly train employees on how to use their biometric systems. Agency employees should be trained to perform their duties efficiently and how to protect and safeguarding the biometric information at their command. A senior official should be designated as the compliance officer to ensure that database information is protected (see Woodward, 1997).

6. To prevent constitution challenges to the use of biometric in correctional fa-
    cilities, manufacturers should work closely with legal scholars to ensure that
    their systems are secure and free from constitutional challenges.

7. State governments should pass laws restricting the movement of biometric
    databases. They should not allow "function creep," where information col-
    lected by a biometric system in corrections is used in other state agencies
    (see Gugliotta, 1999).

8. Manufacturers should conduct pilot tests on the biometric systems and de-
    vices to identify the error rate before they market their products. Training
    and familiarity with the systems can reduce false rejections. Banks may want
    to lower the number of the false rejection since telling customers that they
    are not who they are does not go over well. Entries to military intelligent net-
    work, however, may require a high rejection rate since critical data to na-
    tional security is at stake (Esser, 2000).

9. Congress should mandate biometric regulations based on a privacy bill,
    such as a Code of Fair Information Practice (CFIP). The adoption of a bio-
    metric requirement at the federal level is an effective way to balance privacy
    concerns with the benefits of biometrics (Woodward, 1998).

10. Given the extraordinarily serious implications of biometric technologies
    and the absence of any effective protections, a ban should be placed on all
    applications until after a comprehensive set of design requirements and
    protections has been devised, implemented, and is actually in force. Only
    in this manner can biometric technology providers and scheme sponsors
    be forced to balance the interests of all parties rather than serving the inter-
    ests of only the powerful and repressing the individuals whose biometrics
    are to be captured (Clarke, 2001).

SUMMARY

Biometrics, which is used to identify or authenticate a person based on his or her physical
characteristics such as a fingerprint, retina, iris, hand, face, or voice, is becoming more
prevalent in correctional agencies. Various forms of biometric scans are used by correctional
agencies to verify prisoners, to control access for correctional facilities, and to regulate the
movement of probationers and parolees.

   Although biometric technology is more secure, efficient, and time saving than traditional methods of identification and verification, such as password and personal identification numbers, it is relatively new. Its use, therefore, raises a series of concerns. One major
issue is privacy. There are concerns as to what extent personal information collected by biometric systems will remain private. The accuracy and reliability of biometric technology
have been questioned, and there are practical problems associated with this new technology. There is also the issue of alternative secure methods of identification and verification

of special needs individuals, such as those who are blind and those who have lost limbs, who may not be able to use this technology. This will be an issue that correctional agencies will have to address as the use of the technology expands. As the sophistication of biometrics increases, the identification schemes operated by correctional agencies would require regulation in order to achieve the appropriate balance between personal and social needs of corrections.

Although some efforts have been made by the federal government to study the legal and constitutional issues related to the use of biometrics, more needs to be done. The federal and state governments need to establish privacy requirements and standards for the use of biometrics. They also need to train their personnel to adequately and efficiently operate biometric systems. Finally, it is important that manufacturers of biometric systems increase their effectiveness and minimize the social, legal, and ethical problems associated with their use.

Biometric technology seemed tailor made for a system that is based on controlling people's movements, such as corrections, since identification and authentication are fundamental requirements for security in corrections. Although at present only a few correctional agencies use the technology, it is possible that its use in corrections will expand drastically in the next decade. This expansion will serve to depersonalize not only inmates and their visitors but employees as well. This could further alienate offenders from society.

REFERENCES

American Civil Liberty Union. (2001). *Q&E on Facial Recognition. http://www.aclu.org/issues/privacy/facial_recognition_faq.html*

American Civil Liberty Union. (2002, January 3). *Drawing a Blank: Tampa Police Records Reveal Poor Performance of Face-Recognition Technology. http://www.aclu.org/news/20011n010302a.html*

AutoMon. (2001). *Kiosk Information Systems Joins Forces with AutoMon Corporation Partnership Automates Paper-Based Law Enforcement Procedures and Allows Officers to Focus on High-Risk Cases. http://www.kiosks.org/articles/prlIllOlb.html*

Beiser, V. (1999, August 21). *Biometrics Breaks into Prisons. http://www.wired.com/news/technology/0,1282,21362,00.html*

BI Incorporated. (2000). *BI VoiceID Compliance Monitoring as Easy as a Phone Call. http:~www.bi.comrrechnology/voiceid.html*

Biometric Consortium. (2002, January 30). *Biometrics. http://www.biometrics.org/*

Bone, M., & Crumbacker, C. (2001). Facial Recognition. *Corrections Today*, pp. 62–64.

Bratcher, D. (1999, May 1). *Lares Technology Announces the Visitor Authentication Station.* Lares Technology. *http://www.lares.com/news/press/19981106.html*

Breithraupt v. Abram 352 U.S. 432 (1957).

Business Wire. (2001, November 1). *TELEQUIP to Provide Inmate Calling Systems for AT&T. http://www.TNETIX.com/news/default.asp?a=detail&p=1&r=107*

Cade, B. S., & J. Richards. (1996). Permutation tests for least absolute deviate regression: *Biometrics,* v. 52, p. 886–902.

Campbell, J. P., Alyea, L. A., & J. Dunn, J. (1997). *Biometric Security: Government Applications and Operations,* at 1 in CardTech/SecurTech (CTST). Government Conference Proceedings. *http://www.biometrics.org/REPORTS/CTSTG961*

Center for Criminal Justice Technology Newsletter. (2001, June 18). *Biometrics At York County (Pa) Prison. http://www.mitretek.org/business_areas/justice/cjiti/ccjtnews/weekly/vol5-4.html*

Chandrasekaran, R. (1997, March 30). Brave New World: ID Systems Using the Human Body Are Here, But Privacy Issues Persist, *Washington Post,* p. H1.

Chen, H. (1988). *Medical Genetics Handbook.* St. Louis, MO: W. H. Green.

Clarke, R. (2001, April 15). Biometrics and Privacy. Xamax Consultancy Pty Ltd. *http://www.anu.edu.au/people/Roger.Clarke/DV/Biometrics.html#Id&Auth*

Colatosti, T. (1998, November 18). *Wisconsin Department of Corrections Chooses Visage.* Visage Technology, Incorporated. *http//www.visage.com*

Coleman, S. (2000). Biometrics. *FBI Law Enforcement Bulletin,* 69(6):8–9.

Desmarais, N. (2000, November/December). *Biometrics and Network Security.* Information Technology Interest Group, New England Chapter. *http://abacus.bates.edu/acrlnec/sigs/itig/tc_nov_dec2000.htm*

Elrick, M. L. (2001, July 31). *Cops Tap Database to Harass, Intimidate.* Free Press. *http://www.freep.com/news/mich/lein31_20010731.htm*

Esser, M. (2000, October 1). *Biometric Authentication. http://faculty.ed.umuc.edu/-meinkej/inss690/messer/Paper.*

Finger-scan.com. (1999). *Finger Scan Technology. http://www.finger-scan.com./finger-scan_technology.htm#Optical,Silicon,Ultrasound*

Gaudin, S. (2000, May 8). *Biometric Eyes the Enterprise.* Network World Fusion. *http://www.nwfusion.com/research/2000/0508feat2.html*

Gugliotta, G. (1999, June 22). *No Laws Yet Govern Biometrics, Legal Experts Say.* Seattle Times. *http://seattletimes.nwsource.com/news/nation-world/html98/priv_19990622.html*

Gunnerson, G. (1999, February 23). *Are You Ready for Biometrics? http://www.zdnet.com/products/stories/reviews/0,4161,386987-2,00.html*

Hall, J. A. Y., & Kimura, D. (1994). Dermatoglyphic Asymmetry and Sexual Orientation in Men. *Behavioral Neuroscience,* 108:1203–1206.

Hansell, S. (1997). Is This an Honest Face? Use of Recognition Technology Grows in Everyday Transactions, *The New York Times,* August 20, p. D1.

Harby, K. (1996, April). Optics: A Discerning Eye, *Science America,* p. 38.

IOSoftware. (2000). *Biometrics Explained. http://www.iosoftware.com/biometrics/explained.htm*

Jacobson, L. (1999, March 20). *Playing the Identity Card.* National Journal. *http://www.infowar.com/p_and_s/99/p_n_s_041799a_j.shtml*

Jain, A. K., Hong, L., & Kulkaeni, Y. (1998). *A Multimodal Biometric System Using Fingerprints, Face and Speech.* 2nd International Conference on Audio- and Video-Based Biometric Person Authentication (pp. 182–187), Washington, DC, March, 22–24.

Kelley, D., & Oien, K. (2000, May 3). *Implementing Biometric Technology to Enhance Correctional Safety and Security. http://tunxis.commnet.edu/ccjci/futures/classviii/kelley_oien.html*

LeVay, S. (1996). *Queer Science: The Use and Abuse of Research into Homosexuality.* Cambridge, MA: MIT Press.

Markowitz, J. (2000). *Speech Recognition and Speaker Biometrics. http://www.jmarkowitz.com/pubs.html*

McManus, K. (1966, May 6). At Banks of Future, an Eye for an ID, *Washington Post,* p. A3.

Miller, B. (1996). *Everything You Need to Know about Automated Biometric Identification.* CardTech/SecurTech (CTST) Government Conference Proceedings, p. 1.

Mintie, D. (1999). *Biometrics in Human Services. Biometrics in Human Services User Group Newsletter,* 3(5). *http://www.dss.state.ct.us/digital/news16/bhsug16.html*

Moskowitz, R. (1999, January 25). *Are Biometrics Too Good? http://www.networkcomputing .com/1002/1002colmoskowitz.html*

National Biometrics Test Center. (2000). *Biometrics Publications.* San Jose State University. *http://www.engr.sjsu.edu/biometrics/publications.html*

National Law Enforcement and Corrections Technology Center. (2000, October). *TechBeat Fall 2000. http://www.nlectc.org/txtfiles/tbfall2000.html*

Newcombe, T. (1997, March). *Technology Focus. http:/lwww.govtech.net/publications/gt/l997/ marlmarch97-technologyfocus/march97-technologytocus.phtml.*

Nuger, K. P. (2000, February 2). *Biometric Applications: Legal and Societal Considerations.* National Biometric Test Center. *http://www.engr.sjsu.edu/biometrics/publicationSconsideratio.html*

Page, D. (1998). *Biometrics: Facing Down the Identity Crisis. High Technology Careers Magazine. http:~www.hightechcareers.com/docl98/biometrics198.html*

Pavis, T. (1998, May 6). *Bill Clamps Down on Biometrics. Wired News. http://www.wired.com/news/ politics/0,1283,12128,00.html*

Perkey v. Department of Motor Vehicles 721 P.2d. 50 (Gal. App. 1986).

Ritter, J. (1995). Eye Scans Help Sheriff Keep Suspects in Sight. *Chicago Sun-Times,* June 22, p. 18.

Schmerber v. California 384 U.S. 757 (1966).

Schneier. B. (1999). Biometrics: Uses and Abuses. *Communications of the Association for Computing Machinery (ACM),* 42(8):136.

Security Information Management Online Network (1999, July 23). *Ohio Department of Rehabilitation and Corrections Signs New Contract with Viisage. http://www. simon-net.com/PressRelease.asp?lD=2107*

Skinner v. Railway Labor Executives' Association, 489 U.S. 602, 616 (1989).

Speir, M. (2000, June 5). *Voice Verification: Veritel Corp.'s Veritel Voice.* Federal Computer Week. *http://www.fcw.com/fcw/articles/2000/0605/web-biorev3-06-05-00.asp*

The Corrections Connection. (2001). *Florida DOC Increases Security with Identification Technology. http://www.corrections.com/technetwork/thtml.*

Tierney, T. (1995). Eyes Have It in Future of Law Enforcement: Technology Expands to Identify Suspects, *Chicago Tribune,* June 27, p. 1.

Trone, K. (2001, December 11). *Committee Debates Privacy Concerns. The Desert Sun. http://www.thedesertsun.com/news/stories/local/1008035701.shtml*

U.S. Department of Justice. (2001, August 21). *National Correctional Population Reaches New High.* Washington, DC: U.S. Government Printing Office.

Vernonia School Dist. 47J v. Acton, 515 U.S. 646, 652 (1995).

Weaver, J. A., & Beitzel, G. W. (1996). *Fingerprints, Digital Photos and Digital Signatures: Pennsylvania Automated Recipient Identification System (PARIS).* CardTech/SecurTech (CTST) Government Conference Proceedings, p. 1.

Wildes, R. P. (1997). Iris Recognition: An Emerging Biometric Technology, *Proceedings of the Institute of Electrical and Electronics Engineers (IEEE),* 83:1348–1350.

Woodward, J. D. (1996). Biometrics Offers Security—But Legal Worries, Too. *American Banker,* August 23, p. 11.

Woodward, J. D. (1997). Biometric Scanning, Law & Policy: Identifying the Concerns—Drafting the Biometric Blueprint. *University of Pittsburgh Law Review,* 59:97.

Woodward, J. (1998, May 20). Biometrics and the Future of Money. Testimony before Subcommittee on Domestic and International Monetary Policy, Committee on Banking and Financial Services. 106 Congress, Washington, DC.

Young, K. (1999, February 8). *Biometric Security. PC Magazine. http:~www.zdnet.com/products/stories/reviews/0,4161,387177,00.html*

ZdNet. (1999). *How Biometrics Works. http://www.zdnet.com/products/stories/reviews/0,4161,2199371, 00.html*

Zunkel, R. (1998). Hand Geometry Based Verification. In A. Jain, R. Bolle, & S. Pankanti (eds.), *Biometrics: Personal Identification in Networked Society* (pp. 87–102). Norwell, MA: Kluwer Academic Publishers.

Prisoners' Constitutional Rights

Kate King

OVERVIEW

Prior to the onset of prison litigation in the 1960s, prisoners' rights were whatever the prison administration allowed. Convicted felons, according to *Ruffin v. Commonwealth* (1871), were considered "slaves of the state" and therefore, civilly dead. The Virginia court wrote in *Ruffin* that "[A prisoner] has, as a consequence of his crime, not only forfeited his liberty, but all his personal rights except those which the law in its humanity accords him."[1] Because prisoners were considered civilly dead, they held the status of nonperson; thus the courts were free to ignore their petitions for relief.[2] This attitude prevailed until the 1960s. Palmer and Palmer identified three reasons why the courts avoided prisoners' issues: Judges felt they had no expertise in the area of prison administration; they viewed the running of American prisons as a function of the executive branch; and they feared intervention might jeopardize the safety of prisoners and staff.[3] A fourth reason prisoners' lawsuits were ignored, according to Branham and Krantz, was the simple dislike that judges had for prisoners' lawsuits.[4]

Judges' views changed significantly, however, during the "cultural revolution" of the 1960s. Social wrongs were acknowledged and Americans called for reform. Oppressed groups, including minorities, women, and prisoners, found a receptive audience within the federal courts for their complaints. Inmates filed thousands of petitions, and in many cases judges became involved in the day-to-day running of state prison systems (e.g., *Ruiz v. Estelle,* where the entire Texas correctional system was ruled unconstitutional).[5] Because correctional employees were being held liable for the violation of prisoners' rights, inmates felt empowered. When prison officials realized that federal judges were serious about prisoners' rights and willing to hold wardens and commissioners in contempt of court, or order money damages paid to inmates, the administration of prisons in America began to change.

Areas addressed by prisoner lawsuits included access to the courts, classification, discipline, prison conditions, officer brutality, solitary confinement, the quality of food, ventilation, medical care, inmates' right to help one another file lawsuits, correctional staff training, suicide policies, overcrowding, fire safety, the right to worship, good time credits, censorship, and more. The ripple effect of judicial intervention into the management of state prisons was extensive. Prison directors took notice of the lawsuits in other jurisdictions. Many who were not personally challenged brought their own policies into conformance with these rulings in order to deter future lawsuits, or, in the event they were sued, to bolster their own defense. Thus, court decisions regarding one state system often influenced prison administration in many others. Ironically, some prison directors began to welcome lawsuits because when they lost, the legislature gave them needed funds to improve their prisons.

As with all social movements, this one also ran out of steam. New appointees to the United States Supreme Court in the 1970s held different views than their predecessors regarding prisoners' rights. Their views echoed society's emerging get-tough attitude toward crime, and this brought a shift in the federal courts' response to prisoner lawsuits. An attitude of deference to correctional administrators emerged, signaling a slowdown of the prisoners' rights movement. While inmates retain some civil rights, judges are now leaving the daily operation of prisons in the hands of correctional professionals. Today, according to the Supreme Court, inmates possess limited rights to free speech, religious freedom, the right to marry, access to the courts, equal protection of the law, procedural due process, and the right to be free from cruel and unusual punishment.[6]

SOURCES OF PRISONERS' RIGHTS

Bartollas defines a right as "a claim by an individual or group of individuals that another individual, a corporation, or the state has a duty to fulfill."[7] Prisoners' rights derive from the United States Constitution, state constitutions, and federal and state statutes. These rights are not absolute, however. They must be interpreted in light of the legitimate institutional needs of the prison administration. These needs include institutional security, order and discipline, and the rehabilitation of the inmate. The courts have recognized that prisoners are entitled to due process of law. Due process involves the "procedural and substantive rights of citizens against government actions that threaten the denial of life, liberty, or property."[8]

The constitutional amendments that are relevant to the study of prisoners' rights are the First, Fourth, Fifth, Sixth, Eighth, and Fourteenth. In addition, section 1983 of the Civil Rights Act of 1871 (42 U.S.C. 1983) provides prisoners with the ability to sue government employees who violate their civil rights while acting under color of law. The United States Supreme Court ruled, in *Monroe v. Pape* (1961), and again in *Cooper v. Pate* (1964), that section 1983 applies to inmates, opening the door for state prisoners to challenge their treatment by prison officials in federal court.[9]

Inmates can legally challenge prison policies, actions of employees, or conditions of their confinement in other ways. These include a state or federal habeas corpus petition, a state tort lawsuit, and a petition for injunction.[10] A petition for habeas corpus requests that the court order a hearing to determine if a prisoner is being illegally confined. A tort is a civil wrong, a wrongful act, or a wrongful breach of duty other than breach of contract. This action in state court gives the inmate an opportunity to claim that a correctional employee failed to fulfill a legal obligation, and, thus, to collect money damages. When a prisoner files a petition for injunction, he or she is requesting that the court order the prison to refrain from committing a particular act, such as holding the inmate in unsanitary conditions.

MAJOR ERAS OF PRISONERS' RIGHTS

Hands-Off Era

As mentioned previously, during the hands-off era, prisoners, considered civilly dead and were basically ignored by the public and the courts. This attitude, "out of sight, out of mind," ensured that prisoners who were subjected to cruel and inhumane treatment and conditions had nowhere to turn for help. Written pleas were intercepted by guards, who read outgoing inmate mail, and often ended up in the garbage. Those petitions that did get through to the courts were routinely dismissed. Most judges felt they had neither the power nor the obligation to provide relief to prisoners. The result was that prison officials were allowed to do virtually as they pleased, answering to no one. The consequences of this indifference to the treatment of inmates were disastrous. In many American prisons, inmates suffered in squalid, deplorable conditions, enduring inhumane treatment, even torture. (See *Holt v. Sarver* [1970], where the district court ruled the entire Arkansas prison system violated the Eighth Amendment's ban on cruel and unusual punishment.)[11]

Hands-On Era

Society's changing attitudes regarding punishment and rehabilitation, and the civil rights movement, led to the demise of the hands-off era, which had prevailed between 1776 and 1961.[12] The hands-on, or activist, approach grew strong in the 1960s with the federal courts' recognition that prisoners were indeed persons, and thus entitled to basic constitutional rights. However, social change rarely occurs overnight. Earlier events had paved the way for the hands-on era, including the Supreme Court's ruling in *Ex parte Hull* (1941), which held that state officials may not interfere with a prisoner's right to petition for a writ of habeas corpus, and *Coffin v. Reichard* (1944), where the Sixth Circuit Court of Appeals extended habeas corpus hearings to consider conditions of confinement.[13] Unfortunately, these early decisions were not widely followed. Large-scale prison reform would have to wait until society was ready to demand it. The turbulent 1960s and the increasing militancy of the disenfranchised caught the courts' attention, ushering in the era of prisoners' rights.

During this period of judicial activism, inmates challenged virtually every aspect of corrections. Inmates did not win all of the lawsuits they filed, but the ones they did win changed corrections enormously. Specific constitutional rights were enumerated, requirements of due process were clarified, censorship was limited, conditions of confinement were addressed, appropriate sanctions and restrictions were defined by the courts, and legal liabilities were denoted. Epitomizing the movement, Supreme Court Justice Thurgood Marshall declared in *Wolff v. McDonnell* (1974) that "A prisoner does not shed his basic constitutional rights at the prison gate."[14] Justice Marshall made it clear that no matter how despicable their crimes, prisoners do have rights that are protected by the United States Constitution.

Due Deference

By the end of the 1980s, the federal courts had again shifted their attitude toward prisoners. They had become less sympathetic to their complaints and less willing to grant prisoners' petitions. Silverman notes several reasons for this trend: Prison populations had grown tremendously, jurisdictions had limited financial resources to deal with the population growth, public attitudes had become tougher toward criminals, the makeup of the Supreme Court changed as liberal justices retired and were replaced by more conservative justices, and correctional practices overall had improved.[15]

Foreshadowing the shift, the Supreme Court ruled in *Meachum v. Fano* (1976) that "Given a valid conviction, the criminal defendant has been constitutionally deprived of his liberty to the extent that the state may confine him and subject him to the rules of its prison system so long as the conditions of confinement do not otherwise violate the constitution."[16] The Supreme Court further indicated its reluctance to expand inmate rights in *Bell v. Wolfish* (1979), stating that "maintaining institutional security and preserving internal order are essential goals that may require limitation or retractions of the retained constitutional rights of both convicted prisoners and pretrial detainees."[17]

By 1987, the attitude of the highest court was clear. In *Turner v. Safley*, the Court stated it would not intervene in prison operations so long as there was a "'valid, rational connection between the prison regulation and the legitimate governmental interest put forward to justify it."[18] Subsequent Supreme Court decisions have cemented this position that the lower courts should defer to the judgment of prison officials except in the most obvious situations of deliberate indifference to constitutional violations.

Another factor in the shifting attitudes of the judiciary toward prisoners' rights was the existence of frivolous lawsuits. Schmalleger and Smykla define frivolous lawsuits in this way: "Lawsuits with no foundation in fact. They are generally brought for publicity, politics, or other reasons not related to the law."[19] The perceived flood of frivolous lawsuits, combined with the get-tough attitude of the 1980s, led many judges to reexamine their positions regarding inmate lawsuits.

RELEVANT AMENDMENTS IN CORRECTIONAL LAW

The First Amendment

While the courts have ruled that prison security frequently outweighs the individual rights of prisoners, they have acknowledged several First Amendment rights that prisoners retain. First Amendment issues involve the censorship of mail, freedom of speech and expression, freedom of association, and freedom of religion.

Censorship of Mail

Censorship of mail has been the focus of much prisoner litigation. The federal courts have addressed this issue primarily because restrictions also affect nonincarcerated individuals. The Supreme Court held in *Procunier v. Martinez* (1974) that "censorship of prison mail works a consequential restriction on the First and Fourteenth Amendment rights of those who are not prisoners."[20] Because of this collateral effect on nonincarcerated persons, restrictions "must further an important governmental interest unrelated to the suppression of expression."[21] Thus, prison officials may not simply censor mail because what is written is unflattering or untrue. To censor an inmate's incoming or outgoing mail, that mail must threaten security, internal order, or an inmate's rehabilitation. Restrictions cannot be overly broad. The result of this decision was a major increase in the amount of contact prisoners had with the outside world. In *Pell v. Procunier* (1974) inmates challenged prison rules that prohibited them from conducting interviews with the press. The *Pell* decision changed the standard set in *Martinez* (proving a substantive government interest was at risk) to the less stringent reasonable relationship test. That is, if a restriction is reasonably related to a legitimate correctional goal, it does not violate the constitution.[22] This decision reinforced prisoners' right to personal expression but also gave prison officials a major role in determining when the interests of the prison were at risk.

In 1987, the Supreme Court decided *Turner v. Safley*, upholding a ban on inmate-to-inmate correspondence. In this decision, the high court explained how a lower court could determine if the complained of rule was reasonable. The court must look for a valid, rational connection between the rule and a legitimate government interest; the court must ask if the right should be protected for some other reason than claimed by the inmate; the court should ask what impact protecting the right might have on the prison; and the court should ask if there are any alternatives to restricting the constitutional right in question.[23] The *Turner* decision, like *Pell*, reminded prison administrators that inmates do have certain First Amendment rights. At the same time, the court further explained how and why prison officials could place limits on those rights.

In *Thornburgh v. Abbott* (1989) the Supreme Court overruled *Procunier v. Martinez*, officially replacing the substantive government interest test with the reasonable relationship test. This case addressed conditions under which mailed publications may be rejected by the warden. It held that a magazine or other published material may be seized if it contains procedures for making bombs or other incendiary devices, if it is related to escape, if it gives instructions on brewing alcoholic beverages, if it is written in code, if it describes or encourages physical violence, if it instructs in criminal behavior, or if it is sexually explicit and by its nature threatens security, order, and discipline.[24] The Court felt that overruling *Martinez* was necessary because some lower courts were still using the *Martinez* standard instead of the lower reasonable relationship test first mentioned in *Pell*.

Freedom of Speech and Assembly

The courts have been reluctant to extend first amendment protection to prisoners' freedom of speech or right to assemble. In *Roberts v. Pepersack* (1966) a lower court approved the punishment of a prisoner who circulated materials urging fellow inmates to protest against the prison administration for maltreatment. The court stated that "In a prison environment where the inmate tends to be more volatile than on the streets, strong restraints and heavy penalties are in order."[25] In *Jones v. North Carolina Prisoners' Labor Union* (1977), the Supreme Court upheld prison regulations restricting inmates from soliciting other inmates to join their union and prohibited union meetings, as well as outside mailings to the union. The Court stated that First Amendment rights "must give way to the reasonable considerations of penal management" and "may be curtailed whenever the institutional officials believe that such associations are likely to disrupt order and stability. It is enough to say they have not been conclusively shown to be wrong."[26] So, to win a freedom to assemble lawsuit, an inmate must prove conclusively that the prison administration is wrong in fearing that the assembly might disrupt institutional order and stability.

Freedom of Association

According to Branham and Krantz, the constitutionally protected freedom of association is narrowly defined in the prison context.[27] Two questions must be addressed regarding inmates' freedom of association: (1) Do prisoners have any constitutional right of association? and (2) If yes, to what extent can the prison restrict those rights? Several court decisions are enlightening. In *Rowland v. Wolff* (1971) a prison's decision to deny visitation of relatives, based on an informant's tip regarding smuggled contraband, was upheld.[28] The District Court in Georgia ruled in *Polakoff v. Henderson* (1973) that prisoners have no constitutional right to conjugal visits,[29] and in *Block v. Rutherford* (1984), the Supreme Court held that the "Constitution does not require that detainees be allowed contact visits when responsible, experienced administrators have determined, in their sound discretion, that such visits will jeopardize the security of the facility."[30] Clearly, the courts have deferred to the judgment of prison officials in this area. However, they have also emphasized that restricting inmates' freedom of association based on legitimate institutional needs does not deny the right but merely its expression.

Freedom of Religion

Freedom of religion in prison has been extensively litigated. Early petitions were filed by Black Muslims who challenged prison administrators' restrictions on their worship. In *Fulwood v. Clemmer* (1962) the federal court of appeals for the District of Columbia ordered prison officials to recognize the Muslim religion and to allow members of that faith to hold services.[31] The Supreme Court ruled in *Cruz v. Beto* (1972) that Buddhists must be given a reasonable opportunity to practice their faith. Specifically, the Court held that "If Cruz was a Buddhist and if he was denied a reasonable opportunity of pursuing his faith comparable to the opportunity afforded fellow prisoners who adhere to conventional religious precepts, then there was palpable discrimination by the State."[32] In 1975, the U.S. Court of Appeals for the Second Circuit held in *Kahane v. Carlson* that an orthodox Jewish inmate has the right to a diet consistent with his religious beliefs unless the government can show cause why it cannot be provided.[33]

The Supreme Court revisited the scope of an inmate's right to practice his or her religion in *O'Lone v. Estate of Shabazz* in 1987. The Court held that not allowing Muslim inmates to stop working on Friday afternoons and hold worship services was constitutional because of the burden it would place on security staff. The Court held that the restrictions placed on Muslim inmates were reasonably related to legitimate prison concerns and stated that it would not substitute its judgment for that of prison officials regarding difficult and sensitive matters related to the running of a prison.[34] Interestingly, in 1993, Congress passed the Religious Freedom Restoration Act, concerned about restrictions on the free exercise of religion. Bartollas (2002) notes that prison administrators' requests to exclude prisoners from coverage were rejected. This Act changed the standard imposed by the Supreme Court from reasonable relationship to compelling state interest. That means that prison officials may not restrict inmates' exercise of religious freedom unless they can show the restriction is necessary to achieve a compelling government interest. This is a much tougher test.

The Fourth Amendment

The Fourth Amendment prohibits unreasonable searches and seizures. While many cases have been filed, the courts have consistently held that this protection does not extend to prisoners. In *Moore v. People* (1970), the court held that searches conducted by prison officials were not unreasonable as long as they were not conducted for the purpose of harassing or humiliating prisoners.[35] *U.S. v. Hitchcock* (1972) added that evidence found in the search of a prison cell could be used in court, since it was not reasonable to expect the same level of privacy in a prison cell as in a home or automobile.[36] In *Bell v. Wolfish* (1979), the court stated that "shakedowns" (unannounced cell searches) were a necessary component of institutional security and inmate and staff safety. In addition, the *Bell* court held that strip searches, including body cavity searches after contact visits, were allowable when the institution's need for such searches could be established.[37] *Hudson v. Palmer* (1984) upheld the right of officials to search cells and confiscate any materials found. The court ruled that "a prisoner has no reasonable expectation of privacy in his prison cell entitling him to the protection of the Fourth Amendment against unreasonable searches."[38] Also in 1984, the court held in *Block v. Rutherford* that prisoners had no right to be present while cell searches were conducted.[39]

Prisoners have also used the Fourth Amendment as a basis for challenging pat searches and body cavity searches. The courts have ruled that these searches may be conducted in the name of institutional security and order, but a balance must be struck between the inmates' privacy rights and the prisons' legitimate needs. In the case of female officers conducting pat-down searches on male inmates, the Ninth Circuit Court of Appeals held that "Routine pat down searches, which include the groin area, and which are otherwise justified by security needs, do not violate the Fourteenth Amendment because a correctional officer of the opposite gender conducts such a search."[40]

The Fifth Amendment

The Fifth Amendment relates to prisoners primarily when they are charged with crimes separate from the offense for which they are incarcerated. The ruling case is *Baxter v. Palmigiano* (1976) wherein the Supreme Court ruled that if inmates are required in prison disciplinary hearings to furnish testimony that might incriminate them in further criminal proceedings, they may not be forced to waive immunity.[41]

The Sixth Amendment

For prisoners, the Sixth Amendment is relevant to a speedy trial, although it is infrequently cited. The Sixth Amendment may be invoked by a prisoner who has pending charges in a forthcoming trial. Because a prisoner's ability to defend himself or herself may weaken over time, the courts have held that prison officials must make a "good faith effort" to bring the prisoner to trial.[42]

The Eighth Amendment

The Eighth Amendment prohibits the imposition of cruel and unusual punishment. Eighth Amendment cases have focused on conditions of confinement and the treatment of prisoners, as well as torturous executions. Major Eighth Amendment rulings have been handed down in the areas of overcrowding, solitary confinement, corporal punishment and physical abuse, excessive use of force, medical care, prison conditions, and inadequate nutrition. Cruel and unusual punishment has not been specifically defined. Rather, the courts have developed three principal tests to determine whether conditions or policies are unconstitutional. In *Lee v. Tahash* (1965) the court formed the "shock the conscience" test, which asks if the circumstances in question are of such a character as to shock the general conscience of society or violate fundamental fairness.[43] The second principle stems from the decision in *Weems v. United States* (1910), which declared that punishment could not be unnecessarily cruel.[44] The final test asks if the punishment exceeds legitimate penal aims.

Prison Conditions

In *Pugh v. Locke* (1976), the federal court used the "totality of conditions" as a standard by which to evaluate whether prison conditions in Alabama violated the Eighth Amendment.[45] Using this standard, the court ruled that while some aspects of prison life were acceptable, when all factors were combined, the totality of conditions did violate the prisoners' right to be free from cruel and unusual punishment. An Oklahoma court also applied the totality of conditions standard in *Battle v. Anderson* (1977), where inmates were sleeping in stairwells, garages, and libraries and not given access to bathroom facilities.[46] In *Wilson v. Seiter* (1991) the Supreme Court expounded on the totality of conditions test stating that some conditions may establish an Eighth Amendment violation "in combination" when each would not on its own, but "only when they have a mutually enforcing effect that produces the deprivation of a single, identifiable human need such as food, warmth, or exercise."[47] In addition, the Court held that prisoners must not only prove that prison conditions are objectively cruel and unusual, but also that they exist because of the deliberate indifference of officials. This is a difficult test, indeed.

Solitary Confinement

The courts have ruled that solitary confinement, per se, is not unconstitutional; however, the conditions in which inmates are held, and the length of time they spend in solitary confinement, may violate the Eighth Amendment. In *Fulwood v. Clemmer* (1962) the court ruled that prison officials must assess, on a case-by-case basis, the effect of solitary confinement on a prisoner's mental condition. *Wright v. McMann* (1972) held that inmates cannot be deprived of clothing needed for warmth in solitary confinement,[48] and *Hutto v. Finney* (1978) held that solitary confinement must be limited to 30 days.[49] Most courts recognize that isolation of some inmates is necessary to the orderly management of a prison but draw the line when conditions are barbarous, shocking, or disgusting.

Physical Abuse

Corporal punishment of inmates is now considered abuse and is prohibited by the Eighth Amendment. *Jackson v. Bishop* (1968) held that whipping constituted cruel and unusual punishment, and in 1971, a New York decision outlawed the use of corporal punishment to enforce prison discipline.[50] Carlson et al. (1999) note that the use of corporal punishment tends to fail the third test of cruel and unusual punishment, going beyond legitimate penal aims.[51]

While the use of force is legitimate in certain situations, excessive use of force in prison can have serious legal repercussions. In evaluating a prisoner's claim that his or her Eighth Amendment rights were violated, the courts will examine the intent of the officer(s). In *Whitley v. Albers* (1986) the Supreme Court ruled that only the "unnecessary and wanton infliction of pain" constitutes cruel and unusual punishment, and that to establish an Eighth Amendment violation, one must look at whether force was applied in good faith or "maliciously and sadistically for the purpose of causing harm."[52] The Supreme Court stated in *Hudson v. McMillan* (1992) that "when prison officials maliciously and sadistically use force to cause harm, contemporary standards of decency are always violated."[53]

Medical Care

Incarceration necessarily prohibits inmates from seeking outside medical care. They are dependent on the medical services available to them in prison; thus, there is a duty to provide such services. In 1966, in *Edwards v. Duncan,* the federal court held that the total and intentional denial of medical care to inmates violated the Eighth Amendment.[54] Six years later, *Newman v. Alabama* ruled that prisoners, as a class, do have a constitutional right to medical care.[55] The major case regarding inmates' health care, decided in 1976, remains controlling law. That case is *Estelle v. Gamble.*

Estelle v. Gamble (1976) established that inmates do have a constitutional right to adequate medical care in prison. The Supreme Court set the standard in *Gamble,* by which inmate claims should be evaluated. It held that deliberate indifference to serious medical needs of prisoners constitutes the unnecessary and wanton infliction of pain, thus violating the Constitution.[56] *Gamble* further held that mere medical malpractice did not violate the Eighth Amendment, nor did an inadvertent failure to provide medical care constitute the unnecessary and wanton infliction of pain.

Overcrowding

Inmates have filed many lawsuits claiming that overcrowding constitutes cruel and unusual punishment. The courts have held that overcrowding, by itself, does not violate the Eighth Amendment. It may aggravate a situation, contributing to an Eighth Amendment claim of totality of circumstances, but by itself, overcrowding is not enough to trigger constitutional protection. The major case in this area is *Rhodes v. Chapman* (1981). In *Rhodes*, the Supreme Court ruled that double celling and overcrowding do not constitute cruel and unusual punishment. To prove a constitutional violation, the inmate must show that the conditions involve the "wanton and unnecessary infliction of pain" and are "grossly disproportionate" to the severity of the crime warranting imprisonment.[57]

The Fourteenth Amendment

This amendment applies the Bill of Rights to the states. When prisoners use the Fourteenth Amendment to challenge their treatment in prison, it typically involves issues of due process or equal protection. Due process requires that laws and procedures be reasonable and applied with fairness and equity. Equal protection cases typically center on issues of race, gender, and the availability of services.

The major case regarding due process in prison is *Wolff v. McDonnell* (1974). In *Wolff*, the Supreme Court ruled that basic due process must occur when adverse decisions are made at disciplinary hearings. To meet the basic constitutional requirements, prisoners have a right to receive notice regarding the charges against them, to have a fair hearing, to confront witnesses, to receive sufficient time and assistance, if needed, in preparation for the hearing, and to receive a written statement of the findings of the hearing officer(s).[58] In *Baxter v. Palmigiano* (1976) the Supreme Court held that inmates have no right to counsel in a disciplinary hearing.[59] *Vitek v. Jones* (1980) dealt with the involuntary transfer of an inmate from prison to a mental hospital. The Supreme Court ruled that a hearing and other minimal elements of due process, such as notice and the availability of counsel, were required because in being transferred to a mental institution, the inmate faced a significant deprivation of liberty.[60] In *Sandin v. Conner* (1995), a transfer to disciplinary segregation was held not to trigger the due process protections outlined in *Wolff* because it was not an atypical or significant deprivation of liberty.[61]

In *Washington v. Lee* (1966) the federal court held that the Equal Protection Clause of the Fourteenth Amendment was violated by statutorily imposed racial segregation because there was no compelling state interest in the segregation.[62] In 1968, the Supreme Court reaffirmed the lower court's ruling, when it stated in *Lee v. Washington* that segregation is only justified in temporary situations where violence between the races is imminent.[63]

In *Glover v. Johnson* (1979) female inmates filed a class action suit, claiming they were denied educational and vocational opportunities that were available to male prisoners. The court ruled that an equal protection violation had occurred when female prisoners were offered fewer and lesser quality programs than male inmates.[64] However, in *Pargo v. Elliott* (1995), the Eighth Circuit ruled that because of differences and needs, identical treatment is not required by the Fourteenth Amendment. The court stated that there was no evidence of "invidious discrimination"; therefore, no constitutional violation had occurred.[65] Nonetheless, female prisoners have won the majority of cases seeking equal treatment.

CONCLUSION

The prisoners' rights revolution began in the turbulent 1960s when federal courts redefined their proper role and the scope of their duties regarding prison conditions and the treatment of inmates. As inmate petitions flooded American courts, judges became aware of the broad range of issues they would address. At the beginning of the twenty-first century, the situation regarding prisoners' rights is this: Enormous changes have been made, but state and federal courts seem reluctant to address remaining problems. Atrocious violations of constitutional rights have been exposed and remedied, yet many problems remain. Two-thirds of the state prison systems are currently operating under consent decrees covering a diverse range of issues, including prison conditions, officer training, food services, disciplinary proceedings, recreational opportunities, fire safety, and mental health care.

Obvious improvements have been made in institutional living conditions and administrative practices. Religious freedoms are protected, due process procedures are followed in disciplinary hearings, communication with the outside is easier, and law libraries and legal assistance are available to prisoners. Despite the improvements, several threats loom in the future. Overcrowding continues to exacerbate other problems in prison; HIV/AIDS will cost correctional agencies enormous amounts of money as prisoners get sick and require care. Aging inmates will need special assistance, special diets, and modified living conditions. All of these areas are ripe for prison litigation.

NOTES

1. *Ruffin v. Commonwealth*, 62 VA.790 at 796 (1871).
2. Mays, G. Larry, and L. Thomas Winfree. 2002. *Contemporary Corrections*, 2nd ed. Belmont, CA: Wadsworth.
3. Palmer, John W., and Stephen E. Palmer. 1999. *Constitutional Rights of Prisoners*, 6th ed. Cincinnati: Anderson.
4. Branham, Lynn S., and Sheldon Krantz. 1997. *The Law of Sentencing, Corrections, and Prisoners' Rights*, 5th ed. St. Paul: West.
5. *Ruiz v. Estelle*, 503 F. Supp.1265 (S.D. Tex, 1980).
6. Branham and Krantz, 285.
7. Bartollas, Clemens. 2002. *Invitation to Corrections*. Boston: Allyn and Bacon.
8. Scheb, John M., and John M. Scheb II. 1999. *Criminal Law,* 2nd ed. Belmont, CA: Wadsworth.
9. *Cooper v. Pate,* 378 U.S. 546 (1964).
10. Hawkins, R., and G. P. Alpert. 1989. *American Prison Systems: Punishment and Justice*, Englewood Cliffs, NJ: Prentice Hall.
11. *Holt v. Sarver,* 309 F. Supp. 362 (E.D. Ark 1970).
12. Silverman, Ira J. 2001. *Corrections: A Comprehensive View,* 2nd ed. Belmont, CA: Wadsworth.

13. Schmalleger, Frank, and John Ortiz Smykla. 2001. *Corrections in the 21st Century*, New York: Glencoe McGraw-Hill.
14. *Wolff v Mc Donnell*, 418 U.S. 539 (1974).
15. Silverman, Ira J., p. 332.
16. *Meachum v. Fano*, 427 U.S. 215 (1976).
17. *Bell v. Wolfish*, 441 U.S. 520 (1979).
18. *Turner v. Safley*, 482 U.S. 78 (1987).
19. Schmalleger and Smykla, p. 295.
20. *Procunier v. Martinez*, 416 U.S. 396 (1974).
21. Ibid.
22. *Pell v. Procunier*, 417 U.S. 817 (1974).
23. *Turner v. Safley*, 482 U.S. 78 (1987).
24. *Thornburgh v. Abbott*, 490 U.S. 401 (1989).
25. *Roberts v. Pepersack*, 256 F. Supp. 415, M.D. (1966).
26. *Jones v. North Carolina Prisoner's Labor Union*, 433 U.S. 119 (1977).
27. Branham and Krantz, p. 319.
28. *Rowland v. Wolff*, 336 F. Supp. 257, D.C. Neb. (1971).
29. *Polakoff v. Henderson*, 370 F. Supp. 690, D.C. GA. (1973).
30. *Block v. Rutherford*, 468 U.S. 576 (1984).
31. *Fulwood v. Clemmer*, 206 F. Supp. 370, D.D.C. (1962).
32. *Cruz v. Beto*, 405 U.S. 319 (1972).
33. *Kahane v. Carlson*, 527 F. 2d 492, 2nd Cir. (1975).
34. *O'Lone v. Estate of Shabazz*, 482 U.S. 342 (1987).
35. *Moore v. People*, 171 Colorado 338, 467P.2d. (1970).
36. *United States v. Hitchcock*, 467 F.2d 1107, 9th Cir. (1972).
37. *Bell v. Wolfish*, 441 U.S. 520 (1979).
38. *Hudson v. Palmer*, 486 U.S. 517 (1984).
39. *Block v. Rutherford*, 486 U.S. 576 (1984).
40. *Grummett v Rushen*, 779 F.2d 491, 9th Cir. (1985).
41. *Baxter v. Palmigiano*, 425 U.S. 328 (1976).
42. *Smith v. Hooey*, 393 U.S. 374 (1969).
43. *Lee v. Tahash*, 352 F. 2d 970, 8th Cir. (1965).
44. *Weems v. United States*, 217 U.S. 349 (1910).
45. *Pugh v. Locke*, 406 F. Supp. 318, M.D. Ala. (1976).
46. *Battle v. Anderson*, 564 F.2d 388, 10th Cir. (1977).
47. *Wilson v. Seiter*, 501 U.S. 294 (1991).
48. *Wright v. McMann*, 460 F.2d 126, 2nd Cir. (1972).
49. *Hutto v. Finney*, 437 U.S. 678 (1978).
50. *Inmates of Attica Correctional Facility v. Rockefeller*, 453 F.2d 12, 2nd Cir. (1971).
51. Carlson, Norman A., Karen M. Hess, and Christine M. H. Othrmann. (1999) *Corrections in the 21st Century*. Belmont, CA: Wadsworth.
52. *Whitley v. Albers*, 475 U.S. 312 (1986).
53. Ibid.
54. *Edwards v. Duncan*, 355 F.2d 993, 4th Cir. (1966).
55. *Newman v. Alabama*, 349 F. Supp.278, D.C. Ala. (1972).
56. *Estelle v. Gamble*, 429 U.S. 97 (1976).
57. *Rhodes v. Chapman*, 452 U.S. 337 (1981).
58. *Wolff v. McDonnell*, 418 U.S. 539 (1974).
59. *Baxter v. Palmigiano*, 425 U.S. 308 (1976).
60. *Vitek v. Jones*, 445 U.S. 480 (1980).
61. *Sandin v. Conner*, 515 U.S. 472 (1995).
62. *Washington v. Lee*, 263 F. Supp. 27, D.C. Ala. (1996).
63. *Lee v. Washington*, 390 U.S. 333 (1968).
64. *Glover v. Johnson*, 478 F. Supp. 1075, D.C. Mich. (1979).
65. *Pargo v. Elliott*, 69 F.3d 280, 8th Cir. (1995).

An Alternative to Incarceration: Contemporary Use of Shaming Penalties in the United States

Kathleen M. Simon & Ruth Ann Strickland

BRIEF HISTORICAL BACKGROUND OF SHAMING IN THE UNITED STATES

Early in American colonial history, bizarre, humiliating shame sentences were imposed on criminal offenders. For example, in Williamsburg, Virginia, thieves were nailed by the ear to the pillory with the amount of time they were nailed calibrated to the seriousness of the offense and then the offender was torn from the pillory without first taking out the nail. This literally earmarked the offender for life (Book, 1999). Communities during this period were close knit, and shaming penalties made criminals well known to law-abiding citizens. Shaming also led to public disgrace and shunning. These factors enhanced the effectiveness of shame penalties. Shaming sentences varied according to the severity of the crime including public admonishments, public apologies, confessions, wearing signs, branding, public corporal punishment, and maiming (Blomberg & Lucken, 2000).

Shame sentences eventually fell out of favor in the mid–nineteenth century as Americans moved westward and began to view prisons and jails as a more effective means of punishment. The influx of immigrants and the Industrial Revolution broke up some of the close-knit communities. With the rise of urbanization, relationships between and among neighbors were more impersonal. In addition, shaming penalties declined in popularity because the people began to believe that they were not as effective when the offender was unknown to all community residents. Many Americans also desired a more humane approach to punishment, and by the mid-1800s, imprisonment became the leading form of punishment (Sanders, 1998, pp. 362–363). Yet shaming is still incorporated in the American justice system in that criminal proceedings are public and the mass media may take an interest in them, exposing the accused to possible humiliation and embarrassment not only in their community but nationwide.

Beginning in the mid-1970s, judges in the United States once again started incorporating shame into their sentences. For instance, in *People v. McDowell,* 130 Cal. Rptr. 839,

843 (Ct. App., 1976), a trial court imposed a shame sentence that required a convicted purse snatcher to wear taps on his shoes as part of his probation. Judges, increasingly frustrated with the traditional forms of punishment, are turning to shame sentences more frequently. Although many are reversed on appeal, including the one used in *People v. McDowell,* shaming in judicial sentences persists into the present and is used in all regions of the United States (Book, 1999).

Shaming has returned in part due to concerns expressed by cultural critics such as Christopher Lasch. In *The Revolt of the Elites and the Betrayal of Democracy,* Lasch argued that American society no longer was able to use shame as a method of enforcing shared social norms or legal boundaries. He contended In *The Culture of Narcissism* that failure to use shame would result in a society with no boundaries and no individual responsibility. The return of shaming penalties is attributed also to ordinary law-abiding citizens' frustration with the shamelessness of modern criminals. Shame punishments do not allow offenders to go to prison anonymously and escape public denunciation. Lawrence Friedman, in the Ray Rushton Distinguished Lecture Series, although no advocate of shaming sentences, remarked that the use of "get tough" measures historically have not worked (1997, 921). Shame sentences may serve as a practical alternative to incarceration in a time of overcrowded prisons and jails.

Others agree that get-tough measures are not working, particularly the advocates of restorative justice and reintegrative shaming (Braithwaite, 1989; Braithwaite & Roche, 2001, pp. 63–79). With the rise of the victims' rights movement, new models are used to explain the criminal process. One new model based on victims' rights—the nonpunitive model of victims' rights—emphasizes restorative justice and advocates alternatives to a punitive approach (Presser & Gaarder, 2000). The principle of restorative justice stresses that punishment alone is not the key to changing criminal or abhorrent behavior. Direct involvement of victims and the community is central to the process of resolving a crime (Wakimoto, 1999). Alternative strategies, such as apologies, shaming, and informal restitution, are embraced by this model's advocates. This outlook on the criminal process may, in part, explain the revival of interest in shaming sentences (Roach, 1999).

SHAMING PENALTIES: DEFINITIONS

Three bodies of literature on punishment may shed light on the use of shaming. Expressive theories of punishment view penalties as a means to unequivocally stigmatize certain behaviors. Moral educative theories of punishment see punishments as a means of setting and maintaining boundaries of acceptable behavior. Finally, reintegrative shaming stresses that although society should express its disapproval when social norms are violated, it should also demonstrate concern for the individual's well-being. This approach views degradation as alienating and asserts that it leads to even more antisocial behavior (Tonry, 1999, pp. 1764–1767).

Shaming penalties may be retributive and expressive—allowing society to vent its moral outrage by shedding light on an offender's unacceptable behavior. This type of shaming sentence can turn to degradation and go beyond simple embarrassment. Shaming may also be used for its perceived deterrent effects. If a behavior is disgraced in a particularly public and humiliating fashion, advocates of shaming believe it will deter others from engaging in like behavior. Finally, shaming may be employed for rehabilitative and reintegrative purposes—to express disapproval but also help the individual become a more cooperative, social being in the community (Hubacher, 1998, pp. 555–556).

Today, shaming penalties take many forms. Kahan (1996, pp. 633–635) identified four forms: stigmatizing publicity, literal stigmatization, self-debasement, and contrition. A fifth type—reintegrative shaming—is discussed by John Braithwaite.

The first and most common type of shame penalty is stigmatizing publicity. Stigmatizing publicity employs a variety of techniques such as publishing offenders' names in newspapers, pasting their names on billboards or broadcasting their names on community access television. Many municipalities and judges use this form of shaming.

Another form of shaming—literal stigmatization—subjects the offender to ridicule. Judges may require offenders to wear T-shirts declaring their status as a convicted burglar. Or, others may require drunk drivers to wear bracelets that boldly designate that they are DUI convicts. Other less dramatic uses may require display of bumper stickers or posting of signs at residences to warn others of their criminal proclivities. One judge in Florida said that as a result of the bumper sticker penalty, drunk driving in his county dropped by one-third (Massaro, 1991, p. 1887). Literal stigmatization is the scarlet letter sentence employed earlier in American history but recycled for modern use.

Self-debasement involves use of shaming to publicly disgrace an offender. Some sentences require offenders to stand in public places, such as courthouses, with signs announcing their offenses—forcing them to face public ridicule and derision. More creative use of shaming as self-debasement occurred in New York, where a slumlord was sentenced to house arrest in one of his dilapidated tenements where tenants greeted him with a banner that read "Welcome, you Reptile!"

A combination of literal stigmatization and self-debasement occurs with sex offender registration requirements employed by numerous states. Although this measure is aimed at protecting the community, it may stigmatize and debase sex offenders, who are required to reveal their offense to the community or county of residence. In some communities, Web pages exist that allow citizens to search and find sex offenders who reside in their county.

Contrition is based on apology and forgiveness and follows in part the reintegrative model of shame sentencing. As part of restorative justice and a shaming ceremony, some communities require public apologies and use community-based sanctions to ensure victim restitution. Various offenders have been ordered to run apology advertisements, announcing their conviction and apologizing to the community. In Tennessee, a judge ordered a defendant who helped steal a vehicle to confess before a church congregation (Massaro, 1991, pp. 1888). In Maryland, offenders were required to apologize on their hands and knees for their crimes (Schuler, 1995). Such apologies may not necessarily mesh with reintegrative shaming and may result in self-debasement. Apology rituals are used more frequently in cases in which the offender has a family connection to the victim or close community ties.

In contrast to stigmatizing shaming strategies, Braithwaite focuses on reintegrative shaming. Reintegrative shaming expresses disapproval of a person's bad deeds but still recognizes the good qualities of an individual. Braithwaite's theory of reintegrative shaming—as opposed to disintegrative or stigmatizing shaming—rests on holding offenders accountable for their harmful behavior but also on forgiveness and acceptance back into their families and communities. Stigmatization alone does not encourage forgiveness or reintegration (Bennett, 1996, p. 4). Braithwaite describes reintegrative shaming as shaming followed by reintegration efforts as the community forgives and allows the offender to reenter without feeling like an outcast (Braithwaite, 1989, pp. 100–101).

Braithwaite (2000) argues that societies can condemn the wrongdoing while still showing respect for the individual. He claims that societies that employ stigmatization or disrespectful shaming are prone to higher crime rates whereas societies that employ reintegrative shaming experience lower crime rates. He states also that a communitarian society, with a sense of interdependency and a strong family system, enhances the effectiveness of shaming ceremonies. Unemployment, family disintegration, and cultural diversity may weaken interdependency and also undermine the effective use of shaming (Braithwaite, 1989, p. 100).

ARGUMENTS FOR SHAMING SENTENCES

It Works in Certain Settings

While little data exist today to illustrate the effectiveness of shaming sentences in deterring crime or reducing recidivism, much data exist to illustrate the failure of traditional forms of sentencing. Research suggests that prison stays of more than two years are counterproductive, leading to dissolution of families and community ties and ultimately recidivism (Rottman & Casey, 2000; Viano, 2000). Many scholars believe that sentencing nonviolent offenders to prison is outmoded and only makes offenders more hardened and violent when they are released (Etzioni, 1999). Increasingly, Braithwaite's theory is used to explain crime rates and recidivism rates in a variety of cultural settings. Empirical evidence indicates some successes associated with shaming (Miethe et al., 2000; Morris & Maxwell, 2001; Morris & Young, 2000).

It Deters

One goal of shaming, according to advocates, is to change behavior and to deter others from engaging in similar offensive behavior. Judges across the United States use shame sentences to "send a message" of deterrence and to foster a belief that the justice system works. Many see it as rehabilitative and incorporate it into probation sentences. Since 1988, Judge Ted Poe in Houston, Texas developed a reputation for using shame sentences. Poe believes that public punishments can right wrongs and prevent recidivism through humiliation. He sentenced a man who committed perjury to carry a sign that read "I lied in court. Tell the truth or walk with me." He required teenagers who vandalized schools to return to school and apologize to all the students and explain their actions. Poe and many other advocates of shame sentences believe that these types of penalties force offenders to think carefully before committing future misdeeds. Furthermore, he believes it sends a message to the general public and discourages them from committing similar acts (McMurry, 1997, pp. 12–14).

John Braithwaite (1989) argues that the United States should never have separated shame and punishment. In his view, linking the two—shame and punishment—is essential to deterrence. Intense, visible shame provides the incentive to forgo antisocial behavior, and reintegrative shaming allows the repentant criminal to gain readmittance into society (Mokhiber, 1990).

It Encourages Reliance on Alternative Sentences

Dan Kahan and others believe that the return of shame sentences is an opportunity because such approaches can make alternative sentences more acceptable. He argues that shaming punishments are appropriate for crimes such as petty theft, driving under the influence, assault, perjury, burglary, embezzlement, toxic waste dumping, and drug distribution. He also believes that traditional alternative sentences, such as community service, are not shameful enough and do not adequately express the public's moral outrage (Schuler, 1995). Unlike Braithwaite, he advocates using the full spectrum of shaming penalties from reintegrative to disintegrative shaming.

It's Fiscally Sound

Book (1999) argues that if used appropriately, shame sentences could be an efficient, fiscally sound, and positive means to deter crime and reduce recidivism. Shaming is fiscally sound because it is cheaper than imprisonment. Unlike other alternatives to incarceration, shaming allows an expression of moral outrage. Although studies do not definitely suggest that shaming penalties deter crime, many believe that shaming should work due to the unpleasant consequences associated with shaming. According to Kahan (1996, pp. 639–640), shaming triggers certain psychological responses that augur its success, such as reinforcing the idea the lawbreaking is a disgrace and encouraging conformity with the law, marking the offender's misdeeds as contrary to community norms, and promoting confidence in the law that deviant behaviors will be condemned.

It Helps Offenders Avoid the Criminological Influences of Prison

Shaming avoids the afflictive elements of imprisonment. Many offenders who are incarcerated, especially first-time offenders, become hardened criminals—they learn by example. Prisons are a training ground for how to become a better criminal. Those who are imprisoned experience greater difficulty when trying to reintegrate into society. When given a choice, offenders typically select shaming over incarceration. Shaming can be supplemented with imprisonment or other penalties to allow for a flexible response to a variety of criminal acts. Adding shame to conventional punishment reduces society's overreliance on incarceration (Kahan, 1996, p. 642).

It Resonates

Enhancing society's ability to condemn deviant behaviors sets shaming apart from fines and community service. Even though all offenders may not experience shame when shaming penalties are imposed, shaming sentences still resonate with the public. Public opinion surveys suggest that the public is ready to endorse shaming sentences if they can be shown to work (Alter & Wingert, 1995, p. 46). Recent research suggests that shaming in conjunction with restorative justice is effective in reducing recidivism, particularly with juvenile offenders (Miethe et al., 2000; Morris & Maxwell, 2001; Morris & Young, 2000, p. 19). The public also supports restorative justice measures for nonviolent offenders (Cullen et al., 2000).

Anecdotal Evidence of Success Exists

Additionally, anecdotal evidence suggests some shaming successes. Judge Ted Poe of Texas, in an interview on *NBC Nightly News*, claimed that over a ten-year period of imposing shaming penalties, 69 of the 72 offenders he shamed did not return to his courtroom again—intimating that shaming reduces recidivism (Faw, 1998). Mississippi Judge John Whitfield claimed that after one year of using shaming sentences, the recidivism rate in his jurisdiction fell to 18 percent compared to a national average of 62 percent (Gurdon, 1998). In Anoka, Minnesota, reintegrative shaming used for juveniles and their parents appears to work, with only 7 of 300 youth becoming repeat offenders. After eighteen months of applying the principle of reintegrative shaming to those who solicit prostitutes, the city of Minneapolis, Minnesota has witnessed a decline in recidivism (Grant, 1999). Each john may choose a shaming session or traditional punishment. Those who choose shaming must confront a group of forty volunteers in the immediate community, who chide him for contributing to the poor quality of life in the community (Powell, 1998, p. 1A). Also, Kansas City, Missouri has used "John TV" to televise the names, dates of birth, and faces of those accused of prostitution-related crimes. After six months, arrest rates for solicitation dropped by one-third and prostitution arrest rates for women halved ("Kansas Puts Faces on Suspected 'Johns' on TV," 1997).

ARGUMENTS AGAINST SHAMING SENTENCES

It's Degrading:

Opponents of shaming, such as the American Civil Liberties Union, believe that the government should not involve itself in the process of degradation associated with shaming penalties. Civil libertarians fear the message sent by shaming sentences and argue that use of degradation in punishment may foster disrespect for the law and citizens toward one another. They further contend that humiliation and degradation do not result in rehabilitation and may produce more anger and resentment (*Harvard Law Review,* 1998, pp. 1972–1973). They view the Minneapolis shaming sessions as ineffective and argue that these practices threaten legal rights and constitute improper use of police power (Anderson & Giobbe, 1998, p. 15A). They protest "John TV" as violating the presumption of innocence standard ("Kansas Puts Faces on Suspected 'Johns' on TV," 1997).

It Fosters the Labeling Effect

In fact, shaming may produce more criminality through the labeling effect. Judges face the arduous task of predicting when shaming will work and determining when an offender is susceptible to shame. The typical risk analysis that occurs now in regard to sentencing an offender to incarceration does not apply to shaming penalties. R. Dean Wright, a sociology professor at Drake University, argues that shaming penalties only work in a few instances where criminals still care about what their community thinks of them—for instance, older, middle class shoplifters (Shatzkin, 1998, p. A20).

It May Be Too Retributive

According to opponents, shaming sentences are too retributive. They can result in self-destruction, with documented incidences of suicide linked to shame sentences. Shame may impose unwarranted hardships on the shamed offender, making reentry into society difficult if not impossible. Of course, Kahan and other supporters counter that all criminal sanctions impose a difficult risk calculus on judges—no one knows the emotional or psychological toll these sanctions may have. Critics of shaming penalties do not fault imprisonment sanctions on the grounds of proportionality.

It Does Not Work in Modern Cultures

Shaming tools, opponents argue, are less effective in modern cultures because for shaming to work a certain social intimacy must exist where criminal offenders are known by others in the community. In urban environments, the fear of community disgrace may be virtually nonexistent. Individuals are less knowledgeable about members of their community and therefore less able to inflict shame (Massaro, 1991, p. 1912). Modern American society may not be culturally conducive to shaming. Requirements for shaming include close-knit, smaller communities where members are interdependent and have the same moral and behavioral expectations. Shaming must involve individuals who are valued by the offender, and offenders must experience the fear of being abandoned. In the United States, personal autonomy, a "mind your own business" mentality, and moral relativism inhibit shaming. Transience has only heightened independence and contributes to a decline in social affiliations that allow for informal social control. Furthermore, the disintegration of the family unit takes away one more source of shared cultural shame values (Woods, 1997, p. 37).

It Expands the Net of Social Control

Restorative justice may inspire shaming without an emphasis on reintegration. Shaming, with its use of conditional sentences, could expand the net of social control. It could extend sentences for longer periods than would otherwise be sanctioned in actual prison terms. For some victims' rights and crime control advocates, an apology or show of contrition is simply not enough. For some civil libertarians, a tendency to denounce offenders for their misconduct is too tempting when shaming techniques are used, and for them, this undermines the principle of reintegration (Roach, 2000).

It's Too Soft

Some opponents of shaming believe that shaming penalties are the easy way out and should not be used in lieu of prison time. In 1998, Governor Don Sundquist of Tennessee vetoed legislation aimed at public shaming of DUI offenders—forcing them to pick up litter on the side of the road wearing an orange "I AM A DUI OFFENDER" vest. Sundquist justified his veto decision by arguing that the shaming penalty should be employed along with the jail time, not as an alternative to incarceration. Tennessee's 1982 DUI law mandates two days of jail time for first-time DUI offenders. The vetoed bill would have required offenders to pick up trash for six eight-hour sessions (or two days) while wearing the orange vests. The sponsors of the legislation believed the public embarrassment was worse than serving the jail time. Representatives of Mothers Against Drunk Drivers (MADD) concurred with Sundquist's veto and argued that drunk drivers were a menace to society and belonged in jail (Branson & Dries, 1998, p. A1).

Its Impact Will Decrease across Time

While shame penalties may appear novel at first and attract the appropriate amount of public denunciation of those crimes, eventually, if implemented broadly, shame sentences would expand and become commonplace. Opponents argue that the bombardment that would occur from the daily announcements of criminal acts might decrease the drama and the impact of shaming punishments. Eventually, the public might start ignoring this information and avoid it much like they use their remote television control to screen out annoying commercial advertisements. If shamings are well publicized but do not capture public attention, their possible deterrent effects are undermined (Massaro, 1991, pp. 1931–1932).

It's Cruel

Other opponents call shaming penalties cruel and dehumanizing. Government should set examples for others, and by incorporating debasement and degradation as punishment, the government sends the wrong message. In one case, a man convicted of domestic violence was ordered to let his spouse spit in his face. This type of punishment may create the impulse to demean people (Reske, 1996). They also fear it could lead to a form of lynch mob justice if proper restraint on how the public exercises its shaming authority is not used. It may appeal to the lowest, meanest common denominator of mass mentality and may be injurious to democracy (Whitman, 1998, p. 1090). Rehabilitation is less likely under these circumstances, especially if the offenders already do not cherish societal approval (Martinez, 1997, p. F1). Criminals, once shamed, may have no motive to change.

EXAMPLES OF HOW SHAME PENALTIES ARE EMPLOYED

The types of shame penalties employed in the United States vary but are concentrated in the areas of literal stigmatization and stigmatizing publicity, particularly in the South. Some are self-debasing and few rely solely on contrition. Most of these penalties are not based on the concept of restorative justice. The following vignettes illustrate the use of shaming penalties by individual judges. These judges either have employed shaming penalties more frequently than other judges or have used them in a particularly creative way, earning them prominent media coverage.

Judge Leon Braun

For over five years, Dougherty County, Georgia judges have employed literal stigmatizing shame penalties to straighten out first-time offenders. In September 2000, the lastest instance involved Daniel Alvin, convicted of eight counts of theft ("Jury Still Out on the Effectiveness of Public Shaming of Criminals," 2000). He stood before Judge Leon M. Braun, Jr. as a husband and father. His wife was pregnant and he had fathered eight-year-old, disabled twins. His crime was conning victims into paying for Atlanta Hawks basketball tickets and bus rides to the games when in fact these services were never delivered. Judge Braun offered a choice —spend six months in prison or five weekends in jail combined with walking around Fulton County Courthouse for thirty hours carrying a sign that announced "I AM A CONVICTED THIEF." Alvin chose the shame sentence. Although his service of the sentence carried a significant amount of embarrassment for his family and himself, he spent only a small amount of time in jail and he was able to avoid a family breakup (Woolner, 1997). The Superior Court Chief Judge Loring Gray, Jr. in this judicial district claims that the public humiliation sentences have been used in approximately a dozen cases and that they are applied primarily to thieves, burglars, and shoplifters as an alternative to sometimes harsh prison terms ("Jury Still Out on the Effectiveness of Public Shaming of Criminals," 2000).

Judge Ted Poe

Creative yet controversial, Judge Ted Poe, a state district court judge of Harris County, Texas, has employed a wide array of creative shame sentences. He ordered a father of 13 illegitimate children, who appeared before him on forgery charges, to attend Planned Parenthood meetings. He forced a drunk driver who killed two people in an automobile accident to hang a picture of his victims in his prison cell and to spend ten years there. A piano teacher, who molested two students, was ordered to not play the piano for 20 years and the piano was given to a school (Reske, 1996). Another drunk driver, convicted of manslaughter, was forced to speak to students about the dangers of drunk driving, carry a sign that advertised his crime, serve a prison term and go to boot camp, and erect a memorial at the accident's scene (Duin, 1998, p. A1). In another case, a man who abducted his own children was sentenced to six months in jail and 20 hours of shoveling horse manure (Sanders, 1998, p. 368).

Judge Thomas Brownfield

In Pittsfield, Illinois, a rural farm community, Judge Thomas Brownfield ordered a person convicted of aggravated battery to post a sign on his property that said "Warning: A Violent Felon Lives Here. Travel at Your Own Risk." The judge reasoned that a lengthy prison stay was too harsh for this defendant and gave him probation instead and a requirement to post this sign (Hoffman, 1997, p. A1; Massaro, 1997, p. 690). This probation condition was later reversed by the Illinois Supreme Court.

Judge L. Todd Burke

Rebecca Escobar of Wilkes County, North Carolina was driving while intoxicated and as a consequence, her automobile collided with another, killing Faye Schnablegger. Escobar was a first-time offender, but under North Carolina law, she was eligible to serve about one year in jail. After her conviction on the charge, Superior Court Judge L. Todd Burke crafted a sentence he hoped would "send a message." His split sentence required Escobar to spend ninety days in jail, relinquish her driver's license indefinitely, maintain the site where the cars crashed, and walk around the flagpole at Wilkes County Courthouse carrying a sign that states "I am a convicted drunk driver, and as a result I took a life." The judge believed this type of public sanction would have a greater impact on Escobar and would also give notice to the general public about the consequences of drunk driving (Rochman, 1999, p. A1).

More recently Judge Burke required a Greensboro, North Carolina man who was convicted of taking indecent liberties with a child to carry a sign that read "I am a twice-convicted sex offender" once a month for one hour outside of the courthouse. A 21- to 26-month sentence was suspended requiring Daniel Keith Talton, the convicted sex offender, to serve five years of intensive probation, to carry the sign, and to avoid contact with the victim or anyone under the age of eighteen who was not attended by an adult supervisor (Fuchs, 2001, p. B1).

Judge Janette Dunnigan

Circuit Judge Janette Dunnigan of Manatee County, Florida sentenced Reuben Nation to wear a sign that read "Convicted Sexual Offender" in front of his home. In addition to the sign condition, she sentenced Nation to 11 months and 29 days in jail to be followed by two years of community service and 13 years of probation. He was required to undergo electronic monitoring and complete a sex offender treatment program. Also, he was prohibited from living within 1000 feet of a school, day care center, or playground or any other places where one might find children. The prosecutor originally requested three to six years in prison in accordance with state sentencing guidelines but acceded to the judge's decision. Judge Dunnigan later claimed that she did not intend to shame or punish Nation with the sign requirement but merely wanted to warn the public of his predatory behavior (McMaster, 1997, p. 1B).

Judge Larry Schack

Circuit Judge Larry Schack of St. Lucie County, Florida imposed a stigmatizing publicity sentence on Kenneth Boatwright, who pleaded guilty to felony petty theft. Boatwright has 14 prior petty theft convictions. As part of a plea bargain, in addition to a nine-month jail sentence, Boatwright agreed to place an advertisement in a local newspaper one column wide and four inches long with his photograph and a statement that read, "I am a convicted thief." Schack has used a variety of shaming sentences, such as requiring defendants to wear T-shirts advertising their convictions, sex offenders to post signs on their front doors warning children to stay away, and public apologies of defendants to their victims (Maddox, 1996, p. A1; Nesmith, 1996, p. 1A).

Judge Nile Aubrey

In March 2000, Pierce County Judge Nile Aubrey of Tacoma, Washington ordered a seventeen-year-old convicted of theft to pay a fine, spend 90 days in jail, and wear a sign announcing "I am a car thief" for 16 months of supervised probation ("Public Humiliation Makes a Comeback" 2000). Whether the sentence will hold up on appeal or not does not seem to deter judges from employing public humiliation in their sentencing arsenals.

Judge Paul Lenz

For Dan Pannell, a former funeral home worker convicted of stealing money left as memorials, Judge Paul Lenz rendered a shame sentence. Pannell could reduce his jail time—a sentence of 100 days—by standing in front of the cemetery wearing a sign that read, "I stole from the families of the dead." By wearing the sign for eight hours a day for three days and agreeing to community service, Pannell could cut the sentence to 40 days in jail. Pannell's lawyer, however, indicated that his client was unlikely to take the judge up on the offer and simply wanted to put the incident behind him ("Thief Can Cut Jail Time by Wearing 'Stole From Dead' Sign at Cemetery," 2001).

Judge Robert Crawford

Since 1996, Circuit Judge Robert Crawford of Wisconsin has employed shaming penalties on a regular basis. From sandwich board marches to shaming speeches, Crawford regularly imposes shaming penalties (Doege, 1997, p. 1). His sentences lean toward self-debasing rituals. Crawford is not the only Wisconsin judge to incorporate shame into his sentencing. The idea of using shame for nonviolent offenders as an alternative to jail time was not limited to Judge Crawford. The County Board of Milwaukee in 1996 voted 14–11 to direct a group to study the possibility of developing and implementing shaming penalties for cost-saving and deterrence purposes. Opponents of these practices preferred jail, fines, or community service over humiliation (Doege, 1996, p. 4; Schuldt, 1996, p. 3). A survey of

Wisconsin's 234 circuit court judges on a variety of administration of justice issues revealed that 75 percent of them disapprove of shame penalties as a sanction alternative (Unmhoefer, 1997, p. 12).

Judge Shirley Strickland Saffold

In Cleveland, Ohio, Judge Shirley Strickland Saffold ordered an HIV-positive male hooker to go on TV and admit that he carried the HIV virus and had engaged in prostitution while infected. This sentence resembled *The John Hour* employed by Ed Koch, then mayor of New York, much earlier. *The John Hour* was used to embarrass men who were convicted of soliciting prostitutes and to deter other men from doing this (Kaplan, 1998, p. 75). "John TV" was also adopted in Kansas City, Missouri. Color photographs of men and some women appear with each name, birthdate, and place of residence and statements from those who were arrested for a prostitution-related offense (Walsh, 1997, p. 10A). Stigmatizing publicity episodes such as these are on the rise.

Judge Michael Cocconetti

Judge Michael Cocconetti of Painesville, Ohio has issued shame penalties using both literal stigmatization and contrition. Three men who tossed rocks from a railroad bridge at a passing driver had to hold a three-foot-by-ten-foot banner for five hours on Christmas Eve that read, "We threw rocks from a Rte. 2 bridge. WE'RE SORRY." They had also to pay for the $150 sign. They pled no contest to placing injurious objects on a roadway. Two men who caused a public disturbance were ordered to apologize in a local newspaper ad. A wallet thief was ordered to hang posters apologizing to any victim who wanted an apology (Martin, 1999, p. 1A). Some local residents rejected these shame penalties, believing jail time was more appropriate ("Judges Mete Out Punishments That Don't Fit the Crimes," 2000, p. 6B).

Everyone Gets Into the Act

Not only are judges imposing shame penalties, but sheriffs as well may get into the act. Mecklenburg County sheriff Jim Pendergraph's office will begin posting on an Internet site the names of everyone wanted in hopes of shaming them into turning themselves in ("Mecklenburg Sheriff to Post Wanted's Names on Internet," 2000). Also, a South Dakota legislative study committee—the interim Judiciary Committee of the Legislative Research Council—passed a resolution recommending to the chief justice of the state Supreme Court that people ordered to do community service, such as work crews, wear distinctive clothing. All but one of the eight committee members approved the proposal and thought that shaming and guilt were appropriate to achieve deterrence. Concerns regarding the labeling of primarily youthful offenders were dismissed as "coddling" ("Legislative Committee Supports Outfits to Embarrass Offenders," 1998).

The lieutenant governor of Alabama proposed a law in 1997 that would use public shaming against drunk drivers. The law would require repeat DUI offenders to have the letters DUI prominently displayed on their vehicle license plates (Owens, 1997, p. A7). Similarly, the Texas legislature examined a law that would mandate distinctive license plates for

DWI offenders (Woods, 1997, p. 37). In Dallas, Texas, shoplifters are ordered to stand outside department stores with signs that advertise their crimes. In Boston, Massachusetts, men who are found soliciting prostitutes are forced to clean the streets (Gahr, 1997, p. 38).

GUIDELINES FOR EMPLOYING SHAME PENALTIES

It appears that shame sentences have made a comeback. Various governmental and nongovernmental agents use shame as a way to fight crime. Since shaming sentences and techniques are in use and will be in use despite heavy criticism, it is more pragmatic to suggest ways to employ shame penalties that will yield the best results.

Aaron Book suggests that shame penalties generally should be used only for nonviolent offenders. Shame, if imposed on angry individuals, could result in a destructive shamerage spiral (1999, p. 684). Others recommend that judges should use shaming selectively, carefully evaluating whether an offender and society are best served by a shame sentence, incarceration, or some other alternative. Much like the risks of incarcerating an offender for too little time or for too long, shaming penalties also carry risks. Some offenders are immune to shaming, and the threat of public rebuke carries no significance (Sanders, 1998). Consequently, judges have to make individualized decisions. Across-the-board imposition of shame penalties could be as destructive as across-the-board imposition of prison sentences.

Generally, shaming should be optional; allow the defendant to choose between a shame penalty or a traditional punishment. Shame sentences should be offered as an alternative to traditional penalties, and acceptance should be voluntary. More effective usage of shaming seeks to reintegrate the offender into society. Combining shame penalties with community service ensures that the offender gives something back to the community and that others in the community are aware of the possible consequences of committing similar misdeeds. Under these general guidelines, shaming may work.

REFERENCES

Alter, Jonathan, & Wingert, Pat. (1995). The Return of Shame. *Newsweek* (6 February):21, 24.

Allen, Scott. (1999). Pollution Down So Should the Laws Go? *The Boston Globe* (13 September), p. C1.

Anderson, Marna, & Giobbe, Evelina. (1998). Shaming Tactics Erode Rights, Won't Do Much to Deter Crime. *Star Tribune* (4 July), p. 15A.

Bennett, Katherine Jean. (1996). *A Family Model of Shaming and Delinquency: A Partial Test of Braithwaite's Reintegrative Shaming Theory*. Dissertation, Doctor of Philosophy (Criminal Justice), December. Sam Houston State University, Huntsville, TX, 179 pp.

Blomberg, Thomas G., & Lucken, Karol. (2000). *American Penology: A History of Control*. New York: Aldine de Gruyter.

Book, Aaron S. (1999). Note: Shame on You: An Analysis of Modern Shame Punishment as an Alternative to Incarceration. *William and Mary Law Review* 40:653. *http:web.lexis-nexis.com/*

Braithwaite, John. (1989). *Crime, Shame and Reintegration*. Cambridge: Cambridge University Press.

Braithwaite, John. (2000). Shame and Criminal Justice. *Canadian Journal of Criminology* 42(July):281–298.

Braithwaite, John, & Roche, Declan. (2001). Responsibility and Restorative Justice. In Gordon Bazemore and Mara Schiff (eds.), *Restorative Justice Community: Repairing Harm and Transforming Communities*, (pp. 63–84). Cincinnati, OH: Anderson Publishing Co.

Branson, Reed, & Dries, Bill. (1998). Sundquist Vetoes DUI Trash Duty to Shame Offenders. *The Commercial Appeal* (24 April), p. A1.

Cullen, Francis T., Fisher, Bonnie S., & Applegate, Brandon K. (2000). Public Opinion about Punishment and Corrections. *Crime and Justice*, 27:1–67.

Doege, David. (1996). Experts Question Shaming Penalties. *Milwaukee Journal Sentinel* (21 December), p. 4.

Deoge, David. (1997). Shaming Sentences Group Is Diverse; Crawford Admits He's Made Some Mistakes But He'll Continue to Practice. *Milwaukee Journal Sentinel* (6 April), p. 1.

Duin, Julia. (1998). Perpetrators Sentenced to Humiliation in Texas: Judge Orders '90s Version of Scarlet Letter. *Washington Times* (5 September), p. A1.

Etzioni, Amitai. (1999). Back to the Pillory? *The American Scholar* 68(Summer):43–50.

Faw, Bob. [reporting] (1998). New Trend across Country of Publicly Shaming or Humiliating Criminals as Punishment for Their Crimes. *NBC Nightly News* 6:30 P.M. ET (3 December).

Friedman, Lawrence M. (1997). Dead Hands: Past and Present in Criminal Justice Policy. *Cumberland Law Review* 27:903–926.

Fuchs, Mike. (2001). Sex Offender Will Wear Sign Stating Crime; Legal Experts Call It 'Shaming' Punishment. *Greensboro News & Record* (26 April), p. B1.

Gahr, Evan. (1997). Can Shame Tame Cons? *Insight on the News* (31 March), p. 38.

Grant, Ashley H. (1999). Minneapolis Police Return the Old-Style Justice. Associated Press State and Local Wire (6 March).

Gurdon, Hugo. (1998). A Laughing Stock—by Order of the Court, Football Thugs Beware: 'Name and Shame' Works in the US, says Hugo Gurdon. *The Daily Telegraph* (23 June), p. 17.

Harvard Law Review. (1998). Development in Law: Alternatives to Incarceration. 111(May):1967–1990.

Hoffman, Jan. 1997. Crime and Punishment: Shame Gains Popularity. *New York Times* (16 January), p. A1.

Hubacher, Art. (1998). Every Picture Tells a Story: Is Kansas City's "John TV" Constitutional? *Kansas Law Review* 46(April):551–591.

Judges Mete Out Punishments That Don't Fit the Crimes. (2000). Editorial. *The Plain Dealer* (3 January), p. 6B.

Jury Still Out on Effectiveness of Public Shaming of Criminals. (2000). Associated Press. *Chattanooga Times/Chattanooga Free Press* (16 September), p. B8.

Kahan, Dan M. (1996). What Do Alternative Sanctions Mean? *University of Chicago Law Review* 63(Spring):591–652.

Massaro. Toni M. (1997). "The Meanings of Shame: Implications for Legal Reform." *Psychological, Pubic Policy and Law* 3 (December): 645–703.

McDermott, Kevin. (1999). Tax Scafflows Are Warned Names May Go On Web. *St. Louis Post-Dispatch* (6 April).

McMaster, Kellie. (1997). Judge Joins Creative Penalty Approach: An Order That a Sexual Offender Post a Warning Sign on His Door May Be Novel in Manatee County, but Similar Tactics Are Used Elsewhere. *Sarasota Herald-Tribune* (Manatee Edition) (10 July), p. 1B.

McMurry, Kelly. (1997). For Shame: Paying for Crime Without Serving Time, But With a Dose of Humility. *Trial* 33(May):12–14.

Mecklenburg Sheriff to Post Wanted's Names on Internet. (2000). Associated Press State & Local Wire. (5 October).

Miethe, Terance D., Hong Lu and Erin Reese. (2000). Reintegrative Shaming and Recidivism Risks in Drug Court: Explanations for Some Unexpected Findings. *Crime and Delinquency* 46(October):522–541.

Morris, Allison and Warren Young. (2000). Reforming Criminal Justice: The Potential of Restorative Justice. In *Restorative Justice: Philosophy to Practice*. Heather Strang and John Braithwaite, eds. Burlington, VT: Ashgate Publishing Co., pp. 11–31.

Morris, Allison and Gabrielle Maxwell. (2001). Restorative Conferencing. In *Restorative Justice Community: Repairing Harm and Transforming Communities*. Gordon Bazemore and Mara Schiff, eds. Cincinnati, OH: Anderson Publishing Co., pp. 173–197.

Nesmith, Susannah A. (1996). Judge Hopes New 'Scarlet Letter' Shames Criminals. *The Palm Beach Post* (2 December), p. 1A.

Owens, Gene. (1997). Alabama Looks at "Scarlet Tags" for Drunk Drivers/But Will they Create a Cool Fad for the Young? *Greensboro News Record* (4 February), p. A7.

Powell, Joy. (1998). The Power of Shame Put to the Test. *Star Tribune* (17 June), p. 1A.

Presser, Lois and Emily Gaarder. (2000). Can Restorative Justice Reduce Battering? Some Preliminary Considerations. *Social Justice* 27 (Spring): 175–195.

Public Humiliation Makes a Comeback. (2000). *The News Tribune* (21 March), p. B8.

Reske, Henry J. (1996). The Scarlet Letter Sentences: As Convicts Who Are Ordered to Shovel Manure and Post Warning Signs Have Learned, Shame Is Making a Comeback. *American Bar Association Journal* 82(January):16.

Roach, Kent. (1999). Four Models of the Criminal Process. *Journal of Criminal Law & Criminology* 89(Winter): 671–716.

Roach, Kent. (2000). Changing Punishment at the Turn of the Century: Restorative Justice on the Rise. *Canadian Journal of Criminology* 42(July): 249–280.

Rochman, Bonnie. "Sentenced to Public Shaming," *News & Observer* (Raleigh, NC) (29 November 1999), A1.

Rottman, David and Pamela Casey. (2000). Therapeutic Jurisprudence and the Emergence of Problem-Solving Courts. *Alternatives to Incarceration* 6 (Spring):27–30.

Sanders, Scott E. (1998). Scarlet Letters, Bilboes and Cable TV: Are Shame Punishments Cruel and Outdated or Are They a Viable Option for American Jurisprudence? *Washburn Law Journal* 37 (Winter): 359–382.

Schuldt, Gretchen. (1996). County to Study Possibility of Shaming Non-violent Offenders. *Milwaukee Journal Sentinel* (9 November), p. 3.

CASE

People v. McDowell, 130 Cal. Rptr. 839 (Ct. App. 1976).

chapter 13

Arresting Decline and Unlocking Potential: The Standards and Accreditation Approach to Professionalizing Jails

Scott Blough & Keith N. Haley

INTRODUCTION AND BACKGROUND

The Fear and Reality of Jail

When you list what Americans fear most, going to jail has to be near the top. Jail, in fact, is a key component of the American philosophy of punishment. That fear of being locked up is often implanted early in the mind of a child when, in the presence of a police officer, a parent says, "You better be good or I'll have that police officer take you to jail."

Jail may be both America's top fear and its worst nightmare. The United States is home to 3365 jails, 47 of which are private, housing as many as about 605,000 inmates on any given day (Bureau of Justice Statistics, 2000). As broad as the range of jail capacity in the United States is (21,302 for Los Angeles; to small jails with 10 inmates), the gap in quality is as wide between the most sophisticated jails and the enigmatic detention facilities that are not that far removed in appearance and hospitality from the dungeons of the past. Most jails, like prisons, are filled to capacity in many jurisdictions in the United States. In 1999, America's jails were operating at 93 percent of the rated capacity for the nation. In the United States, our incapacitation rate is 222/100,000 residents (Bureau of Justice Statistics, 2000), up from 163/100,000 in 1990.

The Functions of Jail in Society

Jails, of course, perform a critical set of functions in society. While the types of jail facilities are often lumped together, they are generally broken down into several categories, ranging from large full-service jails to small temporary holding facilities. Nearly half of all people in jail are convicted and serving sentences of confinement for crimes. Others, comprising a number of near equal size, are in jail only for the purpose of awaiting trial.

Many others are in jail for shorter periods of time and will be released when they have secured the services of a bond agent or are transferred to another category of jail facility that is allowed to detain them for a longer period of time. Still others will be released in a short period of time because the police and the prosecutor decide that there is not enough evidence to proceed with the case. Traffic offenders can spend a portion of their time in jail as they prepare to pay their traffic ticket, go to court, or until they can secure the services of a bond agent.

Other jail residents are most ill suited for their stay in a local jail because they actually belong somewhere else. A mass exodus from mental hospitals in the United States during the 1970s has resulted in a new inmate population. This population, the mentally ill (see Chapter 9), comprises at least 8 percent of the jail population (Kerle, 1998) and may be as high as 16 percent (U.S Department of Justice, 1999). Even when the mentally ill are sent from jails to hospitals and mental institutions for a psychiatric diagnosis, they are often returned within hours to the jail because the mental health facilities are not equipped to handle them. A severe shortage of mental health services in America's jails is apparent, but it has been difficult to attract the resources needed to offer such services at the jail or some other location (Walsh & Bricout, 1997). There are also special needs inmates with one or more of the following conditions: suffering from substance abuse; having an HIV-positive condition; or living with tuberculosis or another infectious disease. Finally, there is always the ever-present risk of suicide in jail facilities (see Chapter 7), particularly among young white males who have been arrested and booked for nonviolent offenses and are intoxicated at the time of confinement. Suicide is the leading cause of death in jails, where more than 400 occur each year (Hayes, 1999). In Table 13–1, Schmalleger and Smykla (2001) provide a comprehensive list of the purposes of jails.

Table 13–1   The Varied Purposes of Jails

- Receive persons awaiting arraignment and hold them pending trial, conviction, or sentencing.
- Readmit probation and parole violators and bail-bond absconders.
- Detain juveniles until custody is transferred to juvenile authorities.
- Hold mentally ill persons until they are moved to appropriate health facilities.
- Hold individuals for the military.
- Provide protective custody.
- Confine persons found in contempt.
- Hold witnesses for the courts.
- Hold inmates about to be released after completing a prison sentence.
- Transfer inmates to federal, state, and other authorities.
- House inmates for federal, state, or other authorities because of crowding of their facilities.
- Operate some community-based programs as alternatives to incarceration.
- Hold inmates sentenced to short terms (generally under one year) of incarceration.

Frank Schmalleger and John Ortiz Smykla, *Corrections in the 21st Century.* Glencoe/McGraw-Hill, 2001, p. 91.

METHOD

Objectives of Chapter

The objectives of the study reported in this chapter are to

1. Discuss the role of the standards and accreditation process as a means of acquiring professional status in law enforcement and corrections, and particularly in jail administration.
2. Identify the key public and private stakeholders in the jail standards-setting process in a community.
3. Describe the jail standards creation, revision, and approval processes in Ohio.
4. Describe a typical jail inspection in Ohio from the perspective of a participant-observer.

HISTORY OF JAIL STANDARDS AND ACCREDITATION

Jail standards did not always exist. Before the 1960s, very few jails complied with established standards (Schmalleger et al, 2001). The National Sheriffs Association (NSA), the American Correctional Association (ACA), and a few progressive states led the movement toward improving the management, operations, and living conditions in the nation's jails. Health standards have been developed by the National Commission on Correctional Health Care (NCCHC). NCCHC offers its own accreditation program to jails across the United States. The sheriffs developed the NSA Jail Audit, which closely resembled the Standards for Adult Local Detention Facilities first created by the American Correctional Association in December of 1971. The ACA has said in the foreword to its latest standards document that executive, legislative, and judicial branches of local, state, and federal jurisdictions frequently refer to its standards as the professional benchmark.

Types of Standards

Standards can be classified in a number of ways. Some are indeed *general* in that the standard may say that there has to be a written policy on visitation, while another *specific* standard may require definite candle watts for the lighting that illuminates inmates' cells or visitation areas. Most all standards are written with the intention of being *minimum*. State and local authorities are encouraged to exceed minimum standards and realize that minimum standards always represent a compromise among all parties with a collective interest and are often constructed merely to bring the substandard members up to a minimally acceptable level. Complying with minimum standards in an old jail facility can be an expensive proposition to city councils and county commissions.

Some standards are *mandatory* and some are *voluntary*. States will often have standards applying to jail facilities and other kinds of government services in both categories. Mandatory standards often have the force of law behind them in relation to compliance. Voluntary standards are often more elaborate in terms of scope and amenities, which add costs but are nevertheless important in making a jail a hospitable and satisfactory place for inmates to reside. Voluntary standards also have a way of migrating into the mandatory category as a progression of jail administration professionalism takes hold in a state. There are still several states where all jail standards are only voluntary (e.g., Wyoming and Idaho).

Standards may also be examined in relation to the standards-setting agency. While not all states have standards for jails, a majority of the states do. Along with the standards comes the responsibility of measuring compliance. Some states with standards have no inspection capability built into their standards machinery, making it easy to avoid or delay needed improvements that cost money for new staff and facility construction and renovation.

Ohio was a leader in setting statewide jail standards by creating the Bureau of Adult Detention (BAD) in 1976, which included an inspection capability in a team of four regional inspectors (Kerle, 1998). Although the jail standards are backed by the force of administrative law, the philosophy of BAD and its inspectors seems to be to "work with the locals" in improving their jails. The Ohio Bureau of Adult Detention is a unit of the Ohio Department of Rehabilitation and Correction. Since its inception, BAD has made revisions to its jail standards.

Jail standards can be categorized by the type of facility to which they apply. The ACA classifies jail facilities according to three major categories: general purpose detention facility or jail; holding or lockup facility; and a hybrid type of facility that contains a mixture of long-term, short-term, and holding units. Ohio has 246 jails in the following categories: 95 full-service jails; 16 minimum-security; 100 five-day; and 35 eight-hour (Blough, 2001). Minimum standards are both alike and different among the four categories. Table 13–2 provides a view of the average daily population of Ohio's jails by type of facility from 1997 to 2001.

Table 13–2   AVERAGE DAILY POPULATION IN OHIO'S JAILS 1995–1999

Facility	1997	1998	1999	2000	2001
FSJ	13,783	14,959	15,951	16,133	16,644
MSJ	923	735	704	719	762
5D	371	377	380	371	420
8HR	39	29	43	51	51
TOTAL	15,116	16,100	17,078	17,274	17,877

Annual Jail Report 2001, Division of Parole and Community Service, Bureau of Adult Detention, Ohio Department of Rehabilitation and Correction.

The total average jail population in Ohio has obviously gone up each year from 1997 to 2001, as it has in virtually every other part of the nation. The average jail population in Ohio's short-stay facilities, however, has remained constant overall since some police agencies have forgone the luxury and liability of maintaining a five-day or eight-hour facility. Prisoners requiring this kind of service have been housed in either full-service or minimum-security jails of their own or at other city or county agencies. Regional jails have slowly begun to replace smaller, inefficient, and substandard facilities (Wilbur, 2000), thereby actually causing a slow decrease in the number of jails in America. Ohio's Corrections Center of Northwest Ohio (CCNO), a regional jail, is an excellent example of successful regionalization. CCNO from its inception has served five counties and the city of Toledo, defying the much-bandied position that such regional cooperation is not possible. The average daily population for all four types of facilities in Ohio has increased approximately 18 percent since 1997 and about 3 percent over the 2001 figure (Blough, 2001).

While the full and partial privatization of jails has taken hold in some states, this has not been the case in Ohio. Correction Systems, Inc. is an example of a successful publicly owned for-profit corporation that began with jail operations in Orange County, California and is now operating 12 correctional facilities, 11 in California, one in Lincoln County, New Mexico, and three halfway houses in Texas (Martin, 2001).

The Critical Role of the Jail Inspector in Assuring Quality

Inevitably, the agency responsible for the quality of a state's jails has to determine if the standards are being met. A number of scenarios would be possible to envision. Inspections at the jail could be unannounced. Inspectors could arrive at any hour of the day or night prepared to assess the jail and its personnel on one or all of the state's standards. The inspection could indeed be a terror for the local jail administrator.

In Ohio, the BAD jail inspection process is anything but a terror, the acronym attached to the jail inspector's agency title notwithstanding. In fact, what transpires is a well-planned visit where a professional dialogue occurs between the jail manager and the regional state inspector.

To understand the jail inspection process, one needs to become familiar with the mission of the jail inspector. This was perhaps best characterized in the publication *Competency Profile of a Detention Facility Inspector* (National Institute of Corrections, 2000):

> An effective Detention Facility Inspector is one who assesses compliance with applicable standards and promotes professionalism through inspections, technical assistance, investigations, studies, and staff development to ensure safe, secure, effective and legally operated jails.

Jail inspectors are much more than auditors of standards. They are required to provide ongoing technical service to jails throughout the year. This service includes training, policy analysis, investigations, explaining legal case studies, and conducting staffing analyses. The actual jail inspection tops off the list of responsibilities.

Rosazza (2000) describes several different types of jail inspections in his book *Jail Inspection Basics*: physical plant, operations, management, complaints and grievances, complete inspections, partial inspections, and financial examinations.

The physical plant inspection examines the facility in its entirety. An operational inspection examines facility operations involving, for instance, security, intake and release, medical services, food service, visitation, mail, discipline, and classification. In a management inspection, critical management issues, primarily related to the jail management's responsibility to direct, supervise, and train its staff, are reviewed, inspected, or audited. The complete inspection is a look at the total facility and its operation. A partial inspection involves examining something less than the whole. A grievance and complaint inspection includes investigating complaints made to judges or the state's governor that have been referred to the jail inspector for action. Financial inspections and audits address commissary accounts and other aspects of inmate funds. Most inspectors, however, are not qualified to conduct financial audits.

Ohio's Jail Inspection Process

In Ohio, the jail inspection process consists of two equally important phases. The two-part process concerns the physical plant and the administrative aspects of the jail. The physical plant inspection is an on-site viewing by the inspector of the facility in its entirety. Rosazza (1990) includes buildings, grounds, capital equipment such as generators, audiovideo communications systems, and fire systems as part of the physical plant inspection. A physical plant inspection is crucial to meeting standards since much of the physical plant issues concern life, health, and safety standards.

The jail inspector conducts a physical walk-through of the entire facility, focusing on such things as space for housing, programming, recreation, cleanliness, and facility maintenance. Moreover, the jail inspector does a cursory review of health and safety issues, such as food storage, means of egress and fire notification, and fire suppression devices. The inspector may choose to speak with inmates and verify that certain types of materials are available to inmates, such as inmate rules, toiletries, reading matter, and writing materials.

In conjunction with the physical plant inspection, inspectors generally complete a cursory review of policies and procedures that are in place within the jail. This process also involves reviewing documentation to ensure that policies and procedures are implemented within the jail. That documentation might include such material as jail logs, visitor logs, clothing exchange logs, and grievance forms. The policies and procedures are reviewed to ensure compliance with the minimum standards for jails in Ohio, which are part of the state's administrative code. The jail administrator has the opportunity to review and amend policies and procedures during this process. To accomplish this, the jail inspector communicates regularly with the jail administrator during the days following the inspection. The end result of this interaction generally produces policies and procedures that comply with the standards.

In addition to the jail inspectors' duty to inspect the physical plant and policies and procedures of the jail, they also need to maintain a liaison with the fire and health inspection authorities. This liaison activity ensures that the jail is complying with fire and health regulations since failure to meet these standards would have a serious impact on life, safety, and health conditions in the jail. Jail inspectors review the fire and health inspection reports and follow up with correspondence to ensure that deficiencies noted by these authorities are corrected.

After the inspection is completed, a report is issued to the necessary responsible authorities. In Ohio, this includes the agency head, the county and/or city executives, and the administrative judge of the jurisdiction inspected. Those jurisdictions that are out of compliance with standards are required to submit a plan of action, which details the plans that will bring the jurisdiction into compliance. This portion of the inspection process is referred to as compliance monitoring. The inspector reviews the plan of action and makes periodic inquiries into the timeliness of the progress toward the agreed-upon improvements. The progress monitoring is ongoing throughout the year and may require additional physical inspections by the jail inspector.

Ohio has utilized the partial inspection process throughout the past 20-year cycle that concluded in 2002. This process involved utilizing some standards from each of the different categories in order to provide a representative sampling of total jail operations. Each year, inspectors reviewed approximately 10 percent of the 313 minimum standards for jails in Ohio. This review provided BAD with valuable insight into the training and technical assistance needs of local jail jurisdictions.

Participant Observation in a Jail Inspection

During the fall of 2000, one of the authors, Keith Haley, accompanied by a visiting University of Bucharest Professor, Theodora Ene, participated in a scheduled jail inspection at the municipal jail in Bedford Heights, Ohio. The jail inspector met us at the jail early in the morning and the inspection began.

The first part of the inspection included a clear description by the jail inspector to the local jail administrator as to what was going to happen. The two of them systematically went down a detailed list of standards and compared them with the written policies and procedures in the local agency's manual. Any problems with compliance were noted, and any clarifications that were needed from either side's point of view were dealt with immediately. After the administrative portion of the inspection, the BAD inspector and the jail administrator made a thorough physical inspection of the jail. After the physical inspection, the jail inspector spent an hour or so preparing his notes and completing forms required by the state. Finally, the BAD jail inspector and the jail administrator sat down for a final conference and went over the results of the inspection and discussed what follow-up steps would be needed. The entire four-hour process was conducted in an atmosphere of civility and professionalism with the intention of improving the jail always foremost in the minds of the participants.

Ohio's Revision of Standards Process

In the summer of 2000, Ohio embarked on a project entitled Revision of the Minimum Standards for Jails in Ohio. The goal for this project was that the new standards had to be directive, measurable, objective, and specific. The mission of the committee that worked on this project was as follows:

> The Ohio Minimum Jail Standards' Revision Committee will assist the Bureau of Adult Detention, Department of Rehabilitation and Correction by providing their professional input and expertise in revising and recommending standards that promote safe, secure, efficient and lawful jail systems by developing Minimum Standards that are directive, measurable, objective and specific. The Minimum Standards will reflect current trends, technology, and law.

The process began with the organization of the Ohio Minimum Jail Standards Revision Committee. This committee was composed of people from a variety of disciplines, including corrections, law enforcement, training, academia, law, architecture, and medicine. The committee, which consisted of more than 30 members, was divided into 8 subcommittees for the standards review process. These subcommittees were charged with reviewing standards associated with the following areas: reception and release; classification, housing, and administrative segregation; security; sanitation, environmental conditions, and food service; communication, visitation, telephone and recreation, and programming; medical; discipline, violations and penalties, disciplinary hearings and grievances; and staff and staff training.

Each subcommittee utilized a variety of resources, including standards from the American Correctional Association, National Commission on Correctional Health Care, other states, and case law. The subcommittees were scheduled to meet twice and draft recommendations for presentation to the full committee, which met in late November of 2000. After the subcommittee presentations, the recommendations were distributed to the committee members for individual comment. Those comments were collated and returned to the committee members before the final committee meeting that was held in February 2001. A consensus was reached on the recommendations at the February 2001 meeting and the new standards were submitted to the Department of Rehabilitation and Correction's Legal Division for review.

After the internal review, the new standards were sent to the Ohio Joint Committee on Agency Rule Review (JCARR), where they subject to the same scrutiny that all prospective administrative rules undergo. The minimum standards for jails in Ohio received the support of the legislature and became effective on January 1, 2003.

ACCREDITATION AND CERTIFICATION

More than one agency has a stake in the accreditation process. The American Correctional Association is a big player, and its document, Standards for Adult Local Detention Facilities (SALDF), is more than a primer on what both the ideal and minimum standards are in jails of various types. Now the ACA, along with the assistance of the American Jail Association, is leading in the development of the fourth edition of the SALDF. In fact, the entire revision process is focused on developing "performance-based" standards that are bound to cause a stir among the jail management community (Miller, 2000). Just as the "objectifiers" and "quantifiers" have complicated the accreditation process for higher education and other service industries, the movement has captured the allegiance of the leadership of the ACA. Inevitably, the quantified, performance-based approach to standards means developing scores of measures that need to be quantified, implemented, and recorded. This sea change in the way accreditation will be accomplished may not please jail administrators and their staff unless they have a stake in being evaluators and trainers in the ways of the new performance-based system. A jail is a 24/7 busy operation, and there will not be a lot of time to take measures of performance in a plethora of categories.

RESULTS AND DISCUSSION

Jail Inspection Standards and Procedures

The results of this study show that jail quality is indeed a major concern in California, Texas, Florida, and Ohio. Standards and procedures have been implemented to ensure that local and regional jail facilities not only meet the necessary requirements related to life, health, and safety but that benchmarks for any other conditions in the jails of these states have been established. Table 13–3 contains a glimpse of jail standards and compliance procedures in the four states in this study.

The four states in this study have developed an array of standards that set the minimum levels of acceptance in many categories of jail service. The number of standard categories or chapters range from a low of 10 in California to 24 in Texas. Within each of the state's chapters, however, are many subsections dealing with finite specifications that must be met. Inspections occur at least every year, and in California and Florida the audits are conducted twice a year. The frequency of audits in jails is unusual given that law enforce-

Table 13–3   JAIL INSPECTION STANDARDS AND INSPECTION PROCEDURES

State	Number of Standard Categories	Frequency of Inspections	Number of Inspectors	Number of Jails
California	10	Biannual	6	449
Texas	24	Annual	4	274
Florida	20	Biannual	152[*]	105
Ohio	12	Annual	4	252

[*]Florida utilizes volunteer jail and other corrections personnel to inspect.

ment agency and educational institution accreditation visits are much less frequent, although when the critical social justice function of the jail is considered along with its potential for harm, frequent inspection and oversight are justified. States perform this inspection process with a minimum number of inspectors. The number of inspectors utilized in Florida is unusual until you consider that the inspectors are trained volunteers who work in jails or other aspects of corrections. Conversely, one can readily surmise that covering the state of Texas or California with only four and six inspectors respectively requires a Herculean effort.

Compliance and Sanctions

While good will and positive intentions will go a long way in improving any public service, the progress in jail quality needed force behind the compliance effort to professionalize jails. Table 13–4 portrays the jail compliance and sanction features for California, Texas, Florida, and Ohio.

Compliance with state jail standards for adult detention facilities is mandatory in three of the four states in our study. In California the jail standards are not mandatory for adult detention facilities but do require compliance for juvenile detention in an adult facility and juvenile detention facilities.

In all four states the standards are created and enforced at the state level. In California and Ohio, the state corrections agency is the governing body over jail standards. In Texas and Florida, a special body has been formed to deal with jail standards compliance.

Table 13–4   COMPLIANCE AND SANCTION FEATURES

State	Governing Agency	Mandatory/ Voluntary	Force of Law	Sanctions
California	Board of Corrections	Voluntary[*]	Yes	Juvenile only
Texas	Commission on Jail Standards	Mandatory	Yes	Yes
Florida	Florida Model Jail Standards Committee	Mandatory	Yes	Public scrutiny
Ohio	Department of Rehabilitation and Correction	Mandatory	Yes	Yes

[*]Standards are mandatory only for juvenile institutions and confinement.
Table adapted from T. Rosazza and J. Nestrud, State Jail Inspection Programs: State of the Art. *American Jails*, March/April 2000.

In Texas that body is the Commission on Jail Standards, and in Florida it is the Model Jail Standards Committee.

Rosazza (2000) found that sanctions can be plotted on a continuum, ranging from informal persuasion to formal action under the authority of a state body and approved by a court of law. A number of enforcement sanctions are available to the state agency: petitioning of courts; directives requiring compliance by independent commissions; orders by jail inspectors (the equivalent of getting a ticket from a law enforcement officer); restricted use of the jail; orders to close the facility; withholding state subsidies; placing the jail on probation; and decertification. Coupled with persistent informal persuasion, enforcement continues until the jail comes into compliance with the deficiency.

Range of Standards in Professional Jails

Table 13–5 contains a list of all of the distinct categories of standards that could be identified when all four states' sets of standards were examined.

Excluding definitions, an examination of the combined sets of jail standards for California, Texas, Florida, and Ohio reveals 34 distinct categories. Those standards range in significance from rather mundane things such as clothing, bedding, and linens to life, security, safety, and health concerns. Some might say there are life, health, and safety standards and then there are the rest. The first group, by nature, is the most critical and has the potential to severely sanction or close a jail. Consequently, issues such as suicide prevention and response, fire safety, inmate protection, religion, and sanitation are readily apparent in the standards of all four states in this study.

Beyond these necessary categories, there are categories dealing with jail administration, inmate comforts, rules of procedure for inmates and staff, and various special categories that relate to a state's particular concerns. Fees for service, for example, are a widely discussed and controversial topic within the jail administration community. While some counties and communities have entered into this arena, many have not. Licking County, Ohio is one county whose jail has pioneered the inmate fee-for-service. Sheriff Gerry Billy, a successful multiple-term sheriff and a leading jail consultant, has been able to reduce jail costs and build inmate responsibility by making them attach value to what they receive while residing in the jail.

Texas has a specific category of standards addressing the work assignments of inmates. Haley and Collins (2000) found in their study of state corrections department Web sites that Texas is proud of its approach to making as many inmates as possible work to assist in curtailing prison costs. In fact, Texas inmates are required to get up at 3:30 A.M. in order to prepare for the day's work assignment.

While some commentators critical of the progressive jail administration movement may say that 34 chapters of standards among these four states may be too responsive to the concerns and comforts of inmates, the jail may represent one of the best checkpoints in society to determine how far democracy and its principles reach. Democracy has to live in our

Table 13–5 RANGE OF STANDARDS BY TOPIC IN CALIFORNIA, TEXAS, FLORIDA, AND OHIO

1. Reception and Release
2. Admission and Classification
3. Food Service
4. Security and Control
5. Housing
6. Sanitation and Environmental Safety
7. Communication and Telephone
8. Inmate Recreation and Programming
9. Visitation
10. Staffing
11. Staff Training
12. Medical/Mental Health Services
13. Prisoner Supervision, Order, Discipline, Administrative Segregation, Grievance, Hearings
14. Management
15. Records and Public Information
16. Inmate Clothing and Personal Hygiene
17. Bedding and Linens
18. Employee Regulations
19. Pharmacy
20. Storage and Handling of Individual Prescriptions
21. Inmate Privileges
22. Contraband
23. Direct Supervision Jails
24. Minimum Construction Standards
25. Admission, Classification, Housing, and Release of Juveniles
26. Rulemaking Procedures
27. Construction Rules and Approval
28. Life Safety Rules
29. Education and Rehabilitation Programs
30. Work Assignments
31. Fees
32. Variance Procedure Rules
33. Compliance and Enforcement
34. Rules of Practice in Contested Cases

schools, businesses, political life, and criminal justice system. If democracy lives in our jails, where society confines some of its most undesirable people, then it probably lives everywhere else. *The Miami Herald* recently published a feature article describing the philosophy, administration, and operations of Haiti's jails. In stark contrast to the standards and accreditation approach to improving American jails, prisoners are the last concern of the Haitian government. There are no standards.

PROGNOSIS FOR JAIL STANDARDS AND ACCREDITATION

Improvement Will Be Evolutionary

The magnitude of the problem of bringing more than three thousand jails in America up to standard and maintaining them at a sufficient level of quality will require time and patience. Jails cannot merely suspend operations in their communities while a substantial number of improvements are made that satisfy standards developed by the host state or some national accrediting body. Jails perform a public safety function above all else, and the performance of this function will supersede all others, no matter that inmates may be served in a substandard environment.

The cards are stacked against rapid and wholesale improvement of the jails for a number of other reasons. Many of the nation's jails are old, and to bring them into the modern era on several of the categories of standards would require funding in some areas beyond what a community is able to pay. Jails are not a priority for most people in a society, and that is not likely to change no matter how prosperous a community becomes. Because a jail serves an unpopular and sometimes dangerous clientele, some citizens and criminal justice professionals suggest that the conditions in jail ought to be worse than they are in order to act as a deterrent to crime. Undoubtedly the popularity of the *www.crime.com* Web site, which features live Web cams on prisoners in Maricopa County, Arizona, is a result of the public's curiosity about criminals in confinement and may involve a slightly sordid enjoyment about seeing the deprivation of rights and privileges of prisoners.

A Difficult Sale for Performance-Based Standards

The probability that the jail administration community will accept a performance-based approach to standards and accreditation is not high. The American Corrections Association's Performance-Based Standards Project is well underway. This draft represents the fourth version of the standards for adult detention facilities. The problems are likely to come at the point of implementation and reporting. The required elements in the new process are standard; outcome measure; expected practice (previously called standard); comment; protocol; and process indicator. Busy sheriffs, police chiefs, and jail administrators are not going to accept the sale of this cumbersome review process easily. It may be one of the best examples of overshooting the mark that we will see in criminal justice in some time. Accreditation does not go down smoothly for most criminal justice executives, since they are by nature action-oriented people. A complicated, protracted approach to complying with jail standards will only aggravate the situation. Accreditation in law enforcement experienced a similar resistance to hundreds of standards. Not until the number of standards was cut in half did acceptance for the Commission on Accreditation for Law Enforcement Agencies begin to grow. There is a natural give and take between any accrediting body in a professional field and the accredited. "Trimming back" the enthusiasm of an accrediting body from the world of the ideal to what is practical is a common occurrence.

The Profession of Jail Management and Operations

In little more than two decades jail administration has attained professional status in the eyes of those who manage jails. We now accept that there is a substantial body of knowledge necessary to master in order to properly manage and operate a jail. The National Institute of Corrections offers training to obtain the designation of certified jail manager, which further exemplifies the professional growth of the field. Jail professionals themselves sit in judgment of their peers by means of creating standards, implementing them, and ensuring compliance. Jail operations are now recognized as crucial work within the criminal justice discipline. Sanctions with the force of law are now available to bring those who do not meet standards into compliance. All of these features are the earmarks of a profession. The work of jails has arrived at the doorstep of professional status. Recognition of this achievement by those outside criminal justice will be the last step to move jail administration to true professional status.

Regionalization of Jails

While simply not possible in many parts of the nation, regional jails are a wise solution for small and large communities to join together in sharing the cost and responsibility of providing secure, safe, and sanitary confinement for its prisoners of many varieties. The Corrections Center of Northwest Ohio is an example of cooperation between four rural counties, one urban county, and a large city (Dennis, 1998).

A regional jail will more than likely start with not only a new facility but also with fresh thought about corrections and visionary leadership necessary to sustain the joint enterprise. The likelihood of a professional jail administrator being employed who will insist upon the highest possible level of professional service is much higher in a regional jail than in an array of disconnected smaller jails in a section of a state containing several counties and cities.

The Confusion, Clamor, and Competition among Accrediting Bodies

Health organizations, state corrections departments, federal corrections bodies, architectural associations, special accreditation committees appointed by the states, and the private associations of law enforcement executives are all involved in some aspects of the jail professionalization and accreditation movement. Beyond these organizations you have county executives and commissions, legislative bodies, and employee associations all wanting some say in the administration and operations of a jail. Finally, there are the courts and the legal community, who are all too willing to step in and resolve the conflicts among parties. It is a wonder that progress is made when the large number of stakeholders is considered.

The Professional Jail as Democracy's Triumph over Oppression

We suppose that one of the best tests of the professional status of a jail in America is whether or not the common citizen could spend a day and night in confinement and abound with the belief that they were safe and cared for. To leave a jail and to be able to say that would require far more from a jail than simply meeting the life, health, and safety standards. Are we willing to go beyond merely what is necessary in jail administration and operations? If we are, then professional status and formal accreditation are due to those that perform jail work.

Democracy and totalitarianism lie at the opposite ends of the political and human rights continuum. If America is to remain the "beacon on the hill" that the rest of the world admires and emulates, jails will have to accept their responsibility to advance the cause of liberty and justice. When the guilty and innocent, the rich and the poor, the citizen and the alien, the skilled and unskilled, and the powerful and the weak can all enter and leave our jails having the same just experience, one more chapter in the triumph of democracy over oppression will have been written.

CONCLUSION

While both feared and neglected, the jail performs one of the most important functions in a free society. The jail may, in fact, be the virtual fulcrum on the balance between order and liberty in a democracy. The jails in California, Texas, Florida, and Ohio operate under sets of elaborate standards that not only attend to the life, health, and safety concerns of their clients and staff but set minimum conditions that must be met in regard to other amenities of the jail environment, regardless of the inmates' length of stay.

Law enforcement, state corrections departments, county commissions and administrators, city councils and managers, health agencies, the courts, and special regulating bodies created by state legislators are some of the major stakeholders in the jail standards and accreditation endeavor. As is always the case in standards setting, there is seldom unanimous consent on the resolutions concerning even the major issues. Jails, in the last analysis, are costly to build, operate, and maintain. Much of the work of the standards setting and inspection bodies in California, Texas, Florida, and Ohio consists of informal persuasion in trying to get local detention facilities to attain both mandatory and voluntary compliance with established standards.

The role of the jail inspector is crucial in improving jails in states included in this study. These inspectors act as enforcers, consultants, and advisors to jail administrators trying to improve their jails while they continue to perform the critical role of admitting, housing, and releasing inmates for a number of constituents. Unfortunately, there are not enough jail inspectors in any of the states. Inspectors operate under the direction of either state corrections departments or special boards and committees that are created by the legislature for the purpose of creating and enforcing jail standards.

Periodic revision of standards is a necessary but difficult task. As rules in jail court cases and the latest in recommended professional practices become known, new standards are in order. The authors can attest to the immense challenge it is to revise an entire set of standards for a state. All who participate in such an effort must be dedicated to improving the jails of their state and the nation.

Jails in America are on a steady but deliberate path toward improvement. It is unlikely that the proposed performance-based standards now being formulated by the American Jail Association and the American Correctional Association will be well received since the performance standards will be much more labor intensive than the previous process of maintaining standards.

Jail administration has indeed arrived as a professional field within law enforcement and corrections. The last three decades of progress in improving jails is a tribute to those visionary practitioners who led the charge in changing jails from America's dumping ground to the point of there being another triumph of democracy over oppression. While much work remains to get all jails on par with some of the finest detention facilities, the die is cast and there is no chance of turning back now.

REFERENCES

Blough, S. (2001). *Annual Jail Report*. Columbus, OH: Ohio Department of Rehabilitation and Correction.

Bohm, R., & Haley, K. (1999). *Introduction to Criminal Justice*. New York: Glencoe/McGraw-Hill.

Bureau of Justice Statistics. (1999). Jail Statistics. *http://www.ojp.usdoj/gov/bjs/jails.htm*

Bureau of Justice Statistics. (2000). Jail Statistics. *http://www.ojp.usdoj/gov/bjs/jails.htm*

Dennis, J. (1998). Cooperation Works: Six Ohio Jurisdictions Join Forces to Create Regional. *Corrections Today* 60(6): 128.

Haley, K., & Collins, J. (2000). *Virtual Corrections: A Content Analysis of State Corrections Department Web Pages*. A paper presented at the annual meeting of the Academy of Criminal Justice Sciences, March, New Orleans, 2000.

Harrington, S. (1999). New Bedlam: Jails Not Psychiatric Hospitals, Now Care for the Indigent Mentally Ill. *The Humanist* 59(3): 9.

Hayes, L. (1999). Suicide in Adult Correctional Facilities: Key Ingredients to Prevention and Overcoming the Obstacles. *Journal of Law, Medicine, and Ethics* 27(3): 260.

Kerle, K. (1998). *American Jails: Looking to the Future*. Boston: Butterworth-Heinemann.

Martin, K. (2001). *Privatization on the County Level*. The Corrections Connection News Center, *www.correctionsconnection.com*

Miller, R. (2000). *Phase One: Developing Fourth Edition Standards for Adult Local Detention Facilities*. American Correctional Association, Lanham, Maryland.

National Institute of Corrections. (2000). *Competency Profile of a Detention Facility Inspector*.

Rosazza, T., & Nestrud, J. (2000). State Jail Inspection Programs: State of the Art II. *American Jails*, March/April 2000.

Schmalleger, F., & Smykla, J. (2001). *Corrections in the 21st Century*. New York: Glencoe/McGraw-Hill.

Walsh, J., & Bricout, J. (1997). Services for Persons with Mental Illness: Implications for Family Involvement. *Families in Society: The Journal of Contemporary Human Services*, 78(4): 420.

Wilbur, H. (2000). The Importance of Jails. *Corrections Today* 62(6): 8.

chapter 14

Inside the Jail:
A Look at Building Design
and Inmate Supervision

Christine Tartaro

HISTORY

Jail design in the United States experienced few major developments prior to the early 1970s. For approximately two hundred years, architects relied on the same general facility design that was used for such prisons as Auburn Penitentiary, built in 1821, or Eastern State Penitentiary, built in 1829. Eastern State Penitentiary was the symbol of the Pennsylvania system of prison discipline. The Pennsylvania system sought to keep inmates physically separated at all times, with inmates serving their entire sentences in their individual cells. There was to be no interaction among inmates or between inmates and guards, and inmates were even forbidden to speak to each other through the cell walls. Prison officials working under this model went so far as to place hoods over inmates while they were being moved within the facility to prevent contact with other inmates (Rothman, 1998). Supporters of the Pennsylvania system believed that it was only through silence and reflection that an inmate could be reformed.

Inmates at Auburn were permitted to work together, but only in silence. The enforcement of silence was to allow them time to reflect on their misdeeds as well as prevent them from discussing their criminal lifestyles, thereby encouraging continuation of that behavior upon release. When inmates were not working or eating, they remained in their cells alone and silent (Rothman, 1998). Since the goal of architecture is to complement the purpose of an institution (Nelson, 1983), both the Auburn and Pennsylvania system facilities were built in such a way that did not foster communication or interaction among inmates and between inmates and staff. Inmates residing in both prison systems were expected to spend whatever time they had in their cells alone and silent (see Chapter 3).

As Farbstein (1986) noted, the purpose and management of correctional facilities has changed over the past 200 years. Prisons and jails have become instruments in the delivery of services. It is no longer desirable, nor feasible, to isolate inmates for the duration of their stay in prison or jail. Inmates work in the institution, participate in education programs, and receive visits from family. Jail architects of 200 years ago did not envision these types of activities within the correctional facilities. The architects of the past also did not anticipate the problems of having to supervise a population that consists of large proportions of people who are at risk for suicide. Nor were issues of vandalism or the stress and safety of prison staff as pressing as they are today. These problems prompted officials from the Federal Bureau of Prisons to support the development of new ideas in jail design and supervision.

This chapter provides a review of three design and supervision strategies that are found in jails nationwide today. The linear intermittent design is a traditional setup that has remained popular over two centuries. Podular indirect and podular direct supervision are more recent design approaches.

LINEAR INTERMITTENT

Nearly all prisons and jails from the eighteenth century through the 1970s adopted a similar interior prison design. While the outward appearance of prisons differed significantly, the inside of these institutions can be described as having a linear intermittent design and supervision strategy. *Linear* refers to the architectural design of the facility (Zupan, 1991), which includes a rectangular design with corridors leading to either single or multiple occupancy cells (Nelson, 1983). Corridors are usually arranged either at acute or right angles (Nelson, 1983; Zupan, 1991). The placement of cells along these corridors presents a dilemma for corrections officers: Either they use electronic equipment to monitor the inmates or conduct surveillance by entering the corridors periodically. The former presents two problems. First, using cameras to monitor inmates further isolates inmates from staff, thus preventing staff from being able to defuse problems before they escalate (Zupan, 1991). Second, upon detecting an infraction on camera, it will take time for corrections officers to reach the cell and intervene.

The second supervision option within a linear design is referred to as intermittent surveillance (Zupan, 1991). Corrections officers frequently monitor inmates by periodically walking through the corridors and looking into cells. The bars lining the cells keep inmates and officers separated. Nelson (1983) and Zupan (1991) note that this design and method of supervision presents numerous security problems. The absence of corrections officers from the inmates' living areas essentially gives inmates control over the jail cells and dormitories. The lack of constant supervision makes prevention of assaults, rapes, homicides, suicides, vandalism, and gang formation unlikely (Zupan, 1991; Zupan & Stohr-Gilmore, 1988). During the periods when officers are not observing inmates from the corridors, inmates have the opportunity to plan escapes and create weapons (Nelson, 1983). Even when officers patrol, subtle forms of misconduct, such as extortion, gambling, or drug use, may remain undetected (Zupan & Menke, 1991). Under this system, officers can only react to problems when they occur. If they detect a problem during their patrols or are alerted to a problem in another way, officers are sent into the housing areas to address the problem. Inmates will be separated and sanctioned accordingly. Again, a significant issue here is the fact that officers will not be able to reach inmates in danger for some time, perhaps not until someone has been seriously injured.

Another important feature of the linear intermittent design that is thought to contribute to violence and disorder is the message that the environment sends to its inhabitants. As was noted, intermittent surveillance does not provide constant inmate supervision, which may provide inmates with the opportunity to be violent and destructive. In anticipation of this behavior, these jails have been equipped with vandal-resistant furnishings (Nelson, 1986; Zupan, 1991). Expensive steel or concrete beds and steel toilet seats and sinks are used, since they are more difficult to damage than wood furniture or porcelain fixtures. Heavy metal doors and bars are also used to prevent escapes (Zupan, 1991).

Research on the impact of environmental cues on behavior has been conducted in the community as well as within the correctional setting. Zimbardo's (1970) work on violent and destructive behavior provides evidence of the importance of the environment on human actions. Zimbardo argued that many behaviors considered pleasurable are not carried out because the actions do not conform with norms of social appropriateness. However, such behavior can be expressed provided that "deindividuation" occurs. Zimbardo (1970) defined this as

> a complex, hypothesized process in which a series of antecedent social conditions lead to changes in perception of self and others, and thereby to a lowered threshold of normally restrained behavior. Under appropriate conditions what results is the "release" of behavior in violation of established norms of appropriateness (p. 251).

In order for destructive, antisocial behavior to occur, Zimbardo reasoned that "releaser" stimuli (e.g., damage on a car that indicates that it has been abandoned) must be present.

Several researchers contend that the linear intermittent jail setting can encourage antisocial behavior. Wener and associates (1993) argue that this setting sends a message that animal-like behavior is expected of the inmates, since they are placed in cages while staff maintain a safe distance on the other side of the bars. Resser (1989) explained that "vandal-proof" fixtures express to an inmate that "you are a vandal" and "you cannot damage this fitting." Resser believes that inmates are likely to respond negatively to this message and participate in destructive behavior. Environmental "stressors" in jails, such as lack of privacy, boredom, excessive heat, noise, unpredictability (inmates are uncertain about their fate), and crowding, may influence inmates' physical and mental health as well as social behavior (Zupan, 1991; Zupan & Menke, 1991).

Bowker (1980) summarized the environment of correctional facilities with the following: "It is more than a play on words to say that prison assaults occur in an environment that is itself an assault upon the senses. The noise is deafening, the architecture obnoxious, and most of all, the prisoners have little control over their fate" (p. 30). A jail setting with graffiti on the walls and damage to fixtures may provide the "releaser" stimuli that Zimbardo presented as a precursor to destructive acts. An example of this can be found in a New York City jail. The jail's living areas changed to include normal furniture, clear glazing instead of glass, and frequent interaction between officers and inmates. Violence and vandalism in the living areas were dramatically reduced. Despite this improvement in one area of the jail, problems persisted in the intake and receiving areas. Those areas were not changed and remained the same as traditional facilities in design and operation. Graffiti and vandalism remained a problem, and staff and inmates believed that intake and receiving were the most dangerous areas in the facility (Wener et al., 1993).

PODULAR INDIRECT/REMOTE SUPERVISION

After over 150 years of using the linear intermittent design, architects and jail administrators gradually began to explore other options. One of these options is referred to as the podular indirect supervision approach (also referred to as podular remote supervision). A podular design allows for a manageable size of inmates in housing units. *Manageable* has been defined as varying from groups of twelve to twenty-four (Bayens et al., 1997b) to groups of sixteen to forty-six (Zupan & Stohr-Gilmore, 1988). Cells, often single occupancy, in these facilities are clustered around a common dayroom (Nelson, 1986). The de sign of the facility improves the sight lines of corrections officers, thereby allowing for constant supervision, as opposed to periodic monitoring associated with the linear jails. Corrections officers supervise inmates from a nearby control booth and call for assistance if a problem occurs in the living units.

Research has indicated that officer sight lines have the potential to impact the number and type of assaults in correctional facilities. Atlas's (1983) study of crime site selection for assaults in two medium and two maximum security prisons provides a good example of this. More serious assaults occurred in areas with poor supervision, and that, according to Atlas, indicates a level of planning on the part of the assailants. If offenders are planning violent encounters, improved sight lines may reduce such incidents.

The podular indirect supervision model has been supported by civil service unions, since officers spend most of their time in the safety of the control room (Nelson, 1983). The management philosophy in these jails remains remarkably similar to that of linear intermittent facilities. Specifically, podular indirect supervision jails and linear intermittent designs share two basic beliefs: (1) Staff and inmates should not interact with each other; and (2) vandal-resistant fixtures should be placed throughout the jails. Both of these beliefs stem from the conviction that inmates are dangerous and destructive. The primary function of the staff in podular indirect facilities is to operate the control room, observe inmate behavior, and call for backup in the event of a problem. There is no contact with inmates unless infractions are detected or inmates need to be moved, and corrections officers communicate with inmates through an intercom system (Farbstein & Wener, 1989). Farbstein and Wener (1989) reported that although corrections officers felt safe in the control booths, they expressed apprehension about entering the living units unless the inmates were locked down. Since officers rarely entered the living areas, there was little contact with inmates, so they had little knowledge of individual inmates or problems brewing inside the pods.

PODULAR DIRECT SUPERVISION

History

The podular direct supervision model originated at three Metropolitan Correctional Centers (MCCs) operated by the Federal Bureau of Prisons (BOP) (Nelson & Davis, 1995). The BOP was aiming to depart from the traditional jail design and create a prototype for the nation (Gettinger, 1984). According to Nelson and Davis (1995), the BOP adopted the philosophy that "If you can't rehabilitate, at least do no harm" (p. 2). Architects were commissioned to design three facilities in New York, Chicago, and San Diego. The BOP directed the architects to include four characteristics: individual rooms for inmates, living units that house fewer than fifty inmates, direct supervision of inmates by officers, and restricted movement within the facility (Gettinger, 1984).

The newly designed jails in San Diego and New York opened in 1974, and the institution in Chicago opened in 1975 (Nelson & Davis, 1995). Evaluations of the new facilities had favorable findings. Violent incidents in the three facilities dropped 30 to 90 percent (Wener et al., 1993).[1] Although these institutions experienced sharp reductions in assaults, suicides, graffiti, and vandalism, local jail administrators were apprehensive about adopting this design. Rather than believing that the changes in environment and supervision were responsible for the more peaceful conditions, local and state officials assumed that the federal facilities were holding less violent prisoners[2] (Nelson & Davis, 1995).

In 1981, the Contra Costa County detention center in California opened the first local podular direct supervision facility, thus marking the birth of the "new generation jail" philosophy (Zupan, 1991). The facility featured an "open booking" area with a large lounge, television sets, coffee machines, and comfortable furniture. Intoxicated inmates and others who were not able to adapt to the normalized booking or living area were placed in a more secure setting, and inmates under the influence of alcohol were monitored by volunteers from Alcoholics Anonymous (Gettinger, 1984; Zupan, 1991). Contra Costa County's experience with this model was as positive as that of the Metropolitan Correctional Centers, with assault rates 95 percent lower than in the old facility.

Critics were quick to assume that, like the MCCs, the Contra Costa County Jail housed "softer" inmates. As Gettinger (1984) noted, the jail population consisted of few misdemeanants, with most inmates charged with burglary, narcotics offenses, armed robbery, murder, or escape. The inmate population was also racially mixed with blacks, whites, and Hispanics. As the MCCs and the Contra Costa County facility continued to be successful, other counties followed their example. By 1995, 147 of these facilities housing over 70,000 inmates were operational (Kerle, 1995).

Facility Design

Bayens and associates (1997b) identified three characteristics of the physical layout of the new generation jails. First, self-contained living areas, similar to those found in podular indirect supervision jails, are to be constructed. This concept was adopted from the Federal

Bureau of Prisons' unit management approach. Unit management calls for the creation of a manageable size of inmate housing groups (Nelson, 1988) that allow for concentration of services (e.g., having visiting rooms, recreational facilities, and education and counseling areas within the unit), thus reducing the movement of inmates. The availability of services within the pod frees the staff from having to transport inmates as well as provides inmates with more freedom of movement throughout the pod (Farbstein, 1986).

Second, interaction space must be provided. Living areas where inmates can socialize in a normal environment are essential. These rooms should have comfortable furniture and a tile or carpet floor. In addition to this, many podular direct supervision facilities provide ample telephones, television sets, and recreation areas. The comfortable furnishings serve to reduce stress by making the unit look and sound "noninstitutional" (Wener et al., 1985). The absence of bars and vandal-resistant settings reduces the high noise levels often found in correctional facilities. Competition for telephones and use of television sets frequently turns violent in traditional facilities. LaVigne (1994) found that at one point, fights over phone use in Rikers Island accounted for 25 percent of all inmate violence in that facility. In an attempt to lessen the competition for such resources, podular direct supervision facilities commonly provide several phones and other equipment (Wener et al., 1993).

Third, personal space is to be provided, commonly in the form of single-occupancy rooms. The rooms provide inmates a place to which they may retreat if they want to be alone. The rooms give inmates their own private space, and the ability to enter and exit the rooms as they wish gives them a feeling of control. The combination of the three aforementioned factors is intended to normalize the environment, thus providing inmates with positive expectations for their behavior (Wener et al., 1985).

Supervision

Past research has indicated that officers in traditional facilities have at times relinquished power to inmates in exchange for their cooperation (Sykes, 1972; see Table 14–1). The ability of inmates to run even a portion of the facility creates the opportunity for exploitation of weaker inmates and manipulation of the staff. The leadership vacuum that is likely to develop in the absence of staff control may be prevented with constant staff presence and interaction in the living areas. New generation jails aim to establish control over every part of the institution (Zupan & Stohr-Gilmore, 1988) by utilizing corrections officers' interpersonal communication skills.

In contrast to the reactive approach officers take in linear intermittent or podular indirect facilities, officers in new generation jails work to prevent negative behavior before it occurs (Nelson, 1983; Wener et al., 1993). Bayens and associates (1997a) define direct supervision as a "method of correctional supervision in which one or more jail officers are stationed inside the living area and are in direct physical interaction with those housed within the pod throughout the day with the ultimate goal of keeping negative behavior in check" (p. 54). Officers with extensive training in interpersonal relations and conflict management remain in the pods at all times (Zupan & Stohr-Gilmore, 1988). Since they are located in

Table 14–1   COMMON CHARACTERISTICS OF DIFFERENT JAIL DESIGNS AND SUPERVISION STRATEGIES

Characteristics	Linear Intermittent Design	Podular Indirect Supervision	Podular Direct Supervision
Physical design	Cells lined along corridors Single/multiple-occupancy cells or dormitories Vandal-resistant floors, fixtures, and furniture	Cells positioned around a dayroom Single/double-occupancy cells Vandal-resistant floors, fixtures, and furniture	Cells positioned around a dayroom Single/double-occupancy cells Wood, fabric, porcelain, and tile fixtures and furniture
Supervision	Physical barrier between officer and inmates Intermittent supervision Enter living areas in response to problems	Physical barrier between officer and inmates Constant supervision Enter living areas in response to problems	Inmates and officers located in living area together Constant supervision Located in living areas to prevent problems

the living areas with inmates, it is expected that officers will detect signs of tension between inmates and defuse the problem by either talking to them or by restricting their privileges.

The work of officers in traditional facilities has been described by Zupan and Menke (1988) as "fragmented, routinized and menial—in a word, impoverished" (p. 615). Although the officers interact with inmates most frequently, they have little say in the decision-making processes in jails (Zupan, 1991). Officers' work in new generation facilities, however, involves communication skills, crisis management techniques, and other skills, making the job quite different from what jail officers have been used to for the past 150 years. Officers are expected to handle minor incidents within the pods, usually by temporarily locking down an inmate in his or her cell, but inmates are also given the opportunity to regain privileges by improving their behavior (Farbstein & Wener, 1989; Senese, 1992). Removal of an inmate from the pod and placement in a more secure, less enjoyable portion of the facility is also an option. Since the environment within the pod is "normalized," inmates have much to lose by being removed (Farbstein & Wener, 1989). Due to the changes in roles and expectations of corrections officers, training is a critical component of the podular direct supervision concept. One official at the Manhattan House of Detention remarked, "I don't care what you do with the walls, if the staff isn't confident, if they don't believe they can do it, if you don't have a support system to make sure they can succeed, the best design will be defeated" (Krauth & Clem, 1987, p.50).

Zupan and Stohr-Gilmore's (1988) study of podular direct supervision facilities illustrates the importance of training in the functioning of these jails. One of the four institutions evaluated by the researchers differed in its training procedures. While other facilities held six- to eight-week training sessions for their officers, one jail only provided two weeks. The jails that required six to eight weeks of training covered communication skills, but the facility offering the two-week session involved work found in traditional facilities, with emphasis on physical control of inmates. When the facility opened, inmates were occasionally locked into cells without supervision, contrary to the direct supervision philosophy. Inmates living in this facility had more negative evaluations of the facility and staff than those living in a true podular direct supervision jail. Houston and associates (1988) found similar results in another facility. The researchers examined a county jail system as it moved into a new facility. The new jail contained officer workstations within inmate living quarters, a common characteristic of direct supervision jails. Despite the change in architecture, the county provided no training for officers as they made the transition to the new facility. The researchers found that the new environment had little effect on inmate and staff attitudes about their living and work environment, respectively.

RESEARCH ON DIFFERENT FACILITY DESIGNS

Evaluations of the three architectural and management designs can be divided into two categories. The first category involves before-and-after designs of facilities that moved from a linear intermittent design to podular direct supervision. The second involves cross-sectional comparisons of facilities using different architecture and management designs.

Pre- and Posttests

Wener and colleagues (1993) reported the changes in vandalism and violence rates in the MCCs and other facilities that adopted podular direct supervision. As was mentioned previously, violent incidents in the three facilities dropped 30 to 90 percent. The Pima County, Arizona facility had drastic declines in vandalism and graffiti. The number of damaged mattresses dropped from 150 per year in the linear intermittent facility to none in two years in the podular direct supervision facility. An average of two television sets per week was in need of repair in the old facility, compared to two in two years in the new jail. Inmate clothing was also destroyed less frequently, falling from an average of ninety-nine sets of clothes destroyed per year to fifteen sets in two years.

The Manhattan House of Detention (nicknamed "The Tombs" for its poor conditions) was a violent, graffiti-ridden facility that was ordered closed by a federal judge in 1974. The judge cited problems with brutality, noise, and overall inadequacies in the institution (Gettinger, 1984). The inside of the building was renovated and the officers were trained to perform direct supervision. After the change, the facility had no homicides, suicides, sexual assaults, or escapes for the first two years. The incidence of less serious infractions also declined (Gettinger, 1984; Wener et al., 1993).

Senese (1997) followed the progress of one facility as it moved from linear intermittent to podular direct supervision. Senese found a decline in property destruction and a 27 percent average reduction in contraband, inmate on inmate violence, suicide, attempted suicide, and escapes. Property theft, however, increased. In a similar study, Jackson (1992) reported that the podular direct supervision model received favorable inmate evaluations of the climate and relationships with officers. The overall assault rates declined by over 50 percent after the move to the new facility, and attempted suicides also declined. There was an increase in contraband incidents, but the author speculates that this was a result of a recent ban on cigarettes.

Bayens and associates (1997a, 1997b) compared seventy categories of rule infractions during a five-year period of operation of a linear intermittent jail with the first five years of operation of a new generation jail. Serious offenses, such as rape, aggravated battery, and arson, occurred less frequently in the podular direct supervision jail, with a 58 percent average reduction in offenses in the new jail. Less serious violent offenses, such as fighting, battery of staff, and battery of inmates, decreased an average of 59 percent, attempted suicides decreased 89 percent, and successful suicides decreased 75 percent. Overall, the new generation jail had a reduction in staff reports of negative inmate behavior in fifty-one of seventy categories of infractions.

One important finding of Bayens and colleagues (1997b) was the effect of overcrowding on inmate infractions in the podular direct supervision facility. As the institution's population exceeded rated capacity, the number of inmate rule infractions increased 116 percent. Farbstein, Liebert, and Sigurdson (1996) noted that some of the six podular direct supervision jails included in their audit had problems related to crowding, reduced staffing, limited training, fewer programs, and ineffective classification. Farbstein and colleagues concluded, "Thus, as robust as direct supervision might be, it cannot be treated with indifference or allowed to degenerate too far without serious consequences" (p. 4). This brings attention to the fact that serious problems can occur if new generation jail administrators and county officials are not vigilant with respect to crowding conditions and staffing problems.

Cross-Sectional Comparisons of Facilities

Farbstein and Wener (1989) compared seven facilities, all of which were podular direct or podular indirect supervision. Staff surveys, inmate surveys, and site visits were used to assess the relationships between inmates and staff, the amount of reported violence in each facility, and the extent to which the environment is "normalized." The authors reported that direct supervision administrators rated their facilities better on safety and reported fewer incidents of violence. Inmates and officers reported having more positive contact with each other than those residing and working in the podular indirect supervision facilities. Additionally, the environment was found to be "softer" and more "normalized" in the new generation jails. Direct supervision jails also seemed to respond more positively to overcrowding problems. However, researchers cautioned that overcrowding interferes with some of the goals of direct supervision jails, such as the ability to have frequent interaction with inmates.

Williams, Rodeheaver, and Huggins (1999) surveyed inmates and officers in a traditional linear jail, an indirect supervision facility, and a podular direct supervision facility. Inmates residing in the podular direct supervision jail reported more positive feelings toward officers, higher feelings of safety, and less concern about guarding their belongings. The number of disciplinary infractions was also lower in the podular direct supervision jail. Officers in the jails, however, did not report feeling any safer in the new generation jail than they did in the linear facility.

Zupan and Stohr-Gilmore (1988) compared four podular direct and three linear intermittent jails. They found that inmates' evaluations of the jail climate were more positive in the new generation jails. Inmates in the podular direct supervision jails experienced less anxiety and had fewer anxiety-related physical health symptoms.

One study compared recidivism rates for inmates in a traditional facility with inmates in three new generation institutions. Applegate and colleagues (1999) were interested in the presence or absence of differential recidivism rates given the controversy surrounding the placement of inmates in a more comfortable new generation jail. Supporters of a more punitive correctional setting believe that harsh treatment inside a jail will deter inmates from recidivating. Supporters of a softer approach may argue that a more positive jail experience might prompt inmates to become involved in positive programming, thus increasing the chances of a positive reintegration. The researchers found no significant differences in recidivism for inmates residing in the linear intermittent and podular direct supervision jails.

A NOTE OF CAUTION

Although administrators and officers were reluctant to believe that new generation jails would provide a more pleasant work and living environment for officers and inmates, the design is now being considered a viable option for addressing the needs of county corrections systems. As counties decide to retire their current institution and build a new jail, more and more decision makers are choosing the new generation option. Nevertheless, those responsible for choosing a jail design, overseeing the construction, and supervising the operation of these institutions do need to be careful. Partial implementation of programs is a problem that affects every aspect of the criminal justice system. Decision makers hear about a promising new technique, facility, or program and decide to adopt it, but for whatever reason, be it financial issues, philosophical differences, or poor communication with the parties involved, not every aspect of the new program is included. In a survey of seventy-six podular direct supervision jails, Tartaro (2002) found that few of these institutions actually normalized the living areas with wood and fabric furnishings and many kept furniture in the living areas bolted to the floor. Jails participating in this survey also provided limited general and communication skills training for officers.

As discussed earlier, Zupan and Stohr-Gilmore's (1988) evaluation of different jails revealed that the new podular facility that did not provide the recommended training for its officers did not benefit from the new design and supervision to the extent that the jails that fully implemented the program did. Several researchers have also cautioned that although direct supervision jails may provide counties some benefits, housing inmates above the capacity level might diminish the benefits derived (Bayens et al., 1997b; Farbstein et al., 1996).

The new generation jail approach seems to be a promising option for corrections systems, but only when all of the components are included. This means that the proper furniture and fixtures need to be used, officers must be trained appropriately, officers must be placed inside the living areas, and jails must not become overcrowded. Failure to integrate all of the components of the new generation jail design has the potential to make the atmosphere of the new jail resemble that of the traditional institutions.

NOTES

1. It should be mentioned that the conditions of confinement in the New York MCC were the subject of a lawsuit (*Bell v. Wolfish* 441 U.S. 520 1979). The complaint cited overcrowded conditions, specifically double bunking, inadequate recreational facilities, and lack of educational facilities. The court found that the conditions did not constitute punishment, which is prohibited prior to adjudication of guilt (del Carmen et al., 1998).

2. There is some merit to the state and local administrators' theory. Until recently, federal institutions have been less violent than state and local facilities. Congress has passed legislation to broaden the category of federal offenses, resulting in younger, more violent inmates entering the federal system (Welch, 1996). However, the violence levels in federal prisons did not begin to change until the late 1980s and early 1990s, well after the introduction of podular direct supervision in Chicago, New York, and San Diego.

REFERENCES

Applegate, B. K., Surette, R., & McCarthy, B. J. (1999). Detention and Desistance from Crime: Evaluating the Influence of a New Generation Jail on Recidivism. *Journal of Criminal Justice.* 27(6):539–548.

Atlas, R. (1983). Crime Site Selection for Assaults in Four Florida Prisons. *The Prison Journal.* 58(1):59–72.

Bayens, G. J., Williams, J. J., & Smykla, J. O. (1997a). Jail Type and Inmate Behavior: A Longitudinal Analysis. *Federal Probation.* 61(3):54–62.

Bayens, G. J., Williams, J. J., & Smykla, J. O. (1997b). Jail Type Makes Difference: Evaluating the Transition from a Traditional to a Podular, Direct Supervision Jail across Ten Years. *American Jails.* 11(2):32–39.

Bowker, L. H. (1980). *Prison Victimization.* New York: Elsevier.

Del Carmen., R., V., Ritter, S. E., & Witt, B. A (1998). *Briefs in Leading Cases in Corrections* (2nd ed.). Cincinnati, OH: Anderson Publishing Company.

Farbstein, J. (1986) *Correctional Facility Planning and Design.* New York: Van Nostrand Reinhold.

Farbstein, J., Liebert, D., & Sigurdson, H. (1996). *Audits of Podular Direct-Supervision Jails.* Washington, DC: National Institute of Corrections.

Farbstein, J., & Wener, R. (1989). *A Comparison of "Direct" and "Indirect" Supervision Correctional Facilities.* Washington, DC: National Institute of Corrections.

Gettinger, S. H. (1984). *New Generation Jails: An Innovative Approach to an Age-Old Problem.* Longmont, CO: NIC Jails Division.

Houston, J. G., Gibbons, D. C., & Jones, J. F. (1988). Physical Environment and Jail Social Climate. *Crime and Delinquency.* 34(4):449–466.

Jackson, P. G. (1992). *Detention in Transition: Sonoma County's New Generation Jail.* Washington, DC National Institute of Corrections.

Kerle, K. (1995). Direct Supervision: The Need for Evaluation. *American Jails.* 9(3):5.

Krauth, B., & Clem, C. (1987). *Direct Supervision Jails: Interviews with Administrators.* Corrections Information Series, NIC Information Center, Boulder, CO.

LaVigne, N. (1994). Rational Choice and Inmate Disputes over Phone Use on Rikers Island. In R. V. Clarke (ed.), *Crime Prevention Studies,* Vol. 3 (pp. 109–125). Monsey, NY: Criminal Justice Press.

Nelson, R. (1983). New Generation Jails. *Corrections Today.* 45(2):108–112.

Nelson, W. R. (1986). Can Cost Savings Be Achieved by Designing Jails for Direct Supervision Inmate Management? *Proceedings of the First Annual Symposium on Direct Supervision Jails,* Jay Farbstein and Richard Wener (eds.). Boulder, CO: National Institute of Corrections.

Nelson, W. R. (1988). The Origins of the Podular Direct Supervision Concept: An Eyewitness Account. *American Jails.* 2(1):8–16.

Nelson, W. R., & Davis, R. M. (1995). Podular Direct Supervision: The First Twenty Years. *American Jails.* 9(3):11–22.

Resser, J. P. (1989). *The Design of Safe and Humane Police Cells.* Royal Commission into Aboriginal Deaths in Custody.

Rothman, D. J. (1998) Perfecting the Prison: United States, 1789–1865. In Norval Morris and David J. Rothman (eds.), *The Oxford History of the Prison* (pp. 100–117). New York, Oxford: Oxford University Press.

Senese, J. D. (1997). Evaluating Jail Reform: A Comparative Analysis of Podular/Direct and Linear Jail Inmate Infractions. *Journal of Criminal Justice.* 25(1):61–73.

Senese, J. D., Wilson, J., Evans A. O., Aguirre, R., & Kalinich, D. B. (1992). Evaluating Jail Reform: Inmate Infractions and Disciplinary Response in a Traditional and a Podular/Direct Supervision Jail. *American Jails.* 6(4):14–23.

Sykes, G. (1972). *Society of Captives: A Study of a Maximum Security Prison.* Princeton, NJ: Princeton University Press.

Tartaro, C. (2002). Examining Implementation Issues with New Generation Jails. *Criminal Justice Policy Review.* 13(3):219–237.

Welch, M. (1996). *Corrections: A Critical Approach.* New York: McGraw-Hill.

Wener, R., Frazer, W., and Farbstein, J. (1986). *Correctional Facility Planning and Design,* 2nd edition, Van Nostrand: Reinhold, New York.

Wener, R., Frazier, F. W., and Farbstein, J. (1993). Direct Supervision of Correctional Institutions. In National Institute of Corrections (eds.), *Podular, Direct Supervision Jails* (pp. 1–8). Longmont, CO: NIC Jails Division.

Wener, R., Frazier, W., and Farbstein, J. (1985). Three Generations of Evaluation and Design of Correctional Facilities. *Environment and Behavior.* 17(1):71–95.

Williams, J. L., Rodeheaver, D. G., & Huggins, D. W. (1999). A Comparative Evaluation of a New Generation Jail. *American Journal of Criminal Justice.* 23(2):223–246.

Zimbardo, P. (1970). The Human Choice: Individuation, Reason and Order versus Deindivduation, Impulse and Chaos. In W. J. Arnold and D. Levine (eds.), *Nebraska Symposium on Motivation,* Vol. 17 (pp. 237–307). Lincoln: University of Nebraska Press.

Zupan, L. L. (1991). *Jails: Reform and the New Generation Philosophy.* Cincinnati, OH: Anderson Publishing Co.

Zupan, L. L., & Menke, B. A. (1988). Implementing Organizational Change: From Traditional to New Generation Jail Operations. *Policy Studies Review.* 7(3):615–625.

Zupan, L. L., & Menke, B. A. (1991). The New Generation Jail: An Overview. In Joel A. Thompson and G. Larry Mays (eds.), *American Jails* (pp. 180–194). Chicago: Nelson-Hall Publishers.

Zupan, L. L., & Stohr-Gilmore, M. K. (1988). Doing Time in the New Generation Jail: Inmate Perceptions of Gains and Losses. *Policy Studies Review.* 7(3):626–640.

Correctional Education: The History, the Research, and the Future

Dale J. Ardovini-Brooker

INTRODUCTION

Prison is a cold, remote place that for most people exists somewhere else. The image is not accidental by any means. The idea is to remove the criminal from the rest of society and hide him or her from the general public. Sykes (1958) describes the prison as a place that deliberately deprives offenders of a number of things the rest of society has relative easy access to. He is careful to emphasize that such deprivation, not in its material but rather in its nonmaterial or symbolic form, is what distinguishes imprisonment from punishment. What the deprivation process does to an inmate is to separate him or her from the rest of society and breaks the person down to being known for the act that he or she committed. Education plays a significant role in the prison experience by redefining the inmate as a student who possesses certain skills. Presently, education programs are structured such that prisoners can have an opportunity at reshaping and redefining their lives into meaningful ones.

Correctional education embraces a diverse blend of postsecondary education programs, vocational programs, GED programs, as well as adult basic education programs in a number of different prisons from minimum to maximum security. The main focus of this chapter is on the vocational and postsecondary education that occurs inside prison. The first section provides a historical overview of the evolution of correctional education, from its religious and moral teachings in the earliest prisons to the teaching of various computer applications and sociology courses offered in the contemporary prison setting. The second section of the chapter discusses the issues confronting prison higher education, paying close attention to the moral and ideological issues arising in the tension of what prisoners themselves are and, accordingly, what prisons should or ought to be. The third section provides a review of the empirical literature as it relates to correctional education and recidivism. The last section presents a research agenda to look at the various components of the correctional education process.

HISTORY OF CORRECTIONAL EDUCATION

The Beginnings: 1798 to 1870

Indications are that the first school was introduced in 1798 at the Walnut Street Jail. It was opened to provide a beneficial leisure time occupation—learning reading, writing, and arithmetic. This falls in line with the idea that prisoners must be able to have a certain amount of freedom in order to maintain order within the larger institution. In 1801, New York State elementary education was taught to inmates during the winter months by the better-educated inmates. This is basically the way things operated in terms of correctional education. There were no outside interactions; inmates trained other inmates, and just as they were responsible for maintaining order, they were also the ones who did the teaching. In 1825, the Boston Prison Discipline Society was created. Its focus was on religion and the inmate's salvation being achieved through Sabbath schools and by the development of industrious habits under strict supervision. Sabbath schools became a feature in a number of prisons in the northern United States. "The Sabbath schools did provide the infant stage of prison education and inmates were more aptly prepared for a satisfactory adjustment to society upon release than many of us realize" (Roberts, 1971, p. 4).

There was a difference between the Pennsylvania system in the 1820s and the Auburn system in the 1840s, in New York State. Under the Pennsylvania system, only basic forms of education were practiced, such as the study of morals and religion, which was headed by the chaplain, who went from cell to cell in the prison visiting the inmates. This was the product of Quaker reformers, who believed in a system within the prison that required total separation. However, from this we see the first real prison teacher, the chaplain who discussed readings of the Bible. Under the Auburn system, "[R]ather than being seen as fellow beings capable of the entire range of human intelligence and emotion, convicts were now thought to be something as man and beast who needed first to be broken and trained" (Silva, 1994, p. 21). Also under this system, the administration was unimpressed by the cottage work coming from the Pennsylvania system and chose to use the inmates as workers; this was their function, and this of course left no time to engage in educational endeavors. However, in 1847, in New York, the first legal recognition of academic education was put into effect: A law provided for the appointment of two instructors for each prison (Auburn and Sing Sing). As the chaplains had done in the Pennsylvania system, these instructors would also pass from cell to cell and teach the "three Rs." One of the problems with this system of education was that the visits were few and far between, thereby bringing into question the purpose of such a process.

Brockway's Era, 1870 to 1929

Zebulon Brockway's (warden at the Elmira Reformatory on New York in the 1870s) influence on prison reform and more specifically prison education is crucial in this historical analysis. As Roberts (1971) notes, "Brockway gave education for the first time an important place in the correctional process" (p. 8). Brockway worked on developing his educational system by enlisting specialists. In 1878, selected inmates were placed in charge of elementary classes meetings six times a week, and Dr. D. R. Ford of the Elmira Women's College was hired to conduct courses in physical geography and natural science for advanced inmates. It is here that the beginnings of postsecondary education (academic and vocational) begin to take shape. Most of the education that was going on at the time was still being done by inmates to other inmates.

A Special Note on Texas

Rambo (1933) reveals in his thesis a number of interesting points regarding the early history of correctional education in Texas. He makes note that the first law providing for any form of education in the Texas Prison System was passed in 1895 (Rambo, 1933, p. 2). This law gave management the right to have the chaplain carry on any kind of schoolwork that he saw fit. There was no schoolwork done under this law. The next law regarding education came about in 1911; it provided for industrial education and stated that all illiterates must attend school. The law was amended in 1927 and provided for a full-time educational director. The first prison schoolwork was done within the walls of the Huntsville unit in 1911. The State Department of Education donated books, and the best-educated prisoners did the teaching. In the spring of 1911, 68 students were enrolled. In the next few years, schoolwork was unsettled. Schools were reorganized and abolished several times because of numerous reasons, chief among which was lack of funds. In 1921, in addition to education on the Huntsville unit, elementary grades were taught on the Eastham and Ferguson Farms. In 1927 schoolwork was suspended. It was reorganized in the late fall. The subjects taught included reading, writing, arithmetic, spelling, English geography, civics, and Spanish. "In the spring of 1929, the desire of the convicts to become educated had spread so rapidly and so many had sought the opportunity to attend school, that the management appropriated money from the treasury of the amusement funds to re-establish a school on the Eastham Farm" (Rambo, 1933, p. 4). "The greatest movement in school work came in 1931 and 1932. New books were bought and obtained from the state; new ideas were introduced; and, in general, a complete new system was organized. The enrollment grew from less than eight hundred men to over two thousand."

As the 1920s approached, there became more of an emphasis on correspondence courses between inmates and teachers on the outside. The earliest came from Columbia University in New York. In 1924, there is evidence of the first personal contact between inmates and college faculty at Rockview Prison in Pennsylvania. At Ohio penitentiary in 1924, 200 prisoners enrolled in correspondence courses from everything on poultry raising to advertising and commercial art. It is here that we may have for the first time a linkage between postsecondary education and recidivism; it was reported that a survey of convicts completing these courses indicated them as successful after release from prison (Smith, 1930). There were regional differences in terms of prison education programs. California led the way in prisoner education. In 1928, San Quentin Prison reported that, in addition to those inmates enrolled in basic literacy, grade school, and high school studies, there were 438 prisoners enrolled in University of California Extension Division courses. In Illinois, Iowa, Kansas, Massachusetts, Minnesota, New Jersey, New York, Pennsylvania, and Wisconsin, inmates were enrolled in extension courses, primarily from their land-grant colleges and state education agencies. In New York, at Clinton Prison, inmate teachers participated in weekly Normal School training sessions offered by the civilian head teacher so they could be certified by the state Board of Regents as elementary school teachers. In 1927, a large percentage passed the certification test successfully. At the New York State Reformatory at Elmira, in keeping with Brockway's traditions of linking education with parole, compulsory education up to the eighth-grade level was required, and both academic and trade classes were held in 30 classrooms throughout the day. In Pennsylvania, five professors from State College taught vocational courses to some 50 inmates at Bellefonte Prison. It is clear though, that the mid- to late-1920s witnessed the first articulation between prisons and colleges, although systematic college course offerings and degrees would not come for several more decades (Silva, 1994).

Education as Correctional Treatment: 1929 to 1965

During this period, there were two significant developments regarding correctional education: (1) the recognition that education is an essential element in a modern program of correctional treatment; and (2) the belief that such education should be of the same type and quality that has been found effective in adult education programs in free society (Roberts, 1971). One of the significant events to occur in this period was the 1933 Englehhardt Commission, which was appointed to study the scope of education in New York State. One recommendation clearly states,

> The term education as used in correctional work should be interpreted very broadly. Education in terms of the three Rs alone, or of vocational training, organized and administered in the manner of traditional schools is inadequate in correctional work. Education can and must be administered in terms of individual needs. There must be a complete background of information upon which an educational diagnosis can be made and the administrative set-up for training must permit the use of teaching methods applicable to diagnostic procedure. Education must be directed purposefully towards specific objectives. Teaching must be very largely in terms of guidance. It may be, but it is not necessarily, concerned with textbooks, classrooms, and the ordinary appurtenances of the traditional school. The objective is always the attainment of some well defined end, such as changing attitudes, increasing vocational efficiency, elimination of complexes, the development of willingness and skill for cooperative living after release (Wallack et al., 1939, p. 19).

In terms of individual needs, we see that in today's setting this is a crucial element of correctional education. There are three basic levels that most programs focus on: (1) adult basic education; (2) vocational education/training; and (3) postsecondary academic education. The focus has also shifted from just creating a worker for the labor force to creating a resocialized community member.

During World War II, little attention was paid to prison education. After the war, the G.I. Bill flooded colleges and universities with veterans. Adult education was now being reexamined and higher education became the norm; this allowed prisoner education to become a more acceptable notion. The first-degree program was initiated by Southern Illinois

University at Carbondale at the Menard State Prison when, in 1953, 25 inmates registered for classes. Part of the University Studies degree program, inmate-students were funded by state aid and university grants. These initial efforts in prison higher education lasted until the early 1980s. The 1950s saw a slow and sporadic development in prison college programs. In 1954, only one other college was involved in prison education, the University of Maryland, which offered one course per semester at Maryland State Penitentiary. By 1965, more than 10 years after the first college program was initiated, only a dozen postsecondary college programs were operating on a regular basis in the nation's state and federal prisons.

A Special Note on Texas

Gathright's doctoral dissertation (1999) notes some significant historical developments in the correctional education process in Texas. A need was established for vocational instruction based on the rise of prison industries in the Texas prison system. Through the 1940s, inmates received training in skills needed for those industries. Instruction was provided by inmate teachers with college degrees, headed by a civilian director and a civilian librarian, a practice that continued until the 1970s. The late 1940s and 1950s saw the rise of a more organized system of education under the leadership of Prison Director O. B. Ellis, who oversaw the initiation of GED classes in 1956. Vocational classes were offered in the following areas: construction, cooking and baking, television repair, brick laying, welding, auto mechanics, carpentry, commercial sign painting, laundry services, and poultry husbandry (Stone et al., 1974). Funds from the Texas Prison Rodeo were devoted to the financing of these education programs. The 1960s marked a decade of dynamic change for the now-named Texas Department of Corrections. The system, under the Director George Beto, established an Adult Basic Education (ABE) program and worked with local colleges to establish a continuing education department in 1965. Included in these colleges were Lee College, Alvin Junior College, and later Sam Houston State University. These colleges continue to serve offenders seeking postsecondary education inside Texas prisons.

The Rehabilitation Model Meets with the War on Crime: 1965 to the Present

According to Silva (1994), the single most important event in the development of higher education for prisoners occurred in 1965. Congress passed Title IV of the Higher Education Act. Grants became available to inmate-students, who could usually qualify for the maximum funding possible because of their minimum income. The availability of these grants allowed students the opportunity to participate in an institution many would not have access to in the free world.

Project Newgate (see also Seashore et al., 1976) was one of the most ambitious college prison programs according to Silva (1994). In 1967 and 1968, the Office of Economic Opportunity funded five college programs. The five programs were at prisons in Rockview, Pennsylvania; Saint Cloud, Minnesota; Ashland, Kentucky; Sante Fe, New Mexico; and Englewood, Colorado. Three other non–Project Newgate sites—Lompoc, California; Manard, Illinois; and Eastham, Texas—were included in the final 1972 study. The initial concept of

Newgate was to establish, as nearly as possible, a campus experience within the prison walls. Inmates who had begun their degree programs in prison would be encouraged and financially supported to continue their studies on the campuses of the cooperating colleges. Three primary sources of success were included in the final Project Newgate report: (1) lessened recidivism, (2) achievement of stability, and (3) realization of life goals.

Beginning in 1965, there was a rapid expansion of prison college programs. In 1967, Marin Junior College was offering an associate's degree to inmates at San Quentin. In 1968, there were college programs in 13 states and the District of Columbia and in the Federal Bureau of Prisons. By 1970, 33 states offered college programs on their prisons. In 1973, there were 182 programs; by 1976, 237 programs; and by 1982, 350 programs (Silva, 1994).

A Special Note on Canada
Weir (1973) discusses the history of correctional education in Canada. He notes that education programs were implemented initially to assist those who did not have a chance to get a good education on the outside. It was a way to make up for what adults lacked as children. Education had started to be viewed as a major institution within the larger institution of the penitentiary. Weir notes that part of the history for both Canada and the United States is that correctional education, more specifically vocational education, was crucial for job skills, which then in turn could translate into the inmate, once released, becoming part of the workforce and staying out of further trouble. Weir notes that "the real concern was to provide programs of adult education that would contribute to the maturation of those inmates exposed to it, provide programs of vocational training designed to teach the occupational skills required to compete in the competitive 20th century labor market, and while in doing so, hopefully bring about changes in behavior and attitudes to the extent that substantial numbers of inmates who enter our institutions each year would avoid wasting the remainder of their lives in the shadow world of the criminal" (1973, p. 44).

A Special Note on Texas
Texas, with its growing correctional population, has the highest number of inmates enrolled in academic programs. Tables 15–1 and 15–2 show data on last year's enrollment figures for students in the Continuing Education Program in the Windham School District.

Table 15–1 CONTINUING EDUCATION PROGRAM PARTICIPANTS DURING **2000–2001**

Total Participants	*9578*
Two-year college academic	6490
Four-year college academic	894
Graduate college academic	130
Vocational college credit	2984
Vocational college noncredit	688

Table 15–2   Degrees and Certificates Awarded during 2000–2001

Total Degrees and Certificates Awarded	*3776*
Associate degrees conferred	373
Bachelor degrees conferred	61
Master's degree conferred	6
Junior college vocational credit certificates	1760
Junior college noncredit certificates	1576

A Special Note on New York

In 1996, New York Governor George Pataki commuted the lengthy prison sentences of seven people, six of whom, he noted on their behalf, had dutifully earned college degrees in prison. What was so interesting about this particular moment was that in 1995, Pataki eliminated the college program from the New York State budget. There has been a serious decline in the availability of college prison programs in New York. While the number of high school equivalency degrees in New York rose from 2779 awarded in 1991 to 3216 in 1999; college degrees went from 1078 in 1991 to only 70 in 1999 (New York State Department of Correctional Services, 1989).

These special notes on Texas and New York and their current correctional education situation are a point for discussion about the current state of affairs in terms of corrections. On the one hand, Texas continues to serve a great number of offenders and continues to provide a variety of correctional education programs, while New York has removed the funding for certain programs and seems to be moving in a different direction. These events could very well have an effect on what inmates do once they are released from incarceration. This issue will be the focus of the rest of this chapter.

GENERAL ISSUES RELATING TO CORRECTIONAL EDUCATION

Throughout the history of correctional education, there have been a number of debates as to what education programs in prison should be able to accomplish. The area that has been discussed the most is the effect of the correctional education process on recidivism. There has been a great deal of debate as to whether or not the process or some other variable is actually associated with the behavior of an offender once released from prison. Rehabilitative programs that were operated in the 1940s to the 1960s were reported on by Martinson (1974), and it was noted that these programs had no real effect on recidivism. This led to a public sentiment against rehabilitative efforts aimed at those incarcerated. This became known as the "nothing works" ideology.

It was believed that rehabilitative efforts could be enhanced if the incarcerated offender sought spiritual enlightenment. In the 1960s postsecondary programs began to be offered in correctional settings. In an overview of the effectiveness of prison education programs, Linden and Perry (1983) pointed out that the 1950s and 1960s were a period of optimism, whereas the 1970s were characterized by Martinson's "nothing works" ideology. They argued that prison education programs can produce desirable results: "Most evaluations have shown that inmates make substantial improvements in learning, but this does not necessarily have an impact on rates of post-release employment and recidivism. The review of the literature suggests that programs will be most likely to succeed if they are intensive, if they can establish an alternative community within the prison and if they offer post-release services to inmates" (p. 43). Also, "The research suggests that programs will have the most impact if inmates are intensively involved in the educational process and if they get peer support for these activities. Second, if the reduction of recidivism is seen as a goal of prison education programs, support services should be provided to an inmate upon release to enable him to continue his education or to assist him in finding a job where his new learning can be used" (p. 55).

Gehring (2000) critiques the research that has been done in the field of correctional education and notes that "lack of education is related to—but does not cause—crime. Yet data is often presented so audiences will assume education reduces recidivism. The fact, of course, is that education helps people pursue social aspirations, it does not make them into good community members." (p. 198). He also explores the idea that the educational program itself should not be evaluated (in terms of its effectiveness) on what the participants do once released rather recidivism should be measured at the individual level. Gehring (2000) explores another issue relating to correctional education, that "many institutional systems foster a seemingly inherent, anti-education bias among staff" (p. 201) and this should be considered when looking at attitudes about recidivism. Johnson and colleagues (1997) lend support to Gehring's argument about the antieducation bias. In their survey of wardens, 41 percent of those surveyed wanted college education to be either reduced or eliminated. Further results from the survey indicate that 68 percent of wardens noted that college education services have been reduced or eliminated in the past year.

> The ideologically tinged perspective toward prisons as places *for* [emphasis in the original] punishment as opposed to imprisonment *as* [emphasis in the original] punishment gives rise to the principle of least eligibility and calls into question *any* [emphasis in the original] service or program that prisons might provide. When coupled with the cost consciousness and budget constraints present in many states (and the federal government), prison programs become an easy target for righteous criticism and elimination (Johnson et al., 1997, pp. 38–39).

Jones and d'Errico (1994) also note that correctional education is called into question (by those within the system and law makers as well) about how it serves the offender while incarcerated. "Whether a college education is appropriate for prisoners is largely an ideological or moral question, and the answer to this depends on one's expectation of what it means to be a prisoner. The answer, in short, depends on how different people believe a prisoner ought to be treated during incarceration" (Jones & d'Errico, 1994, p. 4). They also bring into question whether the correctional education process serves to educate or correct the prisoner. It is noted by these authors that correctional education is a process that takes place and should take place because the prisons should have been in the process of reforming the prisoner all along. In essence, the correctional education process serves as a supplement to incarceration in terms of producing a person that will be ready to be part of the community once released. Jones and d Errico go on to discuss what types of things prisoners should be learning in the process. They indicate that teaching liberal arts and humanities to offenders can produce critical thinking skills instead of what they call, "rigid, personal dogma" (1994, p. 10).

Correctional education programs include programs such as life skills, ABE (adult basic education) and GED classes, vocational training, and correspondence courses. A stated goal of most prison education programs is to return the offender successfully to society (Duguid, 1982). As correctional thought has moved from penology (punishment) to corrections (treatment) to opportunity (social programs), legislatures have begun to mandate educational programs for offenders. For example, Texas offenders with less than a sixth-grade functional level must attend ABE classes until such time as they can test higher.

Enocksson (1981) argues that just examining recidivism rates, as a prime criterion for the success of a correctional education program, is not helpful to the field of study. She believes that certain things about the program should be investigated to understand how it affects the offenders who go through the process. One of the variables she promotes as being important to understanding the phenomenon is the number of people who complete the program. For postsecondary education, an academic degree would indicate completion of a program as well as a vocational certificate. It is also argued that criminal behavior should not be focused on after the offender is released it should be on what type of employment is gained upon release. "Work has a central position on all of our lives because it is an economic necessity and consumes much of our time and effort" (Enocksson, 1981, p. 9).

EMPIRICAL RESEARCH RELATING TO CORRECTIONAL EDUCATION AND INMATE BEHAVIOR

Gerber and Fritsch (1995) evaluated and summarized research that focuses on the correctional education process and its outcomes. The three areas of education are (1) precollege, or what is known as adult basic education; (2) college education; and (3) vocational education. They note, "The available studies on the relationship between college education and post release employment and education are methodologically weak, but consistently show positive consequences for society. We recommend reserving judgment on these two outcomes until more rigorous studies are conducted" (p. 129). They also found that not only do these studies examine the educational process and its effect on recidivism, but also found research on the effects of correctional education on the postrelease participation in education of offenders and disciplinary problems of those correctional education participants inside the prison where the process was taking place. Most of the studies in the three areas showed support for the idea that correctional education reduces recidivism. The authors also point out that future work needs to examine other issues not found in the reviewed material. Many of the studies that were reviewed by Gerber and Fritsch are reviewed more carefully in the following sections.

Precollege Correctional Education Research

One of the earliest evaluations of prison education programs looked at the effects of attendance at the full-time day school of Wisconsin State Prison on recidivism rates. In this study, Schnur (1948) compared the recidivism of 680 former prison students with 1082 controls over a two-year period following release form prison. While the experimental and control groups were unmatched, an attempt was made to standardize the two groups on the basis of factors associated with both recidivism and participation in the school program. After the standardization, the two groups were compared and it was found that there were relatively small but statistically significant differences in recidivism rates between them. One additional finding of relevance to policymakers was that no effects were observed until the men had attended school for six months or more.

Saden (1962) looked at 1000 inmates who were paroled from Michigan State Prison between 1945 and 1949 also found that former prison students were more successful on parole than were nonstudents. However, in this study there was no matching or random assignment nor was there an attempt to control for differences between the two groups (the school group was younger and had slightly less involvement in crime than the nonschool group).

Mace (1978) studied the effect of correctional education on the adjustment of former inmates back into society as measured by their postrelease recidivism. The sample consisted of 320 adult inmates paroled from West Virginia prisons. Mace found that (1) educational participants has significantly lower recidivism rates than did nonparticipants and remained out of prison for significantly longer periods of time; (2) inmates who completed their GED were significantly less likely to recidivate than were nonparticipants; and (3) college participation was found not to have any statistically significant effect in reducing the number of former inmates who recidivated.

Cogburn (1986) studied the recidivism rates for inmates who earned a diploma or a GED while incarcerated. The sample consisted of 2844 inmates in the Alabama Department of Corrections. The data were collected from the records of inmates from 1976 through 1986. Cogburn found that (1) of the 2844 who were part of the study, 1182 earned diplomas, 284 earned diplomas and GED certificates, and 1378 earned GED certificates only; (2) 70 percent of those inmates who received a diploma or a GED certificate did not return to prison, 11 percent did return to prison, and less than 20 percent were still incarcerated; and (3) the overall recidivism rate for inmates who received a GED was 12.9 percent, 13.3 percent for diploma recipients, and 16.9 percent for those inmates who received both a GED and a diploma (pp. 6–10).

A study conducted by the New York State Department of Correctional Services (1989) examined the recidivism rate of inmates who had earned a GED while incarcerated. The population of this study consisted of 15,520 inmates (4226 who earned a GED and 11,294 who did not earn a GED) who were released in 1986 and 1987. A chi square test was used in treating the data. The analysis revealed that inmates who received a GED while incarcerated returned at a lower rate than those inmates who did not receive a GED. Additionally, the data indicated that a significant difference existed between the recidivism rate of inmates who earned a GED and those who did not. Moreover, the study concluded that a positive relationship existed between completion of a GED diploma while incarcerated and the likelihood of returning to prison.

Vocational (Correctional) Education Research

Anderson (1981) sampled correctional clients paroled from the Vienna, Illinois Correctional Center during the years 1972 through 1976. The sample included male parolees who had received vocational training and academic education. Comparisons were made with parolees who had received neither vocational training nor academic education during the same time period. A random sample of 400 was selected. Some had no information available; of the 238 left, 122 had vocational training and 70 had academic training (GED/college courses). Some had both. Case files were reviewed and data were collected. "Level of vocational training" refers to the proportion of time trained within vocational areas. For some trade areas, there were several levels of training that produced one or more certificates. Welding, food service, and drafting were three trade areas that produced a parole violation rate of 0 to 14 percent. The one parolee in horticulture and the two in Emergency Medical Technician (EMT) also completed parole without violation. Vocational training was shown to be positively correlated with parole success. Those who enrolled in vocational training were less likely to commit further felonies. Major findings were as follows: (1) As the type of vocational certificate becomes better (more hours and a higher level of training), the length of employment while on parole becomes longer; (2) parolees who received vocational training had significantly fewer arrests on parole than those parolees who did not receive vocational training; (3) parolees who had no vocational training or lower levels of vocational training were more likely to have their parole revoked than those parolees who had higher levels of vocational training; (4) parolees who received vocational training were employed, on parole, significantly longer than those parolees who did not receive vocational training; (5) there was little relationships between type of vocational training and initial job placement on parole, and this strongly suggests the need for a coordinated job placement program; (6) as the grade point average in vocational training increases, so does the number of months working on parole, and this relationship is statistically significant; and (7) those parolees who were enrolled in academic course work while at the institution were significantly more likely to take vocational training or further course work while on parole (Anderson, 1981).

Schumacker and colleagues (1990) examined adult releasees who had vocational/academic training and compared them to a control group of releasees who did not receive vocational training. A fourth group that received only academic training while incarcerated was also studied. A total of 760 releasees were studied for 12 months. Background variables, such as vocational enrollment and completion, academic background, employment, and violation status over the 12-month period, were included. A stratified proportional sampling procedure was used to select and equate inmate groups. Parole officers recorded the month-to-month status of each releasee during the time on parole. They found that (1) the vocational and vocational/academic groups had the highest employment rates and lowest criminal activity rates after 12 months of tracking; (2) the control group had the highest criminal activity rate; (3) when compared with vocational noncompleters, data indicated that vocational completers (vocational completers were those who finished a vocational course of instruction) had a higher employment rate and fewer arrests; (4) the vocational noncompleters, however, had higher employment rates and fewer arrests than the control group; (5) the academic group had the lowest employment rate and second highest criminal activity rate at 12 months compared with those releasees who had less than a GED; and (6) the completion of a GED or higher increased postrelease success over those with less than a GED (Schumacker et al., 1990).

Anderson and colleagues (1991) compared adult releasees who had vocational or vocational and academic training to a control group of releasees who chose not to enroll in vocational or academic training. A fourth group, who received only academic coursework while incarcerated, was also studied. A total of 760 releasees were studied for 12 months. Violation/nonviolation was the dependent variable. It was cross tabulated with fourteen independent variables, focusing especially on education and/or vocational program involvement while incarcerated. Violation was defined as "returned to prison because of parole violation," "committing a new crime" (also resulting in parole violation) or "being absent without permission (also a parole violation). Chi square analysis was done to examine the relationship between violators and nonviolators. Chi square analysis indicated that seeking and obtaining a job was essential to remaining on parole. Parolees who had no prior documented history of abusing alcohol or drugs were no more successful on community release. Anderson and colleagues (1991) profile a successful parolee and an unsuccessful one based on a number of independent variables. Parolees who did not have a known record of alcohol and/or drug abuse were more successful on community release. Important positive background characteristics included being married, participating in academic/vocational programs while incarcerated, not being a minority group member, and being a first-time (incarcerated) felony offender. The profile of the parole violator, in terms of background characteristics, is a single male who does not seek nor obtain a job following release, has a known history of abusing alcohol and/or drugs, has not taken academic or vocational courses while incarcerated, is a minority (e.g., black, Asian, Hispanic), and more often is a repeat offender.

Postsecondary Academic Correctional Education Research

Chalfont (1972) evaluated a prison education program at the Lorton Institute in Virginia. It was not initially set up as a controlled experiment. A matched control group was formed of prison college applicants who failed to enter the program because of early parole, change of plans, or other reasons. The experimental group consisted of 73 inmates, while the post hoc control group consisted of 32 inmates. The program consisted of instruction in sociology, mathematics, and English at the first-year university level. Inmates who completed the equivalent of first-year university were permitted to attend second-year classes at Federal City College in Washington, D.C. Extensive support services were provided to help inmates adjust to the academic and social pressures of college routine. In addition, financial support and employment assistance was provided for some released inmates. Evaluating the success of the program in terms of the absence of arrests, Chalfont's findings indicate that 58 percent of the experimental group and 56 percent of the control group could be classified as successes. However, those inmates who were arrested but had their cases dismissed were redesignated as successes; 70 percent of the experimentals were successful as compared to 59 percent of the control subjects.

Duguid (1982) examined the University of Victoria correctional education program for a follow-up study. He examined a group of 65 men during a three-year period to see if they would return to prison after being provided with a college education while incarcerated. At the end of this three-year period, Duguid found that the rate of recidivism for the students was 14 percent as compared to 52 percent for the matched group of nonstudent prisoners.

Linden and colleagues (1984) examined two penitentiaries in Canada, a maximum and medium security facility. They used an experimental design to see if those inmates who went through a university-level education program for five months would recidivate when released. The sample size was 66, with pretests and posttests. No statistically significant results were found between the control and experimental groups. They note that one of the deficiencies of the program was its length; since it only lasted five months, the effectiveness of the education is in question. The program did accomplish the goal of providing inmates with university-level training. The inmates and prison staff had positive assessments and a high level of satisfaction with the program. The program seemed to have a positive effect on the inmates' discipline, noting that they had better records after entering the program than before.

Offenders involved in educational programs within maximum and medium security correctional institutions were selected in the study conducted by Knepper (1989). A study of 526 offenders enrolled in these programs and released on parole between January 1980 and December 1985 was identified. The study population was divided into four groups: (1) a "college" group, composed of offenders who completed at least 12 credits toward an associate of arts degree; (2) a "vocational" group, consisting of those enrolled in vocational programs; (3) a "secondary" group of those completing secondary-level academic work; and (4) an "elementary" group of those offenders completing instruction in remedial academic studies. Knepper found that while offenders who participated in college programs in prison had significantly lower needs assessment scores on parole, suggesting fewer adjustment problems, they were also found to have a higher level of recidivism. It was also discovered that offenders who participated in college programs while in prison and do not recidivate while on parole successfully complete parole at a lower level of supervision.

O'Neil (1990) examined students in the Prison College Extension of Alexander City Junior College in Alabama. There were 129 postsecondary education participants and 129 non-postsecondary education participants who were randomly selected. Those who had postsecondary education were found to be slightly statistically significant in terms of their recidivism as compared to those who had no post-secondary education. Participation of the incarcerated in correctional education programs seems to result in some decrease.

Lagenbach and colleagues (1990) studied a televised instructional system that provided postsecondary education to inmates. They found lower rates of recidivism in the student group. Attempts were made at making causal inferences but were unsuccessful because of an uncontrolled variable (the inmates' employment status once released and education level). Behavior in terms of misconduct (while incarcerated) on the part of the offender indicated no difference between participants and nonparticipants.

Seashore and colleagues (1976) studied college education in prison. An extensive study was conducted of selected college programs in state and federal prisons throughout the country. The research consisted of on-site observations of program operation as well as the analysis of each program's impact on the postprison "success" of former students. Over 350 former program participants were found and personally interviewed. The Project was known as Project Newgate. For the study recidivism was broken down into four categories other than not being arrested or no violations occurring. The researchers indicate things such as returning to prison on a new conviction; technical violations or jail for 60 says to a year; technical violation or jail for 30 to 59 days; and minor difficulties and less than 30 days in jail. No consistent differentiations in terms of recidivism between groups (college program participants and nonparticipants) appeared. The researchers note that the programs or background experiences seemed not to have played a role in whether or not someone recidivated. In some instances the control group had a lower recidivism rate than the college participants. The authors note,

> At first glance some may interpret these data as indicating that participation in a prison college program has no bearing on whether a participant will recidivate. However, this would be a hasty conclusion and one too often made in studies of this kind. Although it may be valid to say that no relationship has been demonstrated one way or another, one must keep in mind that participation in college prison programs could have an impact on its participants' behavior and attitudes, but one which either is not measured or is being offset or obscured by the impact of other yet unidentified variables (Seachore et al., 1976, pp. 184–185).

Rose and Nyre (1979) studied the influence of post secondary education programs available to inmates in the state of California regarding their recidivism rate, educational opportunities, and the need for such programs. The population consisted of 38 public and private state agencies, including correctional institutions and postsecondary institutions. The data were collected through a variety of research tools such as questionnaires, interviews, case studies, and educational records. Rose and Nyre found that (1) quite a number of ex-offenders who participated in correctional education programs have gone on to four-year institutions; (2) the availability of education programs in the California prisons has facilitated an increase in enrollment in these programs; and (3) the program offerings include a wide range of both academic and vocational courses that can accommodate a wide range of student interest and stability.

Thorpe and colleagues (1984) studied the recidivism rate of former inmates who had earned a degree while incarcerated in a New York State prison. The sample consisted of 276 former inmates. The research found that (1) the graduates recidivated at an overall rate that was lower than the rate for all releases (14 percent versus 20 percent) and (2) those graduates who did recidivate remained free for a longer period of time than was predicted. The researchers concluded that the inmates' motivation and capabilities and the impact of the educational program might jointly contribute to the lower recidivism rate.

Wolf and Sylves (1981) evaluated the effectiveness of the Higher Education Opportunity Program (HEOP) in New York State. This program allowed inmates to enroll in courses leading to postsecondary degrees at an accredited institution. College courses were taught at the institution, or in some cases inmates attended classes at college campuses but returned to the correctional facility at the end of the day. Data were compiled on a sample of 277 former male inmates who participated in the program and had since been paroled. Information collected included the subjects' individual and demographic characteristics, criminal experiences, time spent, credits earned, courses taken, services received, academic achievement in the program, subsequent criminal record, employment, income, and educational status after classes. The data indicated that (1) there were positive program results despite short periods of participation; (2) over half of the subjects attended college and 75 percent had been employed after release; and (3) the group's recidivism rate was comparatively low.

Holloway and Moke (1986) assessed the impact of an educational program during incarceration upon an offender's postrelease behavior. It hypothesized that inmates obtaining associate degrees would experience more successful reintegration (meaning they would not be reincarcerated, they would not be arrested, and they would be employed full time in the first year of parole) than nondegreed inmates. Subjects participating in the study were 300 residents of the Lebanon Correctional Institution, a medium security prison in Ohio for adults under thirty years of age. Ninety-five of the 300 inmates earned associate degrees while incarcerated. These individuals were compared with two other groups: 116 offenders who received high school diplomas and 106 offenders who were high school dropouts. The research revealed that by the end of the first year on parole, more than two-thirds of the college graduates were employed, compared to approximately 60 percent of the high school graduates and 40 percent of the high school dropouts, suggesting that a linear relationship exists between the level of education an inmate acquires while in prison and the likelihood of obtaining and retaining employment. The research also found that college education during incarceration contributes to inmates' postrelease success in regard to arrest and recidivism.

Blackburn (1981) studied the relationship between recidivism arte and participating in a postsecondary educational program. The focus of this study was on whether or not there was a significant difference in the length of time each group remained free before incarceration. Blackburn found that the recidivism rate for nonparticipants was higher than for participants (58 percent as compared to 37 percent). However, there was no difference found in the amount of time each group remained free.

Lockwood (1991) studied a college education program in New York State to assess the effects upon the participants. One of the variables examined by Lockwood was the number of credit hours that a student took while incarcerated. What was found was that there was lack of support for the idea that college education in a correctional program reduces recidivism. Furthermore, persons with more than 60 college credit hours were actually more likely to be reincarcerated than those with fewer than 30 credit hours.

Women and Research on the Postsecondary Correctional Education Process

In recent years a great deal of attention has been paid to the increasing number of women who are being incarcerated. Women are the fastest growing segment of the prison population, and many are taking notice. One serious deficiency in the correctional education research is the lack of focus on women and how they, as a group, are affected by education programs they are offered. Fine and associates (2001) analyzed 274 female inmates who participated in college programs while incarcerated and compared them to 2031 women who did not attend college while incarcerated. Findings show that women who attended college while in prison were significantly less likely to be reincarcerated (7.7 percent) than those who did not attend college while in prison (29.9 percent). Beyond the traditional approach to this type of research, Fine and colleagues (2001) also evaluated the impact of the college program on the safety and management of the prison environment by surveying faculty members and interviewing correctional officers and administrators. Findings indicated that the prison environment was safer and more manageable with fewer disciplinary actions. The researchers also tried to understand the personal and social effects of the college programs on students and their children. This was done through one-on-one interviews conducted by inmate researchers and focus groups with inmates, children, university presidents, and faculty. Lastly, as part of the research objectives, Fine and colleagues (2001) examined the impact of the college experience in the transition home from prison by interviewing former inmates and analyzing the reincarceration rates described previously. This comprehensive approach to studying the correctional education process provides a guide for future research on the correctional education process.

Summary

Correctional education has a long history in the United States as well as a significant history in the state of Texas. This history lends itself to an understanding of where the phenomenon is in contemporary context and where it is headed. This is crucial to understanding the nature of the research that was described in the last three sections of this review. There are a number of issues surrounding the correctional education process, from whether or not it should be implemented to what the process is best suited for in terms of reforming, rehabilitating, or preparing the offender for when he or she returns to the community. Much of the empirical research finds that there is a great deal of support for the hypothesis that inmates that go through the education process are less likely to recidivate when they return to society as compared to those who do not participate. The research is limited in the sense that there are no real comparisons made between the individuals who do participate. For example, no study really examined the relationship between the type of education (vocational and postsecondary academic/college) an inmate received while incarcerated and compared the groups' recidivism to find out which group was better off once released. This is a shortcoming that other studies must explore. Other shortcomings include the lack of research focusing on racial groups and the impact race has not only on the education process but on the postrelease period. Finally, while some recent work has focused on women in the correctional education process, more must be done.

CORRECTIONAL EDUCATION RESEARCH AGENDA

While there is a great deal of attention paid to the outcome of the correctional education process in terms of recidivism and postrelease employment, there is little work done on how the process works within the correctional setting. Some research does focus on what the educational process does in terms of reducing the amount of disciplinary actions among participants, but again, there seems to be a need for more research to be done. Many researchers come to study correctional education from the outside and often staying outside without even talking to one subject who is actually going through the process. Studies that exist with regard to prisoner attitudes focus on what prisoners consider to be the meaning and value of rehabilitation. The following questions need to be explored to better the research that has been done in the field:

1. **What purpose does it serve the prisoner who is going through the process?**   This gets to how the correctional education process effects the prisoner while incarcerated, which in turn could lead to other outcomes once released. As Taylor (1994) notes about his experience as a student in the correctional education process, "I had found my lifeline, the exploration and development of my intellect. I thrived on the positive challenge and surprised myself with my academic savoir-faire. I could actually witness the results of my cognitive growth in my test scores and term paper grades" (p. 126). Many of the studies cited previously and a great deal of other literature on the correctional education process note that cognitive development is crucial in the process and that it does happen, but there has been no real empirical research done on it rather; it is simply assumed by many in the field of study. Duguid (1982) notes that the cognitive deficiency model assumes that prisoners are simply deficient in certain analytic problem-solving skills, interpersonal and social skills, and ethical/moral development. These are assumptions that we place onto the person going through the process; there may be some other purpose for engaging in the process. One idea stemming from this is the development of a typology of students based on why they engage in the process and what purpose it serves them. Basically, why would prisoners want to learn about sociology or psychology when they could be playing dominos or watching television? One hypothesis is that most of the participants in the correctional education process (more specifically the vocational or college process) hope it

will assist them in getting paroled and in turn into something useful once released from prison. An alternative hypothesis is that the prisoner goes through the process out of sheer boredom. Another hypothesis is that the prisoner was denied the opportunity on the outside to go through the education process properly and in the prison setting it is more convenient. This hypothesis could lead to the development of a theory about the correctional education process and how it serves the underprivileged minorities that are incarcerated.

2. **What does the process do to the individual while incarcerated?**   There are a number of factors to consider for this question. While there are those who believe the educational process is strictly developing the morals or ethics of the prisoner or that his or her cognitive development is what is being transformed miss the perception of the subject going through the process while part of the total institution. While these issues may be of some importance on a more microlevel, it is important to hear about the experiences that go on from the people in the process. This is important especially if any type of longitudinal study is to be undertaken. There is no doubt that once a prisoner has acquired a degree or has taken a number of classes that something has changed within his or her minds, but what has changed? Another related question here is, What courses changed them the most and why did they have an effect on them? A course in economics may not have the same effect as a course in criminology or psychology. Are different courses more influential, was it an instructor, was it something learned in the class, or was it something derived from the class that assisted in the change?

3. **How does the environment play a role in the education process?**   Taylor (1994) goes into detail about how he studied so that he could drown out the "cell house's roar" and how study groups were formed whereby inmates quizzed each other over meals and tutored each other. He notes how careful he had to be with his study group at recreation time because the policy was that any meeting over three or more offenders in a nonsport activity was considered an "illegal gathering." As long as a Bible was displayed so that it was perceived of as a religious activity not to be considered "illegal," the group could study. Another aspect to consider here is the idea that prisoners are dehumanized while incarcerated and their voices are silenced; prisoners are only allowed to speak to prison personnel when spoken to. Could it be that the environment in the larger institution silences the prisoner and the education process and the classroom dynamic is such that it allows the prisoner a chance to speak out without having to worry about what a correctional staff member might hear? As Mason (1994) notes about her experiences, "Within the first two weeks of prison, you realize that the environment is oppressive. If you are fortunate enough to have access to higher

education while incarcerated then you will have intellectual stimulation that you will not find anywhere else in the system" (p. 135). She goes on to note how the environment itself does not foster self-esteem and how the administration and officers were angry about the educational process taking place because the prisoners were getting something for free that they could not afford. This of course could be open to another idea for research in the form of a survey done to find out how correctional officers feel about the education process. One could hypothesize from what Mason (1994) notes that correctional officers will most likely have negative attitudes about the correctional education process, even more so for those prisoners acquiring a college degree.

4. **How are women affected by correctional education and how are their experiences different from or the same as those of their male counterparts?**   This type of comparative approach is essential in understanding the correctional education process. While Fine and colleagues (2001) is a start in the right direction for analyzing women who go through the process, most research has avoided including women, which provides an unclear view of the process. As Mason (1994) notes in her piece, the Department of Correctional Education school in Virginia only offered classes on business and cosmetology, and then there was the occasional night class offered by the local community college but the only degree it offered was in executive housekeeping. Due to the fact that women (even though they are increasing significantly) still make up a small number of the total prisoners in the United States, often states only have one facility for women, and this poses a significant problem in providing services to them such as correctional education. This too must be considered in the research. Theoretically one could argue that as a minority, the educational process for women is an enlightenment and an opportunity for them more so than their male counterparts. This is due to the fact that women have been socialized to be motherly and nurturing and maybe not independent and free to do what they wish. An education for women while incarcerated could also translate into more of an opportunity than they had prior to the institutional setting. This particular research idea must be considered by criminologists in future studies of correctional education.

CONCLUSION

Our efforts as researchers studying the correctional education process have the potential to contribute to the knowledge about the processes that go inside the prison walls. At the moment the potential remains just that, a suggestion of things to come. There are certain challenges to studying the process of correctional education because of its nature and the various perspectives from which to approach the task from. In this chapter, the foundation for the process was laid down by examining the historical development of the process. The issues surrounding the correctional education process were examined: Is it part of the rehabilitation ideology, or does it fit into the "nothing works" paradigm? These are questions that were posed and by continuing the research, an answer may be found. The empirical research that is currently available was included for a better understanding of where the field is situated, and then a research agenda was proposed to move in another direction. This direction is away from the focus on the outcomes to examining what truly affects the outcomes, the correctional education process itself. There is still a great deal of work to be done, and this area lends itself to a great deal of in-depth evaluations. It's up to those in the field to take the time to seek out active research agendas in this area.

REFERENCES

Anderson, D. B. (1981). The Relationship Between Correctional Education and Parole Success. *Journal of Offender Counseling, Services & Rehabilitation,* 5:13–25.

Anderson, D. B., Schumacker, R. E., & Anderson, S. L. (1991). Releasee Characteristics and Parole Success. *Journal of Offender Rehabilitation,* 17:133–145.

Basch, C. E. (1987). Focus Group Interviews: An Underutilized Research Technique for Improving Theory and Practice in Health Education. *Health Education Quarterly,* 14:411–448.

Blackburn, F. S. (1981). The Relationship between Recidivism and Participation in a Community College Program for Incarcerated Offenders. *Journal of Correctional Education,* 32:23–25.

Chalfont, C. (1972). The Lorton Prison College Project: Third Year Final Report. Washington, DC: Department of Corrections.

Cogburn, H. E. (1986). *Recidivism Study: Positive Terminations.* J. F. Ingram State Technical College ED 302315), pp. 4–10.

Duguid, S. (1982). Rehabilitation through Education: A Canadian Model. *Journal of Offender Counseling, Services & Rehabilitation,* 6:53–67.

Enocksson, K. (1981). Correctional Programs: A Review of the Value of Education and Training in Penal Institutions. *Journal of Offender Counseling, Services and Rehabilitation,* 5:5–18.

Fine, M., Torre, M. E., Boudin, K., Bowen, I., Clark, J., Hylton, D., Martinez, M., Roberts, R. A., Smart, P., & Upegui, D. (2001). *Changing Minds: The Impact of College in a Maximum Security Prison: Effects on Women in Prison, the Prison Environment, Reincarceration Rates and Post-Release Outcomes.* The Graduate Center of the City University of New York, New York, NY.

Gathright, G. L. (1999). *An Analysis of the Principles of Adult Learning Scale in a Correctional Education Setting.* Doctoral dissertation, Sam Houston State University.

Gehring, T. (2000). Recidivism as a Measure of Correctional Education Program Success. *Journal of Correctional Education,* 51:197–205.

Gerber, J., & Fritsch, E. J. (1995). Adult Academic and Vocational Correctional Education Programs: A Review of Recent Research. *Journal of Offender Rehabilitation,* 22:119–142.

Holloway, J., & Moke, P. (1986). Post Secondary Correctional Education: An Evaluation of Parolee Performance. ERIC Microfiche ED 269 578.

Johnson, W. W., Bennett, K., & Flanagan, T. J. (1997). Getting Tough on Prisoners: Results from the National Corrections Executive Survey, 1995. *Crime & Delinquency,* 43:27–41.

Jones, R. L., & d'Errico, P. (1994). The Paradox of Higher Education in Prisons. In Williford, M. (ed.), *Higher Education in Prison: A Contradiction in Terms?* (pp. 1–16). Phoenix, AZ: The Oryx Press.

Knepper, P. (1989). Selective Participation, Effectiveness, and Prison College Programs. *Journal of Offender Counseling, Services & Rehabilitation,* 14:109–135.

Langenbach, M., North, M. Y., Aagaard, L., & Chown, W. (1990). Televised Instruction in Oklahoma Prisons: A study of Recidivism and Disciplinary Actions. *Journal of Correctional Education,* 41:87–94.

Linden, R., & Perry, L. (1983). The Effectiveness of Prison Education Programs. *Journal of Offender Counseling, Services & Rehabilitation,* 6:43–57.

Linden, R., Perry, L., Ayers, D., & Parlett, T. A. A. (1984). An Evaluation of a Prison Education Program. *Canadian Journal of Criminology,* 26:65–73.

Lockwood, D. (1991). Prison Higher Education and Recidivism: A Program Evaluation. *Yearbook of Correctional Education 1991*:187–201.

Mace, J. L. (1978). *The Effect of Correctional Institutions' Education Programs on Inmates' Societal Adjustment as Measured by Post-Release Recidivism.* Doctoral dissertation, West Virginia University.

Martinson, R. (1974). What Works?—Questions and Answers about Prison Reform. *The Public Interest,* 35:22–54.

Mason, C. (1994) A Prisoner's View. In Williford, M. (ed.), *Higher Education in Prison: A Contradiction in Terms?* (pp. 135–138). Phoenix, AZ: The Oryx Press.

New York State Department of Correctional Services. (1989). *Follow-Up Study of a Sample of Offenders who Earned High School Equivalency Diplomas while Incarcerated.* Albany, NY: Department of Correctional Services.

O'Neil, M. (1990). Correctional Higher Education: Reduced Recidivism? *Journal of Correctional Education,* 41:28–31.

Rambo, E. S. (1933). *A Study of Education in the Texas Prison System with Recommendations for Instruction in Industrial Subjects.* Thesis, Sam Houston State University.

Roberts, A. R. (1971). *Sourcebook on Prison Education: Past, Present and Future.* Springfield, IL: Charles C. Thomas.

Rose, C., & Nyre, G. F. (1979). *Inmate and Ex-Offender Post Secondary Education Programs in California.* Los Angeles, CA: Evaluation and Training Institute.

Saden, S. J. (1962). The Educational Treatment Program for Corrections at Jackson, Michigan. *Journal of Correctional Education,* 15:22–26.

Schnur, A. C. (1948). The Educational Treatment of Prisoners and Recidivism. *American Journal of Sociology,* 54:142–147.

Schumacker, R. E., Anderson, D. B., & Anderson, S. L. (1990). Vocational and Academic Indicators of Parole Success. *Journal of Correctional Education,* 41:8–13.

Seashore, M. J., Haberfeld, S., Irwin, J., & Baker, K. (1976). *Prisoner Education: Project NewGate and Other College Programs.* New York: Praeger Publishers.

Silva, W. (1994). A Brief History of Prison Higher Education in the United States. In Williford, M. (ed.), *Higher Education in Prison: A Contradiction in Terms?* (pp. 17–31). Phoenix, AZ: The Oryx Press.

Smith, A. F. (1930). *The History and Present Status of Prison Education in the United States.* Master's thesis, Boston University.

Stone, W., McAdams, C., & Kollert, J. (1974). *T.D.C.: A Brief History* (Division of Research and Development Report). Huntsville, TX: Texas Department of Corrections.

Sykes, G. (1958). *The Society of a Maximum Security Prison.* Princeton, NJ: Princeton University Press.

Taylor, J. M. (1994). Cogito, Ergo Sum. In Williford, M. (ed.), *Higher Education in Prison: A Contra-diction in Terms?* (pp. 125–134). Phoenix, AZ: The Oryx Press.

Thorpe, T., MacDonald, D., & Bala, G. (1984). Follow-Up Study of Offenders who Earn College De-grees while Incarcerated in New York State. *Journal of Correctional Education,* 35:86–88.

Wallack, W. M., Kendall, G. M., & Briggs, H. L. (1939). *Education Within Prison Walls.* New York: Co-lumbia University Press.

Weir, J. D. (1973). A History of Education in Canadian Federal Correction. In Roberts, A. R. (ed.), *Readings in Prison Education* (pp. 39–47). Springfield, IL: Charles C. Thomas.

Wolf, J., & Sylves, D. (1981). The Impact of Higher Education Opportunity Programs. Post Prison Experiences of Disadvantaged Students: A Preliminary Follow-Up of Ex-Offenders. *JND Research,* 1–177. Willimasville, NY: New York State Education Department.

chapter 1 6

California, Texas, and Florida: The Big Three in Corrections

Donna M. Vandiver

INTRODUCTION

California, Texas, and Florida each house the largest numbers of prisoners as compared to any other state. At the end of year 2000, these states combined held approximately 392,000 inmates (Beck & Harrison, 2001), which accounted for approximately 30 percent of all state and federal inmates. This chapter provides an overview of each state's correctional system. For each state, an overview is provided of the administrative outlay, number and characteristics of prisoners, types of prisons, prisoner characteristics, and types of programs. Emphasis is placed on services available to offenders with special needs, including women, mentally ill, elderly, substance abusers, and those with serious medical problems.

The Departments of Corrections in California, Texas, and Florida each have responded differently to the pressing issues facing today's correctional facilities. The administration of any prison system is greatly affected by external factors, such as the public outcry for crime control. The nation's increasing willingness to incarcerate a large proportion of our citizens has been translated by elected legislators into more prison construction and more stringent punishments. While prison populations have increased every year since 1972, a slight decline (.5 percent) occurred in the last six months of 2000 (Beck & Harrison, 2001). Perhaps the modest recent decline in the prison population is indicative of a rethinking of an incapacitation and "get-tough" model of justice. Each of these states has been affected by its aggressive legislation: California's prison population has increased substantially by its "Three Strikes, You're Out" legislation, and Florida incorporated an 85 percent law, requiring inmates to serve at least 85 percent of their sentences. The administration of Texas prisons has been affected by *Ruiz v. Estelle*, which called for an overhaul of the prison system.

Large prison populations call for alert and creative administration. Figuratively, prison administrators are often caught between a rock and a hard place; literally, they are caught between societal demands for crime control and the reality of dealing with the prisoners, who are neither predictable nor easy to manage. Most prisons operate under a vague mission statement including elements of rehabilitation and deterrence. While the rehabilitation era of the 1960s and 1970s does not drive the current philosophy of incarceration, remnants can still be found. For instance, a large percentage of prisons offer programs to assist offenders with special needs. In fact, 95 percent of state prison facilities screen inmates upon intake or provide some type of treatment for mental illness (Beck & Maruschak, 2001). Approximately one out of every 10 inmates in state prison facilities receives psychotropic medication. Many inmates enter the facility with a host of problems, including histories of physical and/or sexual abuse (Harlow, 1999). In a recent survey, 19 percent of state inmates told interviewers they had been physically and/or sexually abused prior to their incarceration. Women inmates report an even higher rate of abuse—50 percent of women inmates report such abuse. Many prisoners also enter the system with substance abuse problems. Approximately half of state inmates in 1997 reported using alcohol and/or drugs while committing the crime that led to their incarceration (Mumola, 1999). Additionally, most prisons provide substantial medical treatment to meet the health needs of prisons. Each of these issues is reviewed in an assessment of the correctional systems in California, Texas, and Florida.

CALIFORNIA

At the end of the year 2000, California housed 163,001 inmates (Beck & Harrison, 2001). The total number of private and public adult correctional facilities as of year 2000 was 86 (Beck & Harrison, 2001). In terms of prison construction, California added 73,000 beds from 1990 to 2000, the second largest increase among all of the states. As of the second quarter of 2001, 93 percent of the inmates were male and 7 percent were female (CDC, n.d.b). In regard to race, 29 percent were white, 31 percent black, 34 percent Hispanic, and 5 percent classified as "other." The most common offenses committed were crimes against person (44 percent), followed by drug offenses (28 percent), property offenses (21 percent), and other offenses (7 percent). Approximately 600 (594) inmates have received a death sentence. The average sentence length is approximately 3.5 years (41.4 months), while the average time served is slightly less than two years (23 months). The average annual cost to house a single inmate is $25,607 (CDC, n.d.b). The 2000–2001 Budget Act established a $4.8 billion budget.

Three Strikes and You're Out

The trend for most states has been to respond to the public's outcry for a tough stance on crime with an adoption of a uniform standard that applies to everyone who commits similar crimes. For California, this meant adopting a "Three Strikes, You're Out" sentencing policy. In general, this means that anyone who has been found guilty of three serious felonies would receive a sentence of no less than 25 years and no longer than a life sentence. While the first two felonies must be a *serious* felony, the third can be *any* felony. Additionally, the sentence is doubled for those who receive a second serious felony. The law also reduces the amount of good time that can be earned to no more than 20 percent of their original sentence for the second serious felony. Typically an inmate can earn up to 50 percent of good time credit (Greenwood et al., 1994).

The Three Strikes law and was enacted into law in March of 1994. This law has created a great deal of controversy, which was explored during its development. A private research organization, RAND, explored many of the arguments both for and against the implementation of this law. In summary, the supporting arguments for the law included the following: protection of the public through incapacitation of chronic offenders, deterrence of repeat offenders, economic advantage by preventing the costs of processing criminals several times through the criminal justice system, and justice obtained by revoking the freedom of those who have caused others harm. The criticisms of the law included the following arguments: the utilization of incarceration despite its in effectiveness in reducing violent crime rates, dramatic increase in prison expenses, lengthy sentences that surpass offenders' peak years may be unnecessary, expenses associated with the increase of trials due to delimiting the plea bargain process, contrary benefits of alternative sentencing that can be more beneficial in reducing crime and would cost less, and unnecessary harshness for several types of crimes, such as drug possession (Greenwood et al., 1994).

The Three Strikes legislation has been a source of controversy, especially in light of the burgeoning prison populations. Some of the most recent arguments against the legislation have led to legal action. The bill AB 1790 was introduced in January of 2002 for the purpose of curbing the Three Strikes legislation. This bill would allow offenders to file for resentencing hearings if they had a serious but nonviolent strike in the past. It has been reported, however, that California's former governor, Gray Davis, supports the Three Strikes legislation in an effort to take a no-nonsense stance toward crime (Livingston, 2002).

Earlier, in November of 2001, the Ninth Circuit Court of Appeals ruled that the Three Strikes law constitutes cruel and unusual punishment under the Eighth Amendment when a person is sentenced to a lengthy sentence for a minor crime. In that particular case, Leandro Andrade was given a 50 years to life sentence for shoplifting videotapes from a local retailer. Andrade had several prior burglary charges; thus, the typical six months jail sentence was escalated to a 50 year to life prison sentence. In the opinion, Judge Paez stated that the grossly disproportionate sentence did constitute cruel and unusual punishment. The U.S. Supreme Court had rejected hearing a similar case in 1999, in which a man received 25 years to life for stealing a bottle of vitamins (Hoppin, 2001). The future of the Three Strikes legislation, therefore, is questionable. The direction that California and other states will take is not clear at this time.

Programs

While one of the purposes of corrections is punishment, it is important to note that a large percentage of inmates are, in fact, returned to society. This had created a demand for innovative and effective correctional programming. Only those inmates who receive life without parole, a death sentence, and those who die prior to serving their entire sentence do not return to society. The largest proportion of offenders will return to society with the hopeful expectation that they will not engage in further delinquency. The recidivism rates of prisoners postincarceration indicate that states are not taking advantage of that opportunity. In an assessment of over 16,000 prisoners released from 11 states in 1983, 63 percent were rearrested for a serious misdemeanor of felony within three years, while 41 percent returned to prison (Beck & Shipley, 1989). This is indicative of high recidivism rates among prisoners; thus, the opportunity to decrease recidivism exists. Incarceration provides states with the opportunity to monitor the behavior of inmates around the clock and to develop programs to meet their needs for the purpose of addressing issues that could prevent further delinquency.

California offers many programs to inmates for the purpose of ensuring, "public safety, public service." (CDC, n.d.a). This includes education, vocational, and health programs, including a state-of-the-art medical facility; the latter features an acute care hospital in Corcoran and a female health care program.

Employment/Vocational Programs

Joint Venture

California has implemented a unique employment program; it differs from traditional prison employment programs in that it allows inmates to work with private employers within the confounds of prison, earning above-average wages (CDC, 2001). Proposition 139 was passed in 1990, which allowed the Director of Corrections to recruit private businesses that can set up their business inside prisons. The program is defined in Proposition 139 (Article 1.5; 2717.1) as "a contract entered into between the Director of Corrections and any public entity, nonprofit or for profit entity, organization, or business for the purpose of employing inmate labor." As of September 1, 2001, the Department of Corrections had 12 active employers who employed 306 inmates across 10 California prisons. Unlike other prison employment programs, Joint Venture *mandates* that prison employees be paid the same wages as the employer's noninmate employees. Inmates, therefore, earn wages equal to free-world employees working for the same company. Other inmate programs, such as New York's Corcraft program, offer prison employees no more than 17 cents an hour.

The wages inmates earn from the Joint Venture program are, however, subject to substantial deductions. Taxes are automatically withheld from the inmates' pay. Inmates are required to pay room and board fees. Some inmates may be required to contribute a portion of their monies to a victim compensation fund. Some inmates have money held out to support their families and to place in savings. From July 1991 to August 2001, all inmates earned a total $14.6 million in wages. The inmates paid $2.3 in taxes, $2.5 in room and board fees, and $2.5 to victims and victim compensation organization funds. Inmates were also able to provide $1.7 million to their families and save $3.2 in savings. These numbers are couple for all incarcerated individuals. Also, many of the prisoners have the opportunity to work with the same company after they are released from prison. This potentially provides of-fenders with a decreased chance of recidivating once released from prison (CDC, 2001).

Sharing Technology with Schools

The California Department of Corrections established a computer refurbishing program in 1994. Inmates are trained to rebuild donated computers, which in turn are placed in K–12 public schools. The program was developed by a nonprofit, private organization, Detwiler Foundation. Various individuals and companies/groups donate computers to the prisons. Thirteen different prisons participate in the program, which allows inmates to learn new vi-tal skills and meets the needs of public education by providing students with computers. These 13 prisons refurbished more than 35,000 computers by the end of 1997, saving the state an estimated $33 million (CDC, n.d.d).

Women and Health

Women are being incarcerated at higher and higher rates. At the end of year 2000, women accounted for 6.6 percent of all state and federal inmates (Beck & Harrison, 2001). While the percentage of women offenders may seem low, women are being incarcerated at higher rates than their male counterparts. From 1990 through the end of 2000, the number of fe-male inmates increased by 108 percent compared to a 77 percent increase of male inmates. Women bring salient issues with them and specific health concerns. California has re-sponded to women's needs by expanding their health care services through the develop-ment of several programs and medical facilities.

Mother Infant Program

Another growing concern of prison administrators is female prisoners who bring problems to incarceration facilities. In 1999 an estimated 721,500 state and federal prisoners were parents to 1,498,800 children under age 18 (Mumola, 2000). In response to the situation, California has established seven community-based facilities throughout the state in which female inmates live with their young children (CDC, n.d.a). Mothers attend classes on par-enting and receive employment training. Treatment for drug rehabilitation is also available if needed.

Health Care Needs

To meet the health care needs of male and female inmates, the California Department of Corrections has implemented at least three health care programs/hospitals: Acute Care Hos-pital, Paris-Lamb Health Center, and HIV Center Program. The Acute Care Hospital has been in operation since June of 1993. It is described as a state-of-the-art hospital serving the needs of inmates, including serious offenders, in a safe environment. It is located in Cor-coran's maximum security facility. The Paris-Lamb Health Center is located at the Central California's Women's Facility. This Center is the only such licensed facility in the nation. It is a 39-bed skilled nursing facility for women, providing a full range of health care services. In response to the growing number of HIV cases within the prison system, an HIV Center Program was developed and has been operational since February of 1993. The facility is located at Vacaville. It provides both inpatient and outpatient care, including medical and psychological services (CDC, n.d.a).

Recently, a 31-year-old inmate who was serving a 14-year sentence for robbery received a heart transplant, which could cost as much as $1 million. It should be noted that the decision to select a recipient for the heart transplant was not made by the California Department of Corrections, but by the doctors at Stanford. Some of the criteria for choosing the most appropriate candidate include overall health, likelihood of death without the transplanted heart, the patient's proximity to the donor, immunological compatibility, and the patient's ability to handle the lifestyle changes associated with the transplant. Whether the person is incarcerated is *not* a consideration. At the time the inmate received the heart, 4119 patients were on the waiting list for a new heart (Landsberg, 2002).

Offering inmates state-of-the art health services does not always go over well with the taxpayers who are left to pick up the tab. As noted by the *Los Angeles Times* (see Landsberg, 2002), denial of adequate medical treatment has been ruled as a violation of the cruel and unusual clause of the Eighth Amendment by the Supreme Court (see *Estelle v. Gamble*, 1976). Also, earlier in 1996 a federal court ordered California to provide a kidney transplant to an inmate. The California Department of Corrections, therefore, had little option but to allow the inmate to have the heart transplant.

Substance Abuse

The dramatic growth in California's prison system has been attributed to its aggressive approach toward drug offenders (Zimring & Hawkins, 1992). From 1980 to 1990 the percentage of incarcerated male drug offenders increased by a factor of 15. Women drug offenders increased from 13 percent of the female incarcerated population to 39 percent over the same time span. During this timeframe legislation was adopted that aggressively pursued drug offenders, which had a dramatic affect on prison populations. As noted by Zimring and Hawkins (1992, p. 32), "For that reason alone [drug offenders comprising a large portion of the increasing prison population], the drug offense category would be a candidate for special consideration in the design of policies to restrain the growth of California prison population."

Capital Punishment

Executions in California were first authorized in 1851. Counties were allowed to execute inmates until the legislature passed an amendment in 1891 limiting execution to state prisons. In 1937, the mode of execution was changed from hanging to lethal gas. From 1967 until 1992, no executions were held due to various State and United States Supreme Court decisions, despite a statute enacted in 1977 allowing executions. In April of 1992 Robert Alton Harris was executed in San Quentin's gas chamber. In 1993 inmates were allowed to choose lethal injection or lethal gas; however, in 1994 it was ruled that the gas chamber violated an inmate's Eighth Amendment protection from cruel and unusual punishment. In 1996, William Bonin, a serial killer, was executed by lethal injection (CDC, n.d.c).

Currently all male death row inmates in California are housed at San Quentin State Prison, a maximum security unit (CDC, n.d.c). The females are housed in the California Women's Facility at Chowchilla. As of the end of year 2000, California had 586 inmates under a death sentence, the largest number of individuals under a death sentence in all of the states (Snell, 2001). Yet this state has a very low execution rate, especially for a populous state. For instance, in the year 2000 only one person was executed. Eight other states exceeded California by executing more than one person in the year 2000 (CDC, n.d.c).

The California Department of Corrections has posted the procedures of an execution on its Web site. It explains that two reports are filed prior to the execution. These reports are filed 20 days and seven days prior to the execution date. Each report contains psychiatric report, chaplain's report, summary of inmate's behavior, and a cover letter from the warden. The condemned inmate's attorney may submit current psychiatric information seven to 30 days prior to the execution if the results have a bearing on the inmate's sanity. A board of psychiatrists considers the information in preparing its preexecution psychiatric reports. During the 24-hour period prior to the execution, the warden allows final visitation from spiritual advisors, friends, and approved family members. The inmate is relocated to the death watch cell, which is adjacent to the execution chamber, at 6 P.M. the day before the execution. Three members of the staff supervise the inmate. The inmate then receives his final meal. The chaplain and the warden meet with the inmate between 7 and 10 P.M. Approximately one-half hour prior to the execution, the inmate is given a new pair of denim pants and blue work shirt. The inmate is then escorted into the death chamber, at which time the staff strap down the inmate. A cardiac monitor is attached to the inmate and two IVs are inserted. The second IV is put in place in case the first one malfunctions. The door is closed and the execution order is given by the warden. After the injections have been administered, a physician declares the death. The family may claim the body; otherwise, the state will make burial arrangements. Up to 50 witnesses are allowed. This includes the warden, the attorney general, 12 reputable citizens, 2 physicians, 5 friends/family of the inmate, 2 spiritual advisors, 17 representatives of the news media, 9 state-selected witnesses, and 4 staff escorts.

TEXAS

The Texas prison system holds the second largest inmate population in the United States. At the end of 2000, Texas housed 157,997 inmates (Beck & Harrison, 2001). Texas was one of 13 states, however, that experienced a decline in its prison population during the year 2000. The population of inmates in Texas declined 3.2 percent. Texas led the nation in prison construction by adding 109,975 beds from 1990 through the end of 2000. As of 2000, Texas exceeded every other state by occupying 127 public and private adult correctional facilities. Texas also leads the nation in the number of executions it performs (Snell, 2001).

Thirty-five percent of the inmates in Texas are between the ages of 30 and 39; this is the largest cohort of inmates. It is followed by those between the ages of 22 to 29 and 40 to 49, respectively (see Figure 16–1). Ninety-four percent of the inmates are male, while 6 percent are female. The majority (50 percent) of inmates were incarcerated for violent offenses, followed by inmates who have committed property crimes (21 percent), drug-related offenses (19 percent), and other crimes (10 percent) (Fabelo, 2001).

The Texas Department of Corrections has a nine-person board, each of whom is elected by the governor. The Department of Corrections is broken into three divisions: institutions, parole supervision, and probation. The Texas Department of Corrections has been heavily influenced by a series of lawsuits, including *Ruiz v. Estelle* (1980), which outlined many of the guidelines that the prison system was required to follow. Texas, like California, provides many programs to prisoners both while they are incarcerated and after they have been released. Some of the programs available to prisoners include a corrections industry program, which offers a broad range of job training skills, as well as an educational program. This allows prisoners to attain their GEDs and even their college degrees while incarcerated. Treatment programs are available to those with a specialized need (i.e., history of substance abuse). For those prisoners who are dying, a special needs parole program has been established that allows certain prisoners to apply for early parole. Recently, a prisoner utilized this program to escape from prison. Mentally ill prisoners are also provided with treatment while incarcerated, as well as postrelease. Texas, again like California, enforces the death penalty. A brief historical overview and some of the current issues surrounding death row inmates are explored.

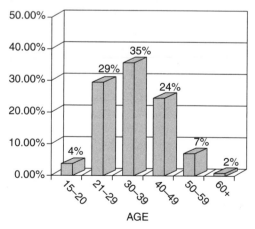

Figure 16–1 Age distribution of Texas inmates

Ruiz v. Estelle

The case of *Ruiz v. Estelle* had a profound effect on the Texas Department of Corrections; it changed the way the system was viewed. It also changed the way the system was run. As noted by sociologist, Ben Crouch, "The Court case of *Ruiz v. Estelle* that was filed in the early 1970s changed everything" (Texas A&M University General Libraries–Press Releases, 2001). He explained that "It was the confrontation of two realities: a prison system that was believed to be the best in the world, operating with realism and integrity and a prison system that was referred to as the best existing example of slavery."

Summarizing this case does not do it justice, as it affected almost every aspect of the correctional system in Texas. A brief background of the case may be helpful in understanding the importance of this case. In 1972, David Ruiz filed a federal lawsuit against the Director of the Estelle prison unit, the Texas board of corrections, and several wardens challenging the constitutionality of the prison's living and working conditions of the prison (Crouch & Marquart, 1989). Ruiz was known as a "writ-writer," an inmate who assists other inmates in preparing cases against the prison system. Ruiz's petition became a class action lawsuit after it was combined with six other similar cases filed. Judge Justice, who is described as a judicial activist, heard the case. The lengthy 159 day trial began on October 2, 1978 and concluded on September 20, 1979. Judge Justice wrote an opinion that was almost 250 pages. He implemented changes to many of the policies and practices. He outlined a wide range of required changes in the following areas: prisoners' access to courts; disciplining procedures; unit size, structure, and location; overcrowding; sanitation; fire safety; health care; security and supervision; sanitation; and workplace safety and hygiene. The judge issued a timeline of dates by which the system had to be in compliance in various areas. A special master was appointed to assist in ensuring the conditions were met (Crouch & Marquart, 1989).

The reluctance to address the judge's order was evident when the state appealed the decision to the Fifth Circuit Court of Appeals. The Fifth Circuit overturned some of the Judge Justice's order, yet many of the provisions were left in tact. The Fifth Circuit still ordered a reduction in overcrowding, building smaller prisons closer to large cities, changes in how the correctional officers are trained, implementation of adequate fire safety codes, increased inmate access to law libraries, development of plans for new prisons which were to be submitted to the court, and implementation of adequate health and safety standards as designated by existing laws (Crouch & Marquart, 1989).

Compliance with the court was no easy task. In order to implement such broad and sweeping changes, budgetary issues had to be addressed. Overcrowding became a focal point because of the substantial costs associated with alleviating the problem. Even though tents were brought in from the Texas National Guard for temporary housing, long-term relief was not in sight. In the early 1980s, the board of corrections ordered that no new prisoners be admitted into the prison system. The new prisoners were held in already overfilled jails. The board of corrections asked the legislation for $85 million to assist in relieving the overcrowded prisons. The legislature allotted $58 million. A subsequent request was made by the Director of Texas Department of Correction for $1.5 billion to build new maximum security prisons. The legislature passed a budget of only $620 million. The successive legislative sessions began to focus more on community corrections rather than its usual get-tough policy (Crouch & Marquart, 1989).

This case has shadowed the Texas correctional system for a quarter of a century, and the effects of the lawsuit have been felt elsewhere as inmates in other states adapted the lawsuit. In hindsight, this case provided the blueprint for how Texas operates its prison system. It also provided a heads-up to other state prisons administrations for several reasons. It allowed others to see what the consequences are of running an inhumane prison. Furthermore, it sent a message to other states that court intervention was not a remote possibility. Moreover, once the courts intervened, their sweep of control could devastate long-standing correctional practices.

Health Issues and Programs

It is essential that the health of prisoners be maintained while they are incarcerated. As prisoners serve longer sentences, it is inevitable that health concerns arise. Approximately one in four state inmates has been injured while in prison (Maruschak & Beck, 2001). Forty percent of state inmates over the age of 45 reported some type of medical problem since admission. The dramatic growth in the number of inmates over the age of 65 has compounded the problem. Housing elderly inmates costs three times as much it as does to house younger inmates. Many states have incorporated hospice units into at least one state facility.

Texas Special Needs Parole

Texas has incorporated a program to address, in part, the problems of inmates who are aging and/or in grave physical condition. The special needs parole program allows inmates who have been given less than six months to live to ask for early parole (Fabelo, 2000a). Inmates who are at least 60 years of age and have a health condition requiring medical services 24 hours a day may be eligible, as well as those with a physical disability causing substantial limitations in their ability to function. Any inmate who has committed an aggravated violent crime is not eligible for the program. Parolees do not return home but are housed in state nursing homes. Those who apply for early parole are heard by the parole board and a decision is made whether the individual is eligible for an early release. The purpose of this program is "to identify eligible specials needs offenders in TDCJ facilities or county jails who could be diverted from incarceration to more cost effective and appropriate treatment alternatives" (TDC, n.d.b). It can cost approximately $34,000 per year to incarcerate an offender with a serious medical condition (Fabelo, 2000a). Housing an inmate in a nursing facility, however, generally costs slightly less than $7000 per year. From 1995 through the end of 1999, a total of 444 were released through special needs parole.

When Things Go Wrong: Case in Point: Often when a new program, such as the special needs parole in Texas, is implemented more problems are created than solved. Steve Russell, a prisoner in Texas, utilized the Texas Special Needs Parole program to escape. Russell had a history of several jail and prison escapes (McVicker, 1997, 1998a, 1999, 2000). He once posed as a doctor by dyeing his white prison uniform green and walking out the front door. On another occasion he posed as a state district judge in a phone call to the district clerk's office in which he was able to reduce his bail low enough that he could meet his bond (McVicker, 2000). When questioned about his numerous escapes by reporters he stated, "I didn't break out . . . I asked if I could go home, and they opened the door" (McVicker, 1998a). Russell had a history of white-collar offenses, including embezzling $800,000 from a medical management company (McVicker, 1999). As reported in the *Houston Press*, Russell "convinced a prison doctor that he was dying of AIDS, obtained a medical parole and had his parole officer notified that he was dead" (McVicker, 1999). Russell, therefore, applied for and was granted parole through the special needs program. Once he was granted early release, he was moved to a nursing home. He was then given permission to leave the facility for medical treatment. It was reported that Russell had died. Later, it was revealed that Russell was not dead. He was captured in Florida.

In another incident in 1998, an inmate was released through the special needs parole program due to a grave illness. The inmate was later involved in the brutal murder of a cabdriver. He and two teenagers held up the cabdriver and shot her several times (McVicker, 1998b).

Problems: Many problems with the special needs parole program were outlined and discussed in a report released by the Criminal Justice Council. For instance, it was noted that no formal referral process exists that identifies offenders who are eligible for such services. Many of the referred cases to the program do not meet the eligibility requirements. In general, the number of cases referred declined substantially (54 percent) from 1995 to 1999. Of those who were referred to the program, most did not substantially benefit from the program for various reasons. For example, in the fiscal year of 1999, approximately one-half (47 percent) of those who were referred were eligible. Of those, 23 percent died during the process, 27 percent refused to participate in the program, 12 percent were released prior to the parole board review, and 38 percent or 139 inmates were actually referred to the parole board. Of those, 30 were approved; however, 7 of the 30 died prior to release. Thus, of the 782 that were referred to this program in 1999, 23 were successfully released from this program.

Recommendations from the Criminal Justice Policy Council included improving the referral process, which would include a computerized system that would identify inmates who would benefit from the program. It was also suggested to include inmates projected to die in the twelve months rather than six months. Another recommendation was made to implement reassessment plan for inmates six months after release (Fabelo, 2000a).

Mentally Ill: (Continuity of Care Program)

In 1998, there were approximately 144,000 mentally ill inmates in the Texas criminal justice system (Fabelo, 2000b). In response, Texas created an agency, Texas Council Offenders with Mental Impairments, to meet their needs. While this agency is responsible for a broad range of aspects related to the mentally ill offenders, one of its programs is highlighted here for the purpose of discussing the special needs of mentally ill offenders. This program provides pre- and postrelease services to those inmates who have been identified as mentally ill.

The continuity of care program identifies inmates who have a mental illness and are going to be released soon. Those inmates are provided with aftercare treatment services. Thus, inmates who are receiving psychotropic medications while incarcerated to control their mental illness would be able to continue taking their medication after being referred to a mental health treatment center. Inmates who have a mental illness and are released from incarceration are provided with follow-up through a 90-day report (TDC, n.d.a).

While an evaluation of this particular program has not been published, results from a similar program developed in New York indicate that those who participate in the program did not experience a significant reduction of arrests (Versey et al., 1997). The study focused on a continuity program established in seven New York jails and provided postrelease mental health services to those who had a mental illness. Postrelease services included medication, counseling, and access to inpatient services. While the findings of this localized program may not apply to all such programs, it is indicative that even more aggressive treatment may be needed to reduce future criminal behavior among the mentally ill.

Substance Abuse

Texas has been addressing the needs of offenders with substance abuse issues for an extended period of time through four different programs: In-Prison Therapeutic Community (IPTC), Substance Abuse Felony Punishment (SAFP) (for probationers), Pre-Release Substance Abuse Program (PRSAP), and Pre-Release Therapeutic Community (PRTC). These intensive rehabilitation programs were developed in response to a directive from the 1997 Texas Legislation. Each of these programs, with the exclusion of SAFP, is designed for incarcerated offenders. SAFP is a program designed for probationers. A summary of these programs is presented in Table 16–1 (Fabelo, 2001).

Sex Offender Treatment Program and InnerChange Freedom Initiative

In addition to these four programs, two other intensive rehabilitation programs were developed in response to the directive from Texas Legislation: the Sex Offender Treatment Program (SOTP) and the InnerChange Freedom Initiative (IFI) program. The SOTP began in 1996 with voluntary participation. It serves approximately 300 inmates each year. The program became mandatory in 1998 for offenders who met specified criteria, but it included many voluntary participants. Of offenders who were released in the fiscal years 1997 and 1998, 13 percent were arrested for a new offense. For those who did participate in the program, 24 percent were arrested. More specifically, 2 percent of the program participants as compared to 6 percent of nonprogram participants were arrested for a new sex offense (Fabelo, 2001).

The IFI is an 18-month biblical principle–based program that attempts to assist inmates in making better decisions in their life. It began in 1997 and is funded by Prison Fellowship Ministries, and participation is voluntary. It serves slightly more than 200 inmates each year. Because this program has not been operating for an extended period of time and began with only 37 participants, it has not undergone an evaluation (Fabelo, 2001).

Table 16–1   SUMMARY OF SUBSTANCE ABUSE PROGRAMS AVAILABLE IN TEXAS

Program	Year Program Originated	Description
In-Prison Therapeutic Community (IPTC)	1992	• Serves inmates with a release date w/n the following 12 to 14 months; all inmates have been paroled and must complete program for release. • 9 to 12 month program involving intensive treatment, followed by 3 months of treatment at a residential facility and 3 to 9 months of outpatient counseling.
Substance Abuse Punishment Facility (SAFP)	1992	• Serves probationers who have a substance abuse program. • Program participation is a mandatory condition of probation. • 9 to 12 month intensive treatment in a secure facility, followed by 3 months of treatment at a residential and 3 to 9 months of outpatient counseling.
Pre-Release Substance Abuse Treatment Program (PRSAP)	1976	• Serves offenders who have a release date within the following 6 months. Most of the offenders are being released through mandatory release, while others have been paroled. • 4 to 6 months of substance abuse with 3 phases.
Pre-Release Therapeutic Community (PRTC)	1996	• Treatment includes individual of counseling, anger management, life skills training, and drug/alcohol education. • Serves inmates with a substance abuse problem and/or educational/vocational deficit. • Most inmates in this program are released through mandatory release. • Inmates have a discharge date within the following 6 months and plan to live in the Dallas area. • Postrelease services are provided at the Dallas Day Reporting Center.

Source: Fabelo, Tony (2001). *Evaluation of the Performance of the Texas Department of Criminal Justice Rehabiliation Tier Programs.* Austin, TX: Criminal Justice Policy Council.

Education/Vocational Programs

Windham School District

The Texas Department of Corrections has established the Windham School District, which provides educational programs for offenders. A literacy program assists inmates to learn basic skills and prepares inmates to earn a GED. Inmates who have disabilities are provided with special educational services, and inmates who do not speak English fluently are taught English as a second language. Additionally, college-level courses are also made available to inmates who have earned a high school diploma or GED.

Texas Correctional Institutions

The Texas Department of Corrections offers a broad range of employment to inmates. Several factories have been established throughout the state to make furniture, garments, bound books and Braille books, boxes, license plates, signs, plastic goods, validation stickers, mattresses, mops and brooms, shoes, soaps, and retreaded tires. Inmates, therefore, have the opportunity to work in a print shop, computer recovery program, metal sign plant, or a textile mill. It is evident that Texas offers a vast range of vocational opportunities for its inmates (TDCJ, 2001b).

The Death Penalty

Texas has a long history of execution, dating back as far as 1819. From 1819 to 1923 the executions were carried out by hanging. In 1924, the electric chair became the sole means of execution. Prior to 1924, counties were responsible for executions. In 1924, five offenders were put to death by electrocution. Lethal injection was adopted as the means of execution in 1977. Since 1996, the offender's family members and friends have been allowed to witness the execution. Since the U.S. Supreme Court reinstated the death penalty in 1976, Texas has led the nation in the number of executions (TDCJ, 2001a).

Death row inmates are housed in the Polunksy Unit (TDCJ, 2001a) but are executed at The Walls unit in Huntsville, Texas. Death row inmates are housed in single-person cells that measure 60 square feet and have a window (TDCJ, 2001a). The inmates are allowed recreation, but not with any other inmates. Some death row inmates are allowed to have radios. While the average time for an offender to spend on death row prior to execution is 10.6 years, two inmates, Joe Gonzales and Steven Renfro, spent less than one year on death row. Two other inmates (Excell White and Sammie Felder), however, spent 23 and 24 years on death row. Both inmates were executed in 1999. The three lethal drugs injected successively are sodium thiopental, pancuronium bromide, and potassium chloride. In order, the drugs sedate the person, collapse his or her lungs and diaphragm, and stop the heartbeat. The drugs cost approximately $86.00 per execution.

As of the year 2000, 450 inmates were under a death sentence. This is the second largest population of inmates held under a death sentence; only California outnumbers Texas with a total of 586 inmates on its death row. It should be noted, however, that Texas performs a higher number of executions than any other state. In the year 2000, 40 inmates were executed in Texas, while only one was executed in California. Oklahoma had executed the second highest number of inmates by executing 11. Thus, the number of inmates executed in Texas far outweighs the number in any other state. In fact the number of inmates executed in Texas accounted for slightly less than half of the total number of executed inmates, which was 85, in the nation during the year 2000 (Snell, 2001).

FLORIDA

While Florida's inmate population of 71,319 pales in comparison to Texas' 157,997 and California's 163,001 (as of the end of 2000) prison population, it is the third largest prison population in the United States (Beck & Harrison, 2001). It also should be noted that New York State has an inmate population of 70,198, making it the state with the fourth largest prison population. Florida has 106 state public and private adult correctional facilities. Florida has not experienced a decrease in its prison population as California and Texas have; it has, however, seen a slower increase (FDOC, 2000–01c). From 1996 to June of 2001, the inmate population increased only 11.3 percent over this five-year period. It experienced a mere 1 percent increase from mid-2000 to mid-2001.

As of June 30, 2001, the majority of the Florida inmates were male (94 percent), while 6 percent were female (FDOC, 2000–01c). From mid-1992 to mid-2001, the percentage of black inmates decreased 4 percent, from 58 percent to 54 percent. The majority of inmates were serving time for drug offenses (18 percent), burglary (17 percent), murder/manslaughter (15 percent), robbery (14 percent), and violent personal offenses (12 percent), which included carjacking, aggravated assault, and others. On average, offenders are serving a substantial portion of their sentences; offenders released in December of 2001 had served an average of 83 percent of their sentences (FDOC, 2001a). The average annual cost to house an inmate in one of their major institutions was $18,159 (FDOC, 2000–01a).

The 85 Percent Law

By 1998 Florida was one of 27 states and the District of Columbia that had implemented a truth-in-sentencing law, requiring inmates to serve at least 85 percent of the sentence (Ditton & Wilson, 1999). These states were provided incentive grants for a federal program by instituting this guideline. Florida'a law affected inmates who were committed on or after October 1, 1995 and required them to serve at least 85 percent of their sentences. As of June 30, 2001, 63 percent of the inmates were serving under the 85 percent law (FDOC, 2001).

Programs

The Florida Department of Corrections developed the Office of Program Services to meet the needs of inmates. This office focuses on four different areas: academic education, vocational education, substance abuse treatment, and transition skills. Inmates who participate in these programs experience reduced idleness, while institutional security increases. Participation in programs increases inmates' ability to adjust to life inside the institution. It has been shown, furthermore, that those who complete programs while incarcerated have lower rates of recidivism. A Priority Program Ranking System was implemented that seeks to identify inmates with the highest need level through a process of screening, prioritizing, and placement into appropriate programs (OPPAGA, 2000).

Academic Education

Almost 80 percent of Florida inmates do not meet a ninth-grade educational level. Four different education programs have been implemented in Florida prisons: the mandatory literacy program, adult basic education, general education development, and special education. Inmates who have at least two years remaining on their sentence and do not meet a ninth-grade reading level are required to participate in the mandatory literacy program. This program includes 150 hours of literacy training. The adult basic education program focuses on reading, writing, and math skills. The general education development program is designed for inmates who score higher than the ninth-grade level. It is similar to any other type of GED program. Inmates who have disabilities and meet the requirements by state and federal law to receive special services are provided with special education (OPPAGA, 2000).

Vocational Education

Florida Department of Corrections offers vocational education programs in 44 occupations at 44 of their institutions (OPPAGA, 2000). The programs range from construction trades to more technical positions such as computer programming and architectural drafting. The majority (83 percent) of Florida inmates do work, participate in programs, or both (University of Florida, 1998). The inmates who do not work are physically unable to work or in an area where work is not possible (i.e., processing through the reception and orientation center or on death row). Inmates who work may be involved in a variety of types of jobs. For instance, some may be involved in new construction, renovations, and repairs. Additionally, two types of community work squads programs are available to inmates, which include working with the Department of Transportation and the Public Works/Interagency Community Service. Inmates who work with the Department of Transportation perform various types of roadway work on the state's highways. They also assist in natural disasters, including severe storms and hurricanes. Those who work with the Public Works/Interagency Community Service perform roadway work on city and county roads instead of state highways. They also maintain grounds, which includes mowing, litter removal, painting, and various repairs. The inmates work with state in local governments in clean-up projects after a natural disaster has occurred. In one fiscal year (1996–1997), it was estimated that the free inmate labor saved taxpayers $23.5 million.

Seven of the prison units in Florida utilize chain gangs. The chain gang squads are closely supervised and work in areas outside of the prison facility. They are under the supervision of armed correctional officers. There is typically one supervising officer per 10 inmates, but this can vary depending on the security level of the inmates. The inmates do wear ankle shackles but are not shackled to one another. The chain gangs perform work for the cities, counties, state agencies, and nonprofit organizations (University of Florida, 1998).

In addition to these unpaid employment programs, Florida has incorporated an employment program similar to Joint Venture program in California. Florida's Prison Industries Enhancement program is a joint private–public agreement that allows inmates to earn wages comparable to free-world employees. Up to 80 percent of the inmates wages can be automatically deducted for incarceration costs, crime victims restitution fund, child support, taxes, and other court-ordered fines (Mahtesian, 1997).

Substance Abuse Treatment

Slightly more than 60 percent of Florida inmates enter the prison with a history of substance abuse. Most of the substance abuse services are contracted through private agencies. In Florida the substance abuse programs are divided into three modalities. The first modality involves a four- to six-month intensive outpatient program. The second modality is a residential therapeutic community program that is more extensive than the first modality. The third modality is an outpatient program designed for relapse prevention as well as a transitional program. Additionally, two programs have been created to meet the needs of inmates who have not only a substance abuse history but also have psychological disorders (OPPAGA, 2000).

Transition Skills

Approximately 90 percent of inmates who enter prison facilities will return to society, thus, it is important to prepare prisoners adequately for their transition from prison back to the community. Most inmates view a two-hour prerelease video. Additionally, a transition and life skills program is available, which is a 100 hour program. This program includes decision-making skills, job readiness, and money management (OPPAGA, 2000).

Inmates who have been released from prison in Florida may have an option that other states do not have. A private, nonprofit program, Prison Rehabilitative Industries and Diversified Enterprises, Inc. (PRIDE), employs about 4300 ex-cons in 56 industries across the state. Some of the industries include farming, eyeglass manufacturing, car and truck renovations, and printing. It was found in a 1994 study that the recidivism rates of PRIDE employees were rather low; only 12.6 percent of the ex-cons who worked at PRIDE for at least six months went back to prison within a two-year period. In Florida the recidivism rates are approximately 50 percent. It has been indicated that other states, including California, have looked into developing similar programs in their states. The CEO of Florida's TaxWatch boasted that PRIDE is one of the best programs in the country (Mahtesian, 1997).

Death Penalty

Florida is one of 38 states that currently utilize the death penalty. Florida has had the authority to execute inmates since 1923. From 1972 until 1976 the death penalty was declared unconstitutional by the United States Supreme Court (see *Furman v. Georgia*). After the Supreme Court ruled that the death penalty was *not* unconstitutional in *Greg v. Georgia* (1976), Florida reinstated the death penalty and executed John Spenkelink in 1979.

Slightly fewer than 400 (371) inmates were on death row as of June 30, 2001. The mode of execution in Florida is death by lethal injection. Lethal injection has been utilized since the fiscal year 1999–2000. Terry Sims was the first inmate to die by lethal injection in Florida. He was executed on February 23, 2000. The executioner, whose identity is not revealed, is paid $150 per execution. Each death row inmate is housed in a cell that is 6′ × 9′. The height of each cell is 9.5′. As of June 30, 2001, 368 of the death row inmates were male and 3 were female. The majority (227) were white, while 133 were black and 11 were classified as neither black nor white (FDOC, 2000–01b).

Male inmates on death row are housed at Union Correctional Institute or Florida State Prison. The female death row inmates are housed at Broward CI, which is also called Pembroke Pines. Death row inmates in Florida wear orange T-shirts, which distinguish them from the other inmates. As of the end of the year 2000, Florida had 371 inmates under a death sentence, the third largest number of inmates under a death sentence (Snell, 2001). Florida was outnumbered only by Texas and California. Florida has the fourth highest number of performed executions, with a total of six executed inmates in the year 2000. Only Virginia, Oklahoma, and Texas, which executed 8, 11, and 40 inmates respectively, outnumbered Florida (FDOC, 2000–01).

CONCLUSION

California, Texas, and Florida lead the nation in terms of the number of incarcerated offenders. California has been affected by the implementation of a get-tough sentencing policy—Three Strikes, You're Out. A consequence of this legislation was inflating incarceration rates, especially for women offenders. In order to meet the needs of incarcerated offenders, programs were implemented addressing specialized populations of offenders. California has sentenced more offenders to death than any other state. However, it has a very low rate of performed executions.

The current Texas prison system is the product of a lengthy history of court battles, mainly that of *Ruiz v. Estelle*. With its high rate of incarceration and the demands of the courts, this state has had to operate its prisons in a tedious balancing act. After *Ruiz*, this prison system had no option but to implement policies and procedures that recognize the inmates' rights. The implementation of innovative programming is not without problems, however. For instance, the implementation of a special needs program allowed an avenue for an inmate to escape, drawing the media's attention once again to the management of correctional facilities. *Ruiz* affected practically every aspect of the Texas Department of Corrections, placing a great deal of strain on the agency as a whole. In addition to *Ruiz*, Texas is also known for its exceedingly high rates of execution. It executes more offenders than any other state.

Florida has the third largest number of incarcerated offenders, yet it houses less than half of the number of inmates incarcerated in Texas. The Office of Program Services is responsible for the academic, vocational, and substance abuse treatment, as well as transition skills program. Each program offers a variety of services to inmates, each focused on increased coping mechanisms and preparation for their release. Florida, like California and Texas, does hand down death sentences.

California, Texas, and Florida house approximately 30 percent of all incarcerated offenders. Because of the large population of inmates and the public's demands for a tough stance toward criminals, these states have acted swiftly by implementing strict sentencing schemes. Texas has been affected by court intervention to revamp its prison system in order to preclude violations of inmate's personal rights. The recent trend of severe legislation and sentencing for offenders appears to be dissipating; what is replacing it, however, is not fully apparent at this time. Paying particular attention to these three states may provide a glimpse of the trends in corrections, which appear to recognize prisoner's rights, respond to the need of preventing recidivism, and address each prisoner's needs with various treatment-oriented programs.

REFERENCES

Beck, A. J., & Harrison, P. M. (2001, August). *Prisoners in 2000.* Washington, DC: U.S. Department of Justice Statistics, Bureau of Justice Statistics.

Beck, A. J., & Maruschak, L. M. (2001, July). *Mental Health Treatment in State Prisons, 2000.* Washington, DC: U.S. Department of Justice Statistics, Bureau of Justice Statistics.

Beck, A. J., & Shipley, B. E. (1989, April). *Recidivism of Prisoners Released in 1983.* Washington, DC: U.S. Department of Justice Statistics, Bureau of Justice Statistics.

California Department of Corrections. (n.d.a). *California Department of Corrections: Programs.* Retrieved May 25, 2000 from the World Wide Web: *http://www.cdc.state.ca.us/program/prgrams.html.*

California Department of Corrections. (n.d.b). *California Department of Corrections: Facts.* Retrieved May 25, 2000 from the World Wide Web: *http://www.cdc.state.ca.us/factsht.html.*

California Department of Corrections. (n.d.c). *California Department of Corrections: Capital punishment in California.* Retrieved May 27, 2001 from the World Wide Web: *http://www.cdc.state.ca.us/issues/capital/capital2.html.*

California Department of Corrections. (n.d.d). *Sharing Technology with Schools.* Retrieved January 20, 2002 from the World Wide Web: *http://www.cdc.state.ca.us/program/cfspage.htm.*

California Department of Corrections. (2001). *The Joint Venture Program.* [Brochure]

Crouch, B. M., & Marquart, J. W. (1989). *An Appeal to Justice: Litigated Reform of Texas Prisons.* Austin, TX: University of Texas Press.

Ditton, P. M., & Wilson, D. J. (1999, January). *Truth in Sentencing in State Prisons.* Washington, DC: U.S. Department of Justice, Bureau of Justice Statistics.

Estelle v. Gamble. (1976). 97 S. Ct. 285.

Fabelo, Tony. (2000a, May). *Overview of Special Needs Parole Policy and Recommendations for Improvement.* Austin, TX: Criminal Justice Policy Council.

Fabelo, Tony. (2000b, August 22). *Presentation to the House County Affairs Committee.* Austin, TX: Criminal Justice Policy Council.

Fabelo, Tony. (2001). *Evaluation of the Performance of the Texas Department of Criminal Justice Rehabilitation Tier Programs.* Austin, TX: Criminal Justice Policy Council.

Florida Department of Corrections. (2001, December). *Time-Served Percentage of Sentence Served in Florida's Prisons.* Bureau of Research and Data Analysis.

Florida Department of Corrections. (2000–01a). *Annual Report: Budget.* Florida Department of Corrections.

Florida Department of Corrections. (2000–01b). *Annual Report: Death Row.* Florida Department of Corrections.

Florida Department of Corrections. (2000–01c). *Annual Report: Inmate Population on June 30, 2001.* Florida Department of Corrections.

Furman v. Georgia. 92 S. Ct. 2726 (1972).

Gregg v. Georgia. (1976). 96 S. Ct. 2909 (1976).

Greenwood, P. W., Rydell, C. P., Abrahamse, A. F., Caulkins, J. P., Chiesa, J., Model, K. E., & Klein, S. P. (1994). *Three Strikes and You're Out: Estimated Benefits and Costs of California's New Mandatory-Sentencing Law.* Santa Monica, CA: Rand.

Harlow, C. W. (1999, April). *Prior Abuse Reported by Inmates and Probationers.* Washington, DC: U.S. Department of Justice Statistics, Bureau of Justice Statistics.

Hoppin, J. (2001, November 5). Circuit Says Three Strikes Can Be Cruel. *American Lawyer Media, L. P.* The Recorder. News, p. 1.

Joint Venture Program. Cal. Penal Code, §§ 2717–2718 (1990).

Livingston, K. (2002, January 16). Three strikes once again in the hot seat. *American Lawyer Media, L. P.* The Recorder. News, p. 1.

Mahtesian, C. (1997, November). Rethinking Prison Labor. *Florida Trend,* feature stories.

McVicker, S. (1997, February 6). King Con; Steven Russell Can Bluff His Way out of Anything—Even Prison. So Why Can't He Stay out of Jail? *Houston Press.* Features.

McVicker, S. (1998a, May 14). Keeping the King Quiet. *Houston Press.* Features.

McVicker, S. (1998b, June 11). The Special Needs of Frank Gonzales Jr. *Houston Press.* Features.

McVicker, S. (1999, September 30). Cell Phones; Not Even Prison Officials Can Silence the Irrepressible King of Con. *Houston Press.* News.

McVicker, S. (2000, August 24). Throwing Away the Key; A Talented Escape Artist and Con Man Gets More Prison Time. Will He Serve It? *Houston Press.* News.

Mumola, C. J. (1999, January). *Substance Abuse and Treatment of State and Federal Prisoners, 1997.* Washington, DC: U.S. Department of Justice, Bureau of Justice Statistics.

Mumola, C. J. (2000, April). *Incarcerated Parents and Their Children.* Washington, DC: U.S. Department of Justice, Bureau of Justice Statistics.

Office of Program Policy Analysis and Government Accountability (OPPAGA). (2000, December). *Review of Department of Corrections.* Report No. 00-23. Chapter 5.

Proposition 139. Chapter 5, Section 5-8, Article 1.5.

Ruiz v. Estelle. 503 F. Suppp. 1265, 1277–1279 (S.D. Tex. 1980).

Snell, T. L. (2001, December). *Capital Punishment 2000.* Washington, DC: U.S. Department of Justice Statistics, Bureau of Justice Statistics.

Texas A&M. Press Release. (2001, February 28). Overcrowding, Inmates' Rights Changed Texas Prison System. Retrieved January 20, 2002 from the World Wide Web: *http://rev.tamu.edu/stories/01/022801-12.html.*

Texas Department of Corrections. (n.d.a). (2001, January 9) *Texas Council on Offenders with Mental Impairments.* Retrieved January 19, 2002 from the World Wide Web: *http://www.tdcj.state.tx.us/tcomi/tcomi-contcare.htm.*

Texas Department of Corrections. (n.d.b). *Texas Council of Offenders with Mental Impairments: Special Needs Parole.* Retrieved November 21, 2001 from the World Wide Web: *http://www.tdcj.state.tx.us/tcomi/tcomi-parpgm.htm.*

Texas Department of Criminal Justice. (2001a, December 10). *Death Row Facts*. Retrieved December 20, 2001 from the World Wide Web: *http://www.tdcj.state.tx.us/id/id-education.htm*.

Texas Department of Criminal Justice. (2001b, November 20). *Institutional Division*. Retrieved December 20, 2001 from the World Wide Web: *http://www.tdcj.state.tx.us/id/id-education.htm*.

University of Florida, Bureau of Economic and Business Research. (1998) *Corrections in Florida: 1998 Opinion Survey*. Gainesville, FL: University of Florida.

Versey, B. M., Steadman, J. J., Morrissey, J. P., & Johnson, M. (1997). In Search of the Missing Linkages: Continuity of Care in U.S. Jails. *Behavioral Sciences and the Law,* 15(4): 383–397.

Zimring, F. E., & Hawkins, G. (1992). *Prison Population and Criminal Justice Policy in California*. Berkeley, CA: Institute of Governmental Studies Press University of California.

part III

Females

Concerns of Female Prisoners

Roslyn Muraskin

Women comprise only 6.4 percent of adult inmates, but they constitute the fastest growing segment of the inmate population. Women's increasing numbers require special examination of the issues particular to their confinement. Seventy-eight percent of women in prison have children. Many of these mothers run single-headed households and leave their children behind when they enter prison. If female inmates do not have family members who can care for their children while they are in prison, they may lose their children to foster care and have their parental rights eventually terminated. Additional obstacles exist for pregnant inmates because of medical concerns and their rights to reproductive choice.

Correctional facilities often do not provide proper gynecological care and have limited prenatal and postpartum care and no abortion services. Inmates who wish to terminate their pregnancy usually must go outside the facility and pay all expenses. Growing attention and awareness of sexual misconduct among corrections staff toward female inmates is also important. In California, for example, women were harassed by prison guards, who unlocked their cell doors at night and permitted male prisoners to enter and abuse them. One female prisoner complained to the facility's administration and was later beaten, sodomized, and raped by three men who had been told of her grievances. Issues facing female inmates are often overlooked because their numbers are not as large as that of male prisoners; however, their concerns are just as legitimate.

"The most perfect social system can only be attained where the laws which govern the sexes are based on justice and equality," according to Susan Grimke, suffragist leader.

According to the U.S. Department of Health and Human Services (2002),

> The struggle to expunge all sex-based laws based on custom, stereotype and paternalism has been largely successful in this country. Sex discrimination has been banned by federal and state law, in employment, education and housing. The right to abortion, while still under attack, is guaranteed by the Constitution. Paternalistic labor laws, that, in the name of protecting women, served to keep them out of better paying jobs, have been abolished.

As a result, women today participate in all realms of society on a more equal basis than ever before.

But legally sanctioned discrimination still exists. Women still earn far less than men for the same work. The "glass ceiling" is still a barrier to women's advancement in the workplace. Women are excluded from certain educational opportunities. And poor women are trapped in a cruel *Catch 22:* effectively denied their right to reproductive freedom through state laws that prohibit Medicaid coverage for abortions, while at the same time punished for bearing children under new welfare laws.

In spite of extraordinary progress, full equality for women remains an unfulfilled goal (p. 3).

During the past twenty years, more and more women have been found to be addicted to drugs/alcohol. Many of these women are poverty stricken, have multiple problems, are in abusive relationships, and suffer from mental illness. These women are entering into the correctional system at unprecedented rates.

The number of incarcerated women, once a minuscule number, tripled during the 1980s alone:

In the 15 years from 1980 to mid-1995, the number of women incarcerated in U.S. prisons rose by 460 percent, compared to an increase of 241 percent for men. The same pattern appears with the jail population. More than three times as many women were in jail in mid-1997 as in mid-1985. On average, the number of women in jail has grown by 10 percent each year from mid-1985 to 1997. These figures represent high present and future costs for these women—both in terms of separation from their families and children and in their inability to contribute economically to U.S. society.

Many of the women entering our criminal justice system are young—under forty years old—and 8 of every 10 are parents. New findings show that up to 80 percent of the women offenders in some State prison systems now have severe, long-standing substance abuse problems. In 1986, Congress significantly increased the penalties associated with crack cocaine. With the setting of mandatory minimum sentences and "three strikes and you're out" laws, many women are now being incarcerated who would previously have remained in their communities under criminal justice supervision.

Women offenders have traditionally represented a small proportion of the total offender population. But over the past decade, the number of incarcerated women has dramatically increased, expanding at rates far higher than for males. The number of women in jails rose from 15,900 in 1983 to 51,6000 in 1996—a 9.5 percent increase per year; women now account for more than 10 percent of the inmates in U.S. jails (U.S. Department of Health and Human Services, 2002, pp. 3–4).

MINORITY WOMEN ARE BEING DISPROPORTIONATELY AFFECTED

According to the U.S. Department of Health and Human Services (2002), "The increasing incarceration of women offenders has had a particularly grave impact on poor women of color. By 1994, the proportion of African American females incarcerated in the United States was higher than for white females. The rising use of crack cocaine among minority women in poverty appears to be a major factor. During the last decade, the number of African

American inmates in State, Federal, and local jails and prisons has grown at a faster pace than for non-minority inmates. The number of black (non Hispanic) women incarcerated for drug offenses in State prisons increased by 828 percent from 1986 to 1991" (p. 4).

WOMEN ARE ENTERING PRISON AT A MORE ADVANCED STAGE OF DRUG ABUSE THAN MEN

These women are experiencing a multitude of psychosocial and medical problems, which include both physical and sexual abuse as well as victimization. "Imprisoned women come mainly from poverty. Female prisoners have very low incomes, are disproportionately from minority groups, such as African American, and Hispanic, tend to be under-educated and unskilled and have sporadic employment history. Imprisoned women are mostly young, single heads of households. More than three quarters of all women in prison have children, and two-thirds of the women have children under the age of 18" (U.S. Department of Health and Human Services, 2002, pp. 5–6).

WOMEN OFFENDERS REQUIRED SPECIALIZED, WOMEN-SPECIFIC SUBSTANCE ABUSE TREATMENT

The Department of Health and Human Services states that "traditional substance abuse treatment models were originally designed for men; they address alcohol and drug addiction from a male perspective. Women's substance abuse is different. Addiction tends to occur more rapidly for women than for men, to involve more than one mood-altering substance, and to produce serious medical consequences over a briefer period of time" (2002, p. 7). Furthermore, "Typically, women offenders with substance abuse problems have been victims of violence—physical abuse, domestic violence, and rape. . . . 46 percent of all drug-dependent women have been victims of rape and from 28–44 percent have victims of incest. Twenty-nine percent report being physically abused as children and 60 percent as adults. Thirty-one percent report emotional abuse as a child and 48 percent as an adult" (2002, p. 7). Traditionally all treatment programs are focused on men. "Addicted women—especially those with children—face a unique set of problems which in the past have precluded successful treatment outcomes: a male-model approach to therapy; programs with inadequate knowledge, capacity, and resources to meet the special needs of women; the chronic medical and complex psychosocial problems unique to women; and the pressure of dependent children" (U.S. Department of Health and Human Services, 2002, p. 7).

FEW APPROPRIATE TREATMENT PROGRAMS FOR WOMEN NOW EXIST WITHIN THE CRIMINAL JUSTICE SYSTEM

According to the Department of Health and Human Services (2002), "Nationwide, there is a lack of comprehensive treatment services available for women offenders. Relatively few treatment programs are geared to the special needs of women and their children, and even fewer treat pregnant women" (p. 8).

TREATMENT SAVES MONEY

The cost of treatment contrasts with the cost of incarceration:

> It costs less money to treat a women offender for substance abuse than to incarcerate her. Effective treatment results in savings to society that outweigh the costs of treatment by a factor of at least 4 to 1. These are the costs for incarcerating and treating a substance-abusing woman: . . . It costs from $20,000 to $30,000 per year to incarcerate a woman in prison or in a woman's jail. It costs $54,209 per bed to build a new State facility and $78,000 per bed for Federal facilities. California alone, which now has about 11,500 women prisoners, has had to build two new State facilities with more than 3,000 beds for women. Foster care for the child of an incarcerated woman adds $3,600 to $14,000 a year, excluding administrative costs to the total (U.S. Department of Health and Human Services, 2002, p. 12).

Moreover, "when women offenders go untreated for their addiction, society also pays a heavy cost in health and social damage. These are young women, likely to become pregnant, many of whom pay for their drugs through high-risk sexual behavior. More women than men in correctional settings now test positive for the human immunodeficiency virus (HIV). If this lifestyle is not interrupted, these women are at risk of HIV not only for themselves, but as a conduit to their babies and to their sexual contacts. The lifetime cost of treating a single HIV-positive individual suggests what a large payoff there can be before effectively treating a substance-abusing woman offender" (U.S. Department of Health and Human Services, 2002, p. 14).

For both male and female offenders, "their untreated addiction exacts a high social cost. With men, their higher rate of violent crime creates major costs to society. Substance-abusing women are responsible for much less social cost resulting from violent crime than men are. However, untreated addiction among women exacts a deep and tragic social cost. For these women, the costs are compounded not only by the health and personal damage to themselves, but by the serious and potentially permanent damage that is done to the physical and emotional well being of their children, as well as the disintegration of their families" (U.S. Department of Health and Human Services, 2002, p. 14).

REFERENCES

Carlacio, J.L. (2003). "Setting a Rhetorical Precedent: The Early Feminist 'Thought: of Sarah Grimke. Unpublished paper for *The Second Biennial Feminism(s) and Rhetoric(s) Conference* "Challenging Rheteroics: Cross-Disciplinary Sites of Feminist Discourse." *http://femrhet.cla.umn,edu/proposals/ carlacios_ jami.htm*

From *Substance Abuse Treatment for Women Offenders: Guide to Promising Practices* U.S. Department of Health and Human Services, 2002. National Institute of Health. Rockville: Maryland.

c h a p t e r   1 8

Women Prisoners

Karen Fein

INTRODUCTION

The rapid increase in the number of women entering our correctional facilities has been astronomical. Although the ratio of women to men in state and federal prisons remains small (men outnumbered women by 15 to 1 as of June 30, 1998), the number of women prisoners has for nearly 30 years been growing faster than the number of men. According to the Bureau of Justice Statistics, between 1983 and 1999 the number of women in jail increased by 51,835 (Stephen, 2001). The Bureau of Justice Statistics reported that the number of male prisoners grew by 80 percent between 1990 and 2001, while the number of female prisoners grew by 114 percent during that same period (Beck et al., 2001). While the numbers may differ a bit from study to study as a result of the methodology used, the higher female rates is consistent. Something has clearly changed, and we can expect consequences of this increased incarceration rate for females.

The data are important. However, we need to remember that these are real people we are reading about. Remember that they are women, individuals in their own right—they are parents, and siblings, and daughters, but first and foremost they are individuals. They are not a small segment of society to which we can easily turn a deaf ear, for they are as much a part of this society as each one of us, as anyone. By virtue of this alone, we need to become familiar with their plight and become involved in the process of working together to ameliorate the factors that have brought us to this point.

People not only get locked up because they are found guilty of doing wrong, they get locked up because we as a society create sanctions that define various behaviors as illegal. Furthermore, and possibly more important, people are incarcerated in response to a social ethos. A prevailing cultural belief and the resulting norms and sanctions are applied with vigor, and we sit back and watch the results. A prime example is when Americans and their political representatives decided to be tough on crime and on drugs. We agreed on harsh penalties and punishments for people who we believed were not responsible enough to stay out of trouble. We set up policies such as "three strikes and you're out" and launched a "war on drugs," casting our nets so wide across the populace that not only were serious violent offenders caught and locked away, but so too were scores of the nonviolent. We filled our prisons and our jails with people who, under our policies, we believed were deserving of our sanctions. had done wrong, that is, whom jails and prisons are meant to hold. There are those who write that our efforts were purposeful: that they were a further extension of a patriarchal society, an effort to further attack and subjugate the women of our society; to punish increasing numbers of women, especially women of color, who had failed in their ascribed social roles as women and mothers—reminiscent of the "witch hunts" in the late 1600s. Still others argue that our efforts were a continuation of a culture of oppression, targeted at certain racial and ethnic groups, maintaining the balance of power (i.e., among the have and the have-nots). These and other theories cannot be ignored. The evidence does show that people from certain racial and ethnic groups are overrepresented in our penal systems. For example, while African Americans make up 13 percent of our nation's population, they make up nearly half of the inmate population (Greenfeld & Snell, 2000). As long as we continue to define the problem as stemming from a person's intrinsic deficits, we do little to address the social, political, and economic factors that likely contributed to maintain these individuals and groups in the lower echelons of the social strata. This is not to say that individuals are nothing more than representations of the broader social context without choice and responsibility for their actions. Rather, it simply recognizes the multiplicity of factors that play a role in each of our life experiences and situations. And so, with this said, let us consider the plight of women offenders as they interact with the criminal justice system.

The goals of this chapter are threefold. First, a description of the correctional institution is presented. Second, a description of women is prison is presented. Third, a discussion of system modifications is offered.

JAILS AND PRISONS

Goffman (1961) defines a total institution as "a place of residence and work where a large number of like-situated individuals, cut off from the wider society for an appreciable period of time, together lead an enclosed, formally administered round of life" (p. xiii).

Though both jails and prisons are total institutions, each possesses unique qualities. It is important to stress these differences. The *jail* is a locally administered and funded confinement facility with authorization to hold persons awaiting adjudication and/or those committed after adjudication to serve sentences of one year or less (Steadman, 1994). The jail may hold persons who are awaiting trial, are being held for another jurisdiction, are serving a sentence of less than one year, or are awaiting transportation to another facility such as a prison or a mental hospital (Moynahan & Stewart, 1980). An important distinction among jail inmates is between those who have been convicted and those who remain unconvicted. According to the Bureau of Justice Statistics (BJS), approximately half of the jail population is unconvicted (Harlow, 1998b).

The *prison,* in contrast, is a state or federally funded institution that houses individuals whose cases have already been adjudicated and who are serving sentences of more than one year. Individuals in prisons are often serving time for more serious offenses than individuals in jails (Irwin, 1985).

An additional important factor differentiating the jail from the prison, in terms of potential for liaison between the community and the correctional institution, is where the inmates resided. For instance, because of the small number of women's prisons, many women are forced to serve out prison sentences in locales far from their homes (Padel & Stevenson, 1988).

This can act as an impediment to continuity of care for those individuals, cutting them off from social support systems and community programs that might provide services during their incarceration as well as upon their release from custody. Without familiar linkages in place for the ex-inmate, obtaining services can be far more difficult and fragmented. Conversely, the jail as a county facility usually holds individuals, both men and women, who are from that specific county. Serving time and being released into one's county of residence may enhance the opportunity for continuous care.

These four differences between prison and jail—local control and local monies as the primary funding source, the short length of stay, the predominance of nonviolent and misdemeanant offenders, and the "local" proximity to an inmate's home community—serve to highlight not only the differences between the two institutions, the jail and the prison, but they also hint at ways to use each institution differently with regard to rehabilitation.

THE WOMEN

The research that has been conducted on incarcerated women has found that these women are economically deprived, undereducated, and unskilled with sporadic employment histories and disproportionately African American or Hispanic, young, single, heads of households, with at least two children under age eighteen (Feinman, 1994; Owen and Bloom, 1995).

Nearly two-thirds of women in jails and prisons were minorities (black, Hispanic, other) (Greenfeld & Snell, 2000). According to the Department of Justice (2002), "relative to their number of U.S. residents, black non-Hispanics were 5 times more likely than white non-Hispanics, over 2 1/2 times more likely than Hispanics, and 11 times more likely than persons of other races to have been in jail" (Beck et al., 2002).

According to Pollack-Byrne (1990), "women inmates come from families marked by alcoholism, drug addiction, mental illness, erratic use of authority, and desertion" (p. 77). In addition, nearly half of all inmates, both male and female, reported that a family member had been incarcerated (Harlow, 1998b). Women were far more likely than men to be serving time for a drug offense and less likely to be sentenced for a violent crime (Gilliard & Beck, 1998). Twenty-seven percent of female inmates were held for drug law violations; this was true for 21 percent of male inmates. Women were twice as likely as men to be held for fraud or theft (Harlow, 1998b). Women offenders tended to be involved in crimes that have an economic motive (Wellisch et al., 1996) and were less likely to commit violent crimes than are male offenders. Currently, women make up 14 percent of violent offenders (Greenfeld & Snell, 2000). This overview paints a picture of women facing a multiplicity of problems.

TRAUMA—PAST AND PRESENT

Women entering jails and prisons have pasts fraught with traumatic experiences. The American Correctional Association (1990) reported that a majority of adult female offenders had been victims of physical abuse and 36 percent had been sexually abused. According to the Bureau of Justice Statistics, a higher percentage of females than males reported having been physically or sexually abused (Harlow, 1998a). Furthermore, for men, the reported abuse generally took place when they were under the age of eighteen; for women, the abuse continued into adulthood (Harlow, 1998a). Owen and Bloom (1995) have found that well over half of the sample in their study of female inmates reported exposure to some form of childhood physical or sexual abuse, adult rape, and/or battering. The literature is ripe with disheartening descriptions of the abuse that these women may have experienced in their childhoods and in their present-day relationships.

For many of these women, the physical and emotional scars of abuse have not yet healed. Their self-esteem and their belief that they can or cannot do better for themselves and their families remain tied to their histories of abuse. To further complicate things, many of these women come to jail or prison on the heels of a domestically abusive relationship and may return to that relationship or to a similar relationship upon release. These women need help to free themselves from the abuse. Judith Herman (1992) wrote that

> The core experiences of psychological trauma are disempowerment and disconnection from others. Recovery, therefore, is based upon the empowerment of the survivor and the creation of new connections. Recovery can take place only within the context of relationships; it cannot occur in isolation (p. 133).

In essence, then, America's correctional facilities are filled with people who likely need guidance and practice at envisioning, much less believing in positive futures changed through empowerment.

Lord (1995) writes that the psychological trauma creates a need "to reconnect to other people and discover once again capacities for trust, autonomy, initiative, competence, identity, and intimacy" (p. 262). In a study conducted by Gray and colleagues (1995), the authors found that many persons in their sample needed help to repair the damage done by victimization. However, few of the women in that study received *any* type of help with building self-esteem, improving communication skills, or managing stress and anger (Gray et al., 1995). The damage from sexual and/or physical abuse can be far reaching. It seems clear that given the incidence of abuse among female inmates, it may be not only appropriate but essential to provide services that focus on these types of traumatic experiences and their consequences. If they could be linked with appropriate community services, it is possible that the services provided in the jail could play an integral part in decreasing the chances of females returning to jail.

SUBSTANCE ABUSE

Consideration must also be given to issues of substance abuse and dependence, since many of the women entering jails and prisons are coming in on drug related offenses. Based on 1999 data, female prison inmates were more likely than male prison inmates to have used drugs regularly (Greenfeld & Snell, 2000). In addition, nearly one in four female prisoners reported committing their offense in order to obtain money with which to buy drugs (Snell, 1994). According to a National Institute of Justice (NIJ) survey of drug-abusing women offenders, "most drug abusing women offenders are indigent, have multiple problems, and possess few personal and social resources" (Wellisch et al., 1994, p. 9). In a more recent study by Wellisch and associates (1996) the authors note that "drug-abusing women offenders generally have a high incidence of medical and psychological problems" (p. 33).

MENTAL HEALTH

Numerous studies have explored mental health issues among prison populations. The fewer number of studies that have been conducted in jails as contrasted with prisons have focused on female jail detainees with specific mental health diagnoses. Teplin and colleagues (1997) found that "many female jail inmates have severe psychiatric disorders and require mental health services" (p. 604). Veysey (1998) added that not only are many women coming into jail with mental illnesses, but that many of these women come into jails with "issues that complicate mental health problems" (p. 371). Some research indicates that women are more likely than men to receive a diagnosis of a severe mental illness (Veysey, 1998). Similarly, Teplin and colleagues (1997) found that women were diagnosed with depression at a rate four times higher than that for men, that depression often goes undetected in jail, and that fewer women than men receive mental health services in jail. The issue of identification of needs and service provision is imperative for the jail detainee with mental health problems, both while in the jail and when released into the community. While often the inmate who is depressed poses less of a management problem than the inmate who might be experiencing symptoms of schizophrenia, he or she is in no less need of treatment.

PARENTING

According to Veysey (1998), 67 percent of women in prisons had one or more children under the age of eighteen. Veysey (1998) also noted that about 70 percent of women in jail or prison lived with their minor children before incarceration. Child custody issues abound for incarcerated females. Pollack-Byrne (1990) wrote that many women expect to maintain or have custody returned to them upon their release from jail or prison. Crawford (1988) found that 68.3 percent of the study's sample had family members who continued to care for the children while the mother was incarcerated. Meanwhile, only 10.6 percent reported that a significant other was caring for the children during their incarceration (Pollack-Byrne, 1990). The difference in percentages between family caring for children and significant others caring for children infers a great deal of responsibility for child care falling to members other than a coparent. Identification of needs and assistance in obtaining help to meet their needs is a paramount issue in the lives of the women and their families.

Finally, in 1990, the American Correctional Association (ACA) estimated that 6 percent of prisoners and 4 percent of jail inmates were pregnant upon admission (Acoca, 1998). It has also been reported that women in community drug treatment who have been referred by the criminal justice system often need legal advice to deal with child protective agencies (Reed, 1987). Given these multiple overlapping problem areas, an effective, comprehensive community-based service system might include domestic violence services, legal aid, substance abuse services, child welfare services, mental health services, as well as educational and employment services.

SERVICE PROVISION

A great deal of energy goes into debates as to whether correctional facilities should be responsible for providing treatment other than that which focuses on the physical health of the residents or medication needs that may arise from mental health issues. However, the question might better be posed as to how best to achieve the goals of the criminal justice system (i.e., retribution, deterrence, punishment and public safety, and rehabilitation). Few would argue the priority of security as the primary goal of the jail or prison. It is essential to maintain the safety of the public and of the institution. In addition, it is clear from earlier discussion that jails and prisons cannot provide the same level or method of treatment. For example, an institution that has three years' time with an inmate can address treatment issues far different from the institution that has an individual for only 11 days. What appropriate role can the jail or prison play? The difficulties these women face do not spontaneously appear upon their incarceration. While it is possible that some symptoms and/or conditions are exacerbated, in most cases incarceration is simply another hardship in a life filled with hardships. The women must contend with numerous problems, and they may very well need assistance in order to triumph over their adversities. It is appropriate and necessary (at the minimum, in order to reduce recidivism) for the institution to provide certain services and treatments to incarcerated individuals. For example, if an inmate is in need of psychotropic medication, the institution must have mechanisms in place to meet these needs. However, jails are not treatment centers with the capability of addressing all of the needs of their inmate populations; nor should they be.

It is difficult to produce a comprehensive list of services available to inmates in jails. The type and availability of jail services depends on numerous factors. Some of these factors may be internal to the institution, such as staffing levels, budgets, philosophy of the jail administration, and size of a particular inmate group. A reason often cited as impeding specific services for women inmates stems from the comparatively small proportion of women as compared to men in jail:

> An accounting of inmate services offered in the Nation's jails indicates that only the largest jails offer educational, counseling and recreational programs to inmates, smaller jails have neither the facilities nor the money to provide inmate programs (Zupan, 1991, p. 59).

It is important to note that no gender distinction is made in Zupin's statement. The research indicates that jail services for all inmates are lacking. But, much like Daly's (1994) statement that "disparity studies adopt an add-women-and-stir posture" (p. 6), those programs that do exist tend to be developed with male inmates in mind.

Other factors may emanate from external forces such as the courts, professional standards of care, and available resources outside the jail. These are discussed later. Internal and external factors are not necessarily mutually exclusive. It is possible, for instance, that the philosophy of a particular jail is reflective of the local community's viewpoints and of the viewpoints of the society at large as well. With many factors at play, it is difficult to generalize from findings that exist with regard to services available in specific jails. Nevertheless, available data would suggest the following as the presentation of the primary issues in relation to service provision in jails.

Legal Considerations

Why provide services at all? Is it because it is the humane thing to do, because society shares the responsibility for creating "rabble," or because it is in society's best interest? The following offers some insight into the mandate for services. Legal standards and legislative mandates, while often ambiguous, do call for, and indeed require, some standard of care. People locked in prisons, jails, mental hospitals, and the like all have rights. While they do not have all of the rights they had as free individuals, the institution that is responsible for maintaining physical custody of the inmate does have the obligation to meet certain needs of the inmate.

So what must the institution provide? Providing a safe environment through the provision of food, shelter, and clothing is mandated. The institution is responsible for keeping the inmate protected while in its care. Yet it is possible to move beyond that into additional and more ambiguous areas.

The leading decisions defining the responsibilities of care focus on the Eighth and the Fourteenth Amendments of the U.S. Constitution. The Eighth and Fourteenth Amendments are referred to in legally securing both convicted and pretrial defendants medical and psychiatric treatment. For convicted persons, the right to care comes from the Eighth Amendment (cruel and unusual punishment). For pretrial detainees, that right is imbedded in the Fourteenth Amendment providing for due process.

The Constitution of the United States guarantees American citizens certain basic rights. We are citizens before, during, and after incarceration. Thus, the responsibility of the institution must remain congruent with the laws and rights governing the populace. This does not mean, however, that there is an obligation under the Constitution for all persons to be treated the same. We have laws, for example, that allow for certain age groups to drive or to buy liquor, while other age groups are prohibited from such behaviors. Unequal treatment must, however, be rational and related to a legitimate interest of the state.

In the landmark case of *Estelle v. Gamble,* the court stated that the government is under an "obligation to provide medical care for those whom it is punishing by incarceration," because the Eighth Amendment prohibition on government imposition of cruel and unusual punishment results in a affirmative duty to give medical treatment to inmates (*Estelle v. Gamble*, 429 U.S. 97, 1976, as cited in Resnik & Shaw, 1980, p. 397). With *Estelle v. Gamble* (50 L Ed 2d 251—1976), described as "the constitutional genesis" of a prisoner's right to treatment, the court employed standards of "deliberate indifference" and "serious medical needs" as the measure of culpability. It should be noted that parity between physical health and mental health as they relate to constitutional safeguards has been widely accepted, though not always implemented.

Serious Medical Needs

The issue of serious medical needs is an important one. The implication is that diagnosis and evaluation have taken place and that without treatment; the individual would suffer pain and negative consequences. Certain types of mental illnesses will likely fit into this "serious medical illness" category, but many other problem areas will not. For example, mild depression would not dictate treatment. Severe depression, in which an individual expressed suicidal ideation or a severe depression such that the individual was unable to perform ordinary tasks, would dictate intervention. Addiction problems would not require intervention from a legal standpoint either. Substance abuse and alcoholism are generally not defined in the courts as serious illnesses per se, but rather they are viewed as conditions that require "rehabilitation," not "treatment" (Cohen, 1991).

The distinction between treatment and rehabilitation is an important one. In the legal world, *treatment* means there is a *disease*, which has been diagnosed and for which an intervention aimed at "curing" the malady could be implemented. Rehabilitation refers to a condition for which the individual holds some degree of responsibility and for which "disease" is not the predicate (Cohen, 1991). While debate certainly exists surrounding these assumptions, the legal arena continues to impose this paradigm. Thus, there is no legal directive for the provision of rehabilitative services to inmates, medical or other (Cohen, 1991).

DELIBERATE INDIFFERENCE

In the language used in the *Estelle v. Gamble* case, the court also discussed "deliberate indifference." Briefly, deliberate indifference "[r]equires more than poor judgment and less than intentional acts or omissions calculated to cause suffering. An excellent rule of thumb is that deliberate indifference to the needs of inmates exists when action is not taken in the face of a strong likelihood that failure to provide appropriate care would result in harm to the inmates"(Cohen, 1991, p. 9).

The Fourteenth Amendment is the Constitutional Amendment referred to in cases of pretrial detainees. Pretrial detainees, most often held in the jail, have yet to be adjudicated. Under Due Process (fourteenth Amendment) these detainees may not be punished. As such, if an inmate is in need of care for a serious medical illness, the institution will not exhibit "deliberate indifference" in failing to attend to the medical/psychiatric needs of that individual, and the individual will not be punished by nonreceipt of care. Being held in jail prior to adjudication does not in and of itself constitute a breach of the inmate's constitutional rights under the Fourteenth Amendment (*Bell v. Wolfish*, 441 U.S. 520, 1979).

It is clear that many of the problem areas thus far described as existing for incarcerated populations would not warrant intervention under the present day understanding of "right to treatment," either for convicted persons or for pretrial detainees who have yet to be adjudicated. There is no such *disease* as "domestic violence." There is no *disease* known as "victim of social realities" or "bad luck." There is no *disease* for female inmates labeled "father of the child cannot be found" and "mother has no support systems." Yet these and other life conditions or situations may have serious consequences for those involved as well as for the society at large, especially in light of the provision or lack of the provision of services in the jail or the community. Much of the research that has been carried out with incarcerated populations has focused on psychiatric illnesses and the need to treat these illnesses while incarcerated. While this is important, many incarcerated individuals do not meet the diagnostic criteria for "mental disorder" but are still in need of services. Thus far, the courts have only spoken to the issues of medical and psychiatric care. However, legal directives and policy are not synonymous. What a court says institutions must or must not do does not mean that institutions may not develop policies on their own that address the needs of their populations.

The use of the courts to address treatment issues within correctional institutions has been the primary avenue toward change. "By the early 1980s, incarcerated women were using the courts to address four primary issues: inadequate medical attention, parental rights, pregnancy care, and sex discrimination" (Rafter, 1990, p. 197). A landmark case in 1974, *Barefield v. Leach,* found that "what Equal Protection Clause requires in a prison setting is parity of treatment, as contrasted with identity of treatment, between male and female inmates with respect to the conditions of their confinement and access to rehabilitation opportunities" (*Barefield v, Leach,* Civ. No. 10282, D.N. Mex., 1974, slip op. at 37–38, as cited in Rafter, 1990). *Glover v. Johnson* and *Canterino v. Wilson,* both important cases for female inmates, began from the findings of *Barefield.* Glover found that the size of the institution (i.e., male institutions as compared to female institutions) was not the factor upon which to base comparisons. The court stated that gender was the critical comparison factor (Rafter, 1990). In *Canterino v. Wilson,* the court found that inmates "were denied access to many vocational education and training programs . . . available to male prisoners" and that of "the programs which are available to females at KCIW [Kentucky Correctional Institution for Women], many are inferior in quality to the corresponding programs at [Kentucky's] male institutions (*Canterino v. Wilson,* 1982, p. 188). However, while *Glover* remains intact, *Canterino,* originally successful in 1982, was struck down by the appellate court in 1989 (Rafter, 1990).

The Equal Protection Clause of the Fourteenth Amendment has been presented in numerous legal arguments regarding equitable treatment in correctional facilities. The particular part of the Clause that relates to issues of equitable treatment is, "no state shall . . . deny to any person within its jurisdiction the equal protection of the laws." In *Reed v. Reed,* it was found that "policies that discriminate on the basis of gender are subject to scrutiny under the Equal Protection Clause," (*Reed v. Reed,* 404 U.S. 71, 75, 1971). However, in *Turner v. Safley* (482 U.S. 78, 89, 1987), the Court noted "that prison laws that infringe upon a prisoner's constitutional rights would be upheld if they are reasonably related to a legitimate penological interest." The Court noted the unique nature of the correctional system, allowing for institutional decisions that may at first appear to be contrary to legal standards such as are found in the Equal Protection Clause of the Fourteenth Amendment. However, this does not mean that the institution has the right to base disparity in the system on such factors as the smaller number of women in correctional facilities as compared to the number of men (*Glover v. Johnson,* 478 F. Supp. 1078, 1979; *Canterino v. Wilson,* 546 F. Supp. 207, 1983).

In *Jeldness v. Pearce,* 30 F.3d 1220, 1229 (9th Cir. 1994), the court found that state prisons receiving federal funds are required by Title IX to make reasonable efforts to offer the same educational opportunities to women as to men. "The number of classes offered should at least be proportionate, not just to the total number of inmates, but to the number of inmates desiring to take educational programs" (*Jeldness v. Pearce,* 30 F.3d 1220, 1229, 9th Cir. 1994).

Todaro v. Ward was a major case that focused upon women's health care in correctional facilities. The *Todaro* case was "a class action suit that charged that the entire health delivery system in a women's prison worked constitutional deprivation. Here, the United States Court of Appeals for the Second Circuit affirmed a district court's conclusion the New York Sate had failed to provide the entire population of the Bedford Hills prisons with access to adequate medical care or with the delivery of treatment prescribed by physicians for inmates (*Todaro v. Ward,* 431 F. Supp. 1129, S.D.N.Y. 1977, as cited in Resnik & Shaw, 1980, p. 340).

In *Jordon v. Gardner,* 986 F.2nd 1521 (9th Circ. 1993), "the court held that subjecting women with a history of sexual abuse to pat searches by men could constitute cruel and inhuman punishment" (Coormaraswamy, 1999, p. 8).

Many state cases have addressed issues of female prisoners in institutions. Yet change through the courts is often implemented only after considerable amounts of time and expense. *Todaro v. Ward* was an excellent example of this. While the court rendered its final decision on July 11, 1977, and the judgment took effect in December of 1977, the plaintiffs' case had begun presentation in the summer of 1974 (Resnik & Shaw, 1980).

Of great import is the Prison Litigation Reform Act (PRLA). On April 26, 1996 the PRLA was promulgated. In short, this Act sought to curtail the Federal Court's participation in what was described by some legislators as "the running of state prisons" (Prison Litigation Reform Act, 18 U.S.C.A. § 3626, Supp. 1997). "The primary recourse pursued by prisoners is to bring suit before the federal courts for mistreatment. The passage of the PRLA is an attempt to limit prisoners' access to such recourse" (Coormaraswamy, 1999).

As stated earlier, while the majority of change has stemmed from court cases, change has also been the product of legislative endeavors. The main role that the legislature has played has been in constructing legal mandates regarding sentencing requirements. The "three strikes and you're out" laws, which numerous states have now adopted in some form or another, have resulted in increases of correctional populations. In addition, while state budgets have supported the physical expansion of correctional environments, there has not been equal support for rehabilitative programs. For example, in the late 1990s, the California Department of Corrections spent approximately $21,000 per prisoner per year. Of that, $11,000 (52 percent) was spent on security measures, $3125 (14 percent) for health care, and $900 (4.5 percent) for education and training (Coomaraswamy, 1999).

It would appear that as a society, we remain fixed in the dichotomy of us versus them and punishment versus rehabilitation. We do not seem to be able to accept that punishment can exist simultaneously with efforts to rehabilitate. We want to stop recidivism—we want people to change for the better, but we do not believe they can or that we should have to help in that process. We want to teach them a lesson, but we do not seem to care what they learn.

PROFESSIONAL STANDARDS

In the 1970s the correctional community expressed a readiness to reexamine standards of care for their incarcerated populations. Steadman and colleagues (1989) noted two factors that have been associated with this change: the courts' willingness to hear inmates' suits against institutions; and the advent of deinstitutionalization, at which time there was a heightened concern among health care professionals regarding medical care in correctional facilities.

Over time, professional organizations have developed and disseminated "professional standards" for mental health care in custodial facilities. Though these standards are not legally binding on the jail or prison, they may encourage states and counties to consider guidelines for effective management and care of their populations. Here again, though, the emphasis is on the treatment of mental illnesses and not rehabilitative "conditions."

The organizations that have been particularly involved in developing and disseminating standards of care include the American Public Health Association (APHA); the American Correctional Association (ACA); the American Medical Association (AMA); the American Association of Correctional Psychologists (AACP); the U.S. Department of Justice; and the National Association of Sheriffs. While there are differences between the standards suggested by the various organizations, they all present recommendations concerned with issues of confidentiality, staffing and professional development, and identification of mentally ill inmates (i.e., screening and subsequent evaluation). Research by Steadman and associates (1989) shows that "perhaps the single most important theme that emerges in the standards is the need for all health care services to be delivered in the context of a formal, structured program" (p. 39). Through inclusion in standards for care, mental health care has been defined as a viable health care need to which the facility must respond.

The issue of diversity of U.S. jails and the limited budgets with which they must function of course affect the nature of that response. Steadman and colleagues (1989) point out that jail administrators have criticized many of the standards given staffing levels, the number of inmates, and the fiscal realities of many local jails as unrealistic. There has also been frustration over the lack of "how to" in the standards. Standards typically do not come with directions for implementation. Nonetheless, the involvement of the various organizations already mentioned as well as others in the promulgation of professional standards of care for correctional facilities is a positive move toward formal inclusion of mental health care within institutional policies.

Based on these and other recommendations, states and counties have developed "minimum standards of care." While these focus largely on the management of the correctional facility, they do touch on the medical and mental health needs of inmates. Nevertheless, tracking whether a county facility meets or does not meet these minimal standards of care remains an issue. Some states do follow through with regular inspections, however; many states do not enforce these minimum standard policies.

Even so, standards (see Chapter 13) and court involvement may do more than impact the mental health services within the jail. By placing the focus on correctional populations, especially jail populations, who are eventually released back into the community, professional organizations may alert community service providers to the issues as well.

WOMEN AND JAIL SERVICES

Bonta and colleagues (1995) state that the underrepresentation of women in conflict with the law has had an important impact on the services provided to female offenders and on theory development and research" (p. 277). According to Wellisch and colleagues (1996), while there are certainly more services now than in the late 1970s, "the increased number of programs has not been sufficient to significantly reduce the discrepancy between those who need services and those who receive treatment" (p. 53). Based on the findings of a study conducted by the National Council on Crime and Delinquency (NCCD), "one of the most universally shared attributes of women in prison is a history of victimization" (Acoca & Austin, 1996 as cited in Acoca, 1998). Yet the NCCD reported that "as with so many of the conditions affecting women most severely, histories of violent physical and emotional trauma are rarely identified or treated in prison and jail settings" (Acoca, 1998, p. 58). Based on structured interviews with 151 women prisoners for the NCCD, Acoca (1998) found that access to all services was extremely limited. She also reported that it was particularly difficult for women to access psychological services, substance abuse services, and acute medical treatment.

The National Institute of Justice (NIJ) study by Wellisch (1996) suggests that "drug treatment alone, without an attendant, comprehensive range of rehabilitation services, can rarely effect stable, long-term behavioral change" (p. 9). That same study reports that few women in need of drug treatment actually receive treatment. This is corroborated by Veysey (1998): "Women are typically underserved in correctional settings in all types of jail programming" (p. 368).

In Teplin's and colleagues' (1997) study on female jail detainees with mental illness, the variables that predicted who received services included current disorder (schizophrenia or manic episodes more likely than depressive disorder), treatment history, and criminal history. It is interesting to note that while a history of psychiatric treatment increased the odds of receiving services, two or more prior arrests decreased the odds of receiving services.

WHAT IS NEEDED?

According to Immarigeon and Chesney-Lind (1992), successful decarceration of women is partly dependent on a well-planned and coordinated assessment of needs, continuous monitoring of progress, and aftercare support services. But current research indicates that women in jail simply do not receive these types of services with any consistency or continuity. Kaplan and Sasser (1996) offered a list of what they see as necessary to "successful community reintegration": On entry, inmates should receive tests of educational and vocational interests and aptitudes. This will help provide appropriate training placement and facilities close to their homes (out-of-state incarceration should be prohibited). Furthermore, inmates should receive more hospitable treatment for inmates' families (including overnight or extended visits), custody of their children for the first few years after birth, and well-designed and comprehensively implemented supportive services after release, including drug and alcohol treatment, vocational training, and social and emotional support (Kaplan & Sasser, 1996; p. 50).

Researchers agree that one of the most important services for incarcerated persons is discharge planning (Kaplan & Sasser, 1996; Veysey, 1998). Kaplan and Sasser (1996) report that a result of the deficiencies in the area of discharge planning services for incarcerated women is that when women are released they may be homeless or "in an environment that is not optimal to maintaining their sobriety and refraining from further criminal activity" (p. 50). This point underscores the importance of the relationship between the correctional facility and the community in the provision of services.

Much of the problem in providing appropriate services to incarcerated persons stems from two areas. The first is that by refusing to provide adequate funding to carry out these service objectives, we let it fall to a system already bursting at the seams, to provide these services on top of what they already are scrambling to achieve. We tell workers who did not hire onto the job to provide social services (correctional officers, for example) that their duties have been expanded, that now they must work to ensure that the inmates receive various program services. However, when we do offer said services, we implant them into the existing correctional system in a parallel manner as opposed to an integrated manner. This does little to foster an attitude of positive regard for these additional goals.

Second, rather than working to have fewer women who require assistance, we argue about whether providing assistance minimizes their experience of punishment. While incarceration may provide a needed respite for a few, for the majority of individuals, being stripped of freedom and existing under the total control of the institution is experienced as punishment. We in America value freedom and choice a great deal. In many ways both are lost to the individual in the institution. Punishment and service provision does not have to be in conflict with one another. It is possible that we would all best be served if we focused on what we can do, *in addition* to maintaining correctional facilities, to turn the tides.

REFERENCES

Acoca, L. (1998). Defusing the Time Bomb: Understanding and Meeting the Growing Health Care Needs of Incarcerated Women in America. *Crime and Delinquency,* 44(1):49–69.

American Correctional Association. (1990). *Task Force on the Female Offender: What Does the Future Hold?* Alexandria, VA: American Correctional Association.

Beck, Allen J., Karberg, Jennifer C., & Harrison, Paige M. (2002). *Vol. NCJ-191702: Prison and Jail Inmates at Midyear 2001.* Washington, DC: Bureau of Justice Statistics, U.S. Department of Justice.

Bell v. Wolfish, 441 U.S. 520 (1979).

Bonta, J., Pang, B., & Wallace-Capretta, S. (1995). Predictors of Recidivism among Incarcerated Female Offenders. *The Prison Journal,* 75(3):277–294.

Canterino v. Wilson, 546 F. Supp. 207 (1983).

Cohen, F. (1991). *The Law of Deprivation of Liberty: Cases and Materials.* Durham, NC: Carolina Academic Press.

Crawford, J. (1988). *Tabulation of a Nationwide Survey of State Correctional Facilities for Adult and Juvenile Female Offenders.* College Park, MD: American Correctional Association.

Daly, K. (1994). *Gender, Crime, and Punishment.* New Haven and London: Yale University Press.

Estelle v. Gamble (50 L Ed 2d 251,1976)

Feinman, C. (1994). *Women in the Criminal Justice System* (3rd ed.). Westport, CT: Praeger.

Gilliard, D. K., & Beck, A. J. (1998). *Vol. NCJ-167247: Prison and Jail Inmates at Midyear 1997.* Washington, DC: U.S. Department of Justice.

Glover v. Johnson, 478 F. Supp. 1078 (1979).

Goffman, E. (1961). *Asylums.* Garden City, NJ: Anchor Books, Doubleday & Company, Inc.

Gray, T., Mays, G. L., & Stohr, M. K. (1995). Inmate Needs and Programming in Exclusively Women's Jails. *The Prison Journal,* 75(2):186–202.

Greenfeld, Lawrence A., & Snell, Tracy L. (2000). *Vol. NCJ-175688: Women Offenders.* Washington, DC: Bureau of Justice Statistics, U.S. Department of Justice.

Harlow, C. W. (1998a). *Vol. NCJ-172879: Prior Abuse Reported by Inmates and Probationers.* Washington, DC: U.S. Department of Justice.

Harlow, C. W. (1998b). *Vol. NCJ-164620: Profile of Jail Inmates 1996.* Washington, DC: U.S. Department of Justice.

Herman, J. L. (1992). *Trauma and Recovery.* New York: Basic books.

Immarigeon, R., & Chesney-Lind, M. (1992). *Women's Prisons: Overcrowded and Overused.* San Francisco: National Council on Crime and Delinquency.

Irwin, J. (1985). *The Jail.* Berkley and Los Angeles, CA: University of California Press.

Jeldness v. Pearce, 30 F. 3d 1220, 1229 (9th Cir. 1994).

Kaplan, M. S., & Sasser, J. E. (1996). Women Behind Bars: Trends and Policy Issues. *Journal of Sociology and Social Welfare,* 23(4):43–56.

Lord, Elaine. (1995). A Prison Superintendent's Perspective on Women in Prison. *The Prison Journal,* 75(2):257–269.

Moynahan, J., & Stewart, E. K. (1980). *The American Jail: Its Development and Growth*. Chicago: Nelson-Hall.

Owen, B., & Bloom, B. (1995). Profiling Women Prisoners: Findings from National Surveys and a CA Sample. *The Prison Journal*, 75(2):165–185.

Padel, U., & Stevenson, P. (1988). *Insiders: Women's Experience of Prison*. London: Virago Press.

Pollock-Byrne. (1990). *Women, Prison, & Crime*. Contemporary Issues in Crime and Justice Series. Pacific Grove, CA: Brooks/Cole Publishing Company.

Prison Litigation Reform Act, 18 U.S.C.A. § (supp. 1997).

Rafter, Nicole Hahn. (1990). *Partial Justice: Women, Prison, and Social Control* (2nd ed). New Brunswick, NJ: Transaction Publishers.

Reed, B. (1987). Developing Women-Sensitive Drug Dependence Treatment Services: Why So Difficult? *Journal of Psychoactive Drugs*, 19:151–164.

Reed v. Reed, 404 U.S. 71, 75 (1971).

Resnik, Judith, & Shaw, Nancy. (1980). Prisoners of Their Sex: Health Problems of Incarcerated Women. In I. P. Robbins (ed.), *Prisoners' Rights Sourcebook*. New York: Clark Boardman.

Snell, T. (1994). *Vol. NCJ- 145321 March 1994: Women in Prison*. Washington, DC: U.S. Department of Justice, Bureau of Justice Statistics (pp. 1–13).

SourceBook of Criminal Justice Statistics. (1998). Vol, NCJ-171146. (Includes 1994, 1995, and 1996 editions.)

Steadman, H. J., McCarty, D. W., & Morrissey, J. P. (1989). *The Mentally Ill In Jail: Planning for Essential Services*. New York and London: The Guilford Press.

Steadman. Henry J. (1994). *Management of Special Populations: Mentally Disabled Offenders*. Final Report.

Stephen, James J. (2001). *NCJ-186633: Census of Jails, 1999*. Washington, DC: Bureau of Justice Statistics. U.S. Department of Justice.

Teplin, Abram, & McClelland. (1997). Mentally Disordered Women in Jail: Who Receives Services? 87(4):604 609.

Turner v. Safley, 482 U.S., 78, 89 (1987).

United States Department of Justice, 1990.

Wellisch, J., Prendergast, M. L., & Anglin, D. M. (1994, October). Drug-Abusing Women Offenders: Survey. In *NIJ Research in Brief*, *http://ncjrs.org:71/0/4/1/pubs/womenoff.asc* (accessed 05/30/97).

Wellisch, J., Prendergast, M. L., & Anglin, D. M. (1996). Needs Assessment and Services for Drug-Abusing Women Offenders: Results from a National Survey of Community Based Treatment. *Women and Criminal Justice*, 8(1):27–60.

Zupan, L. L. (1991). *Jails: Reform and the New Generation Philosophy*. Cincinnati, OH: Anderson Publishing Co.

Psychosocial Rehabilitation Needs of Women Offenders Who Are Deaf: A Case Study

Katrina R. Miller

Abstract

Although female offenders who are deaf make up only a minute group within the state prison population, their psychosocial rehabilitation delivery requirements are unique. A Texas population of seven women offenders who are deaf is described, and a case study is employed with the purpose of identifying and reviewing treatment delivery needs of this population. Among the most pressing needs are access to service providers who sign fluently, ongoing mental health evaluation and treatment, and attention to the functional impact of abuse and victimization. Benefits and drawbacks of four approaches to facilitating service provision within a prison facility are discussed.

Women comprise only 7 percent of the entire state prison population in Texas (Texas Department of Criminal Justice, 2001). Among all offenders who are deaf,[1] the percentage of women offenders who are deaf is consistent with the percentage of women offenders incarcerated overall, although this figure is on the rise (DeBell, 2001; Gondles, 2001; Miller, 2001; Moses, 2001; Texas Department of Criminal Justice, 2001). Traditional approaches to managing female offenders have included little distinction between how the differing rehabilitation needs of incarcerated men and women are addressed by corrections professionals, and many describe women offenders as an especially difficult population to manage (DeBell, 2001). Research focused specifically on the rehabilitation of women offenders has been minimal (Dowden & Andrews, 1999). However, the corrections profession is undergoing a paradigm shift in which the equal treatment of female offenders is viewed as something other than providing them the same treatment that male offenders receive (Gondles, 2001). An impetus to create gender-responsive programming has been recognized (DeBell, 2001; Gondles, 2001). It is understood that women offenders not only have unique health needs but different ways of expressing themselves in the correctional environment.

Specific concerns relating to female offenders include nutrition requirements, reproductive health issues, the care of their children while they are incarcerated, education and career development, and a range of mental health issues (DeBell, 2001). For instance, the rate of past child abuse among incarcerated women is twice that of women in the general public (Tischler, 1999). This is an especially relevant issue for women who are deaf, as 25 percent of females in the general public have been sexually abused as children, in comparison to 50 percent of females who are deaf (Mertens, 1996; Sullivan et al., 1987). Among female inmates in general, 87 percent of those who spent substantial time in foster care or in an institution as children have experienced abuse of some kind (Tischler, 1999). Based on these figures, it could be assumed that past victimization is nearly 100 percent among female offenders who are profoundly deaf, many of whom are placed in residential schools as children (Mertens, 1996; Sullivan et al., 1987).

Additionally, up to 70 percent of women offenders were in physically, emotionally, or sexually abusive adult relationships prior to incarceration (DeBell, 2001). These relationships can impact an individual's functioning in several arenas. Women in abusive relationships are often prevented from working and improving themselves by controlling partners, resulting in a lack of experience with employment, money management, decision making, and other life skills (DeBell, 2001). Thus, they come into the prison system with limited work histories and an average educational achievement at only the seventh to eighth grade level (DeBell, 2001; Texas Department of Criminal Justice, 2001). The educational achievement of women offenders who are deaf is estimated to be much lower, as a study of an entire population of offenders who are deaf found the average educational achievement in this group to be at the third grade level (Miller, 2001).

For women who are deaf, serious obstacles to communication and social development further compound these concerns. For example, 90 percent of children who are deaf are born into hearing families, most of whom are initially unprepared to accommodate their communication needs (Schein, 1996). The development of healthy self-image and essential social skills can be negatively impacted, largely due to language and communication barriers experienced in their families of origin or during their early educational experiences.

While some treatment needs of female offenders can be generalized to women offenders who are deaf, there are important considerations relating to the delivery of services that must be addressed. The purpose of this research is to gain a deeper understanding of the life histories and psychosocial rehabilitation delivery needs of female offenders who are deaf and various approaches to providing these services within the confines of a state prison system.

METHOD

This is study of seven women offenders who are deaf. They represent all of the women within an entire Texas state prison population of 101 offenders who are deaf. Subjects were each identified as an offender who is deaf by the Texas Department of Criminal Justice Physically Handicapped Offender Program (PHOP), which is responsible for the tracking and provision of accommodations to state prison offenders with disabilities throughout the state.

In order to better understand the common experiences of women offenders who are deaf, the common characteristics and experiences of the subjects are grouped together. Additionally, the psychosocial rehabilitation needs of women offenders who are deaf and use American Sign Language are explored from an insider's point of view, using an in-depth case study. A hearing, female researcher skilled in sign language screened each subject during a 15-minute initial contact, at which time language use was informally evaluated, and permission to access prison medical records was requested from each. One subject was then selected for a one-hour, videotaped interview based on two criteria: her status as a female offender who is deaf and her use of American Sign Language as a primary language. To safeguard confidentiality, the names of the subjects have been changed.

RESULTS

The common characteristics of women offenders who are deaf are categorized as personal characteristics, mental health histories, criminal histories, and communication. The case study expands on the experiences of women offenders who are deaf and use American Sign Language. Because there were only seven subjects, each was assigned an arbitrary name in order to personalize the discussion (Table 19–1).

Personal Characteristics

Subjects were predominantly White women in their thirties who were born deaf or hard of hearing (Table 19–1). Four of the women had two or more children. Very little information was available in prison medical files regarding subjects' degree of hearing loss or etiology. Two reported incidences of hearing loss in other members of their families of origin. All had

Table 19–1   CHARACTERISTICS OF WOMEN OFFENDERS WHO ARE DEAF IN A TEXAS STATE PRISON

ID	Race	Age	IQ	EA	Loss	Etiology	Onset	Language	Children
Alisha	W	32	—	5.4	—	rubella	birth	ASL	3
Beverly	W	31	—	3.9	—	fever	3	SimCom	0
Carmen	B	36	70	2.9	severe	—	birth	English	3
Darlene	W	32	—	2.0	—	rubella	birth	ASL	0
Ellie	W	33	—	—	—	—	birth	ASL	0
Francine	W	37	114	3.4	—	—	birth	ASL	4
Gretchen	W	41	115	1.0	—	—	birth	SimCom	2

EA = Educational achievement. Incoming offenders take the Test of Adult Basic Education (TABE) to determine an educational achievement grade level. The EA represents averages of test scores in three subjects: reading, math, and language.

educational achievement grade levels at the fifth grade or below, with the exception of Ellie, who was not able to participate in educational testing due to multiple disabilities. Four
of the women, including Ellie, had significant secondary disabilities (Table 19–2).

Mental Health

Of the women, all had mental health diagnoses on record (including chemical dependency), with the exception of Francine, who chose to refuse access to her medical file (Table
19–2). Francine agreed to participate in the study by answering some questions in person;
however, during the interview she declined to talk about her mental health. Two women
had previous psychiatric hospitalizations, and two others had been hospitalized for chemical dependency prior to incarceration. Four of the women had a history of self-injurious
behaviors, such as wrist slashing or head banging, and two had one or more known suicide
attempts. Although no information was recorded in subjects' medical files regarding past
experiences with abuse, in person, Alisha reported a history of physical, emotional, and sexual abuse as a child. Both Alisha and Carmen reported forming abusive partnerships with
adult males. Carmen had been blinded in one eye as a result of domestic violence.

Criminal Histories

Two of the women had juvenile records. Of these, one had a prior confinement in another
state as an adult. Two women reported that dealing drugs was their occupation. Beverly had
been involved in prostitution since the age of 17. There were a total of eight criminal
charges among these seven women, all but three for violent offenses (Table 19–3). Sentences ranged from three to 15 years.

Table 19–2   MENTAL HEALTH AND OTHER DISABILITIES OF WOMEN OFFENDERS WHO ARE DEAF IN A TEXAS STATE PRISON

ID	Mental Health	Other Disabilities
Alisha	Depression; suicide attempts; victim child abuse	Head injury (car accident)
Beverly	Alcoholism	—
Carmen	Chemical dependency; victim domestic violence	Asthma; blind in one eye
Darlene	Borderline; antisocial; dysthymia	Progressive vision loss
Ellie	Psychotic disorder with paranoia	Borderline intellectual functioning
Francine	Declined to release medical record	—
Gretchen	Bipolar; chemical dependency; suicide attempts	—

Table 19–3   CRIMES AND SENTENCES OF WOMEN OFFENDERS
WHO ARE DEAF IN A TEXAS STATE PRISON

ID	Crime	Sentence
Alisha	Injury to a child	3 years
Beverly	Possession of cocaine	15 months
Carmen	Delivery of cocaine; aggravated robbery	5 years
Darlene	Aggravated assault	5 years
Ellie	Injury to a child under 14	10 years
Francine	Delivery of a controlled substance	—
Gretchen	Aggravated assault on a police officer	8 years

Communication

Of the group, three were primarily English speakers or preferred to use Simultaneous Communication[2] (SimCom; Table 19–1). Four women used American Sign Language. Of the four subjects who were signers, two were experiencing psychiatric symptoms that made it impossible to obtain an interview. Ellie was not capable of providing the necessary information due to difficulty comprehending time referents, and a preliminary contact with Darlene found her bleeding from a large wound on her scalp, caused by several hours of head banging. Due to a history of explosive episodes, she was only able to see visitors with her hands cuffed in front of her body the entire time, and in the presence of two corrections officers.

Francine, who was recently incarcerated, was approached regarding the possibility of an interview, but declined to be videotaped. She burst into tears, exclaiming, "I had a baby when I wasn't married, and I used drugs. You aren't supposed to do that!" Francine's pain was clearly too raw for her to share personal information with a stranger at the time this study was being conducted. Alisha, who was only months away from her release date, was the only subject who both met the study criteria and agreed to participate in an in-depth videotaped interview.

Case Study: Alisha

Alisha is a 32-year-old white female who uses American Sign Language to communicate. She has been deaf since birth as a result of congenital rubella syndrome and is the only person who is deaf in her family of origin. Alisha has been diagnosed with depression and has a history of two suicide attempts. She is serving a three-year state prison term for slapping a three-month-old infant across the face with enough force to cause bruising. Alisha is currently estranged from her husband. She has four sons, one of whom is deceased.

As a child, Alisha attended a state residential school for deaf children. Her mother and one sister knew some signs, and her two other siblings could fingerspell. Alisha describes her relationship with her mother as very close. At the age of six, her parents divorced. Because of the communication barriers and her young age, Alisha did not understand what had occurred, but eventually, fellow students at the residential school she attended explained the concept of divorce to her.

Alisha's mother became romantically involved with a man and moved herself and the children in with him, relocating across the country. His name was Pete. Alisha states that the first time she witnessed Pete slap her mother across the face, she was terrified. She did not know what anyone was saying or why this was happening. Alisha recounts one of many of her own abusive episodes with Pete:

> Pete would make me sit in front of him and practice lipreading. I never understood him, so my mother often walked behind him and gave me signals so that I would know whether to say yes or no. One time he caught her and made her leave the room. I couldn't understand him, so I tried guessing at the answer, but I was wrong. He yanked me up and dragged me into the bathroom and shoved my hand deep into the toilet bowl. I felt totally humiliated.

Although Alisha did not understand much of what Pete said, it was clear to her that her mother was as frightened of him as she was. Pete's abuse escalated into forcing Alisha's hands into dog feces, beatings, and sexual abuse.

In desperation, Alisha moved into her father's household at age 16. Her father soon noticed her listlessness and encouraged her to go to counseling, which she did. However, the depression lingered. By the age of 20, she was married and had recently delivered her first son. She was unable to bond with her son due to what she describes as an underlying dislike of males.

By the time her first son was 3 months of age, Alisha had become physically abusive toward him, wrenching his legs when she was changing his diaper. At this time, Alisha and her husband began having marital problems. Eventually, she had a second son, and then a third, who was removed from the home at three days of age by social services. The deaf community was more critical than supportive toward her, and Alisha began to seek out panaceas to combat her depression, through sexual encounters, drugs, and eventually by slashing her wrists.

Alisha retained custody of her fourth son although she was separated from her husband, as their relationship had become abusive. Her fourth son was about three months old when she committed her offense of record:

> I was in the kitchen and the baby was in his seat on the table. For some reason, I was feeling angry, although it had nothing to do with the baby. I slapped him across the face and when he started to cry, I walked away from him because I didn't want anyone to know what I'd done. He was just an innocent little baby. My husband was visiting the kids at the time, and when he saw the baby's face, he confronted me. That's when I ran upstairs to the bathroom and took some pills. I just wanted to die.

When Alisha was arrested she was not provided with a sign language interpreter. She had the services of an interpreter in court, although she had to stay in the county jail a few extra days until one could be scheduled. In prison, Alisha has participated in a cognitive intervention therapy group. She attends group sessions with the other women offenders even though there is no interpreter. She has learned the behavioral techniques presented in the group through reading the course materials. For example, Alisha has learned about ways to monitor her frustration level and how to take a "time out" when necessary. Today, she takes medication for depression, and she is able to make a connection between her childhood experiences with abuse and her abusive behaviors toward her own children. Of her experiences in prison, Alisha says, "No one really cares about what happens to you here."

DISCUSSION

Unlike the general population of female offenders in Texas, 50 percent of whom are black (Texas Department of Criminal Justice, 2001), all but one of the women offenders in this population who are deaf are also white. Familiarity with the sociocultural aspects of a variety of ethnic backgrounds and the responses of a variety of cultures to disability is an essential consideration for any service provider working with women offenders who are deaf. Ethnically based attitudes toward disability will influence the self-concepts of women offenders who are deaf and persons of color.

For women who are deaf and use American Sign Language, mental health and chemical dependency treatments should be approached with the understanding that storytelling is a cultural norm in the deaf community and that American Sign Language users communicate from the general to the specific (Sabino & King, 2002). The use of visual aids to connect objects and ideas through visual imagery is a recommended technique for counseling clients who are deaf. Therapy should be interactive, taking place with other women offenders who are deaf or women offenders who can use American Sign Language, whenever possible. For abused women offenders who are deaf, women service providers may be more effective in cases in which the abuser was male.

A range of languages, language proficiency, and communication modes was used by these seven female offenders, making it apparent that service providers working with women offenders who are deaf will need to be competent in English and in American Sign Language. Counseling clients who are deaf consider proficiency in American Sign Language an essential skill for service providers (Steinberg et al., 1998). The psychosocial issues of women offenders who are deaf cannot be recognized and addressed by service providers who do not understand American Sign Language and the sociocultural dynamic of the deaf community. For example, many children who are deaf learn sign language at state residential schools. Others learn about divorce, sexual behaviors, and other concepts that cannot be communicated to them in the home unless their parents learn sign language, and few do (Dennis & Baker, 1998). The resulting naïveté may be one reason that children who are deaf are so vulnerable to abuses perpetrated in the residential school setting (Dennis & Baker, 1998; Mertens, 1996; Sullivan et al., 1987). Service providers may need to reeducate women offenders who are deaf about sexuality and abuse.

In Alisha's situation, a service provider knowledgeable about persons who are deaf would recognize the etiology of her hearing loss as a factor that could impact her functionally. Approximately 50 percent of children born deaf due to congenital rubella syndrome experience accompanying psychoneurological symptoms—for example, high impulsivity or a low tolerance for frustration (Chess & Fernandez, 1980; Vernon & Hicks, 1980). The prevalence of multiple disabilities, such as learning disabilities, or the effects of viral illnesses in those who are deaf and exhibit violent behaviors is substantial (Vernon & Greenberg, 1999; Vernon & Hicks, 1980). Service providers must remain alert to functional complications resulting from multiple disabilities in women offenders who are deaf.

The stigmatization of Alisha by the deaf community is not uncommon for people who are deaf and have criminal legal problems (Miller, 2001), but it is an issue that service providers should be aware of so that alternate support systems can be developed. Otherwise, women offenders who are deaf are at risk of becoming marginalized (Cumming & Rodda, 1989), with no sense of group identity or acceptance among hearing people or in the deaf community. A lack of group identification and support from others presents a serious barrier to recovery.

Corollary to this, service providers should endeavor to treat women offenders who are deaf fairly and with respect, with the understanding that like chemically dependent clients, they may experience relapses. When Alisha returns to her community and her daily life is no longer regimented by the state corrections system, she will need substantial aftercare in order to avoid reoffending. Women parolees who are deaf may require a range of services in order to make a successful transition from institutionalization to independent living. These include chemical dependency and mental health counseling services, parenting skills training, respite childcare services, housing, transportation, employment placement, and continued employment supports.

It is important to recognize that the communication abuses of women offenders who are deaf do not end with childhood. In a gross violation of her Constitutional rights and the Americans with Disabilities Act (1990), Alisha reports that she did not receive a sign language interpreter when she was arrested or when she attended treatment in prison. In Alisha's case, she was able to accomplish a great deal independently. However, it should be noted that at the fifth grade level, Alisha had the highest educational achievement of this group of women offenders who are deaf. It will be exceedingly difficult for her cohorts to benefit from treatment-oriented reading materials in the same way that Alisha did throughout her incarceration, as only 22 percent of state prison offenders who are deaf are able to read above the fourth grade level (Miller, 2001).

RECOMMENDATIONS

Beyond barriers that relate to a shortage of service providers available to work with women offenders who are deaf are systemic barriers. Because this population is so small, often facilities do not know how to effectively evaluate, accommodate, and meet the psychosocial service delivery needs women offenders who are deaf. Most women's correctional facilities experience financial constraints in terms of service provision, for example, for the ongoing costs of sign language interpreters. Additionally, it is not the mission of state prisons to provide psychosocial rehabilitation services to offenders.

It just takes one concerned person to make a positive difference in a woman offender's life. As Alisha stated, she did not feel that anyone cared about her while she was in prison. In terms of reintegrating women offenders who are deaf into the community, making contact with them during their incarceration is paramount. There are four key methods to service provision for women offenders who are deaf: advocacy, volunteerism, consulting, and aftercare. Various benefits and drawbacks of each are reviewed next.

Advocacy

Advocacy is a way globally to impact the correctional system. Advocates can ally themselves with prison reform groups such as Citizens United for the Reform of Errants (CURE) to put political pressure on the state prison system, or they can form cooperative liaisons with prison officials, as in the case of the Wisconsin State Council for the Deaf and Hard of Hearing. Most states have a similar body of representation for citizens who are deaf and hard of hearing, but Wisconsin is unique in that a function of their state council is to monitor the number of state inmates who are deaf and hard of hearing (Wisconsin Council for the Deaf and Hard-of-Hearing Meeting Minutes, 2001). Additionally, they serve as watchdogs for potential accommodation issues and collaborate with state prison officials to resolve them.

This approach can be effective if a positive relationship is forged with local facilities, allowing advocates to come in and provide training to corrections personnel. However, some limitations exist in terms of getting policy passed and actually putting that policy into action within a facility. Typically, the advocacy approach requires a high level of follow-up to ensure that recommended actions have been taken and are continued.

Volunteerism

There are several types of volunteerism that can be of benefit to women offenders who are deaf. Perhaps the most common are the prison ministries, which are facilitated by an outside group that arranges to come into an institution and provide religious instruction and spiritual counseling for offenders who want to participate. Representatives of Alcoholics Anonymous (AA) and its affiliates, such as Narcotics Anonymous (NA), can also obtain permission to come into a facility and provide support for women in recovery. Health service–oriented entities sometimes obtain permission to come into a facility and instruct women offenders on female reproductive health, HIV/AIDS awareness, or any number of female health issues. A drawback is that many of the agencies that provide these services do not have sign language proficient staff who can communicate effectively with women offenders who are deaf.

Lastly, social services agencies can obtain grants oriented toward serving victims of abuse and assign service providers to go into a correctional facility to provide counseling.

Because so many women offenders who are deaf have also experienced abuse, this is an angle that may prove effective in securing treatment funding, because funding offender services is rarely a high priority among grantors. A major consideration is that any kind of volunteerism requires a serious, ongoing commitment. Service providers will need to be willing to go into a prison facility on a consistent basis to form rapport with women offenders who are deaf. Volunteerism often appeals to state prison systems because while facilities may recognize the benefits of various treatments, few are financially equipped to provide them, nor are treatment services a priority of most state prisons.

Consulting

Professional consulting is probably the least effective way to initiate services for women offenders who are deaf. Most facilities do not track offenders who are deaf, making them difficult to locate and serve. Facilities generally cannot afford consulting fees and do not seek out consultants unless a serious problem that the public is aware of has already erupted in the state prison system.

Administrators may accept what a consultant has to say, but corrections workers often do not esteem the views of outsiders. Those who work and advance within the corrections system all of their lives are most likely to be recognized as authorities in the workplace. Therefore, in order to gain any measure of success, consultants should focus their energies on providing education and training about deafness to those individuals who have worked in the system the longest and already have the respect of their coworkers. From there, these individuals can influence those they supervise or work alongside.

Aftercare

One potentially effective approach to service provision for women inmates who are deaf is to locate and connect with them prior to and following their release from prison. This is a sorely needed service, as most halfway houses and other facilities are not equipped to serve women who are deaf and use American Sign Language. An important aspect of psychosocial rehabilitation service delivery is consumer choice, or involving consumers in the decision-making process. As women offenders who are deaf will be coming from a highly regimented prison environment that does not foster skill building in this area, education, training, and support will be required for their successful reintegration into society, as will their full participation in the communication required to make these decisions.

By forming a supportive partnership with women parolees who are deaf, service providers can then work together with them to evaluate and work toward meeting their mental health and rehabilitation needs. As identified by this research, effective communication provided in American Sign Language, addressing the functional impact of abuse and trauma, and management of mental illness will likely be chief aspects of effective service provision for women offenders who are deaf.

ACKNOWLEDGMENTS

The Texas Department of Criminal Justice supported this research under Research Agreement #0052-RM00. Points of view are those of the author and do not necessarily represent the position of the Texas Department of Criminal Justice.

NOTES

1. The term *deaf* is used here to indicate a severe to profound hearing loss in which a person is unable to discriminate speech, with or without the use of amplification. The preferred convention of the deaf community to refer to persons who are deaf and use American Sign Language as a cultural group (i.e., as deaf people) has been modified to conform to the rehabilitation and independent living movement's convention of person first language.

2. Simultaneous Communication, or SimCom, is the practice of using American Sign Language signs in English word order, accompanied by spoken English. Due to linguistic diversity among people who are deaf, this technique does not provide effective communication for every woman who is deaf.

REFERENCES

Americans with Disabilities Act. 42 U.S.C.A. 12101 *et. seq.* (1990).

Chess, S., & Fernandez, P. (1980). Neurologic Damage and Behavior Disorder in Rubella Deafened Children. *American Annals of the Deaf,* 125:998–1001.

Cumming, C., & Rodda, M. (1989). Advocacy, Prejudice, and Role Modeling in the Deaf Community. *Journal of Social Psychology,* 120:5–12.

DeBell, J. (2001). The Female Offender: Different . . . Not Difficult. *Corrections Today*, 63(1):56–61.

Dennis, M. J. P., & Baker, K. A. (1998). Evaluation and Treatment of Deaf Sexual Offenders: A Multicultural Perspective. In *Sourcebook of Treatment Programs for Sexual Offenders*. New York: Plenum Press.

Dowden, C., & Andrews, D. A. (1999). What Works for Female Offenders: A Meta-Analytic Review. *Crime and Delinquency*, 45(4):438–452.

Gondles, J. A., Jr. (2001). Female Offenders—The Major Issues. *Corrections Today*, 63(1):6.

Johnson, G. L. & Mosley, A. (August 31, 2001). Texas Board of Criminal Justice. *Statistical Report.*

Mertens, D. M. (1996). Breaking the Silence about Sexual Abuse of Deaf Children. *American Annals of the Deaf*, 141(3):352–358.

Miller, K. R. (2001). *Forensic Issues of Deaf Offenders.* Unpublished dissertation, Lamar University.

Moses, M. (2001). Building Knowledge of Female Offenders. *Corrections Today*, 63(1):120.

Sabino, V. J., & King, C. (2002, April 6). Visual Metaphors in Counseling Deaf and Hard of Hearing People. *BreakOut VII: National Conference on Psychosocial Rehabilitation and Deafness*, Raleigh, North Carolina.

Schein, J. D. (1996). The demography of deafness. In P. Higgins & J. Nash (eds.), *Understanding Deafness Socially: Continuities in Research and Theory.* (pp. 21–43). Springfield, IL: Charles C. Thomas.

Steinberg, A. G., Sullivan, V. J., & Loew, R. C. (1998). Cultural and Linguistic Barriers to Mental Health Service Access: The Deaf Consumer's Perspective. *American Journal of Psychiatry*, 155(7):982–984.

Stringfellow, A. M. (August 31, 2001), Texas Department of Criminal Justice. (2001). 2000 Statisti-cal report. [Online]. Available at *http:www.tdcj.com.*

Sullivan, P. M., Vernon, M., & Scanlan, J. M. (1987). *American Annals of the Deaf*, 256–262.

Tischler, E. (1999). Many Offenders Have Histories of Abuse. *Corrections Today*, 61(3):14.

Vernon, M., & Greenberg, S. F. (1999). Violence in Deaf and Hard of Hearing People: A Review of the Literature. *Aggression and Violent Behavior*, 4(3):259–272.

Vernon M., & Hicks, D. (1980). Relationship of Rubella, Herpes Simplex, Cytomegalovirus, and Cer-tain Other Viral Disabilities. *American Annals of the Deaf*, 125(5):529–534.

Wisconsin Council for the Deaf and Hard-of-Hearing. (2001, December 13). Meeting minutes. Madi-son, Wisconsin.

part IV

Death Penalty

chapter 20

Issues in the Use of Aggravating and Mitigating Circumstances during the Sentencing Phase of Capital Murder Trials

Beth Bjerregaard, M. Dwayne Smith & Sondra J. Fogel

The use of capital punishment in the United States has a long and tumultuous history. Since the founding of this country, the death penalty was a common feature in the criminal justice system of most jurisdictions. It was not until the 1960s that organized opposition to the use of capital punishment developed to the point that it had an impact in the national political arena (White, 1984). The opposition to capital punishment often intersected with other social issues of this era, most notably those involving racial justice and the status of the economically disadvantaged in American society. At the heart of the concerns regarding capital punishment was whether this ultimate sanction was being administered in a manner that provided a fair and just determination of who received death sentences.

The growing concern about the fairness of capital punishment led to a number of legal challenges, the impact of which became particularly evident in 1968; according to available records, this was the first year in which there were no state-sanctioned executions in the United States (Bedau, 1982). This de facto moratorium culminated in the landmark 1972 U.S. Supreme Court decision *Furman v. Georgia*. In this ruling, the Supreme Court, by a 5–4 vote, stuck down death penalty statutes across the country; however, in doing so, the Court made clear that it was the *application* of the statutes, not the punishment itself, that was being invalidated. Specifically, the Court's majority believed that capital punishment, as practiced in Georgia and presumably other states, amounted to cruel and unusual punishment because the manner in which it was administered violated the Eighth Amendment of the U.S. Constitution. The justices in the majority were led to this conclusion by evidence suggesting that the death penalty statutes of Georgia resulted in "arbitrary and capricious" decisions as to who received capital punishment; in essence, this means that the legal facts of death penalty trials were not good predictors of which sentence—life or death—was assessed. Further, the justices believed that Georgia's death penalty practices violated the equal protection clause of the Fourteenth Amendment prohibiting discrimination. Their belief in this regard was influenced by research indicating that black defendants were at greater risk for receiving death sentences, regardless of the legal circumstances of the case. Again, however, the Court indicated a willingness to reconsider their position if states could alter their practices to produce a system that more fairly determined those persons who were selected for execution.

In 1976, the United States entered into a new phase of its history with capital punishment. On July 2 of that year, the U.S. Supreme Court released opinions, all decided by 7–2 votes, that upheld the death penalty statues of three states—Georgia, Florida, and Texas. Because *Gregg v. Georgia* was the first case issued that day, it is largely cited as the decision that marked a return to capital punishment. Subsequently, beginning with an execution in Utah on January 17, 1977, the ensuing years have been termed the "post-*Gregg* era" of capital punishment in the United States (White, 1984).

In rejecting some states' models for capital punishment, the Court suggested that an effective system of capital punishment would allow for each case to be considered individually in light of circumstances of the offense and the offender (see *Roberts v. Louisiana* [1976] and *Woodson v. North Carolina* [1976]). Yet trial courts were not to have unbridled discretion in these considerations. In essence, the Court seemed to signal the desire for a system that was at once more standardized *and* more individualized than previous systems. In order to achieve this, the *Gregg* decision provided a new, and by U.S. judicial standards, unique format for trial courts that were to hear death penalty cases.

THE BIFURCATED TRIAL SYSTEM

In *Gregg,* the Court's majority identified a number of factors incorporated into the Georgia statute that they believed helped to guide the sentencing decision, thereby removing potential arbitrary and capricious aspects of the sentencing process. Although minor variations have been approved for other states, Georgia became the model by which most states restructured their capital punishment statues.

As of this writing, 38 states, as well as the U.S. military and U.S. federal government, have laws that allow for the imposition of capital punishment. As noted, some variation exists among jurisdictions as to the exact nature of their death penalty statues (see Acker & Lanier, 1998). However, all statutes approved by the U.S. Supreme Court have some common elements. First, *Gregg* narrowed "death-eligible" offenses to murders with certain characteristics, now commonly referred to as *capital murders*. (Note: With passage of the *Antiterrorism and Effective Death Penalty Act* [1996], the U.S. federal government expanded death eligible offenses beyond those of capital murder; see Steiker & Steiker [1998] for a discussion of this act and its implications; see Chapter 22). A second—and key—feature of the revised statutes was the creation of a "bifurcated" (two-part) trial process. In the first phase, guilt was to be decided; if the defendant was found guilty, a second phase immediately began to determine whether he or she should be imprisoned for some specified length of time or receive a death sentence. During this phase, the state was required to prove that at least one *aggravating circumstance* (factor) existed that made the murder eligible for the death penalty. However, during the penalty phase, the defendant would be allowed to present *mitigating factors* that might convince the jury to recommend a sentence other than the death penalty.

This crucially important component of capital punishment trials—the sentencing phase, and the introduction of aggravating and mitigating factors—will be the focus of the discussion that follows. Throughout this chapter, examples and illustrations will be drawn from a study conducted by the authors of 635 sentencing decisions in capital murder cases made by juries in North Carolina during the years 1979 to 1994.

THE SENTENCING PHASE: INTRODUCTION OF AGGRAVATING AND MITIGATING FACTORS

As mentioned previously, the model statue approved in *Gregg* required the state to prove during the sentencing phase that the murder had at least one aggravating circumstance that justified imposition of a death sentence. Likewise, it was specified that the defendant would have the opportunity to present any mitigating factors—information that might lessen his or her responsibility for the crime—that might convince a jury to not assess a death sentence. Juries were then required to balance the aggravating and mitigating factors in formulating their recommendation for an appropriate punishment. In Georgia, and in a majority of other states practicing capital punishment, the recommendation of the jury is binding and determines the defendant's fate. However, one variation allowed by the U.S. Supreme Court was that the ultimate decision for sentencing rested with the trial judge. A recent Supreme Court decision has restricted this practice (*Ring v. Arizona* [2002]), and it remains to be seen if judges will retain ultimate authority or if jury decisions will be required and binding in all states. Because we will be discussing data from North Carolina, it should be noted that jury recommendations are binding in that state; further, recommendations for a death sentence require a unanimous decision by the jury.

While most states adopted sentencing schemes similar to that of Georgia, it is worth taking note of some exceptions. Texas and Oregon, for instance, chose to guide jury discretion by a somewhat different method. Rather than proving the existence of specific aggravating circumstances, the jury is required to respond to a set of questions, the answers of which determine the defendant's sentence. Texas is especially notable, because it is the state that has executed the most persons in the post-*Gregg*. In contrast to the more common penalty phase model to be discussed later, Texas juries first hear prosecutors present arguments regarding the defendant, especially his or her likelihood of continuing to pose a threat to society. This is followed by the defense's presentation of mitigating evidence, after which they retire to ponder their answers to the following three issues:

1. Whether the conduct of the defendant that caused the death of the deceased was committed deliberately and with the reasonable expectation that the death of the deceased or another would result;

2. Whether there is a probability that the defendant would commit criminal acts of violence that would constitute a continuing threat to society; and

3. If raised by the evidence, whether the conduct of the defendant in killing the deceased was unreasonable in response to the provocation, if any, by the deceased.

The state must prove each issue beyond a reasonable doubt, and the jury must agree unanimously with their answer to each of these. If the jury answers no, or if their answer is not unanimous on any item, the defendant automatically receives a sentence of life in prison. However, if the jury returns an affirmative finding on each of the above issues, it considers the following question:

1. Whether taking into consideration all of the evidence, including the circumstances of the offense, the defendant's character and background, and the personal moral culpability of the defendant, there is a sufficient mitigating circumstance or circumstances to warrant that a sentence of life imprisonment rather than a death sentence be imposed

If the jury unanimously agrees to answer no, the defendant is sentenced to die by lethal injection. Otherwise, the defendant receives a life sentence.

AGGRAVATING CIRCUMSTANCES

To this point, we have discussed aggravating circumstances without fully defining the meaning of this term. It was recognized by the justices in *Furman* that states often had a wide-ranging array of crimes that were subject to the death penalty, but that it was sought with regularity for only a few of those crimes (Bedau, 1982). To reduce the arbitrarily selective imposition of capital punishment, the justices required that states specify a narrow range of crimes for which a death sentence could be imposed. In subsequent decisions, it became clear that the justices preferred that only certain types of murder be reserved for seeking the death penalty. The model that emerged provided an exact listing of "aggravating" circumstances that made certain murders eligible for imposition of capital punishment. These circumstances were to be determined by state legislatures and listed as part of that state's death penalty statutes. Typically, then, the type of crime eligible for the death penalty is a first-degree murder, the circumstances of which have one or more elements that meet the criteria for an aggravating circumstance. In order to impose the death penalty, it is the prosecutor's duty to demonstrate to the jury that one or more of these factors exists.

While there was an apparent assumption that the list of possible aggravators would be relatively short, the present situation finds considerable variation from state to state in terms of how many, and the nature of, the aggravators specified in those 38 states that practice capital punishment. According to Acker and Lanier (1998), Connecticut shows only seven aggravators; in contrast, Delaware lists the most with 22. As an example from one state, the 11 aggravators specified by North Carolina are shown in Table 20–1.

Table 20–1   NORTH CAROLINA CAPITAL PUNISHMENT STATUTES (§ 15A-2000): AGGRAVATING CIRCUMSTANCES

---

1. The capital felony was committed by a person lawfully incarcerated.
2. The defendant had been previously convicted of another capital felony or had been previously adjudicated delinquent in a juvenile proceeding for committing an offense that would be a capital felony if committed by an adult.
3. The defendant had been previously convicted of a felony involving the use or threat of violence to the person or had been previously adjudicated delinquent in a juvenile proceeding for committing an offense that would be a Class A, B1, B2, C, D, or E felony involving the use or threat of violence to the person if the offense had been committed by an adult.
4. The capital felony was committed for the purpose of avoiding or preventing a lawful arrest or effecting an escape from custody.
5. The capital felony was committed while the defendant was engaged, or was an aider or abettor, in the commission of, or an attempt to commit, or flight after committing or attempting to commit, any homicide, robbery, rape or a sex offense, arson, burglary, kidnaping, or aircraft piracy or the unlawful throwing, placing, or discharging of a destructive device or bomb.
6. The capital felony was committed for pecuniary gain.
7. The capital felony was committed to disrupt or hinder the lawful exercise of any governmental function or the enforcement of laws.
8. The capital felony was committed against a law-enforcement officer, employee of the Department of Corrections, jailer, firefighter, judge or justice, former judge or justice, prosecutor or former prosecutor, juror or former juror, or witness or former witness against the defendant, while engaged in the performance of his official duties or because of the exercise of his official duty.
9. The capital felony was especially heinous, atrocious, or cruel.
10. The defendant knowingly created a great risk of death to more than one person by means of a weapon or device which would normally be hazardous to the lives of more than one person.
11. The murder for which the defendant stands convicted was part of a course of conduct in which the defendant engaged and which included the commission by the defendant of other crimes of violence against another person or persons.

As a general rule, the types of circumstances appearing as aggravators suggest that legislators are particularly concerned with having the death penalty option for offenders who had financial gain as a motive (such as robbery and contract killings), as well as those cases with certain categories of victims such as law enforcement officers and public officials. However, a common aggravator across states is one stating that the murder was particularly reprehensible; in North Carolina, "heinous, atrocious, or cruel" is the phraseology employed. This has proven to be a particularly important aggravator because post-*Furman* research has shown that a jury's finding of a heinous and cruel aggravating circumstance is a strong predictor of death sentences (Baldaus et al., 1990). However, exactly what is meant by *heinous, cruel,* or other similarly descriptive terms is not necessarily clear. Compare two murders: In one case, the victim's head is literally blown off with a close-range shotgun blast; the crime scene presents a horrible image, but the death was virtually instantaneous. In another case, the victim suffers a single stab wound; the suspect flees, leaving the victim to die a prolonged death due to puncture of an internal organ that results in little external blood loss. Our experience with North Carolina trials demonstrated that both situations described have been judged as heinous and cruel by some juries; however, other juries hearing very similar cases have rejected heinous and cruel as an aggravating circumstance. In essence, there appears to be no exact definition of *heinous* and *cruel;* ultimately, that discretion is left to the subjective judgement of the jury.

In contrast to the heinous and cruel aggravator, other aggravating circumstances appear easy to support, such as cases where on-duty police officers are the victims, where multiple victims are killed, or where there is ample testimony that the offender was engaged in a robbery when the murder occurred. However, even seemingly objective factors can be subject to argument and interpretation. As an example, consider the following scenario. A man is accused of murdering another man. Witnesses see the individual leaving the scene after hearing loud voices followed by a gunshot. Police determine that the victim's wallet has been emptied of cash. The accused confesses to killing the other man but offers the explanation that he sought out the victim to demand payment of a long-standing financial debt. The two men argued, a fight broke out, and the perpetrator claims that he killed the individual in self-defense. Before leaving the scene, the offender, in an act of frustration and anger, takes what money the victim had on his person, even though it does not cover the debt allegedly owed the perpetrator. If the prosecution opts to seek the death penalty, it will be the prosecutor's task to discredit the defendant's version of events. Instead, the prosecutor will try to convince the jury that the defendant had a premeditated, financial motive for the murder, having sought out the victim with the intent to take his money and to kill him if he resisted. The nature of these persons' relationship, whether a long-standing debt by the victim can be verified, and the perpetrator's reason for carrying a gun to the crime scene will be but a few of the key points argued by both prosecution and defense to persuade the jury to agree with their version of the events. The perceived presence of an aggravator and the resulting opportunity for the jury to recommend a death sentence hang in the balance.

It is important to note that in those cases where aggravating circumstances may be subject to successful rebuttal, prosecutors may offer a plea bargain of not seeking the death penalty if the defendant will plead guilty, thereby foregoing a long and expensive capital murder trial. Alternatively, for any number of reasons, the prosecutor may elect to pursue a first-degree murder conviction without seeking the death penalty, or opt to seek a lesser charge of murder that does not carry the death penalty as a sanction. It is likely that many—but certainly not all—prosecutors would pursue one of these noncapital options if assigned the case described in the preceding paragraph.

Ultimately, the prosecutor has to draw on her or his experience to know the attitudes and predisposition of the local jurisdiction from which potential jurors are selected. Local norms and customs of the population (e.g., rural vs. urban setting, religious vs. secular orientation, liberal vs. conservative political leanings) are among the influences that prosecutors must consider in deciding whether to seek the death penalty, especially in those cases where the ambiguous presence of aggravators may be disputed by the defense counsel.

MITIGATING CIRCUMSTANCES: THEIR MEANING AND LEGAL DEVELOPMENT

Although the Supreme Court made it clear that in order to achieve individualized sentencing, defendants had to be allowed to present evidence that might deter a jury from recommending a death sentence, the exact scope of the Court's decision was unclear. Following *Gregg,* the vast majority of states provided lists of *statutory* mitigating factors that juries are expected to consider; these are factors that, by legislation, must be considered if a case can be made for them. As an example, the statutory mitigators required by North Carolina are shown in Table 20–2. Variations on these mitigators are found in some version among most states' lists of statutory mitigators.

One detail left uncertain in the *Gregg* decision was whether defendants were limited to introducing *only* statutory mitigating factors. Shortly after the *Gregg* decision, the U.S. Supreme Court addressed this issue in *Lockett v. Ohio* (1978). In the *Lockett* decision, the Court concluded that in order to ensure individualized sentencing, defendants must have the ability to present *any* mitigating evidence relevant to the defendant's character or record or circumstances of the offense. The one stipulation in most states is that trial judges can

Table 20–2   NORTH CAROLINA CAPITAL PUNISHMENT STATUTE (§ 15A-2000): STATUTORY MITIGATING CIRCUMSTANCES

1. The defendant has no significant history of prior criminal activity.
2. The capital felony was committed while the defendant was under the influence of mental or emotional disturbance.
3. The victim was a voluntary participant in the defendant's homicidal conduct or consented to the homicidal act.
4. The defendant was an accomplice in or accessory to the capital felony committed by another person and his participation was relatively minor.
5. The defendant acted under duress or under the domination of another person.
6. The capacity of the defendant to appreciate the criminality of his conduct or to conform his conduct to the requirements of law was impaired.
7. The age of the defendant at the time of the crime.
8. The defendant aided in the apprehension of another capital felon or testified truthfully on behalf of the prosecution in another prosecution of a felony.
9. Any other circumstance arising from the evidence which the jury deems to have mitigating value.

review mitigators prior to their introduction to determine if, in their judgement, a preponderance of evidence supports the claim for a mitigator.

In order to accommodate the wide variety of mitigating factors that can be introduced, most statutes incorporate an open-ended mitigating factor which operates as a "catch-all" category. As shown in Table 20–2, North Carolina provides a statutory mitigator of this nature, one that reads "any other circumstance arising from the evidence which the jury deems to have mitigating value" (*North Carolina General Statutes* §15A-2000 [f] [9] [2000]). The presence of this factor allows jurors to consider all factors that they believe to be important, whether or not they are introduced by the defense.

The ultimate impact of the *Lockett* decision was to open the door for many different types of mitigators to be presented at the sentencing phase of capital murder trials. Importantly, it allowed defense attorneys to go beyond statutory mitigators and attempt to introduce any number of nonstatutory mitigators. Scholars who have studied penalty phase mitigation have classified most statutory and nonstatutory mitigators as falling into three broad categories: (1) those that reduce the defendant's responsibility for participating in the crime; (2) those related to the defendant's lack of future dangerousness or the potential for rehabilitation; and (3) those which demonstrate the defendant's general good character (Garvey, 1998). The extent to which various mitigators of these types are actually introduced by the defense will vary considerably from case to case. As a vivid example, our review of North Carolina cases found the number of mitigators presented by defense counsel to range from only one (the statutory catch-all mitigator) to 56, with the average number being 13.

Although *Lockett* expanded defendants' ability to introduce relevant mitigating evidence, the Court still needed to clarify the relative weight that should be assigned to these factors. In early statues, some states, including North Carolina, required that the jury must agree unanimously that a mitigating factor would be considered in their decision. Ostensibly, even if only one juror failed to accept a mitigator as worthy of consideration, that factor was to be discarded as a consideration in the jury's recommendation. However, this standard was challenged, leading to the Court's decision in *McKoy v. North Carolina* (1990) to prohibit states from requiring jurors to unanimously agree on the existence of a mitigating factor. (To avoid confusion, this decision did not alter the requirement that juries' acceptance of *aggravating* circumstances must be unanimous.) The Court's reasoning was that each juror should be allowed to consider all mitigating evidence that might affect his or her decision and that hindering this process violated the spirit of *Lockett*. As another clarification, the Court ruled in *Hitchcock v. Dugger* (1987) that there cannot be any distinctions drawn between statutory and nonstatutory mitigating factors; that is, nonstatutory mitigators cannot be considered of lesser importance when a jury is formulating a sentencing recommendation.

In theory, it would appear that a combination of Supreme Court decisions have fashioned a system of capital punishment that, through the mitigation component of penalty phases, affords a defendant many opportunities to make a case for avoiding the death penalty. By doing so, a number of the problems raised in *Furman* would seem to be corrected. In practice, however, the picture is not quite as clear, a theme we will explore in the sections that follow. Before doing so, let us note that our lengthy discussion of mitigating circumstances may appear to be an imbalanced coverage in their favor. However, there has been considerably more research done on the mitigation element of capital murder trials than on the presentation of aggravating circumstances, resulting in a substantial larger body of available information.

THE DEVELOPMENT OF MITIGATING FACTORS

In developing a list of mitigating factors to present to jurors, defense attorneys typically attempt to characterize the defendant in a way that radically differs from the person who has just been convicted of murder. The core of their argument is that despite his or her actions, the person's life is worth sparing. Some sets of mitigating factors attempt to explain, though not excuse, the actions of the individual in a way that makes him or her seem less responsible for the crime. In this regard, an effective mitigation will convincingly provide a theoretical framework by which the jury can understand the historical life stresses and events that converged to produce the actions of the defendant (Haney, 1998). Other factors are designed to "humanize" the defendant so that the jury can view him or her whose life has not been totally defined by one regrettable act (Sacco, 1994); implicitly, the intention is to make it clear to the jury that the defendant's life is worth sparing.

There are cases in which the defendant's life provides much material to work with in developing mitigation arguments. Other cases involve defendants who, to say the least, pose serious challenges in developing effective arguments. We noted that in the initial years (late 1970s to early 1980s) of our North Carolina capital trial data, many mitigation presentations were rather limited, relying heavily on statutory mitigators. When nonstatutory mitigators were presented, they were often unfocused and seemingly irrelevant. If anything, we believed that they may have worked against the defendant; indeed it appeared in some cases that a defendant may have received a life sentence in spite of, rather than because of, the defense's presentation of mitigators.

Over time, it was apparent that the development of mitigation presentations became more informative and sophisticated. In most states, as in North Carolina, it is a common practice to hire mitigation specialists, typically a professional from a human service field such as social work, psychology, or counseling with demonstrated expertise and skills in bio-psycho-social assessments. These specialists are skilled in constructing social histories of individuals based on in-depth interviews with the defendant. In addition, discussions are conducted with family members, friends, and other persons familiar with the defendant and his or her environment. This information is often supplemented with reviews of school, medical/psychiatric, employment, and other relevant records. From this array of data, mitigation specialists produce a report for the defense that explains the impact of key life events, influences, and socioenvironmental conditions possibly contributing to the defendant's criminal behavior (Andrews, 1991; Hudson et al., 1987; Reed & Rohrer, 2000). Because of the complexity of the information involved, these specialists may be called on to testify as to their findings; if so, they can expect to be aggressively cross-examined by the prosecution in an attempt to discredit any testimony that may be favorable to the defendant.

In the best of circumstances, the defense has the financial resources available to hire competent, skilled specialists to assist with mitigation. The reality is that a large majority of capital murder defendants are represented by court-appointed attorneys or public defenders whose funds limit the expertise they can afford. This situation varies considerably across states and, together with concerns about defendants' access to attorneys skilled in capital case litigation, remains one of the more controversial areas in the current practice of capital punishment in the United States (Haney, 1998).

PROBLEMS IN PRESENTING MITIGATING EVIDENCE

While the task of discovering and developing information to use as mitigation can pose a number of problems, it is quite another challenge to present this information to the jury in such a way that it may sway them from recommending a death sentence. The following sections provide a sampling—one far from exhaustive—of some of these difficulties.

"Death Qualified" Juries

To serve on capital murder juries, persons in most states are required to indicate that they could recommend a sentence of death. Persons who oppose the death penalty are routinely excused from serving on capital murder juries, a practice that has become known as "death qualifying" juries that are to hear capital murder trials. At first glance, this would seem to make sense. However, according to several studies, this restriction may have several implications for the outcome of the verdict and the ensuing sentence. According to some researchers, the process produces a jury more prone to convict a defendant and, having returned a guilty verdict, attitudinally predisposed toward giving more weight to aggravating factors than to any mitigating factors that might be presented (see Sandys [1998] for a discussion of this research).

Prosecution Rebuttal

While the defense is free to present mitigation factors, the prosecution is afforded an opportunity to challenge any claims made in the presentation. Despite the efforts of mitigation specialists working for the defense (described previously), the prosecution team may have as much, if not more, background information on the defendant, allowing them to introduce evidence that undermines the defense's arguments. For instance, the defense may have people willing to testify that the defendant was a good worker and took care of his mother; the prosecution may counter with a witness who describes the defendant as having a reputation of being a bully who was a constant problem for neighbors. Therefore, the defense must weigh carefully the factors they wish to present, knowing that a successful rebuttal may negatively impact the jury's opinion of all successive mitigation factors to be introduced.

Defendant Noncooperation

For a host of reasons, defendants may be reluctant to aid defense attorneys or mitigation specialists in the development of effective presentation of mitigating evidence. These reasons vary from protection of others to reluctance to reveal personal information such as a history of sexual abuse. There is evidence that younger defendants may even be discouraged from providing such information because it would prove to be embarrassing to surviving family members (Cothern, 2000). In other cases, the defendant, if suffering from a mental illness or low intelligence, may be simply incapable of aiding their attorneys and mitigation specialists in building effective presentations that would influence the jury to forego the death penalty.

Difficulty of Mitigation when Defendant Claims Innocence

Defendants who have maintained their innocence in the guilt phase of the trial are placed in a particularly awkward situation. Throughout the trial, they denied their involvement and attempted to convince the jury that they did not commit the murder for which they were on trial. In returning a guilty verdict, the jury explicitly indicated that it did not believe those claims. At the penalty phase, these defendants are now required to shift arguments and must virtually abandon any mention of innocence to avoid further alienating the jury. In effect, they are required to ask for mercy for a crime they claimed not to have committed. This is precisely the situation that has confronted a number of individuals in recent years who have been released from death rows after having been exonerated of the murder for which they were found guilty (Harmon, 2001).

JURISTS MISUNDERSTANDING OF MITIGATORS IN THE CAPITAL MURDER JUDICIAL PROCESS

Presenting effective mitigating arguments present a formidable challenge for defense attorneys in the sentencing phase of capital murder trials. However, defense attorneys may face another barrier to effective mitigation that makes their task even more difficult. At the outset, the judicial processes surrounding capital murder trials are among the most complex in criminal law; in particular, the instructions given to jurors at the penalty phase of these trials requires them to ponder and to respond to a number of questions that leads to their recommendations for a sentence of life imprisonment or execution. It is no surprise, then, that researchers have discovered a number of ways in which people who served on capital murder juries misunderstood the options before them, especially the role that mitigating evidence is supposed to play.

The confusion and resulting misunderstanding of jurors is a key finding to emerge from the Capital Jury Project (CJP), a program of research begun in 1990 to explore the dynamics by which decisions are rendered in the penalty phase of capital murder trials (see Bowers [1995] for a description of the CJP). The implications of research findings from this project, combined with the work of scholars not affiliated with the project, are particularly revealing and, some would argue, quite troubling. Some of these findings and their implications are discussed in the paragraphs to follow.

A major finding to emerge from the Capital Jury Project was the discovery that jurors were confused by and often misinterpreted what they were required to do by the sentencing guidelines provided them. As some research indicates, these misunderstandings often led to errors that resulted in a death sentence being recommended (Blakenship et al., 1997; Bowers, 1996; Eisenberg & Wells, 1993; Luginbuhl & Howe, 1995). A disturbing error is that some jurors mistakenly interpreted the sentencing guidelines to mean that they were *required* to impose a death sentence if the prosecution proved certain aggravating factors (Eisenberg et al., 1996). For instance, Bowers and Steiner (1998) report that 43 percent of the jurors in the CPJ believed they were required to impose a death sentence if they agreed that the crime had the aggravating factor of "heinous, vile, or depraved" (a version of the "cruel and heinous" circumstance) while 35 percent believed that a death sentence was required if the jury felt the defendant would present a future danger to society. Overall, 49 percent of jurors interviewed believed that a death sentence was *mandatory* if any one of these two aggravating factors was proven. In essence, the jurors believed that if they found one or both of these aggravating circumstances to exist, they had no choice but to impose a death sentence. A implication of this fundamental misunderstanding is that *any evidence presented as mitigation was viewed as irrelevant,* no matter how well it explained the defendant's behavior. It should be emphasized that the jurists were incorrect in their beliefs; the presence of aggravating factors qualifies a defendant for a death sentence but *does not* mandate that it be assessed. Nevertheless, the CPJ research suggests that misunderstandings of this nature probably contributed heavily to the decisions reached by some juries.

Several studies have found that jurors' misunderstandings are often linked to their frustration with the sheer complexity of the instructions accompanying sentencing guidelines. Courts often assume that legal terms, including *aggravation* and *mitigation,* are common sense and should be easily understood (Tiersma, 1995). Further, sentencing guidelines are available to jurors in printed form, and are often read to jurors by the trial judge before they leave the courtroom to begin their sentencing deliberations. However, once in deliberation, there are severe restrictions on the information and/or clarifications that can be provided, often leaving jurors in a state of confusion (Tiersma, 1995). In our study of North Carolina trials, we noted that juries who had requested additional information (such as precise definitions of legal terms) were often told that they must use their own judgment or, alternatively, that the court was not allowed to respond. It is not surprising, then, that one CJP study which included former North Carolina jurors found that their misunderstandings of the process sometimes led them to improperly reject mitigating circumstances (Luginbuhl & Howe, 1995).

A former juror interviewed for the Capital Juror Project seemed to capture the feelings of many others in stating that "the instructions were confusing. Specifically, it was written in legal terminology. Very wordy. He [the judge] gave us a forty-page booklet. Very little help to us. We were not even allowed to ask questions . . . it was not clear at all" (Hoffman, 1995, p. 1151). Absent a clear understanding of their duties and options, jurors are often left to their own interpretations, contributing to the erroneous assumptions such as those described previously.

Other findings of the CJP had similarly negative implications for the successful presentation of mitigators. A prime example is Geimer and Amsterdam (1987–1988), who found that a number of jurors carried a "presumption of death" into their deliberations. That is, these jurors believed that a death sentence was the "default" judgement for those convicted and it was the responsibility of the defense to convince the jury otherwise. At first glance, this may seem to be an unimportant presumption, but it suggests that the burden of the penalty phase rests solely with the defense. This clashes with the assumed intent of a bifurcated trial whereby both prosecution and defense enter the penalty phase with equal standing and must successfully make their respective cases for the sentence they advocate.

Also, Bowers (1996) reports that a number of the former jurors interviewed suggested that they had made their sentencing decision before the introduction of any mitigating evidence; in fact, nearly two-thirds of the jurors admitted that they had discussed the punishment during the guilt phase. Bowers and Steiner (1998) add that 30 percent of another set of jurors interviewed said they were absolutely convinced about what punishment they would recommend before the sentencing phase even began. These findings are echoed by Sandys (1995), who found that the majority of jurors he talked with said that they had *simultaneously* made the guilt and punishment decisions; in effect, for them, there may as well have been no penalty phase.

Even if jurors are open to the idea of mitigating factors in determining a sentence, they may misunderstand the burden of proof necessary to accept a mitigating factor as having relevance. Recalling that prosecutors have the option of challenging any mitigator's validity, both Eisenberg and Wells (1993) and Luginbuhl and Howe (1995) discovered that almost half of the jurors they studies believed that mitigating factors must be proven "beyond a reasonable doubt" (the same as determining guilt) as opposed to the correct standard based on "preponderance of the evidence." When another set of former jurors were questioned directly on this issue, Blakenship and colleagues (1997) found that a substantial majority of them answered incorrectly or indicated that they did not know.

A final difficulty uncovered by the Capital Jury Project is not directly related to mitigation but still plays a role in the difficulties faced by the defense in the penalty phase. As mentioned earlier, juries in some states make recommendations that are binding while others are advisory. Even in the latter cases, however, jury opinions carry great weight. Knowing that the sentence was subject to appeal, several researchers interviewed jurists who believed that their recommendation for a death sentence would be reviewed and possibly changed by another sentencing authority; this led them to downplay the importance of their recommendations in determining the defendant's fate (Costanzo & Costanzo, 1994; Geimer & Amsterdam, 1987–1988; Haney et al., 1994). This assumption runs contrary to a concern expressed by the U.S. Supreme Court in *Caldwell v. Mississippi* (as quoted in Bowers, 1996, p. 222) that it is an "intolerable danger for jurors to believe that the responsibility for any ultimate determination of death will rest with others."

Taking all of the preceding factors into account, it should be clear that convincing a jury to forgo a death sentence is no easy task. Nevertheless, successful mitigation is possible if arguments are properly prepared and presented in a persuasive manner. The choice of mitigators is undoubtedly a crucial factor in the odds of making a successful argument. As evident in the next section, some of the potentially best mitigators available to the defense—those that may validly describe factors that should be taken into account by the jury—must be selected and presented with the utmost of care.

THE USE OF MENTAL HEALTH MITIGATORS

It is common to hear that a person must "be sick"—meaning mentally disturbed—to have committed a murder of which they are accused. Traditionally, the U.S. system of criminal justice has afforded special consideration and leniency to criminals suffering from mental disabilities (Sondheimer, 1990). The general belief is that defendants with mental or emotional problems are less culpable or morally blameworthy than defendants without such conditions. If the defendant lacked the inability to make a free and rationale choice to commit the crime or lacked the ability to control their behavior, the U.S. Supreme Court has recognized that the deterrent and/or retributive doctrines underlying the application of the death penalty will not be served (e.g., *Thompson v. Oklahoma,* 1988; *Penry v. Lynaugh,* 1989). It is significant, then, that research has found a significant proportion of death row inmates to possess some type of mental disturbance (Berkman, 1989; Perlin, 1996; Robinson & Stephens, 1992).

These beliefs/doctrines have been clearly embraced by state legislatures, most of whom have explicitly incorporated mental disorders into their list of statutory mitigating factors.[1] In fact, most statutes model their statutory mitigators after the popular "M'Naghten" insanity defense, including both *volitional* (lacks the substantial capacity to conform his conduct to the requirements of the law) and *cognitive* (lacks the substantial capacity to appreciate the criminality of his conduct) mitigators in their schemes (Acker & Lanier, 1994). Nevertheless, capital murder defendants choosing to present forms of mental disability as mitigators can have a difficult time convincing the jury that such factors should be taken into account when recommending a sentence. A particularly formidable challenge is faced by defendants who previously presented an insanity defense at the guilt phase but failed to convince the jury that their mental disorder was serious enough to warrant being excused from responsibility. At the trial phase, defense attorneys must reargue the same evidence, this time trying to persuade the jury that although the defendants are responsible for their criminal actions, their disorders should serve to mitigate against a death sentence. Generally, for these arguments to be successful, a distinction between two commonly used terms must be impressed on the jury. Because of the similarity in their wording and the evidence being presented, it may be difficult for jurors to separate the concept of mental illness from that of insanity.[2] In reality, one may be mentally ill but not criminally insane. Thus, while not dismissing responsibility, it is possible that defendants' mental illness may have significantly impaired their judgement, leading them to engage in acts that were totally uncharacteristic of an otherwise law-abiding life. It is the defense's task to successfully "sell" arguments of this nature to the jury, the success of which may well determine the defendant's fate.

The Risk of Converted Mitigation

One unique feature of mental health mitigators is that their introduction can have exactly the opposite effect from that which was intended. Noting this, Justice O'Connor, in the *Penry v. Lynaugh* (1989) decision, proclaimed that the defendant's mental retardation and history of abuse in that case presented a "two-edged sword." That is, while evidence of this nature can operate to diminish a jury's view of the defendant's culpability, it may also lead a jury to believe that the defendant will be dangerous in the future and has no realistic hope for rehabilitation (Berkman, 1989; Crocker, 1997; Perlin, 1996; Sevilla, 1999; Sondheimer, 1990). Therefore, defense attorneys are often presented with a taxing dilemma when considering the use of mental health mitigators—by arguing that the defendant's mental illness renders him or her incapable of conforming to the requirements of the law, the jury may develop the impression that the defendant will continue to pose a threat to the community and use it as a rationale for recommending a death sentence. Haney, Sontag, and Costanzo (1994, p. 164) refer to this phenomenon as *converted mitigation,* and it represents a distinct risk that the defense must ponder; that is, whether to put forward evidence that might successfully mitigate the defendant's culpability and possibly spare his or her life, or whether to exclude such evidence because it actually could be used against the defendant to justify imposing a death sentence.

Despite these difficulties and risks, there are data indicating that some juries do indeed consider evidence of problems such as mental retardation and severe mental illness as having mitigating value (Garvey, 1998). This was apparent as we reviewed some cases from North Carolina, where mitigators of this nature appeared to have influenced juries to recommend life sentences rather than execution, even in the case of defendants who seemed prime candidates for a death sentence. On the other hand, there is also evidence that juries may indeed be particularly reluctant to accept these types of factors as relevant (Sundby, 1997) or, as suggested previously, to interpret them as evidence in favor of a death sentence. It is not surprising, then, that there were a number of North Carolina cases where compelling evidence of a history of mental illness and/or childhood abuse did not influence the jury to spare the defendant's life.

Expert Testimony

If making the decision to go forward with mental health mitigators, the usual practice is to have such claims introduced through questioning of an expert witness. Usually, these persons are psychologists, psychiatrists, or other trained professionals hired by the defense to examine the defendant; similarly, other professionals may testify as to the condition being claimed by the defendant and the negative impact this condition has on one's life. Unfortunately for the defense, utilizing expert witnesses can have a negative effect on the jury. Research by Sundby (1997) has suggested that jurors view experts with a certain degree of skepticism. They are doubtful that those professionals, who typically spend little time with the defendant, are able to testify with authority as to both the existence of and the impact of the defendant's mental disorder. Further, jurors often view defense experts as "hired guns" and therefore discount the usefulness of their testimony.

Another risk of introducing mental health mitigators through the use of expert witnesses is that once defendants raise the issue of mental disability, they open the door for the state to counter with testimony from their own mental health experts. Inevitably, the state's experts will provide judgments that the defendant poses a significant threat to society and is unlikely to adjust to life in prison. Testimony of this nature can be especially damaging in states such as Texas that explicitly require juries to consider future dangerousness in determining their sentence recommendations. Referring again to North Carolina trials, we read a number of cases where juries heard testimonies from "dueling" psychiatrists whose descriptions of the defendant left one to wonder if those professionals had examined the same person. While there is no direct evidence that speaks to the impact on juries of such exchanges, it is likely that juries who hear such different testimonies are likely to view the state's expert as the more neutral, and thus believable, party. In these cases, the credibility of the defense's argument can be called into question, creating the possibility of converted mitigation.

CONCLUSION

As our discussion has suggested, the penalty phase of capital murder trials involves a maze of complex and, at times, confounding procedures and testimonies from a number of persons. Yet this phase has become an important component of the system of capital punishment as currently practiced in the United States.

A crucial question is whether the inclusion of a penalty phase has helped to alleviate some of the problematic aspects of capital punishment raised in *Furman,* especially as anticipated by the majority of justices in the *Gregg* decision. Answering in the affirmative, supporters point out that the system as a whole has withstood a large number of varied legal challenges over the past three decades, is practiced by a substantial majority of states in this country and has enjoyed widespread public support throughout that period. Those who remain opposed counter that the system's survival has depended more on political considerations than its legal viability and refer to an impressive body of research indicating that the system remains rife with problems, a number of which were discussed in this chapter (see Smith [2000] for a summary of both sides of this argument).

While the debate over capital punishment continues, one or more capital murder trials is being conducted virtually every week in courtrooms across the United States. These are dramas being played out by a cast of characters attempting to understand and perhaps explain exceedingly disturbing and tragic aspects of human behavior. For most of those trials, the penalty phase brings to a conclusion the proceedings of the drama, with the outcome hinging on jurors' reactions to aggravating and mitigating circumstances. The decisions they render are literally matters of life and death.

BOX 20.1   Women and the Death Penalty

Statistics from the Death Penalty Information Center (www.deathpenaltyinfo.org) show that as of July 1, 2003, there are 49 women on death rows across the United States, constituting approximately 1.4 percent of the nation's total death row population. Three states, including North Carolina, Florida, and California, account for almost a third of all women on death row. Since the death penalty was reinstated in 1976, ten women have been executed. Here are brief summaries of two of those cases.

Margie Bullard ("Velma") Barfield

In 1984, Velma Barfield was executed in North Carolina, becoming the first women to be executed in the United States after the *Gregg* decision. Velma, a grandmother at the time she was put to death, was born in 1932 and experienced a traumatic childhood, including claims of having been beaten and raped by her father. As a teenager, she married her first husband Thomas Burke, with whom she had several children. In 1966, Burke was involved in an accident that left him unable to work and Velma responsible for the family's support. During the next few years, Burke began to drink heavily and

Velma became addicted to prescription drugs, an addiction she sustained until arrested for her crimes. Burke died in a house fire of unknown origins in 1969. In 1970, Velma married Jennings Barfield, but he died under mysterious circumstances only six months later. In the late 1970s, Velma was seeing Stewart Taylor. In January 1978, Taylor became ill, was taken to the hospital, and died several days later. At the request of his family, an autopsy was performed, revealing the cause of death to be arsenic poisoning. After several interview sessions with the Robeson County Sheriff's Department, Velma confessed to poisoning Taylor because she was afraid that he would discover her forgery of one of his checks. When pressed, Velma confessed that during the 1970s, she poisoned two elderly persons for whom she worked as a live-in helper, as well as her own mother. When exhumed, the bodies of all three victims still showed unusually high traces of arsenic in their body tissue. Although she did not admit to any involvement in the death of Jennings Barfield, varying levels of arsenic were also found when his exhumed body was examined.

(continued)

Brought to trial in November 1978, Velma was found guilty of capital murder in the death of Stewart Taylor. In the sentencing phase, the jury answered affirmatively for three aggravating circumstances, failed to find any mitigating circumstances, and recommended a death sentence. Her subsequent legal appeals were rejected as were her appeals for clemency. In 1984, Velma Barfield, wearing pink pajamas to the death chamber, was executed by lethal injection.

Karla Faye Tucker

In 1998, Karla Faye Tucker became the first women executed in the state of Texas since the late 1800s and the next woman in the nation to be executed after Velma Barfield. Tucker's story is representative of many women in prison and particularly on death row. Tucker dropped out of school in the seventh grade and shortly after began using drugs. In addition to her drug habit, she took up prostitution during her teenage years. On the morning of June 13, 1983, Tucker and Danny Garrett, her boyfriend at the time, had been partying and ingesting a multitude of drugs and alcohol. They devised a plan to steal a motorcycle from her friend's currently estranged husband, Jerry Dean, who was also Tucker's ex-lover. After entering his apartment, they were interrupted by Dean. Garrett grabbed a hammer and began to strike Dean multiple times about the head. Dean continued to make noise, so Tucker grabbed a pickax she found in the living room and began beating him. She then discovered Dean had a companion in the apartment, Deborah Thorton, whom she began to

strike as well. Both victims died from the attack. At trial, Tucker was found guilty of capital murder and assessed a death sentence, despite providing testimony that helped to convict Garrett. Garrett was also given a death sentence but later died in prison from liver disease.

Tucker's case came to exemplify a difficult issue associated with capital punishment. As her execution date drew near, Tucker had spent almost 15 years on death row. During that time, she had converted to Christianity and had undergone what many people believed to be a dramatic personal transformation. This lead a number of prominent religious figures and politicians to argue against her execution, stressing that she was a changed person and no longer deserved the imposed punishment; in effect, they advocated an after-the-trial mitigation factor that they believed spoke against her execution. Other persons, including family members of the victims as well as a number of political officials in Texas, responded that death row conversions of this type were common and, though commendable, did not excuse her heinous crime. Tucker's legal appeals were rejected by the U.S. Supreme Court as was a plea for clemency to then-governor George W. Bush, who was later accused of mocking her supporters in a speech. With both protestors and supporters of her execution demonstrating outside the death chamber, Karla Faye Tucker was put to death by lethal injection on February 3, 1998. A made-for-television movie focusing on her last days on death row aired in March 2002.

BOX 20.2   Minorities and the Death Penalty

The impact of race on death sentencing is among the most controversial issues in the use of capital punishment. The Death Penalty Information Center (www.deathpenaltyinfo.org) estimates that since the reinstatement of capital punishment in 1976, approximately 44 percent of the persons executed since 1976 have been minorities; 35 percent were black. Likewise, 55 percent of the approximately 3700 inmates on the nation's death rows are members of a racial/ethnic minority group. But the issue is complex; numerous studies have indicated that it is the race of the *victim,* more so than the race of the defendant, that impacts the defendant's likelihood of receiving a death sentence. It is no surprise then that approximately 81 percent of all those on death row have murdered white victims, despite the fact that national statistics show that only 50 percent of murder victims are white. Some of the issues raised in regards to minorities and the death penalty are evident in the following cases.

William Basemore

William Basemore is one of a number of black defendants who have argued that the process of selecting their jury was biased. In 2001, a Philadelphia common pleas judge agreed, overturning his death sentence and ordering a new trial. Basemore had been convicted in 1988 for the murder of a security guard that took place during a restaurant robbery by a jury that included two blacks. However, the prosecutor had utilized his peremptory challenges to remove 19 potential black jurors from the jury panel. The

judge ruled that the prosecutor's explanations as to why he eliminated the black jurors were "insufficient." What made this case unusual is that the prosecutor had been previously videotaped in the year before Basemore's trial lecturing a group of prosecutors on the topic of jury selection; during his presentation, he discussed strategies on how to eliminate black jurors, providing circumstantial evidence regarding his motives in manipulating the racial composition of the jury. As of this writing, Basemore is awaiting his new trial. However, even if he avoids conviction for that crime, Basemore will not be a free man any time in the near future; in 2001, he was charged with another murder and awaits a separate trial for that case.

Harvey Lee Green, Jr.

Harvey Lee Green, Jr. pled guilty to two courts of first degree murder during a botched robbery in 1983. After a capital sentencing hearing, he received two death sentences. For the most part, Green's background was rather unremarkable. Although he was involved in drug use and minor delinquency as a youth, he joined the Army and appeared to turn his life around. However, during his stint with the military, he served time in the stockade for his tangential involvement in an attempted rape; in his sentencing trial, this incident would be used to support the notion of his having a violent past. Following his discharge from the Army, he returned home to a small town in Pitt County, North Carolina. Although things seemed to go well at first, Green was unable

(continued)

to obtain steady unemployment and, in the words of one of his attorneys, found his life in a downward spiral. On the afternoon of December 19, 1983, after drinking and smoking marijuana, Green was on his way home when he passed a dry cleaning establishment with a 17-year-old high school girl working behind the counter. Concerned about some bad checks he had written, he decided to use a toy gun to frighten the clerk into giving him money. However, during the robbery, a male customer entered the cleaners. A prolonged struggle ensued in which Green finally grabbed a pipe and beat the victims to death. He then took several dollars worth of rolled coins from behind the counter and fled the scene. Several days later, he exchanged the coins for cash, providing police with a lead that identified him as a suspect in the crime. Although initially denying involvement in the murders, Green finally confessed and later decided to plead guilty. Despite widespread local publicity about the murder and the victims, the sentencing trial was held in Pitt County, and Green received two sentences of death.

Over the next 10 years, Green's sentence underwent considerable judicial scrutiny. On two occasions, the case was returned to Pitt County Superior Court to determine whether the prosecutor had improperly eliminated Blacks from consideration as potential jurors, resulting in an all-white panel that returned his death sentences (both victims were also white). On both occasions, despite considerable evidence that trivial reasons were used to dismiss potential black jurors, the conviction was upheld. However, Green was finally granted a new sentencing trial when the North Carolina Supreme Court ruled that the sentencing phase suffered from errors noted by the U.S. Supreme Court in *McKoy v. North Carolina*. Green was retried in Pitt County in 1992; the jury, this time having one black member, again recommended two sentences of death. Despite a vigorous set of legal challenges that included introduction of a study by the authors of this chapter regarding the race-of-victim effect on death sentencing in North Carolina, as well as Green's attorneys presenting examples of cases in Pitt County where perpetrators did not receive death sentences for killing Black victims under similar circumstances, all appeals were denied. Harvey Lee Green, Jr. was executed by lethal injection on September 24, 1999.

BOX 20.3   The Role of the Mitigation Investigator

Dr. Pamela Laughon, an Associate Professor in the Department of Psychology at the University of North Carolina–Asheville, has worked as a mitigation investigator (also known as mitigation specialist) for over 50 defendants facing capital murder trials in North Carolina, South Carolina, and Tennessee. According to Dr. Laughon, the task of mitigation investigators is to conduct a "life
(continued)

study" of the individual. This begins with an extensive interview of the defendant. Then an exhaustive review of available records (medical, educational, financial, criminal, etc.) concerning the person is conducted, followed by lengthy discussions with a variety of people associated with the defendant in various phases of his or her life. To the extent possible, this includes the defendant's loved ones, but extends to persons who may have known the defendant some years earlier. This information is then analyzed to develop a comprehensive picture of the person with a focus on events that influenced his or her development through time.

Dr. Laughon has found that defendants range considerably in their degree of cooperation with her investigation. For instance, she has worked with defendants who are reluctant to have the details of their lives made public, even if such information might assist the defense in arguing against a death sentence. For some defendants, there are past events so painful—for instance, childhood sexual abuse—that they would prefer risking the death penalty rather than having those events dredged up in the public arena of the court. Other defendants simply do not know much about their early lives. These include those who were separated from their families at an early age and have not had contact with them in years or persons whose memory has been impaired from heavy substance abuse. Consequently, these defendants have little to offer that would help them develop their life histories, so she must rely on the memories of persons who knew the defendant as a child.

Dr. Laughon does not testify at trial, but her materials are often turned over to others who do, especially those who serve as expert witnesses to interpret certain aspects of the information she has uncovered. As well, and as an important component of her task, she uses the data she has gathered to aid defense attorneys in developing a mitigation strategy for the penalty phase, a crucial component of which is to determine who might serve as effective witnesses to call on the defendant's behalf. Typically, this defense strategy must be developed before trial, because if the defendant is found guilty, the penalty phase usually begins only an hour or so later.

Dr. Laughon believes that the presentation of mitigators has improved substantially in the six years she has been doing this work. While she finds reconstructing the lives of defendants to be a challenging and fascinating intellectual journey, she also finds it emotionally draining at times. She has become keenly aware of the pain and anguish often experienced by the defendant's family and other loved ones. In many cases, they are both devastated by the defendant's crime and grieving over his or her possible death; but, because of their association with the defendant, they may find themselves humiliated and scorned and have no one to turn to for sympathy or aid in coping with their situation. Dr. Laughon hopes to extend her research efforts to better understand the needs of those whom she terms the "forgotten people" of the capital punishment controversy and to decipher how they might be helped in dealing with the issues they face.

BOX 20.4   The Challenges of Serving as an Expert Witness

Dr. Kathleen Heide is a Professor in the Department of Criminology at the University of South Florida. Also a licensed mental health counselor, Dr. Heide has been called on to conduct mental health evaluations of defendants who have been charged with capital murder and to later serve as an expert witness during at their trials. Usually called to testify by the defense, Dr. Heide attempts to explain the motivational dynamics of the crime and how the social history of the defendant is relevant to understanding who that person is today as well as in the past. To gain this information, Dr. Heide does extensive clinical interviews with the individual and reviews available records to determine a defendant's family history, evidence of childhood trauma, school and work history, relationships with friends and intimates, involvement with drugs, alcohol, gangs, or cults, how the individual deals with feelings, his or her exposure to different media, and the person's absorption in such activities as music, movies, or video games. From this collection of materials, Dr. Heide attempts to understand how these individuals perceive events and interprets them; she is especially interested in whether they see themselves as

accountable for their behavior, whether they believe they have choices in life, and whether they are truly capable of such emotions as remorse, guilt, and empathy. Dr. Heide's research and clinical experience leads her to believe that many homicide offenders are lacking in their development of these personality dimensions.

When cross examined by the prosecution, Dr. Heide often confronts attempts to discredit her testimony, usually by alleging that her analyses and interpretations are flawed. She says that she is able to withstand such strategies because she is confident that she has provided a thorough, careful, comprehensive, and ultimately honest evaluation. She notes that there are occasions when her report is not viewed as helpful to the defendant, so she is not called to testify. However, when the report is perceived as helpful by the defense attorneys, it is often used in their attempts to leverage a plea bargain whereby the state agrees not to seek the death penalty. Examples of the kinds of cases she has dealt with and their varying outcomes can be found in her book *Young Killers: The Challenge of Juvenile Homicide* (Sage Publications, 1999).

BOX 20.5   Developing Mitigation when the Defendant Claims Innocence

What does the defense do in the penalty phase of a trial when the client claims to be totally innocent of the murder with which he or she is charged but is found guilty by the jury? This situation has faced Julianne Holt

on several occasions. In 1992, Ms. Holt was elected as Public Defender for the Thirteenth Judicial Circuit (Hillsborough County) of Florida. Over the past 10 years, her office has
(continued)

defended approximately 30 clients in capital murder trials, roughly 50 percent of whom have maintained that they were not involved in the murder for which they were being prosecuted. In about half of these cases, the jury has rejected the defendant's claim and returned a verdict of guilty, although usually for a charge less than capital murder. However, in a few cases, the defendant was found guilty of capital murder and the trial proceeded to the penalty phase.

When confronted with this dilemma, Ms. Holt's strategy has been to have a different attorney from her office handle the mitigation phase. The logic behind this move is that the credibility of the attorney presenting the first part of the trial may have been compromised when the jury rejected the defendant's claim of innocence. Importantly, the new attorney is careful to avoid the appearance of disputing the jury's decision at the guilt phase, emphasizing instead that the focus now is to

demonstrate why the defendant's life should be spared. Defendants do not usually testify during the penalty phase, especially if their claims of innocence have been rejected, so the hope is that other witnesses can sway the jury to forego recommending a death sentence. In all but three cases, Ms. Holt's strategy has been successful and the defendant received a life sentence.

Is it possible that a defendant could be wrongfully convicted of capital murder then feel compelled to claim responsibility for the crime at the penalty phase in order to seek the jury's mercy? Ms. Holt has not had one of these cases but says that such a scenario is possible. She warns, though, that it would be a risky maneuver; if the defendant is ever granted a new trial, claiming responsibility for the murder at the penalty phase of the original trial could be introduced as evidence that he or she confessed to the crime.

Notes

1. For example, the Model Penal Code includes "extreme mental or emotional disturbance" and whether "the capacity of the defendant to appreciate the criminality of his conduct or to conform his conduct to the requirements of law was impaired as a result of mental disease or defect or intoxication" among its lists of mitigating factors. *Model Penal Code* § 210.6(4)(b)(1980); § 210.6(4)(g)(1980).

2. For example, the statutory mitigators in North Carolina read, "(F)(2) The capital felony was committed while the defendant

    was under the influence of mental or emotional disturbance. (6) The capacity of the defendant to appreciate the criminality of his conduct or to conform his conduct to the requirements of law was impaired. (North Carolina General Statutes § 15A-200 (f) (2) and (6) (2000). According to one court decision, "the test of insanity as a defense to a criminal charge is whether the defendant was laboring under such a defect of reason from disease or deficiency of mind at the time of the alleged act as to be incapable of knowing the nature and quality of his or her act or, if the defendant did know this, was incapable of distinguishing between right and wrong in relation to such act" (*State of North Carolina v. Evangelista* [1987]. Also, see *State of Ohio v. Claytor*

(1991), where the Ohio Supreme Court rejected the appellant's argument that special jury instructions were necessary because of the similarity between insanity and the mitigating factors being presented.

REFERENCES

Acker, J., & Lanier, C. (1994). In Fairness and Mercy: Statutory Mitigating Factors in Capital Punishment Laws. *Criminal Law Bulletin,* 30:299–345.

Acker, J., & Lanier, C. (1998). Beyond Human Dignity? The Rise and Fall of Death Penalty Legislation. In J. Acker, R. Bohm, & C. Lanier (eds.), *America's Experiment with Capital Punishment* (pp. 77–115). Durham, NC: Carolina Academic Press.

Andrews, A. B. (1991). Social Work Expert Testimony Regarding Mitigation in Capital Sentencing Proceedings. *Social Work,* 36:440–445.

Baldaus, D. C., Woodworth, G., & Pulaski, C. A., Jr. (1990). *Equal Justice and the Death Penalty: A Legal and Empirical Analysis.* Boston: Northeastern University Press.

Bedau, H. A. (1982). Background and Development. In H. A. Bedau (ed.), *The Death Penalty in America* (3rd ed.) (pp. 3–28). New York: Oxford University Press.

Berkman. E. F. (1989). Mental Illness as an Aggravating Circumstance in Capital Sentencing. *Columbia Law Review,* 89:291–309.

Blakenship, M. B., Luginbuhl, J., Cullen, F. T., & Redick, W. (1997). Jurors' Comprehension of Sentencing Instructions: A Test of the Death Penalty Process in Tennessee. *Justice Quarterly,* 14:325–351.

Bowers, W. J. (1995). The Capital Jury Project: Rationale, Design, and Preview of Early Findings. *Indiana Law Journal,* 70:1043–1102.

Bowers, W. J. (1996). The Capital Jury: Is It Tilted Toward Death. *Judicature,* 79:220–223.

Bowers, W. J., and Steiner, B. D. (1998). Choosing Life or Death: Sentencing Dynamics in Capital Cases. In J. R. Acker, R. M. Bohm, & C. S. Lanier (eds.), *America's Experiment with Capital Punishment* (pp. 309–349). Durham, NC: Carolina Academic Press.

Cothern, L. (2000, November). Juveniles and the Death Penalty, *Coordinating Council on Juvenile Justice and Delinquency Prevention* (NCJ 184748). Washington, DC: Office of Juvenile Justice and Delinquency Prevention. [Authors' note: This publication is an agency report; it has no volume number or other identifying notations.]

Costanzo, S., & Costanzo, M. (1994). Life or Death Decisions: An Analysis of Capital Jury Decision Making Under the Special Issues Sentencing Framework. *Law and Human Behavior,* 18:151–170.

Crocker, P. W. (1997). Concepts of Culpability and Deathworthiness: Differentiating between Guilt and Punishment in Death Penalty Cases. *Fordham Law Review,* 66:21–86.

Eisenberg, T., & Wells, M. T. (1993). Dealing Confusion: Juror Instructions in Capital Cases. *Cornell Law Review,* 79:1–17.

Eisenberg, T., Garvey, S. P., & Wells, M. T. (1996). Jury Responsibility in Capital Sentencing: An Empirical Study. *Buffalo Law Review,* 339–380.

Garvey, S. P. (1998). Aggravation and Mitigation in Capital Cases: What do Jurors Think? *Columbia Law Review,* 81:989–1048.

Geimer, W. S., & Amsterdam, J. (1987–1988). Why Jurors Vote Life or Death: Operative Factors in Ten Florida Death Penalty Cases. *American Journal of Criminal Law*, 15:1–54.

Haney, C. (1998). Mitigation and the Study of Lives: On the Roots of Violent Criminality and the Nature of Capital Justice. In J. Acker, R. Bohm, and C. Lanier (eds.), *America's Experiment with Capital Punishment* (pp. 351–384). Durham, NC: Carolina Academic Press.

Haney, C., Sontag, L., & Costanzo, S. (1994). Deciding To Take a Life: Capital Juries, Sentencing Instructions, and the Jurisprudence of Death. *Journal of Social Issues*, 50(2):149–176.

Harmon, T. R. (2001). Guilty Until Proven Innocent: An Analysis of Post-*Furman* Capital Errors. *Criminal Justice Policy Review*, 12:113–139.

Hoffman, J. L. (1995). The Capital Jury Project: Where's the Buck?—Juror Misperception of Sentencing Responsibility in Death Penalty Cases. *Indiana Law Journal*, 70:1137–1160.

Hudson, J., Core, J., & Schorr, S. (1987). Using the Mitigation Specialist and the Team Approach. *The Champion*, (June):33–36.

Luginbuhl, J., & Howe, J. (1995). Discretion in Capital Sentencing Instructions: Guided or Misguided. *Indiana Law Journal*, 70:1161–1181.

Perlin, M. L. (1996). Professionalism, Mental Disability, and the Death Penalty: The Executioner's Face is Always Well-Hidden: The Role of Counsel and the Courts in Determining Who Dies. *New York Law School Law Review*, 41:201–236.

Reed, J. G., & Rohrer, G. E. (2000). Death Penalty Mitigation: A Challenge for Social Work Education. *Journal of Teaching in Social Work*, 20:187–199.

Robinson, D. A., & Stephens, O. H. (1992). Patterns of Mitigating Factors in Juvenile Death Penalty Cases. *Criminal Law Bulletin*, 28:246–275.

Sacco, T. M. (1994). Humanizing the Accused: The Social Worker's Contribution in Mitigation of Sentence. *Social Work/Maatskaplike Werk*, 30:159–168.

Sandys, M.. (1995). Cross-Overs—Capital Jurors Who Change Their Minds About the Punishment: A Litmus Test for Sentencing Guidelines. *Indiana Law Journal*, 70:1183–1221.

Sandys, M. (1998). Stacking the Deck for Guilt and Death: The Failure of Death Qualification to Ensure Impartiality. J. Acker, R. Bohm, & C. Lanier (eds.), In *America's Experiment with Capital Punishment* (pp. 285–307). Durham, NC: Carolina Academic Press.

Sevilla, D. M. (1999). Anti-Social Personality Disorder: Justification for the Death Penalty? *Journal of Contemporary Legal Issues*, 10:247–262.

Smith, M. D. (2000). Capital Punishment in America. In *Criminology: A Contemporary Handbook* (3rd ed.) (pp. 621–643). Belmont, CA: Wadsworth.

Sondheimer, J. N. (1990). A Continuing Source of Aggravation: The Improper Consideration of Mitigating Factors in Death Penalty Sentencing. *Hastings Law Journal*, 41:409–446.

Steiker, C. S., & Steiker, J. M. (1998). Judicial Developments in Capital Punishment Law. In J. R. Acker, R. M. Bohm, & C. S. Lanier (eds.), *America's Experiment with Capital Punishment* (pp. 47–75). Durham, NC: Carolina Academic Press.

Sundby, S. E. (1997). The Jury as Critic: An Empirical Look at How Capital Juries Perceive Expert and Lay Testimony. *Virginia Law Review*, 83:1109–1188.

Tiersma, P. M. (1995). Dictionaries and Death: Do Capital Jurors Understand Mitigation? *Utah Law Review*, 1995:1–48. [Authors' note: Volume number is same as year]

White, W. S. 1984. *Life in the Balance: Procedural Safeguards in Capital Cases*. Ann Arbor: University of Michigan Press.

CASES CITED

Caldwell v. Mississippi (1985) 472 U.S. 320.
Furman v. Georgia (1972) 408 U.S. 238.
Gregg v. Georgia (1976) 428 U.S. 153.
Hitchcock v. Dugger (1987) 481 U.S. 393.
Lockett v. Ohio (1978) 438 U.S. 586.
McKoy v. North Carolina (1990) 494 U.S. 433.
Penry v. Lynaugh (1989) 492 U.S. 302.
Roberts v. Louisiana (1976) 428 U.S. 325.
Ring v. Arizona (2002) 122 S. Ct. 2428.
State of North Carolina v. Evangelista (1987) 319 N.C. 152.
State of Ohio v. Claytor (1991) 574 N.E.2d 472.
Thompson v. Oklahoma (1988) 487 U.S. 815.
Woodson v. North Carolina (1976) 428 U.S. 280.

The Death Penalty

Alan S. Bruce & Theresa A. Severance

In civil society, the wicked would walk on every side, and the cry of the oppressed be in vain, the foundations would be destroyed, confusion and misery would prevail were punishment, capital punishment, never executed. (Nathan Strong, 1777, quoted in Masur, 1989, p. 27)

There is growing awareness that serious, reversible error permeates America's death penalty system, putting innocent lives at risk, heightening the suffering of victims, leaving killers at large, wasting tax dollars, and failing citizens, the courts and the justice system. (Liebman et al., 2002, p. i)

INTRODUCTION

- At the end of 2000, there were 3593 people sentenced to death (54.5 percent were white males, 42.2 percent were black males, 1 percent were white females, and 0.5 percent were black females).

- 85 people were executed in 2000; 83 men and 2 women. This was the second highest annual number of executions since reinstatement of capital punishment in 1977 (1999 had 98 executions).

- Of those under a death sentence at the end of 2000, approximately 13 percent were aged 19 or less, 49 percent were aged 40–49, while 2 percent were aged 50 or older.

- In 2000, 80 executions were by lethal injection and 5 were by electrocution.

- At the end of 2000, the average period between the death sentence and execution since reinstatement of capital punishment in 1977 was over 10 years. In

2000 the average period between sentence and execution for those executed was 11 years 5 months (Snell, 2001).

We are currently in the midst of great controversy and difference of opinion concerning capital punishment. Those in opposition to execution (abolitionists) are increasingly influential, as reflected in recent decisions concerning execution of the mentally ill (Bonner, 2001), state moratoriums (Hitt, 2001), and growing international opposition to the use of execution (Schabas, 1996, p. 3). Meanwhile, the greatest number of executions since 1951 occurred in 1999 (98 executions) (Snell, 2001), the federal government has carried out the first federal executions since the early 1960s (Johnston, 2001), and death penalty supporters (proponents) continue to loudly state their case. U.S. Attorney General John D. Ashcroft, a strong proponent of capital punishment, has required at least 12 federal prosecutors who previously recommended against pursuing the death penalty to do so (Eggen, 2002). It appears that the pace of executions might even be increasing with a number of states having recently conducted multiple executions on the same day. For example, on January 8, 1997, Earl Van Denton, Paul Ruiz, and Kirt Wainwright were executed by the state of Arkansas (Bragg, 1997). The United States shares the use of capital punishment for ordinary crimes with 81 other countries, including those countries President George W. Bush identifies as comprising the "axis of evil" (Sanger, 2002): Iran, Iraq, and North Korea (Schabas, 1997).

The current state of affairs mirrors the generally complex and conflicting perspectives on capital punishment. Experience reveals, however, that opinions of both abolitionists and proponents are frequently ill informed and based on alleged "common sense," personal opinion concerning "just deserts," or emotional reaction to media depictions of violent victimization. For many, such factors will continue to form the basis of opinion on capital punishment. Exposure to the facts of execution, however, should promote more informed opinions on both sides of the death penalty debate. While social science cannot provide solutions to such moral dilemmas as whether capital punishment is "right or wrong" or whether justice necessitates "an eye for an eye," its methods can reveal the facts concerning capital punishment. This chapter presents the facts on a range of important capital punishment topics and contributes to a greater understanding of this sanction. To put modern executions in context, we begin with a brief review of the history of the death penalty and discuss factors influencing methods of execution over time.

HOW CAN HISTORY INFORM US?

While modern executions are characterized by secrecy and order and reflect efforts to reduce physical suffering of the condemned (Bedau, 1997; Costanzo, 1997; Johnson, 1998; Lifton & Mitchell, 2000; Marquart et al., 1994; Sarat, 2001), the earliest forms of capital punishment were violent public rituals often resulting in agonizing death. Indeed, history reveals that there are no limits to the brutality of execution methods. The following descriptions are provided not to shock but to demonstrate the variety of barbaric punishments developed over time:

- *Flaying and impaling* involved "skinning the victim alive and then placing his body upon a sharp stake where he remained until death fortunately intervened. In the meantime the victim was left exposed to the hot rays of the sun and the depredations of insects and ravenous birds" (Barnes, 1972, p. 231).

- *Drowning*, in which the victim was repeatedly subjected to partial drowning and revival before death (Barnes, 1972).

- *Burning at the stake* (Barnes, 1972; Newman, 1978).

- *Drawing and quartering*, in which a horse was attached to each arm and leg and driven in opposite directions to rip the body apart (Foucault, 1979; Maestro, 1973).

- *Breaking on the wheel*, in which "[t]he prisoner's arms and legs were propped up on a wheel-like platform and were broken in several places by the use of a heavy iron bar. The mangled remains were then turned rapidly, scattering gore about until the unfortunate victim was dead" (Barnes, 1972, p. 242).

- *Sawing into pieces* was popular in medieval times and the victim was typically hung up by the feet and sawn in two (Barnes, 1972).

In some instances special punishments were reserved for specific offenses. According to Bedau, the following sentence for high treason was passed on seven men in England in 1812:

> That you and each of you, be taken to the place from whence you came, and from thence be drawn on a hurdle to the place of execution, where you shall be hanged by the neck, not till you are dead; that you be severally taken down, whole yet alive, and your bowels be taken out and burnt before your faces—that your heads be then cut off, and your bodies cut into four quarters, to be at the King's disposal. And God have mercy on your souls (Bedau, 1977, p. 27).

While we react with horror to such punishments, often rejecting them as the product of an "uncivilized" past, this view is overly simplistic. To understand the form and evolution of capital punishment, we must view it not simply as the product of increasing civilization but as influenced by significant change in social context.

The extreme violence characterizing early executions reflects a number of dominant beliefs, including the causes of criminal behavior and the need to satisfy otherworldly powers. Early spiritual explanations for criminal behavior (Vold et al., 1998) contributed to the violence of executions. The death of the condemned was believed necessary to appease spiritual powers, while the extreme violence may have reflected the belief that offenders were possessed by dangerous "otherworldly" forces and must be completely destroyed to remove the evil. Possessed by wickedness, the condemned were also regarded as less than fully human and this may have justified the use of such extreme violence.

Early executions also provided useful social functions. It has long been claimed that execution is an effective crime deterrent, and while the validity of this claim will be discussed later, belief in deterrence clearly played a major role in early execution techniques.

The public nature of execution was meant to deter crime by demonstrating the horrible fate of offenders and requiring the punishment of death for a wide range of crimes (e.g., murder, treason, theft of linens; Bedau, 1997) made the threat realistic to all. While the brutal methods and public nature of the execution were meant to deter, so too was the practice of displaying bodies and body parts of the executed. Following his hanging in Aberdeen, Scotland, on November 24, 1752, for example, the body of William Wast

> hung till his bones were bleached by the sea breezes he had once loved. . . . Pinned to its breastbone was a label on which was scrawled an amusing couplet: *I, William Wast, at the point of damnation, Request the prayers of this congregation* (Adams, 1993, p. 21).

Executions may also serve to exhibit the power and legitimacy of authorities while bringing community members closer together (Masur, 1989). Foucault claims that executions are used by those in positions of authority to reinforce their power and demonstrate the degree of injury to them, as representatives of society, caused by the actions of the condemned. Thus violent punishments were often used to show both the power and legitimacy of a monarch:

> The punishment is carried out in such a way as to give a spectacle not of measure, but of imbalance and excess. . . . By breaking the law, the offender has touched the very person of the prince; and it is the prince—or at least those to whom he has delegated his force—who seizes upon the body of the condemned man and displays it marked, beaten, broken. . . . The ceremony of punishment, then, is an exercise of "terror" (Foucault, 1979, p. 49).

Public executions may also have contributed to social cohesion by uniting "the good" in their condemnation and destruction of "the bad." The condemned have been described as scapegoats serving an important purpose: they are marginal members of society who are "*in* but not *of* the community" (Johnson, 1998, p. 28) and symbolize the collective faults of the larger group:

> The scapegoat, thus invested with group guilt and symbolizing all that the larger group fears, can be banished on the scaffold in a ceremony of righteous power, the object of which is to appease God, to unite the "insiders" of the community in their shared status as special in God's eyes and in their own, and, finally, to render the dominant group safe and secure from the sort of earthy dangers represented by the criminal they have offered up for punishment (Johnson, 1998, pp. 28–29).

WHAT MAJOR FACTORS HAVE CONTRIBUTED TO CHANGE?

The publication in 1764 of Cesare Beccaria's essay "On Crimes and Punishments" marks the beginning of the abolitionist movement. Beccaria condemned the use of violent punishment as barbaric and questioned the deterrent power of execution. By introducing the notion of proportionality of punishment, Beccaria reasoned that excessively violent punishment applied arbitrarily would serve as an incentive to offend rather than a deterrent. Beccaria's classical approach marks a major ideological shift concerning criminality. The treatment of offenders had long been dominated by violent punishments. Beccaria, however, characterizes the offender as a rational actor who might actually be encouraged to offend by the threat of disproportionately severe punishment (Maestro, 1973, pp. 29–30)

Economic factors have also contributed to changes in the use of capital punishment. A reduction in population growth coupled with greater demand for products made labor an increasingly valuable commodity. Execution of offenders would clearly reduce the labor force, so alternative methods that served economic ends while satisfying the need to punish offenders were developed. Beginning in the fifteenth century, a variety of punishments reflecting these concerns were introduced (e.g., galley slavery, transportation, penal servitude at hard labor, and the house of correction; Garland, 1990). Each of these methods served as punishment but also contributed to economic need by preserving the life (and thus the labor) of the offender while providing an inexpensive workforce.

Political concerns may also have contributed to general changes in punishment and the use of execution. During the eighteenth century, as highlighted by Beccaria, the excessively violent and arbitrary nature of punishment was increasingly recognized. While executions had once served as an indicator of the power of authority, growing skepticism contributed to changes in public attitudes towards execution. Whereas the public had once united in condemnation of the condemned, public executions became occasions when

> instead of bearing respectful witness, the crowds came to mock the authorities and to transform the condemned man into a popular hero . . . on more and more occasions the crowd revolted against what it saw to be injustice, class law, or the execution of one of its own (Garland, 1990, p. 141).

Such changes in the nature of punishment and execution, while undoubtedly reflecting increasing humanitarian and economic concerns, may also be seen as a political tactic employed by the state in response to public criticism of its actions.

The trend toward "sanitizing" capital punishment may have culminated with the introduction of lethal injection in 1982 (Marquart et al., 1994). Commenting on the potential for painless execution through lethal injection, former President Ronald Reagan compares human execution by lethal injection to euthanasia of an injured horse:

> I know what it's like to try to eliminate an injured horse by shooting him. Now you call the veterinarian and he gives it a shot and the horse goes to sleep—that's it. I myself have wondered . . . if there aren't even more humane methods now—the simple shot or tranquillizer (Costanzo, 1997, p. 14).

The nationwide transition to execution by lethal injection continues: While 21 states authorized the use of lethal injection in 1990, this number increased to 36 of the 38 death penalty states by 2000; and in 2000 an average of 9 out of 10 executions were by lethal injection (Snell, 2001). While lethal injection has clearly become the preferred method of execution, electrocution (in 11 states), gas chamber (in 4 states), hanging (in 3 states), and firing squad (in 3 states) continue to be available (Snell, 2001).

WHO GETS EXECUTED?

Death penalty proponents often claim some offenses are so horrendous that the death penalty is the only appropriate punishment. Typically such offenses involve especially sympathetic victims, such as young children and police officers; extended suffering or torture; or focus on the most notorious atrocities, such as the offenses of Timothy McVeigh or Ted Bundy (Sarat, 2001). The general assumption, then, is that the death penalty will be applied consistently to those who are the worst offenders. While a popular sentiment, examination of the relevant evidence reveals this is not in fact the case and a number of factors other than the nature of the offense determine who qualifies for execution.

Geography

Presently 38 states and the federal government permit use of the death penalty (Snell, 2001), although its use varies considerably. Of the 683 executions between January 1, 1977, and December 31, 2000, 65 percent took place in 5 states (Texas 239/683 = 34.99%, Virginia 81/683 = 11.86%, Florida 50/683 = 7.3%, Missouri 46/683 = 6.73%, and Oklahoma 30/683 = 4.39%) (Snell, 2001). Clearly the chance of being executed is largely dependent on geographical location.

Legal Definition

Examination of capital punishment statutes also reveals considerable variation in the qualifications for death. For example, in Alabama capital punishment requires "(i)ntentional murder with 18 aggravating factors" (Snell, 2001, p. 2); Colorado requires "[f]irst-degree murder with at least 1 of 15 aggravating factors" (Snell, 2001, p. 2); and Wyoming permits execution for "[f]irst-degree murder" and does not specify additional factors (Snell, 2001, p. 2).

Race

Race continues to be an important factor in capital punishment and a common claim is that the death penalty is discriminately applied to members of minority groups. For example, under the leadership of U.S. Attorney General John D. Ashcroft, the Justice Department has been three times more likely to pursue the death penalty in cases involving blacks accused of killing whites than in cases of blacks accused of killing nonwhites (Eggen, 2002). While the reasons for racial differences in the application of capital punishment remain in dispute, there is no argument that the death penalty is applied disproportionately to black males and that there is considerable geographical variation in this application.

- Northeast (Connecticut, New Hampshire, New Jersey, New York, Pennsylvania) 266 prisoners under death sentence, white = 94/266 = 35.3%, black = 161/266 = 60.5%

- Midwest (Illinois, Indiana, Kansas, Missouri, Nebraska, Ohio, South Dakota) 504 under sentence of death, white = 251/504 = 49.8%, black = 251/504 = 49.8%

- South (Alabama, Arkansas, Delaware, Florida, Georgia, Kentucky, Louisiana, Maryland, Mississippi, North Carolina, Oklahoma, South Carolina, Tennessee, Texas, Virginia) 1924 under sentence of death, white = 1059/1924 = 55.04%, black = 840/1924 = 43.66%

- West (Arizona, California, Colorado, Idaho, Montana, Nevada, New Mexico, Oregon, Utah, Washington, Wyoming) 881 total, whites = 581/881 = 65.95%, blacks = 270/881 = 30.65% (Snell, 2001)

Gender

The sentence of death is clearly imposed on males more often than females, as males comprise more than 98 percent of those on death row (Snell, 2001). Gender disparities in capital punishment will be discussed in a later section.

Age

Execution of a juvenile is a relatively rare event in the United States. In 1642 the first confirmed execution of a juvenile occurred in Roxbury, Massachusetts, when Thomas Graunger was executed for bestiality (Streib, 1988). Since then, juveniles have accounted for approximately 2 percent of all recorded executions (Streib, 1998). Our reluctance to execute juveniles is based on a number of popular assumptions endorsed by the U.S. Supreme Court:

> This Court has already endorsed the proposition that less culpability should attach to a crime committed by a juvenile than to a comparable crime committed by an adult since inexperience, less education, and less intelligence make the teenager less able to evaluate the consequences of his or her conduct, while at the same time he or she is much more apt to be motivated by mere emotion or peer pressure than is an adult. (*Thompson v. Oklahoma*, 1988a)

While there is general agreement that juveniles should be held less accountable for their actions than adults, where to draw the line between childhood and adulthood is less straightforward; this is reflected in the different ages used across jurisdictions to legally classify juveniles. There is a similar lack of agreement concerning the minimum age at which juveniles should be executed. While 14 states and the federal system have established 18 years as the minimum age for execution, 4 states use 17 years, 10 use 16 years, 3 use 14 years, and 7 have no specified minimum age (Snell, 2001). Through rulings in two landmark cases, however, the U.S. Supreme Court has settled this issue by establishing a minimum age for execution that applies to all jurisdictions.

Thompson v. Oklahoma (1988):

William Wayne Thompson was 15 years old when he was involved in the murder of his brother-in-law. Thompson's case was waived to the adult system, where Thompson was tried as an adult, convicted, and sentenced to death. The U.S. Supreme Court agreed to consider the claim that execution of someone less than 16 years of age violated the Eighth Amendment protection against cruel and unusual punishment. In its 1988 ruling the Court agreed that Thompson should not be executed and that execution of persons less than 16 years of age did constitute cruel and unusual punishment. The Court did not, however, establish 16 years as the minimum age for all executions and so left open the issue of whether execution should be permitted for 17 or 18 year old offenders (*Thompson v. Oklahoma,* 1988b).

Stanford v. Kentucky (1989):

Kevin Stanford was 17 years and 4 months old when he was involved in the murder of a gas station attendant. Stanford's case was waived to the adult system, where he was convicted of the homicide and sentenced to death. In this instance the U.S. Supreme Court was asked to determine whether execution of someone less than 18 years of age violated the Eighth Amendment protection against cruel and unusual punishment. In this instance the Court rejected the appeal, ruling that is was not unconstitutional to execute someone under 18 years of age, and established 16 as the minimum age for execution (*Stanford v. Kentucky,* 1989).

Mental Capacity

There has long been concern over whether a "decent" society should execute those judged to have less than normal mental capacity, and a distinction is made between those with mental retardation and those with mental illness.

Mental Retardation

According to the American Association on Mental Retardation (AAMR) definition, mental retardation is characterized by three factors: significantly subaverage intellectual functioning, concurrent and related limitations in two or more adaptive skill areas, and manifestation before age eighteen (Ehrenreich et al., 2001).

Subaverage Intellectual Functioning   Intelligence Quotient (IQ) tests provide standardized measures of intellectual functioning and allow comparisons of individual test scores. The average IQ score is 100, with the majority of U.S. citizens scoring between 80 and 120 (Ehrenreich et al., 2001). Ninety seven to ninety eight percent of the population has an IQ of 70 or more. Those suffering from mental retardation have IQ scores of 70 or less and are in the lowest 2 to 3 percent of the population on intellectual functioning (Reed, 1993). The concept of mental age is used to describe reasoning and understanding capabilities. The mentally retarded have a mental age of 12 years or less, meaning that their reasoning and understanding capabilities do not exceed those of a 12 year old child (Reed, 1993).

Deficits in Adaptive Behavior   As a result of mental retardation, people fail to develop age-appropriate life skills and typically operate at a developmental level significantly below societal expectations for their chronological age. An adult suffering from mental retardation "may have trouble driving a car, following directions, participating in hobbies or work of any complexity, or behaving in socially appropriate ways. He or she may have trouble sitting or standing still, or may smile constantly and inappropriately" (Ehrenreich et al., 2001, p. 10).

Manifestation before Eighteen Years of Age   Mental retardation begins prior to eighteen years of age and can be brought about by a variety of factors before, during, or after birth. Causal factors include genetic abnormalities, physical abuse, inadequate prenatal care, and exposure to toxic substances (Ehrenreich et al., 2001). Individuals with mental retardation generally have a history of maladaptive behavior reflected in school reports and other records that document the developmental nature of the condition. Therefore, it is unlikely someone could fake mental retardation to avoid responsibility for their actions (Ehrenreich et al., 2001).

Those suffering from mental retardation are especially susceptible to false confessions and the inherently coercive nature of interrogation; they frequently do not understand the charges being brought against them and do not understand their rights (Editorial, 2002; Ehrenreich et al., 2001; Kennedy, 1985; Reed, 1993). Many are not able to assist with their own defense. The extent of these problems and the childlike temperament of these individuals can best be illustrated through accounts of mentally retarded offenders:

> Earl Washington, whose mental retardation was diagnosed when he was a child, confessed during long police interrogations to a murder that he did not commit. Washington was so suggestible and eager to please, according to a former employer, that "you could get [him] to confess that he walked on the moon." In an effort to show the invalidity of Washington's confession because of his mental deficiencies, his trial lawyer would "pick a day, any day, and tell Washington that day was [his] birth date . . . after prodding and cajoling, Washington would accept the false date" (Ehrenreich et al., 2001, pp. 13–14).

> [Jerome] Holloway was known as "the most retarded man on Death Row anywhere in the nation." He has the mental age of a seven-year old. His IQ is forty-nine, in the moderate range of mental retardation. His intellectual capabilities are in the bottom .01 to .03 percent of the U.S. population. His intelligence is so low that he does not know the alphabet, cannot read or write, cannot count, make change for a dollar, or tell time. He does not know what country he lives in and confessed in court to having assassinated Presidents Lincoln, Kennedy, and even President Reagan (Reed, 1993, p. 119).

> Limmie Arthur (IQ 65) believed that he was sentenced to death because be couldn't read. He diligently tried to learn so he could earn his GED because he thought he would get a reprieve if he was successful (Reed, 1993, p. 15).

It has been argued that execution of the mentally retarded is inappropriate on the grounds that it violates the Eighth Amendment's prohibition against cruel and unusual punishment, and this charge was considered by the U.S. Supreme Court in *Penry v. Lynaugh* (1989). John Paul Penry confessed to the 1979 murder of Pamela Carpenter. Penry's IQ had been measured on a number of occasions and was estimated to be between 50 and 63 (Reed, 1993). In an examination as part of a competency hearing prior to standing trial, it was found "that Penry, who was 22 years old at the time of the crime, had the mental age of a 6 ½-year old, which means that he has the ability to learn and the learning or the knowledge of the average 6 ½-year old kid" (Latzer, 1998, p. 220). Penry was found competent to stand trial, was convicted of capital murder, and was sentenced to death.

The U.S. Supreme Court heard Penry's appeal on January 11, 1989, in *Penry v. Lynaugh*. Two issues of concern were (1) had the jury in Penry's trial been able to consider all relevant mitigating circumstances during the sentencing phase, and (2) did the execution of a mentally retarded person violate the Eighth Amendment prohibition against cruel and unusual punishment. On the first issue the Court agreed that the jury had not had the opportunity to hear the relevant mitigating evidence and Penry was granted a new trial. On the second issue the Court considered whether as a group the mentally retarded, "because of their mental disabilities . . . do not possess the level of moral culpability to justify imposing the death sentence" (Latzer, 1998, p. 221), and whether there is a national consensus against execution of the mentally ill on the grounds that it violates "evolving standards of decency" (Latzer, 1998, p. 221). In its opinion the Court rejected Penry's claim that execution of the mentally retarded was unconstitutional because it could not conclude "that all mentally retarded people of Penry's ability—by virtue of their mental retardation alone, and apart from any individualized consideration of their personal responsibility—inevitably lack the cognitive, volitional, and moral capacity to act with the degree of culpability associated with the death penalty. Mentally retarded persons are individuals whose abilities and experiences can vary greatly" (Latzer, 1998, p. 224). The court agreed that as long as juries had the opportunity to consider mental retardation as a mitigating circumstance in their sentencing decision, execution of the mentally retarded was not unconstitutional.

Recently, however, the U.S. Supreme Court reconsidered the constitutionality of executing the mentally retarded when it heard arguments in the case of *Atkins v. Virginia* (2002). Daryl Renard Atkins was convicted in the 1996 murder of Eric Nesbitt in Yorktown, Virginia, and sentenced to death. During the sentencing stage of the trial the Court heard conflicting testimony concerning Atkins' level of retardation. While one expert stated that Atkins was "mildly mentally retarded with an IQ of 59," another stated he was of "average intelligence at least."[1] Atkins appealed the sentence on the grounds that execution of the mentally retarded violated the constitutional prohibition against cruel and unusual punishment. On June 20, 2002, the court reversed its ruling in *Penry v. Lynaugh* and concluded that execution of the mentally retarded *does* constitute cruel and unusual punishment and is prohibited by the Eighth Amendment. The Court's shift in this instance was claimed to reflect "currently prevailing standards of decency" and to be consistent with a national state-level shift toward prohibiting execution of the retarded (*Atkins v. Virginia*, 2002). As a result of the ruling the mentally retarded can no longer be executed and the debate will likely now return to consideration of how to determine mental retardation.

The Mentally Ill

In *Ford v. Wainwright* (1986) the U.S. Supreme Court dealt with the issue of execution of the mentally ill. Because the mentally ill should not be found fit to stand trial, *Ford v. Wainwright* dealt with the issue of whether offenders who become insane following their conviction and sentencing should be excluded from execution. In this instance a number of justifications are given for excluding from execution all offenders who suffer mental illness. The Court considered historical attitudes toward execution of the insane and noted the common-law standard forbidding execution of the mentally ill (Latzer, 1998). In its opinion prohibiting execution of the mentally ill, the Court states,

> this Court is compelled to conclude that the Eighth Amendment prohibits a State from carrying out a sentence of death upon a prisoner who is insane. Whether its aim be to protect the condemned from fear and pain without comfort of understanding, or to protect the dignity of society itself from the barbarity of enacting mindless vengeance, the restriction finds enforcement in the Eighth Amendment (Latzer, 1998, p. 216).

However, whether those who become mentally ill while on death row can be treated so that they regain sufficient competence to be eligible for execution remains an issue. In 1992 Claude Maturana was sentenced to die for the murder of Glen Estes, whom he shot and tried to decapitate. In 1999 Maturana was diagnosed as a paranoid schizophrenic, declared unfit for execution, and transferred to Arizona State Hospital. Doctors at the hospital refused requests that they try to restore Maturana's sanity so he could be executed as such action was claimed to be an ethical violation. After contacting all 1400 of Arizona's psychiatrists and advertising in newspapers for a doctor to treat Maturana, the state eventually located a doctor in Georgia who examined Maturana and declared him fit for execution (Press, 2001).

The paradoxical practice of treating inmates so that they become well enough to be executed is not confined to mental illness:

> In 1995, Robert Brecheen, a condemned Oklahoma inmate, slipped into a self-induced drug stupor. State prison officials forced him to regain consciousness by having his stomach pumped in a nearby hospital so they could—just 2 hours later—execute him with state-approved drugs (Welch, 1999, p. 169).

Notably, imposing treatment upon an inmate for the purpose of bringing them to a condition in which they are legally fit for execution is opposed by the American Medical Association (Welch, 1999).

WHAT ARE THE MAJOR ARGUMENTS CONCERNING CAPITAL PUNISHMENT?

The continued use of the death penalty in the United States is a controversial issue. In defending their position, several different arguments are used by both proponents and abolitionists. Interestingly, the same argument is often used by both sides, which demonstrates the amount of confusion that exists concerning various aspects of capital punishment. The most common and enduring topics are discussed next.

Retribution

The retribution argument is commonly based on the belief in revenge and the principle of *lex talionis*—an eye for an eye (Welch, 1996). This desire to retaliate against those who have harmed us is deeply rooted in our past (Costanzo, 1997) and serves as a powerful justification for many death penalty proponents (Bohm, 1999; Johnson, 1998; Quinn, 1999). As noted by Bohm (1999), however, retribution is a complex concept. Indeed, in *Furman v. Georgia* (1972) Justice Thurgood Marshall referred to retribution as one of the most misunderstood concepts in criminal jurisprudence. Among the multiple meanings attributed to retribution are the concepts of vindication—in which society "pays" the offender for the harm he has caused—and "just deserts"—meaning the offender repays society for the damage he has done (Bohm, 1999).

Retribution appeals to death penalty proponents on an emotional level, offering an "emotional sense of justice" to victims' families and the public (Quinn, 1999, p. 348). As Johnson states,

> Most death penalty supporters emphasize not the fine points of the law, sociological findings on deterrence, treatises on justice, but an essentially gut-level belief that murderers deserve to die (Johnson, 1998, p. 232).

Abolitionists, however, reject emotion as a justification for the death penalty. They believe executions impede society's moral progress, diminish the value of human life, and reduce the government to the level of the criminal (Costanzo, 1997; Welch, 1996). Costanzo further asserts that

> although individually we all feel the primitive urge to exact revenge against those who harm us, collectively we must strive to be more rational, fair, moral, and humane than the criminals who commit the acts of violence or cruelty that we condemn (Costanzo, 1997, p.141).

Deterrence

The deterrence argument suggests that the death penalty causes would-be offenders to refrain from committing murder; after weighing the costs and benefits of offending, individuals will conclude that murder is not worth the risk of facing execution. Deterrence offers a seemingly scientific rationale for the death penalty (Costanzo, 1997) and one that appears more socially acceptable than retribution (Bohm, 1999). Polls show that the belief in deterrence is one of the most important foundations for death penalty support in the United States (Radelet & Akers, 1996).

Though deterrence is an appealing concept, its usefulness as a justification for the death penalty is problematic. First, the deterrent value of the death penalty is based on the offender's belief that the costs outweigh the benefits. Scholars (e.g., Bedau, 1997) agree, however, that this equation is undermined by an offender's belief that he won't get caught or that he will be punished lightly; an offender acting on impulse or emotion, moreover, may fail to consider the risks at all. The potential costs associated with committing a crime, however, also depend on successful intervention by various agencies within criminal justice system—including law enforcement, the courts, and the correctional system; thus, such costs are conditional upon arrest, prosecution, conviction, and sentencing (Bedau, 1997; Bohm, 1999).

Second, Bedau (1997, p. 127) also points out conceptual problems with deterrence, including the failure to distinguish between deterrence and incapacitation. The goal of physically preventing individuals from recidivating is reached by incapacitation, not deterrence (Bohm, 1999). This is a common misconception not only among members of the general public but politicians as well. Deterrence, however, involves the individual making the decision not to offend rather than being *physically unable* to offend. As Bedau (1999, p. 128) reminds us, however, "you cannot be deterred if you cannot weigh—as the dead cannot—the perceived risks you face in committing a crime."

Third, evidence that capital punishment is an effective deterrent is weak. Scientific evidence of the deterrent value of the death penalty in the United States was first offered in the mid-1970s. Economist Isaac Ehrlich estimated that each execution between 1933 and 1969 had prevented seven or eight homicides (Bohm, 1999; Costanzo, 1997), while one of Ehrlich's students, Stephen Layson, later projected that each execution actually deterred approximately 15 homicides (Bedau, 1997). Both researchers have been heavily criticized by their peers on methodological and conceptual grounds; however, their studies are still frequently cited by death penalty proponents (Bohm, 1999; Radelet & Akers, 1996). Sociologist William C. Bailey has been searching for statistically significant evidence of the death penalty's deterrent effect since the early 1970s. While he has published more than a dozen studies, no data confirming a deterrent effect of death sentences or of actual executions have been identified (Bedau, 1997; Bohm, 1999). Costanzo succinctly summarizes the state of the evidence regarding deterrence and the death penalty by asserting that

> the fragile logic of deterrence theory has crumbled under the weight of research evidence. More than a century of experience and more than 200 pieces of research lead to an inescapable conclusion: The death penalty does not deter potential murderers (Costanzo, 1997, p. 103).

Though the deterrence argument has little scientific support, this appears to have no influence on death penalty proponents, whose belief in deterrence appears to be "rooted in faith rather than facts" (Welch, 1996).

Incapacitation

The death penalty may be considered the most effective method of incapacitation for murderers. According to death penalty proponents, convicted murderers sentenced to life may harm prison staff or other inmates; they may also escape or be released from prison and commit additional felonies (Bohm, 1999; Welch, 1996). Clearly, an executed offender cannot commit additional crimes.

As Bedau (1997) points out, however, such an argument fails to differentiate incapacitation and prevention. Incapacitation is effective only to the extent to which it actually prevents additional crimes; though an incapacitated offender cannot commit additional crimes, this does not mean that he or she necessarily would reoffend if not incapacitated. Moreover, research has found recidivism rates for convicted murderers to be quite low compared to other felony offenders (Bedau, 1997; Welch, 1996) and that capital murderers sentenced to life without parole are no greater threat to prison staff or other inmates than offenders sentenced to death or other terms of imprisonment (Bohm, 1999).

Cost

As correctional systems continue to assume larger proportions of state and federal budgets, the costs associated with various sentencing options become an important issue (Dieter, 1997). Housing and providing for a maximum security prisoner, for example, is estimated to cost approximately $20,000 per year (Bohm, 1999; Costanzo, 1997). The common assumption is that executing an offender would cost less than supporting him for life in a maximum security prison (Henderson, 2000). Historically, executions may well have been an inexpensive method of dealing with offenders, so cost was not an issue (Costanzo, 1997). In contemporary times, however, the costs associated with the death penalty process have soared (Bohm, 1999; Dieter, 1997). The average execution is estimated to cost $2–3 million (Bohm, 1999; Costanzo, 1997).

Though the cost of housing inmates on death row for a lengthy period is obviously quite high, most of the expense capital punishment entails is associated with the trial process preceding life on death row (Bohm, 1999; Costanzo, 1997). The trial process for death penalty cases is necessarily more complicated and time consuming than non–death penalty trials, given the finality of execution (Dieter, 1997; Quinn, 1999). More thorough pretrial preparation, jury selection, expert witnesses, and a separate penalty phase all contribute to the cost of a death sentence. Death penalty cases also require a constitutionally mandated appeals process, which adds to the total cost.

Worthless Appeals?

A common complaint concerning the death penalty is that offenders are permitted endless frivolous appeals that stretch the gap between sentencing and execution to several years at considerable expense to taxpayers and emotional anguish to the victims' families. In his essay "Two Models of the Criminal Process," Herbert L. Packer distinguished between the crime control and due process models. The crime control model describes a criminal justice system that operates on the presumption of guilt and emphasizes a fast and efficient process. Under this model appeals are regarded as unnecessary obstacles to justice. The due process model, in contrast, describes a criminal justice system that operates on the presumption of innocence and values appeals as a necessary obstacle to wrongful convictions (Packer, 1996). Support for restricting appeals opportunities for the condemned is consistent with Packer's crime control model and reflected in legislation limiting death penalty appeals, such as the 1996 Anti-Terrorism and Effective Death Penalty Act. This support also reveals belief that errors are rarely made in capital trials and that, rather than constituting a necessary obstacle for prevention of wrongful convictions and death, appeals are an obstacle to swift justice.

In 1991, at the request of the U.S. Senate Judiciary Committee, Columbia University researchers began to study the appeals process in state capital cases with the main objective of determining how often appeals were successful, or, in other words, whether the appeals process simply prolonged inevitable execution of the guilty (at great taxpayer expense and emotional stress) or was necessary to prevent miscarriages of justice (Liebman et al., 2000). At the state level the appeals process typically consists of the following three stages:

- *First inspection:* State direct appeal. All death penalty cases are automatically subjected to review by the state. Successful appeal at this stage requires the defense to demonstrate that a "serious error"[2] has occurred.

- *Second inspection:* State postconviction review. Typically state post-conviction review is limited to consideration of constitutional issues that were not and could not have been raised under direct appeal.

- *Third inspection:* Federal habeas corpus. A petition may be filed with the U.S. District Court for the jurisdiction in which the defendant was convicted. If the petition is denied and the offender can demonstrate that the petition deals with a "substantial constitutional claim," an appeal may be made to the Federal Circuit Court. Finally, the offender may request that the U.S. Supreme Court review the case. The only guaranteed appeal to the federal courts is at the District Court level (Liebman et al., 2000).

In the flow chart shown in Figure 21–1, Liebman and colleagues (2000) summarize the main findings from their review of death penalty appeals.

[The findings of Liebman and colleagues reveal that for every 100 death sentences reviewed from 1973 to 1995,

- "41 (41%) were turned back at the state direct appeal phase because of serious error" (Liebman et al., 2000, p. 6).

- "Of the 59 that got through that phase to the second, state post-conviction stage, at least 10%—meaning 6 more of the original 100—were turned back due to serious flaws" (Liebman et al., 2000, p. 6).

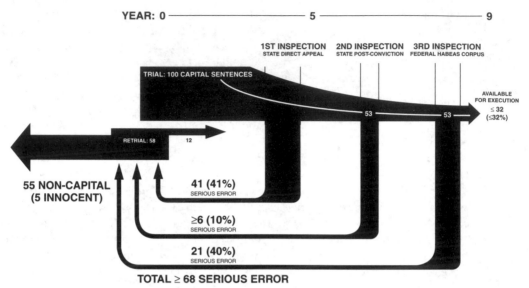

Figure 21–1 The attrition of capital judgments.
Source: Liebman et al., 2000, p. 7.

- "Of the 53 that got through that stage to the third, federal habeas checkpoint, 40%—an additional 21 of the original 100—were turned back because of serious error" (Liebman et al., 2000, p. 6).

- "All told, at least 68 of the original 100 were thrown out because of serious flaws, compared to only 32 (or less) that were found to have passed muster—after an average of 9–10 years had passed" (Liebman et al., 2000, p. 6).

- "Among the individuals whose death sentences were overturned for serious error, 82% (56 in our example) were found on retrial not to have deserved the death penalty, including 7% (5) who were found innocent of the offense" (Liebman et al., 2000, p. 6).

These data indicate that serious errors are not uncommon. Liebman and colleagues identify two factors contributing to the majority of successful appeals:

(1) egregiously incompetent defense lawyers who didn't even look for—*and demonstrably missed*—important evidence that the defendant was innocent or did not deserve to die; and (2) police or prosecutors who *did* discover that kind of evidence but *suppressed* it, again keeping it from the jury (Liebman et al., 2000, p ii).

The findings reveal that far from delaying inevitable execution of the guilty, the appeals process provides an indispensable obstacle to serious injustice and has clearly prevented execution of the innocent. While many argue that the length of the appeals process demonstrates costly inefficiency, Liebman and colleagues reveal that "judicial review takes so long precisely *because* American capital sentences are so persistently and systematically fraught with error that seriously undermines their reliability" (Liebman et al., 2000, p. i).

Arbitrariness and Discrimination

According to Nakell and Hardy (1987), arbitrariness refers to random or inconsistent application of the death penalty, while discrimination concerns using improper criteria (such as race or gender) to influence who is selected for execution. A tiny percentage of all death-eligible offenders—less than 2 percent since 1930—are actually executed (Bohm, 1999), and examination of how the death penalty has been applied over time and across jurisdictions raises troubling questions concerning its arbitrary and discriminatory use (Bohm, 1999; Welch, 1996). Indeed, the U.S. Supreme Court ruled the death penalty was unconstitutional in the 1972 case of *Furman v. Georgia* based on the "arbitrary and capricious" manner in which it was applied (Henderson, 2000).

As a result of *Furman v. Georgia*, states were required to devise procedures to rectify the arbitrary manner in which the death penalty was implemented (Henderson, 2000; Nakell & Hardy, 1987). In practice, however, inconsistencies in the use of the death penalty persist (Bohm, 1999; Nakell & Hardy, 1987; Russell, 1994). Bohm (1999) identifies several reasons for continued arbitrariness in the application of the death penalty, including jurors' error, use of plea bargaining, determination of intent (which in turn influences what charges will be sought), and rule changes resulting from U.S. Supreme Court decisions. Moreover, prosecutorial discretion has been cited as a reason for differential use of the death penalty across jurisdictions (Gross & Mauro, 1989; Welch, 1996).

Males, members of racial minority groups, and the poor are disproportionately represented on death rows across the United States (Costanzo, 1997; Quinn, 1999). While racial, social class, and gender disparities in the death penalty are clearly evident, the extent to which such imbalances result from discrimination is a more complex issue.

Race

Of those executed in 2000, 49 (58 percent) were white and 35 (41 percent) were black (Snell, 2001). The role of racial discrimination in the application of the death penalty remains a very controversial issue (Costanzo, 1997; Quinn, 1999). Historically, racial differences in the treatment of offenders was widely practiced and accepted, as evidenced by the pre–Civil War Black Codes, which "stipulated in law that blacks could be treated far more severely than whites for similar crimes" (Costanzo, 1997, p. 79). While such blatant discrimination seems incomprehensible today, racial bias is still believed to influence decision making at every step of the criminal justice process (Gross & Mauro, 1989).

The U.S. General Accounting Office examined post-*Furman* studies of racial disparities and concluded that "more than half of the studies found that race of the defendant influenced the likelihood of being charged with a capital crime or receiving the death penalty" (Office, 1997, p. 272). In 1987, however, the U.S. Supreme Court ruled in *McCleskey v. Kemp* that proof of *intentional* discrimination against an individual defendant was required to successfully challenge the constitutionality of a death sentence (*McClesky v. Kemp*, 1987). Though racial disparities in the death penalty might suggest a direct association with racial discrimination, proving deliberate discrimination is a difficult task (Russell, 1994).

The impact of victim, rather than defendant, race on death sentences has also been examined. Indeed, according to the U.S. General Accounting Office,

> The race of victim influence was found at all stages of the criminal justice system process. . . . The evidence for the race of the victim influence was stronger for earlier stages of the judicial process (e.g., prosecutorial decision to charge defendant with a capital offense, decision to proceed rather than plea bargain) than in later stages (Office, 1997, p. 271).

Furthermore, these racial disparities persisted when legally relevant variables were included (such as aggravating circumstances). More recent studies confirm this finding, and Bohm reports that

> nearly 80 percent of the victims of those executed under post-*Furman* statutes have been white, and that only 12 percent have been black. Yet, 56 percent of defendants executed have been white, 37 percent have been black, 5 percent have been Latino(a), 1 percent have been Native American and .44 percent have been Asian. Discrimination seems apparent because, historically, capital crimes have generally been intraracial (Bohm, 1999, p. 158).

Social Class

The death penalty is disproportionately applied to poor defendants, as abolitionists point out (Henderson, 2000). Bohm (1999) asserts that the death penalty is unfairly applied to members of the lower class and that this is apparent in the way murder is defined. Annually, about 20 percent of officially recorded homicides qualify for capital punishment. These figures fail to show, however, the thousands of deaths that occur annually due to medical and corporate misdeeds, a significant proportion of which are intentional or negligent (Bohm, 1999).

A more common criticism regarding social class disparities in the death penalty concerns quality of legal representation for the indigent. According to Bright, "[p]oor people accused of capital crimes are often defended by lawyers who lack the skills, resources, and commitment to handle such serious matters. This fact is confirmed in case after case" (Bright, 1997, p. 275). Death penalty proponents may argue that errors caused by ineffective counsel would be detected and amended upon appeal, but this process is far from perfect (Costanzo, 1997).

Gender

Women currently comprise less than 2 percent of death row inmates in the United States (Snell, 2001), while they commit roughly 20 percent of all criminal homicides (Bohm, 1999). Reasons for gender disparities in capital punishment have included how death penalty statutes are interpreted and the paternalistic attitude of key persons within the criminal justice system, such as judges and prosecutors (Morgan, 2000; Streib, 1998). The nature of homicides perpetrated by women is another important consideration: Most women convicted of murder do not have extensive criminal histories, homicides by women typically do not include premeditation or other felonies, and women often act as accomplices rather than the primary perpetrators (Morgan, 2000; Streib, 1998).

Errors and Irreversibility

An enduring concern for both abolitionists and proponents of capital punishment is the potential for executing the innocent. While some continue to assert their confidence that mistakes are not made and that only the guilty are executed,[3] there is clear evidence that the innocent have not only been convicted of capital crimes (Connery, 1996; Radelet et al., 1992) but also executed. When asked whether it is likely that the innocent have been executed, James S. Liebman, coordinator of a Columbia University investigation into the death penalty, stated, "Our judgment is that there is a very high risk that that has happened" (Herbert, 2002). Concern over racial bias and execution of the innocent has led to Federal District Judge Jed Rakoff's ruling that the federal death penalty is unconstitutional as it is a "demonstrably fallible system" (Editorial, 2002) as well as the temporary suspension and investigation of capital punishment systems in Illinois and Maryland (Press, 2002).

As a result of his concern over the capital punishment system in Illinois, Governor George H. Ryan (a proponent of capital punishment) suspended executions in 2000 and created the bipartisan Governor's Commission on Capital Punishment to investigate. Ryan's concerns were prompted by a number of developments, including

- The release of Anthony Porter following an investigation by Northwestern University journalism students. Porter had come within 48 hours of his scheduled execution (Bluth, 1999).

- The release of 13 men from death row over a period of just over 10 years (Governor's Commission on Capital Punishment, 2002).

On April 15, 2002, following a two-year investigation, the Governor's Commission on Capital Punishment released its report. In reviewing the cases of the 13 inmates released from the death row the Commission states,

> All 13 cases were characterized by relatively little solid evidence connecting the charged defendants to the crimes. In some cases, the evidence was so minimal that there was some question not only as to why the prosecutor sought the death penalty, but why the prosecution was even pursued against the particular defendant. The murder conviction of former death row inmate Steven Manning was based almost completely upon uncorroborated testimony of an in-custody informer. No physical evidence linked Manning to the murder he was said to have committed, nor was there any solid corroboration of the alleged statements he made admitting to the murder. Gary Gauger was convicted in McHenry County of the double murder of his parents even though no physical evidence at the scene linked Gauger to either murder, nor was there any satisfactory explanation of a possible motive. The primary evidence against Mr. Gauger were statements, allegedly

made by Gauger, that the police claimed were indicative of guilt, made during an interrogation that was not memorialized. Gauger denied the statements. Following a federal investigation, two other persons were subsequently convicted in Wisconsin of murdering Mr. Gauger's parents. Despite scant evidence, each of these cases resulted in a conviction, and a death penalty (Governor's Commission on Capital Punishment, 2002, pp. 7–8).

Liebman and colleagues identify the following factors as major reasons for the reversal of death sentences, and these further emphasize the importance of the appeals process:

- Trial court errors

- Prosecutor error

- Defense counsel error

- Use of unreliable informants

As a result of their study, Liebman and associates made 85 recommendations for improving the capital punishment system in Illinois, and the committee did not support lifting the death penalty moratorium until the recommendations were in place.

In response to growing concern over execution of the innocent, the U.S. Senate Judiciary Committee recently approved the Innocence Protection Act, 2002, aimed at improving the quality of legal representation in death penalty cases and providing postconviction DNA testing (Stout, 2002). The Act limits DNA testing, however, to instances in which there is believed to be considerable likelihood of wrongful conviction, and so it is likely that only a small proportion of those condemned will have their convictions subjected to the scrutiny of DNA testing.

HOW DOES THE DEATH PENALTY AFFECT THOSE INVOLVED?

At its most basic level, capital punishment is about pain and loss; after all, the death penalty is given because a life was taken, usually in a violent manner. The pain and loss associated with capital punishment, however, are not restricted to murder victims, nor to the condemned. Many others are impacted in a very personal way by a death sentence—including families of both the victims and the condemned and correctional staff.

Although we are regularly exposed to depictions of them—both real and fiction—in the media and popular culture, the trauma and loss faced by homicide victims' families is difficult for most of to fully comprehend. And while we can imagine how we might react if our family members were victimized in such a horrific fashion, we cannot assume that all victims' families will share a similar experience. The circumstances of a particular case—for example, whether the offender is a stranger or an acquaintance—can significantly influence a family's experience (Vandiver, 1998).

In her review of several studies concerning the families of homicide victims, Vandiver (1998, p. 480) identified a number of common themes:

- The loss of close relatives to homicide is a shatteringly traumatic event. The pain, disruption, and trauma caused by homicide cannot be overstated.

- Survivors are not helped, and sometimes further victimized by, the criminal justice system. Both formal and informal supports for homicide victims' survivors are dreadfully inadequate.

- The experience of isolation is very common—at the time they most need contact and support, families often feel the most isolated. The opposite situation of intrusion is often a problem as well, with unwelcome contacts from the criminal justice system, the media, and curiosity seekers.

Clearly, the families of murder victims are impacted by the death penalty on a number of domains.

Another hidden aspect of capital punishment is the impact it has on the families of individuals sentenced to death. The pain and suffering experienced by the families of death row inmates has been depicted in recent years in the media and national television programs such as ABC's *Nightline* and CBS's *60 Minutes*. In her book *Dead Man Walking: An Eyewitness Account of the Death Penalty in the United States*, Sister Helen Prejean (1993) also exposed the lingering anguish placed on these family members.

Though the families of victims and the families of the condemned both experience trauma and loss associated with capital punishment, their experiences differ in some significant ways. Vandiver (1998, p. 486) highlights several key differences:

- The families of condemned prisoners know for years that the state intends to kill their relatives and the method that will be used. They experience a prolonged period of anticipatory grieving, complicated by the hope that some court or governor will grant relief.

- Their relatives are publicly disgraced and shamed they have been formally cast out of society and judged to be unworthy to live.

- The deaths of their relatives are not mourned and regretted the way other violent deaths are; rather, the death is condoned, supported, and desired by many people, and actively celebrated by some.

An often-overlooked aspect of execution is the impact it has on those charged with carrying it out. While the technology of execution has changed to make the process less painful for the condemned, it has also made the process less painful for those who must carry it out. From the invention of the guillotine to lethal injection, methods of execution have been designed to distance the executioner(s) from the condemned, and this practice reveals our awareness that execution is "dirty work" (Lifton & Mitchell, 2000). Efforts to remove individual responsibility with different execution methods include the following:

- Firing squad: One member of the firing squad is given a blank so no one knows for sure that they fatally shot the offender.

- Lethal injection: A number of people are involved in preparing the chemicals and they are administered by machine.

- Electrocution: More than one person "flips a switch" so no one knows who actually turned on the electricity (Lifton & Mitchell, 2000).

Those charged with carrying out executions often spend weeks practicing a strict regimen designed to result in an orderly execution (Johnson, 1998). While it may be popular to conceive of execution as a momentary action in which representatives of the state cause a quick and painless death, we must recognize that it is a complex process for which those involved must train as both members of a team and as individuals.

Though individuals may effectively carry out their role in the team, they still must deal with their involvement at an individual level. As portrayed in the recent movie *The Green Mile*, those involved in execution employ a variety of tactics when performing their duties. Some rationalize that they are just doing their job; if they did not do it someone else would and so why should it not be them? Others focus on what the offender did rather than on the person they have come to know. Others still rationalize that they are simply following the law, that justice is being done; after all, the condemned has had a trial and the opportunity for appeal, so they must deserve the punishment the court has passed (Lifton & Mitchell, 2000). Close relationships between those involved in the execution team provide important support and emphasize that no single person is responsible for killing the condemned (Johnson, 1998).

While many claim they have little difficulty performing their duties others, however, report considerable suffering as a result of their involvement in execution. The following examples reveal the feelings of prison officials involved in executions:

Morris L. Thigpen, former Commissioner of the Alabama Department of Corrections, witnessed 8 executions: "After each execution, I felt as though I left another part of my own humanity and my spiritual being in that viewing room" (Thigpen, 2002, p. 288).

Donald A. Cabana, former Warden at the Mississippi State Penitentiary: "Staring blankly into the witness room, I felt dulled by the terrible reality that was now upon me . . . . I felt the hair on the back of my neck stand up. Positioning myself directly in front of my prisoner, fumbling with the death warrant in shaking hands, I slowly began to read the document. In a quivering, staccato voice, I read for what seemed an eternity (Cabana, 1996, p. 14).

William Leeke, former head of the Department of Corrections for South Carolina: "After it's all over, you feel like you want to go wallow in mud. . . . Because although you didn't do it personally, and even though you don't want to be perceived as a total liberal or soft on crime, you feel like you sort of degraded yourself, and you feel so sorry for the people who had to actually carry out the execution. . . . You can see the visible effects on the people that are doing it, especially the warden who has the responsibility in the death house, the trauma that comes" (Lifton & Mitchell, 2000, p. 103).

Major Kendall Coody, formerly in charge of death row at Angola State Prison, La: "I'm not sure how long I'm going to be able to keep doing this. . . . I've been through five of these executions and I can't eat, I can't sleep. I'm dreaming about executions. I don't condone these guys' crimes. I know they've done terrible things. I don't excuse what they've done, but I talk to them when I make my rounds. I talk to them and many of them are just little boys inside big men's bodies, little boys who never had much chance to grow up. . . . I get home from an execution about two-something in the morning and I just sit up in a chair for the rest of the night. I can't shake it. I can't square it with my conscience, putting them to death like that" (Prejean, 1993, p. 180).

While there are undoubtedly many who claim they would be happy to "flip the switch," it is important to recognize that execution impacts not only the families of both victim and offender but often takes a considerable toll on those who must conduct the execution.

NOTES

1. Atkins received two sentencing hearings following a ruling by the Virginia Supreme Court that a misleading verdict form was used in the first hearing.
2. Serious error is "error that the reviewing court concludes has seriously undermined the reliability of the outcome or otherwise 'harmed' the defendant" (Liebman et al., 2000, p. 4)
3. As Texas Governor, George W. Bush declared his strong support for capital punishment and asserted that he was confident no innocent people had been executed in Texas (Farrell, 2000).

REFERENCES

Adams, N. (1993). *Hangman's Brae: Crime and Punishment in and Around Bygone Aberdeen.* Banchory, Scotland: Tolbooth Books.

Atkins v. Virginia, 260 312 (US 2002).

Barnes, H. E. (1972). *The Story of Punishment: A Record of Man's Inhumanity to Man* (2nd ed., rev. ed.). Montclair, NJ: Patterson Smith Publishing Company.

Bedau, H. A. (1977). Evolution of the Death Penalty in America. In I. Isenberg (ed.), *The Death Penalty.* New York: The H. W. Wilson Company.

Bedau, H. A. (Ed.). (1997). *The Death Penalty in America: Current Controversies.* New York: Oxford University Press.

Bluth, A. (1999, March 12). Illinois Man Is Finally Cleared in 2 Murders. *The New York Times,* pp. 20.

Bohm, R. M. (1999). *Deathquest: An Introduction to the Theory and Practice of Capital Punishment.* Cincinnati, OH: Anderson Publishing Co.

Bonner, R. (2001, August 4). North Carolina to Prohibit Execution of the Retarded. *The New York Times,* pp. 10.

Bragg, R. (1997, January 9). Arkansas Puts 3 Killers to Death by Injection. *The New York Times,* pp. 16.

Bright, S. B. (1997). Counsel for the Poor: The Death Sentence Not for the Worst Crime but for the Worst Lawyer. In H. A. Bedau (ed.), *The Death Penalty in America: Current Controversies* (pp. 275–309). New York: Oxford University Press.

Cabana, D. A. (1996). *Death at Midnight: The Confession of an Executioner*. Boston: Northeastern University Press.

Connery, D. S. (1996). *Convicting the Innocent: The Story of a Murder, a False Confession, and the Struggle to Free a "Wrong Man."* Cambridge: Brookline Books.

Costanzo, M. (1997). *Just Revenge: Costs and Consequences of the Death Penalty*. New York: St. Martin's Press.

Dieter, R. C. (1997). Millions Misspent: What Politicians Don't Say About the High Costs of the Death Penalty. In H. A. Bedau (ed.), *The Death Penalty in America: Current Controversies* (pp. 401–410). New York: Oxford University Press.

Editorial. (2002, July 2). The Death of Innocents. *The New York Times*, pp. 20.

Eggen, D. (2002, July 1). Ashcroft Aggressively Pursues Death Penalty. *Washington Post*, pp. 1.

Ehrenreich, R., Fellner, J., & Smart, M. (2001). *United States: Beyond Reason: The Death Penalty and Offenders With Mental Retardation*. New York: Human Rights Watch.

Farrell, J. A. (2000, May 13). Some Texas Executions Leave Doubts/Despite Bush Claim, Ambiguities Linger. *The Boston Globe*, pp. 1.

Ford v. Wainwright, 477 399 (1986).

Foucault, M. (1979). *Discipline and Punish: The Birth of the Prison*. New York: Vintage Books.

Furman v. Georgia, 408 238 (1972).

Garland, D. (1990). *Punishment and Modern Society: A Study in Social Theory*. Chicago: University of Chicago Press.

Governor's Commission on Capital Punishment (2002). *Report of the Governor's Commission on Capital Punishment*: The State of Illinois.

Gross, S. R., & Mauro, R. (1989). *Death and Discrimination: Racial Disparities in Capital Sentencing*. Boston: Northeastern University Press.

Henderson, H. (2000). *Capital Punishment*. New York: Facts on File, Inc.

Herbert, B. (2002, February 11). The Fatal Flaws. *The New York Times*, pp. 27.

Hitt, J. (2001, December 9). The Year in Ideas: A to Z.; The Moratorium Gambit. *The New York Times*, pp. 82.

Johnson, R. (1998). *Death Work: A Study of the Modern Execution Process* (2 ed.). Belmont, CA: Wadsworth Publishing Company.

Johnston, D. (2001, June 4). As Federal Execution Nears, Groups Call for Moratorium. *New York Times*, pp. 12.

Kennedy, L. (1985). *Ten Rillington Place*. Harper Collins NY, NY Avon.

Latzer, B. (1998). *Death Penalty Cases : Leading U.S. Supreme Court Cases on Capital Punishment*. Boston, MA: Butterworth-Heinemann.

Liebman, J. S., Fagan, J., Gelman, A., West, V., Davies, G., & Kiss, A. (2002). *A Broken System, Part II: Why There Is So Much Error in Capital Cases, and What Can Be Done About It*. New York: Columbia Law School.

Liebman, J. S., Fagan, J., & West, V. (2000). *A Broken System: Error Rates in Capital Cases 1973–1995*. New York: Columbia University.

Lifton, R. J., & Mitchell, G. (2000). *Who Owns Death? Capital Punishment, The American Conscience, and the End of Executions*. New York: William Morrow.

Maestro, M. (1973). *Cesare Beccaria and the Origins of Penal Reform*. Philadelphia, PA: Temple University Press.

Marquart, J. W., Ekland-Olson, S., & Sorensen, J. R. (1994). *The Rope, The Chair, and The Needle: Capital Punishment in Texas, 1923–1990* (1st ed.). Austin: University of Texas Press.

Masur, L. P. (1989). *Rites of Execution: Capital Punishment and the Transformation of American Culture, 1776–1865.* New York: Oxford University Press.

McClesky v. Kemp, 481 279 (1987).

Morgan, E. (2000). Women on Death Row. In R. Muraskin (ed.), *It's A Crime: Women and Justice* (pp. 269–283). Upper Saddle River, NJ: Prentice Hall.

Nakell, B., & Hardy, K. A. (1987). *The Arbitrariness of the Death Penalty*. Philadelphia, PA: Temple University Press.

Newman, G. (1978). *The Punishment Response*. Philadelphia, PA: J. B. Lippincott Company.

Office, U. G. A. (1997). Death Penalty Sentencing: Research Indicates Pattern of Racial Disparities. In H. A. Bedau (ed.), *The Death Penalty in America: Current Controversies* (pp. 268–274). New York: Oxford University Press.

Packer, H. L. (1996). Two Models of the Criminal Process. In B. W. Hancock & P. M. Sharp (eds.), *Criminal Justice in America: Theory, Practice, and Policy* (pp. 155–164). Upper Saddle River, NJ: Prentice Hall.

Penry v. Lynaugh, 492 302 (1989).

Prejean, H. (1993). *Dead Man Walking: An Eyewitness Account of the Death Penalty in the United States* (1st ed.) New York: Random House.

Press, A. (2001, May 8). Mentally Ill Man Awaits Execution. *Milwaukee Journal Sentinel.*

Press, A. (2002, May 10). Maryland Suspends Executions. *The Hartford Courant*, pp. 7.

Quinn, J. F. (1999). *Corrections: A Concise Introduction*. Prospect Heights: Waveland.

Radelet, M. C., & Akers, R. L. (1996). Most Experts Believe the Death Penalty Does Not Deter Crime. In S. E. Schonebaum (ed.), *Does Capital Punishment Deter* (pp. 56–69). San Diego: Greenhaven Press.

Radelet, M. L., Bedau, H. A., & Putnam, C. E. (1992). *In Spite of Innocence: Erroneous Convictions in Capital Cases.* Boston: Northeastern University Press.

Reed, E. F. (1993). *The Penry Penalty: Capital Punishment and Offenders with mental Retardation.* New York: University Press of America.

Russell, G. D. (1994). *The Death Penalty and Racial Bias: Overturning Supreme Court Assumptions.* Westport, CT: Greenwood Press.

Sanger, D. E. (2002, January 30). The State of the Union: The Overview; Bush, Focusing on Terrorism, Says Secure U.S. Is Top Priority. *The New York Times*, pp. 1.

Sarat, A. (2001). *When the State Kills: Capital Punishment and the American Condition.* Princeton, NJ: Princeton University Press.

Schabas, W. (1996). *The Death Penalty as Cruel Treatment and Torture: Capital Punishment Challenged in the World's Courts.* Boston: Northeastern University Press.

Schabas, W. A. (Ed.). (1997). *The International Sourcebook on Capital Punishment.* Boston, MA: Northeastern University Press.

Snell, T. L. (2001). *Capital Punishment 2000* (NCJ 190598). Washington, DC: Bureau of Justice Statistics.

Stanford v. Kentucky, 492 361 (1989).

Stout, D. (2002, July 19). Bill to Prevent Errant Executions Gains in Senate. *The New York Times*, pp. 13.

Streib, V. L. (1988). Imposing the Death Penalty on Children. In K. C. Haas & J. A. Inciardi (eds.), *Challenging Capital Punishment: Legal and Social Science Approaches* (pp. 245–268). Newbury Park: Sage Publications Inc.

Streib, V. L. (1998). Executing Women, Children, and the Retarded: Second Class Citizens in Capital Punishment. In J. R. Acker, R. M. Bohm, & C. S. Lanier (eds.), *America's Experiment with Capital Punishment: Reflections on the Past, Present, and Future of the Ultimate Penal Sanction* (pp. 201–222). Durham, NC: Carolina Academic Press.

Thigpen, M. L. (2002). Managing Death Row: A Tough Assignment. In L. F. Alarid & P. F. Cromwell (eds.), *Correctional Perspectives: Views from Academics, Practitioners, and Prisoners* (pp. 287–288). Los Angeles: Roxbury Publishing Company.

Thompson v. Oklahoma, 487 815, 833–838 (1988a).

Thompson v. Oklahoma, 487 815 (1988b).

Vandiver, M. (1998). The Impact of the Death Penalty on the Families of Homicide Victims and of Condemned Prisoners. In J. R. Acker, R. M. Bohm, & C. S. Lanier (eds.), *America's Experiment with Capital Punishment: Reflections on the Past, Present, and Future of the Ultimate Penal Sanction* (pp. 477–506). Durham, NC: Carolina Academic Press.

Vold, G. B., Bernard, T. J., & Snipes, J. B. (1998). *Theoretical Criminology* (4th ed.). New York: Oxford University Press.

Welch, M. (1996). Corrections: *A Critical Approach*. New York: McGraw-Hill.

Welch, M. (1999). *Punishment in America: Social Control and the Ironies of Imprisonment*. Thousand Oaks, CA: Sage Publications Inc.

The Death Penalty and the War on Terrorism

Neal S. Elover

The question of how to punish criminal defendants has been an ongoing issue since civilization began. This issue continues to be debated in today's legal circles. The question has now become, How should society treat criminal defendants and what if any constitutional rights do they have? One such constitutional right is the Eighth Amendment protection against cruel and unusual punishment.

The direct reference to treatment of criminal defendants in the Constitution is mentioned in the Eighth Amendment, which was ratified in 1791. Many constitutional conventions, such as Virginia, North Carolina, New York, and Maryland, urged the inclusion of the Eighth Amendment in the original Bill of Rights. That rationale for this inclusion stemmed from violations of guaranteed rights as mentioned in the English Bill of Rights. These violations are documented in Blackstone's Commentaries. Punishments in the colonies during the years prior to the American Revolution were severe. As part of the Bill of Rights, the Eighth Amendment was designed to protect the criminal defendant from cruel and unusual punishment.

The constitutions of many American states contain similar provisions to those in the United States Constitution. However, the wording of the provision varies from state to state. The Maryland constitutional convention was one of the states that included a declaration of rights with its Constitution. In Article 16 of the Maryland Declaration of Rights, the guarantee protection afforded criminal defendants by virtue of the Eighth Amendment to the United States Constitution is stated as follows: "no law to inflict cruel and unusual pain and penalties ought to be made in any case, or at any time, hereafter" (Annotated Code of Maryland, Maryland Declaration of Rights). Article 25 of the Maryland Declaration of Rights protects against "cruel or unusual punishment, by the Court of Law" (Annotated Code of Maryland, Maryland Declaration of Rights).

However, the statutory language in the Bill of Rights that mentions the concept cruel and unusual punishment needed to be defined. The court system in its early days tried to define the term in the nineteenth century. In 1878 case of *Wilkerson v. Utah* (99 U.S. 130, 1878), overruled by *Gregg v. Georgia* (428 U.S. 153, 1976), the Supreme Court held that execution by firing squad did not violate the Eighth Amendment. Acknowledging the trouble of defining the terms *cruel* and *unusual,* the Court ruled,

> Difficulty would attend the effort to define with exactness the extent of the Constitution Provision shall not inflicted; but it is safe to affirm that punishments of torture, and all others in the same line of unnecessary cruelty, are forbidden by that amendment to the Constitution (*Wilkerson v. Utah,* 99 U.S. 130, 135–136, 1879).

The issue was not the prosperity of the death per se but the means by which the sentence was carried out. The Court's perception of degree of cruelty was not clarified until 1890. In the case of *In re Kemmler* (136 U.S. 436, 1890), the high court upheld electrocution as a constitutional method of execution. These rulings suggested that punishments inflicted without prolonged pain did not violate the Eighth Amendment to the United States Constitution.

The *Wilkerson* (99 U.S. 130, 1878) and *Kemmler* (136 U.S. 436, 1890) cases did not address whether the phrase *cruel and unusual* referred to punishments practiced in the founding generations or an evolving concept (Bigel, 1997). *In re Kemmler* (136 U.S. 436, 1890) challenged the power of a state to take the life of a murderer by electrocution. It was not then contended, and in the opinion of the Supreme Court, "it could not be, that the Eighth Amendment was intended to apply to the States (Goldberg, 1973). It was urged, however, that the due process clause of the Fourteenth Amendment prohibited the states from imposing cruel and unusual punishments. The Court held that reversal would be proper only if the state "had committed an error as gross as to amount in law on a denial . . . of due process" (Goldberg, 1973), and the state's conclusion that electrocution was a most human mode of execution was not such an error." The Court repeated with the paragraph from the *Wilkerson* case quoted previously and added the following dictum:

> Punishments are cruel when they involve torture or a lingering death; is not cruel within the meaning of that word as used in the Constitution. (Goldberg, 1973, p. 355).

"It implies there something inhuman and barbarous, something more than the mere extinguishments of life" (Goldberg, 1973). Also in the *Kemmler* case, the high court referred to the "burning at the stake, crucifixion, [and] breaking on the wheel" as "in human and barbarous"(Bigel, 1997) punishments and contrasted them with electrocution, which, though technologically novel, appeared to inflict instant death. The Court suggested that it would not confine the meaning of *cruel and unusual* to a specific method of punishment provided that the one adopted inflicted minimal physical suffering (Bigel, 1997).

Two years after *Kemmler,* in *O'Neill v. Vermont* (144 U.S. 324, 1892), the extent of the imposed punishment was challenged in the context of a long prison term and heavy fine, and the Court divided for the first time over the meaning and application of the Eighth Amendment (Goldberg, 1973). The Court declined to consider whether this punishment was cruel and unusual " because as a Federal question, it is not assigned error, nor even suggested in the brief" (Goldberg, 1973 p. 355) and because, in any event, the Eighth Amendment did not apply to the states.

Justice Field, dissenting opinion, would have applied the Eighth Amendment to the states through the privileges and immunities clause of the Fourteenth Amendment. Beyond this, in interpreting the punishment clause, he rejected the traditional reading of the Eighth Amendment, which would limit its application to punishments that inflict such torture as "were at one time inflicted in England" (Goldberg, 1973). Justice Field wrote in his dissenting opinion the following:

> The inhibition is directed, not only against punishments of the character mentioned, but against all punishments which by their excessive length or severity are greatly disproportionate to the offenses charged. The whole inhibition is against that which is excessive either in the bail required, or fine imposed or punishment inflicted (O'Neill case Id, pp. 339–40).

Justice Field concluded that it is against the excessive severity of the punishment, as applied to the offenses for which it is inflicted, that the inhibition is directed. Justices Harlan and Brewer would also have applied the Eighth Amendment to the states, and they too deemed the penalty in issue cruel and unusual.

The Supreme Court again attempted to further define cruel and unusual punishment. In 1919, the United States Supreme Court for the first time ruled that a legislatively established penalty was cruel and unusual. In *Weems v. United States* (217 U.S. 349, 1910), the high court interpreted the cruel and unusual punishment clause of the Eighth Amendment according to the social value of the time. It ruled for the crime of falsifying government records 15 years of hard labor in ankle chains was excessive punishment. The *Weems* standard has been cited by different jurisdictions throughout the years.

In 1958, the United States Supreme Court once again tried to define the cruel and unusual punishment. In *Trop v. Dulles* (356 U.S. 86, 1958), the high court ruled that cruel and unusual punishment clause draws its meaning from "evolving standards of decency" that mark the progress of a maturing society. The Court ruled in the *Trop* case that

> The basic concept underlying the cruel and unusual punishment clause is nothing less than the dignity of man. While the State has the power to punish, the cruel and unusual Clause stands to assure that this power be exercised within the limits of civilized standards (Gardner, 184, p. 184).

The Court has had little occasion to give precise content to the Eighth Amendment, and in an enlightened democracy as ours, this is not surprising. Thus Chief Justice Warren's interpretation of what constitutes cruel and unusual punishment is a fluid concept in which the states of a particular punishment, such as the death penalty, may change as society's values evolve and/or mature.

The dominant cruel and unusual punishment themes in the 1970s and 1980s have been the clause's applications to the death penalty. The Supreme Court has examined the constitutionality of such a penalty, including procedures by which it may be imposed and actual methods of execution. The high court held in a 1972 death penalty case that the death penalty was defective. In *Furman v. Georgia* (408 U.S. 238, 1972) (see Chapter 21), the Court held that those with authority to improve such a sentence could exercise complete discretion over the terms of capital punishment, so imposing the death penalty constitutes cruel and unusual punishment because its application was arbitrary, discriminatory, and capricious. However, in 1976, the Supreme Court declared that capital punishment was constitutional per se and would be used where sufficient "structure" was provided for its imposition. The ruling in *Woodson v. North Carolina* (420 U.S. 280, 1976) invalidated the holding, which made the death penalty mandatory for particular and specified offenses. In *Coker v. Georgia* (433 U.S. 584, 1977), the high court considered the substantive rather than the procedural aspects of the death penalty. This again was another attempt to define the issue of cruel and unusual punishment, and the Court ruled that the punishment for a particular crime had to be proportional to the crime. The high court ruled in the *Coker* case that "a sentence of death was glossily disproportionate and excessive punishment for the crime of rape and was therefore forbidden by the Eighth Amendment as cruel and unusual punishment" (Gardner, 1989, p. 185).

In 1983, the Supreme Court ruled on two important death penalty issues. In *Barefoot v. Estelle* (463 U.S. 880, 1983), the Court was given the chance to specify guidelines for the increasing number of death-sentenced petitioners entering the appellate stages of the federal habeas corpus process. In *Barclay v. Florida* (463 U.S. 939, 1983) the Court ruled that sentences cannot depart from statutory guidelines in determining the aggravating factors for imposing the death penalty. This is the first time that the high court began to look at procedural issues concerning the sentencing of a capital defendant. In 1984, the Supreme Court continued to define the appropriateness of punishment by its ruling in *Pulley v. Harris* (465 U.S. 37, 1984). It ruled that a state need not conduct a comparative proportionality review in capital punishment cases. The high court stated,

> Traditionally, "proportionality" has been used with reference to an abstract evaluation of the appropriates of a sentence for a particular crime. Looking to the gravity of the offense and severity of the penalty, to sentences imposed for other crimes, and to sentencing practices in other jurisdictions, this Court has occasionally struck down punishments as inherently disproportionate, and therefore cruel and unusual, when imposed for a particular crime or category of crime (Gardner, 1989, p. 183).

Also during the 1984 term, the United States Supreme Court set up guidelines for ineffectiveness of counsel in its *Strickland v. Washington* opinion. In later opinions of the United States Supreme Court, the high court ruled on such issues as the use of victim impact evidence, use of mitigating versus aggravating factors in capital punishment sentencing, and the execution of juveniles and mentally ill and retarded inmates.

These opinions solidified the usage of the death penalty in the criminal justice system. But this nation remained divided on how to use the death penalty. Changes in the laws and statutes were needed.

Terrorism, the use of violence, and the threat of violence have created fear in society. Terrorism has dated back to at least the first century, when a Jewish religious sect fought against the Roman occupation of what is now Israel. Terrorism occurs throughout the world and within the United States (domestic terrorism). Throughout the twentieth century, the KKK (Ku Klux Klan) used violence and other tools to keep African Americans separated and segregated from the white population. During the Vietnam War, domestic terrorism was used by antiwar groups. The Unabomber planted or mailed homemade bombs that killed 3 people and wounded 16 others in 16 separate incidents throughout the United States from 1978 to 1995.

Changes were not forthcoming. It was believed that the aforementioned acts of terrorism and violence were isolated. However, with the bombings of the World Trade Center in 1993 and the Oklahoma City in 1995, new anxiety arose regarding the threat of terrorism within the United States. Congress promulgated changes in the federal death penalty statute. These changes were made, and the United States Supreme Court was asked to rule on these changes. Some of these changes were from the newly enacted legislation entitled the Antiterrorism and Effective Death Penalty Act of 1996 and certain provisions of the Federal Death Penalty Act. Challenges to these statutes brought about a renewed debate of the constitutionality of the death penalty. With the execution of Timothy McVeigh, the death penalty debate resurfaced again. However, there are other challenges to the Antiterrorism and Effective Death Penalty Act of 1996 that will face the United States Supreme Court in the future, such as the challenges in the new habeas corpus rules, the mandatory restitution changes, and immigration issues.

On September 11, 2001, terrorist attacks at the World Trade Center in New York City, the Pentagon in Washington, D.C., and a field in Pennsylvania created fear in the nation reminiscent of the 1950s anticommunist sentiments brought on by McCarthyism. In the 1950s, Immigration and Naturalization Service (INS) regulations were created to explain how the federal government would use INS regulations in the fight against terrorism.

With the actions of September 11, 2001, again legislative changes had to promulgate new rules and regulations to deal with terrorism. Changes in the Antiterrorism and Effective Death Penalty Act of 1996 and existing INS rules were passed by Congress and signed into law. Enforcement of these new rules and regulations and amendments to existing statutes began after their passage.

Legal scholars are again debating the new legislative statutes and changes to existing statutes to determine which ones are constitutional and which ones are not. Is it fair to deny basic freedoms that our forefathers wrote in the United States Constitution? The courts will have to separate where the fear of terrorism justifies stripping away an individual's constitutional rights. It appears that the United States Supreme Court will render the ultimate decision.

CREATION OF THE FEDERAL DEATH PENALTY

The federal government has employed capital punishment for certain federal offenses. The United States death penalty laws were first introduced by the First Congress's first crime bill in 1790. Thomas Bud became the first person hung for murder in Maine. Since 1970, 336 men and 4 women have been executed under the federal death penalty law. The federal government has utilized hanging, gas chamber, and electrocution to execute 340 prisoners.

The majority was executed for murder or crimes resulting in murder. There were executions for piracy, rape, rioting, kidnapping, spying, and espionage. Between 1927 and 1963, the United States executed 34 individuals, including 2 women. In 1963, the United States executed Victor Feguer by hanging in Iowa for kidnapping. At that time, Feguer was the last person executed in the United States with a federal death sentence. However, in 2001, two executions took place in the United States. One of the executions was well publicized (Timothy McVeigh). The other one (Juan Garza) was not publicized at all.

In the middle to late 1960s, constitutional issues arose from federal death penalty procedures. Following the United States Supreme Court's capital punishment case decision in 1972 and the reversal of that decision in 1976, legal scholars began to debate the question of whether federal death penalty sentencing was constitutional or unconstitutional. Legal scholars came to the conclusion that federal death penalty sentencing procedures were unconstitutional. However, no one suggested any changes in the death penalty sentencing procedures until 1988.

Congressional attempts during the 1970s and early to late 1980s to enact enforceable death penalty sentencing procedures were unsuccessful. However, in 1988, after numerous attempts, Congress passed the first modern death penalty statute. This statute was known as the "Drug Kingpin" statute and was part of Title 21 United States Code Section 848 (e)–(r)—the Anti-Drug Abuse Act of 1988. This statute brought about the necessary changes in the federal death penalty laws. However, this statute had a major drawback: It was directed at so-called Drug Kingpin murders and to drug-related murders of law enforcement officials in the course of a drug kingpin conspiracy. This statute was modeled after Supreme Court precedents, which declared these types of statutes constitutional after the 1972 ruling in the *Furman* case. Between the enactment of the statute in 1988 and the eventual 1994 expansion of the federal death penalty laws, six persons were sentenced to death for violating Title 21 United States Code Section 848. None of the six have been executed. One of the defendants, John McCullah, had his federal death sentence overturned and was later sentenced to life in prison.

Six years later, in 1994, Congress reviewed again the federal death penalty policy and procedures. Congress passed the Violent Crime Control and Law Enforcement Act of 1994 (Public Law No. 103-322), which included the Federal Death Penalty Act of 1994. This package of legislation expanded the reach of the federal death penalty and modernized the procedures for sentencing for every existing federal capital crime. The federal death penalties that were in effect prior to the expansion of the 1994 federal death penalty act fell into three categories:

1. Crimes involving the physical killing of other persons,
2. Crimes involving dangerous activity that results in death, and
3. Treason and espionage whether or not any death occur (18 USC Sect. 2381 & 18 USC Sect. 794).

The new legislation created a number of new offenses. These new capital offenses fall into these categories:

1. Espionage and treason;
2. Most homicides for which federal jurisdictions; and
3. Continuing criminal enterprise drug offenses that do not involve the killing of anyone but instead involve
   a. Large quantities of drugs or money, or
   b. The attempted murder of any public officer, juror, witness, or member of such person's family (Federal Death Penalty Act of 1994).

The Violent Crime Control and Law Enforcement Act of 1994 was the result of the 1993 World Trade Center bombing. However, some Congressional leaders did not believe that this piece of legislation was strong enough to curb crime. In 1995, another strategic event occurred in the United States. On April 19, 1995, a two-ton bomb exploded just outside the Alfred P. Murrah Federal Building in Oklahoma City, Oklahoma. The bomb, constructed with 4800 pounds of ammonium nitrate and fuel oil and placed in a Ryder van, was parked just below the second-floor daycare center. The explosion killed 168 people, including more than a dozen young children. This was one of the most publicized bombings in the world. At first, people of the United States and the world believed that this bombing was the work of terrorists. Further investigation proved that theory wrong. Timothy McVeigh was responsible for the bombing. He was tried and convicted in Colorado Federal Court of 11 counts of capital murder for the bombing.

USE OF VICTIM IMPACT EVIDENCE

Prior to the penalty phase in the Timothy McVeigh trial, questions were asked as to how victim impact evidence would be admitted during the penalty phase of the trial. Although the Payne Court did set forth a mechanism by which a court may exclude victim impact evidence at sentencing, namely the Fourteenth Amendment Due Process Clause, questions about the scope of allowable victim impact testimony under Payne remained unanswered (Donahoe, 1999). For example, the Court gave no guidance or guidelines as to how many impact witnesses may testify without rendering a sentencing unfair. Moreover, the Court did not explicitly state who might be considered a "victim" for the purpose of impact testimony. In other words, the Court did not clarify whether the opportunity to give impact testimony at capital sentencing is restricted to family members of the deceased or whether the term *victim* may encompass a larger group of persons indirectly affected by the crime (Donahoe, 1999). In the case *U.S. v. McVeigh*, the questions were put squarely before a United States District Court Trial Judge.

Prior to the penalty phase, the United States government notified the Court of its intentions to introduce more than 40 witnesses to testify about the emotional impact of the experience, including four or five individuals who helped with the rescue effort. Attorneys for McVeigh argued the admissibility of any impact testimony from rescue workers. The attorneys stated in their argument the following:

> [If] people who are indirectly affected, even grievously, by an incident, can be allowed to give victim impact testimony about their own condition, where does the line get drawn? For example, . . . there has been an epidemiological study in Oklahoma City to assess

the effects of this on the entire population in the city (Memo Opinion and Order for Change of Venue).

> [M]y concern is that there is only a difference in degree and not between . . . rescue workers who were impacted directly and people who were several miles away and suffered traumatic effects over the next several months (Donahoe, 1999, p. 17).

The government responded by stating that although it would be putting the rescue workers forward as victims, there was no risk of prejudice. The penalty phase evidence would merely present to the jury an objective story regarding a brief [testimonial] snapshot and understanding of the identity of the victim and their background. "The government continued by stating that its proffered testimony was justified in that it would certainly be for less extensive about the background of anyone individual or even all individuals that we offer combined than the defendant will present about himself" (Donahoe, 1999, p. 17).

The trial judge ruled in favor of the government. Judge Matsch allowed rescue workers to testify as victims of the bombing. Judge Matsch qualified his ruling with this observation:

> *Payne v. Tennessee* involved . . . cautions given by every justice who work, and almost every justice wrote in that case. And there simply is no clear guidance as to where the line appropriate, particularly victim impact testimony ends and appeal to passion, the human reactions, emotive reactions or revenge, rage, empathy—all of those things—begins. So I know that these rulings are not going to be consistent with the views of many (Donahoe, 1999, p. 17).

Judge Matsch concluded his ruling by stating that "the experience of those who were called to the scene qualified them as victims within the concept here of victim impact testimony" (Donahoe, 1999).

The government presented 38 victim witnesses during the penalty phase. The jury in the Timothy McVeigh case unanimously recommended for the death penalty. McVeigh attorneys petitioned the court for a new trial. They argued that the volume and quality of the victim impact evidence admitted during the penalty phase precluded the jury from making a reasoned sentencing decision on the evidence and the law. According to McVeigh attorneys, the rescue workers' testimony, in particular, was "graphic and gruesome" and "could not help but inflame the jury" (Donahoe, 1999, p. 20). Also, attorneys for McVeigh argued that they were precluded from objecting to this evidence; as such objections would be viewed by the jury as highly insensitive and would result in further prejudice to the defendant (Annin & Morganthanau, 1997).

The ruling in the *McVeigh* case (Doc. No. 96-CR-68-M, D. Colo. 1997) may significantly expand the pool of individuals who qualify as victims for the purpose of contributing admissible impact information at sentencing (Donahoe, 1999, p. 21). The *Payne* decision only confused the issue of who could give victim impact evidence. The Supreme Court in *Payne* tried to distinguish "direct victims," "or those who suffer physical injury as a result of an unlawful act, and secondary victims," or relatives of homicide victims who experience emotional distress or a change in personal relationships, as viable impact witnesses (Long, 1995). By allowing rescue workers, unrelated to those injured and killed, to testify as to emotional impact of the bombing on themselves and others, the *McVeigh* court added "indirect victims" to the list. Indirect victims have been described as individuals who acute awareness of crimes causes them fear and apprehension, adversely affecting their quality of life (Long, 1995). Some indirect victims can become so traumatized by crime that they develop health problems, both physical and emotional (Elias, 1986; Long, 1995).

The *McVeigh* ruling concerning victim impact evidence was a United States District Court ruling and does not have any binding authority beyond the District of Colorado. However, the *McVeigh* case should not be taken likely. Judge Matsch's decision to augment the scope of permissible victim participation to encompass indirect victims may be consequential in future cases, as his broadening of the definition of *victim* provides an example for other courts to follow in seeking to expand the scope of victim impact evidence. The critical aspect of Matsch's ruling is that it highlighted *Payne's* lack of guidelines for lower courts to follow in deciding whether to exclude, limit, or admit victim impact evidence— and by whom—during capital sentencing. Accordingly, *McVeigh* demonstrates the malleability of victim impact standards as well as the potential for further extension of the boundaries surrounding admissible penalty phase evidence (Donahoe, 1999, p. 21).

With its decision in *Payne v. Tennessee* (501 U.S. 808, 1991), the United States Supreme Court not only endorsed the use of victim impact evidence at sentencing. It also gave the scope of admissible impact evidence room to grow. In the *McVeigh* case, there are at least three areas for potential growth (i.e., who may be considered a "victim" for the purpose of assessing relevant impact, the number of allowable victim impact witnesses, and the extent to which explicit and graphic details may be admitted under the guise of gaining an understanding of the identity of victims, their personal characteristics, and their background). A fourth area for potential growth is whether a victim of a defendant's prior unadjudicated crime can give impact testimony during the defendant's sentencing hearing for a crime with which he or she is subsequently charged. The government's evidence in the Unabomber case served as a convenient reference for victims' inquiry.

According to the United States government, Ted Kaczynski (Unabomber) carried out 16 bombings throughout the United States between 1978 and 1995, killing three people and injuring 29 more (Donahoe, 1999, p. 22). Due to statutes of limitations and venue issues, the United States government only charged the Unabomber with four of the bombings. In its Notice of Intent to Seek the Death Penalty, the United States government listed "victim impact" as an aggravating factor justifying capital punishment (Donahoe, 1999, p. 22).

After the jury was impaneled and the trial was set to begin, the Unabomber plead guilty, admitting to all 16 bombings in return for a life sentence. Therefore, the use of victim impact evidence by the federal government during the penalty phase was moot. During the formal sentencing, the court allowed two victims to give impact statements before the court. The question was to the merits of whether the jury may consider such testimony during capital sentencing proceedings. This allowance will shed more light on the scope of permissible victim impact evidence under *Payne v. Tennessee* (501 U.S. 808, 1991). Given the current state of the law, Donahoe states that there is potential for a defendant's uncharged or unadjudicated crimes to testify regarding the personal impact of those offenses during the penalty phase after the defendant's conviction for a separate crime. Donahoe does not mean to suggest that this type of evidence be admissible. Instead, he wanted to show that it could be by using the facts in the Unabomber case as a model. The mention of a defendant's unadjudicated offenses during capital sentencing, even without victim testimony, has drawn its share of criticism under due process and the Constitution's mandate of accuracy and reliability (Burbach, 1991). Thus, it seems counterintuitive to suggest that victim impact evidence, with all its surrounding controversy, might be coupled with the similarly controversial use of uncharged offenses (Donahoe, 1999, p. 23). Yet this may be the uncharted future of victim impact evidence after the *Payne v. Tennessee* (501 U.S. 808, 1991) decision.

However, the problem of relevance and admissibility of impact evidence from victims of proven yet unadjudicated crimes during the penalty phase of federal case law has been discussed in earlier Supreme Court decisions and certain federal court circuits. According to the United States Supreme Court in *Zant v. Stephens* (462 U.S. 862, 1983), a sentencing jury may properly consider a defendant's prior criminal history as an aggravating factor. The Third, Fourth, Fifth, Nineth, Tenth, and Eleventh Federal Court Circuits have sustained the constitutionality of death sentences based in part on the defendant's unadjudicated criminal history (*Lesko v. Owens,* 1989; *Gray v. Thompson,* 1995; *Clark v. Collins,* 1994; *McDowell v. Calderon,* 1997; *Hatch v. Oklahoma,* 1995; *Devier v. Zant,* 1993) and again in *Williams v. Lynaugh* (814 F.2d 205, (Fifth Cir. 1987), the Court held that evidence of a defendant's unadjudicated violent crimes may be appropriately included in the jury's assessment of his future dangerousness and is probative of relevant elements of the defendant's background (Donahoe, 1999, p. 24). Once established as relevant and unprivileged, such evidence could be admitted and its weight left to the sentencing jury (Donahoe, 1999, p. 24).

At first glance, the value of allowing the jury to hear testimony from victims of a defendant's extraneous violent crimes during the penalty phase may outweigh the costs. It certainly furthers the United States Supreme Court's policy, as set forth in *Gregg v. Georgia* (428 U.S. 153, 1976), to permit the jury to have as much information as possible when making the sentencing decision. More specifically, it could allow a jury to better assess factors such as the defendant's character, moral culpability, blameworthiness, future dangerousness, as well as the harm he or she has caused through his or her criminal acts (Donahoe, 1999, p. 24). In *Simmons v. South Carolina* (512 U.S. 154, 1994), *Eddings v. Oklahoma* (455 U.S. 104, 1982), *Payne v. Tennessee* (501 U.S. 808, 1991), and *Barclay v. Florida* (463 U.S. 939, 1983), the United States Supreme Court recognized these factors as to the jury's decision of whether or not to sentence a capital defendant to death. Furthermore, the fact that a defendant has the opportunity to rebut the prosecution's evidence under *Payne* (501 U.S. 808, 1991), as well as to present mitigating evidence of his or her own, could alleviate a court's concern that testimony from the victims of the defendant's unadjudicated offenses will render the trial unfair.

However, federal appellate courts have not explicitly ruled on the admissibility of victim impact testimony from victims of unadjudicated criminal offenses committed by a defendant during the penalty phase of a capital murder trial (Title 18 USC Section 3663 (a)(2). Victims of a capital defendant's unadjudicated offenses have been called upon to testify as to events of those crimes. While not labeled at all by the courts, victim testimony relating to events of unadjudicated crimes in some cases has closely appeared to be victim impact evidence.

In conclusion, the connection is a philosophical link between retribution as a rationale for capital punishment and victim impact evidence. The question now becomes, Who are the victims and are we seeking retribution for society as a whole? The highest court in the land attempted in the *Gregg* opinion to make a case for society by stating, "The instinct for retribution is part of the nature of man and channeling the instinct in the administration of criminal justice serves an important purpose in promoting the stability of a society governed by law." The *Gregg* (*Gregg* case, 1976, p. 184) court goes on to make clear, inadvertently it seems, that society is not seeking retribution for itself but is simply giving in to the basic instincts of individual." When people begin to believe that organized society is unwilling or unable to impose upon criminal offenders the punishment they deserve, then there are sown the seeds of anarchy—of self-help, vigilante justice, and lynch law." In his dissent opinion in the *Gregg* case (*Gregg* case, 1976, p. 238), Justice Marshall wrote, "It simply defies belief to suggest that the death penalty is necessary to prevent the American people from taking the law into their own hand."

Retribution on behalf of society is an abstraction. It is the victim who may desire retribution. As long as retribution remains a rationale for capital punishment, victim impact evidence, the social and legal medium through which individuals may seek retribution, is sure to follow. But if retribution were to fail as a rationale (which is likely, however far it may be in the future), the argument for victim impact evidence would be severely limited (Donahoe, 1999, p. 31).

The issue of limiting the use of victim impact evidence has reached a critical state in the criminal justice system. Victim impact evidence can become, if it has not already, a major setback in this country's longstanding interest in the sentencing process. Society's increasing demands on behalf of victims have created an "upsurge in punitiveness" (Elias, 1986, p. 123). However, Elias (1986, p. 118), through his research, demonstrates that policies encouraging retribution and punishment do not advance victims' interests or further recovery. Elias's findings suggests that the decline of victim impact evidence—the threat to procedural fairness and rational sentencing—is greater than its supposed increase—the promotion of compassion and redress for victims.

Whatever the case, death penalty issues should not be so vulnerable to interpretation. Capital sentencing procedures should not be seen upon as an experiment. According to Donahoe, by leaving victim impact testimony open for interpretation, as suggested in the *Payne* decision, the Supreme Court of the United States has continued an already considerable risk that unduly prejudicial evidence will be allowed and that arbitrary and emotional capital sentencing decisions will result rather than sentencing decisions that are fair.

CREATION OF THE ANTITERRORISM AND EFFECTIVE DEATH PENALTY ACT OF 1996

The American people long believed that terrorism was a foreign problem. However, this belief changed with the 1993 World Trade Center bombing. The change demonstrated a new anxiety about how easy it would be to bomb any major building in the United States. No one took any considerable action to curb the anxiety of the American people. However, on April 19, 1995, terrorism struck the United States again: the bombing of the Federal Building in Oklahoma City. Legal scholars and legislative leaders were calling for changes in the Federal Death Penalty Act of 1994. Approximately one year after the Oklahoma City bombing, Congress introduced the Antiterrorism and Effective Death Penalty Act (AEDPA) of 1996 (Public Law No. 104–132, 1996). This legislation was the culmination of several bombings of buildings in the United States and new statutes proposed by the Executive and Congressional branches of government. In September 1994, the FBI sent to the Department of Justice a package of antiterrorism recommendations to help tighten immigration rules and regulations along with policy changes. In August 1995, Congress passed an amendment of the Violent Crime Control Appropriations Act of 1995 that amended INA Section 245 (i). Section 245 (i) of the INA allowed illegal aliens, whether illegal border crossers or visa overstayers, to obtain adjustment to legal residence status without having to leave the United States for investigation by U.S. consular officers in the aliens' native country of their possible ineligibility for immigrant status. This amendment was good for three years. However, in July 1997, the amendment of INA Section 245 (i) became a permanent basis of the adjustment of status provision for illegal aliens. Section 245 (i) codified legal residence status for persons entering without inspection or overstaying their visa without having to leave the United States for investigation of their possible ineligibility for immigrant status in their native country.

Approximately 2 months after the Oklahoma City bombing, the Omnibus Counter Terrorism Act of 1995 (Senate bill 390, 104th Congress, 1995) was enacted. This legislation was a response to the 1993 bombing of the World Trade Center in New York City. One week after the Oklahoma City bombing, President Clinton presented an extended and expanded version of the Omnibus Counter Terrorism Act. In the United States Senate, a similar bill, The Comprehensive Terrorism Prevention Act of 1995 (Senate Bill 735, 104th Congress, 1995), was introduced. A conference committee version of the bill was passed in Congress on April 19, 1996. The President of the United States signed this legislation into law on April 24, 1996. The Act's stated purpose was to "deter terrorism, provide justice for victims, provide for an effective death penalty, and for other purposes" (Public Law No. 104–132, 1996). The Antiterrorism and Effective Death Penalty Act was comprised of nine major titles and amending numerous sections of the United States Code.

The Antiterrorism and Effective Death Penalty Act revised the procedures used in the review of federal habeas corpus applications. Some of the revised procedures concern a statute of limitations, restrictions of the review of state-court habeas corpus decisions in the federal court system, and procedures for the discouraging of successive petitions (Martin, 1996). Also, there were provisions concerning the victim and mandatory restitution for certain offenses (AEDPA Sect. 201–211).

However, the majority of the remaining provisions in the Antiterrorism and Effective Death Penalty Act related to terrorist activity. Title III criminalized financial contributions that are made to designate terrorist organization, whether or not they are made for the peaceful or otherwise legal activities of the group. In Title IV, alien-terrorist removal procedures provide for the use of secret and illegally obtained evidence in deportation hearings.

Also under Title IV, deportation can be based solely on membership in one of the designated organizations defined in Title III. Lastly, the criminal removal provision in Title IV leaves the Attorney General no discretion but to order a deportation hearing (Public Law No.104-132).

HISTORY OF FEAR

In order to understand the future impact of the Antiterrorism and Effective Death Penalty Act of 1996 as it pertains to terrorism, it is important to look back at a time in history when the United States became fearful and overreacted to communism. In light of September 11, 2001, few will protest the trial and conviction of Arab terrorists. This reaction is similar to the reaction to communism in earlier American history.

American fear and persecution of communists began in the early 1900s. This fear and persecution lasted for at least 50 years, with arrests, prosecutions, and deportations (Rohr, 1991). By the mid-1900s, a majority of states had enacted legislation with provisions to curb communism in the United States. The United States government also amended the Espionage Act of 1917 with the Sedition Act of 1918 (Public Law No. 65-150 Section 3).

With the Sedition Act of 1918, many constitutional challenges reached the United States Supreme Court in 1919. In the case of *Schenck v. United States* (249 US 47, 1919), the high court upheld the convictions for causing and attempting to cause insubordination in the military and naval forces based on defendants' distribution of leaflets to enlist men opposing World War I and the draft. These convictions were in violation of the Espionage Act of 1917. The Supreme Court concluded by stating that "in ordinary times the defendants in saying all that was said in their circular would have been within their constitutional rights" (*Schenck v. U.S.*, p. 52).

In 1940, the United States government passed legislation to regulate political speech by stating that an alien could be deported based on past beliefs, advocacy, or membership in an organization that advocated forcible overthrow of the United States government (Rohr, 1991). The key provision made membership in such organizations illegal with a penalty of up to 20 years of imprisonment (Rohr, 1991).

The top 11 communist party leaders in the United States were convicted under the Smith Act. The United States Supreme Court upheld the convictions for conspiracy to organize the party for the purpose of advocating and teaching the overthrow of the government "as speedily as the circumstances would permit" (*Dennis v. U.S.*, 1951). In the *Dennis* case, the defendants were convicted for joining "together to advocate a doctrine with no proof of 'imminent danger' " (*Dennis v. U.S.*, 1951). Justice Black wrote a dissent opinion stating that "the only way to affirm these convictions is to repudiate directly or indirectly the established 'clear and present' rule." Justice Black continued by stating "The [first] Amendment as so constructed is not likely to protect any but those 'safe' or orthodox views which rarely need its protection" (dissent opinion in *Dennis*, 1951).

With the Supreme Court upholding the Smith Act, Congress passed and enacted additional statutes in the 1940s and 1950s (Rohr, 1991). In the late 1940s, the Attorney General of the United States published a list of aversive groups. More changes in the statutes of the United States were needed. In 1950, President Truman vetoed the McCarran Act. However, Congress overrode the veto and enacted the detailed and comprehensive McCarran Act in 1950 (*Dennis v. U.S.,* 341 U.S. 494, 581, 1951). This Act required the registration of all communist party members; prohibited any party member from working in a defense facility, holding office with a labor organization, or, among other things, obtaining a passport; and sometimes required the deportation of past or present members (McCarran Act, Public Law No. 82-414). The communist party of the United States challenged the new law in court. The United States Supreme Court had the opportunity to review the McCarran Act and decide whether the communist party of the United States had justification to challenge the new law. The high court reviewed the new law and upheld the McCarran Act and ordered the communist party to register per the provisions of the McCarran Act. This was in spite of the First Amendment right to association and due process challenges (*Communist Party of the U.S. v. Subversive Activities Control Bd.* @103). Again, Justice Black dissented:

> I regret, exceedingly reject, that I feel impelled to recount this history of the Federal Sedition Act, because, in all truth, it must be pointed out that this law—which has been almost universally condemned as unconstitutional—did not go as far in suppressing the First Amendment freedoms . . . as do the Smith Act and the Subversive Activities Control Act (Justice Black, dissenting 367 U.S. 1, 4–19, 1961).

Finally, in 1960, the United States Supreme Court considered the constitutionality of the membership clause of the Smith Act (*Scales v. United States* 367 U.S. 203, 1960). By reading specific intent as to the criminal ends of the organization and active membership into the requirement for conviction under the Smith Act, the high court, in a 5–4 decision, upheld a conviction for membership (*Scales v. United States* 367 U.S. @ 209, 228, 1960). Justice Douglas wrote in his dissent,

> The perils sought to be suppressed are regularly overestimated. History shows in one example after another how excessive have been the fears of earlier generations who shuddered of menaces that, with the benefits of hindsight, we now know were mere shadows. This in itself should induce the modern generation to view with prudent skepticism the recurrent alarms about the fatal potentialities of dissent . . . [T]he lovers of freedom cannot afford to sacrifice their moral superiority by adopting totalitarian methods in order to create a self-deluding sense of security. Suppression, once accepted as a way of life, is likely to spread (dissent opinion in the *Scales* case by Justice Douglas @ 274–75 n. 8).

However, Congress did not listen to Justice Douglas's warning or learn from our history of overreaction. Suppression has spread through many provisions of the Antiterrorism and Effective Death Penalty Act of 1996, affecting the rights of American citizens and legal resident aliens (Beall, 1998).

In several provisions of the Antiterrorism and Effective Death Penalty Act, questions concerning due process issues have been raised concerning the deportation of terrorists and the removal of the criminal alien. The legality of our legal system is put to the test whenever basic due process rights are denied, even when denied to "undesirable" aliens. But what rights are due to a legal resident alien, and how do these rights apply to the Antiterrorism and Effective Death Penalty Act?

It has long been established that a lawful resident alien is protected by the Fifth Amendment and may not be deprived of life, liberty, or property without due process (*Kwong Hai Chew v. Colding*, 1953, & *Landon v. Plasencia*, 1982). In 1953, the United States Supreme Court reviewed the issues surrounding the expulsion of resident aliens. In the case of *Kwong Hai Chew v. Colding* (344 U.S. 590, 1953), the high court wrote the following: "[al]though Congress may prescribe conditions for [a lawful resident alien's] expulsion and deportation, not even Congress may expel him without allowing him a fair opportunity to be heard" (*Kwong Hai Chew,* 344 U.S. @597–98).

Although the rights to due process in deportation proceedings have been established, the specific process of due process is not clear. There is no clear answer to this problem. However, the United States Supreme Court attempted to clear up this problem. In the *Landon v. Plasencia* case (459 U.S. 21, 1982), the Supreme Court employed a three-factor-balancing test that was developed for use in administrative law areas. This balancing test is called the Eldridge test (424 U.S. 319, 1976).

In evaluating the procedures developed in *Plasencia,* the Supreme Court and other lower courts must consider the following factors outline in the Eldrige test. These are

1. The interest at stake for the individual,
2. The risk of an erroneous deprivation of the interest through the procedures used as well as the probable value of additional or different procedural safeguards, and
3. Interest of the government in using the current procedures rather those additional or different procedures (*Plasencia* 459 U.S. @34–37).

Although the Eldrige test is violated by the AEDPA alien-terrorist removal procedures, the AEDPA allows the government, at a resident-alien deportation hearing, to present classified information in a summary report without revealing the classified evidence to the alien, while allowing the judge to examine all the evidence (110 Stat. @ 1262–63). In addition to this provision, unlawfully obtained evidence is admissible against the resident alien (110 Stat. @ 1262). The admissibility can help deport a resident alien based on illegally obtained evidence, even though no crime was ever committed.

By denying an alien the right to know all the evidence against him or her, the government is violating a fundamental element of due process, the right to confrontation (Scaperlanda, 1996). Although the resident alien is entitled to an unclassified summary, the alien is still precluded from cross examining the witness. Also, it is unclear how detailed this unclassified summary must be. According to the AEDPA, the judge shall approve the summary if the judge finds that it is sufficient to enable the alien to prepare a defense (110 Stat, @ 1262). The quality of defense has not been addressed. Legal scholars theorized that the defense provided in the AEDPA would not be as "sufficient" as would a defense with full disclosure of evidence. Also, according to legal experts, this issue is examined by the rule of law known as the preponderance of the evidence (8 USCA Sect. 1534 (g)) used by the government.

The Antiterrorism and Effective Death Penalty Act does make one minor allowance by providing legal counsel to any alien who cannot afford legal counsel (Scaperlanda, 1996, p. 29). The provision is allowed because it takes a lot of evidence to defend a resident alien from deportation. In 1977, Judge Friendly wrote an article concerning deportation hearings and what makes them a fair hearing. He stated in the article the following elements needed for a fair hearing:

1. The right to call witnesses
2. The right to know the evidence against one
3. The right to have the decision based on the evidence presented.

These elements are all ranked higher than the right to counsel (Friendly, 1977).

The *Plasencia* three-factor test can be applied to the AEDPA. Factor one is the individual's interest at stake, and the failure to safeguard the individual's interest is undeniably a "great deprivation of liberty" (Rosenfeld, 1995). In *Plasencia,* the Supreme Court described the interest as "without question, a weighty one" (*Plasencia* case, 1982). The high court continued, "She stand to lose the right 'to stay and live and work in this land of freedom'. Further, she may lose the right to rejoin her immediate family, a right that ranks among the interests of the individual" (*Landon v. Plasencia*).

Factor two (risk of error) is great, and the value of additional procedural safeguards is necessary. As we have seen, the provision in AEDPA concerning counsel for the alien when appropriate does not fully compensate for the loss of the right to confront the accuser and the inability to provide the defense necessary against deportation. Scaperlanda wrote that "any student of our immigration history ought to find the prospect of secret immigration proceedings cause for grave concern" (Scaperlanda, 1996, p. 27). Scaperlanda reviewed two 1950s Supreme Court cases involving secret immigration proceedings. His review showed that these secret immigration proceedings were for national security purposes and eventually were found to be baseless or insignificant to national security (Scaperlanda, 1996, pp. 27–28).

The final factor, the governmental interest in maintaining the secrecy of classified information, is strong, but as Scaperlanda (1996) mentions, information does not always end up being as dangerous to national security as originally presented: Concerning the "repeated, excessive deprivations of individual liberty that have been executed in the name of 'national security,' healthy skepticism is called for whatever this interest is invoked by legislators" (Rosenfeld, 1995, p. 747). Therefore, the government's interest in keeping evidence secret from the alien, except in extreme cases, does not outweigh the individual's interests, particularly when coupled with the risk and history of error (Rosenfeld, 1995, pp. 748–49).

As we have seen, these deportation proceedings appear even more unjust when the alien's deportation is based on membership in a designated organization (Public Law No. 104-132 Sect. 411(1)(c)). The AEDPA reinforced the doctrine of guilty by association. This doctrine provides that aliens can now be deported for association with peaceful aims of organization, rather than only be deported for their own illegal conduct (testimony of James X. Dempsey). However, the 1990 Immigration Reform Act repealed this doctrine by allowing deportation only upon a showing of actual participation in terrorist activity (Gray, 1994).

In addition to the problems with the secret evidence provision, the criminal-alien removal provision of the Antiterrorism and Effective Death Penalty Act also contains due process problems. The court case of *Montero v. Cobb* (937 F.Supp. 88,89 n.1, D. Mass., 1996) set out the major changes:

1. It mandates detention of serious criminal alien during the course of their deportation hearing.
2. There is no longer an exception for aliens who establish that they are not a threat to the community and that there is a strong likelihood that they will appear at future hearings (*Montero*, 937 F. Supp. @92 n.5).
3. Prior to 1996 amendment, Section 1225 (a)(2) contained a number of exceptions that had broadened the availability for bond detention hearings (*Montero* @92).

Lastly, aliens have challenged the mandatory detention provision in the form of writ of habeas corpus (*DeMelo v. Cobb* 936 F.Supp 30, D. Mass., 1996). In the case *DeMelo v. Cobb*, the court at first did not make a decision on this case based on the constitutional issues. However, the decision spent a great deal of the opinion discussing the constitutional issues. The court wrote, "[A]pplication of a putative prohibition against any exercise of discretion of the Attorney General to allow DeMelo's release on bond, pending a hearing regarding deportation, raises serious due process issues" (*DeMelo* @34).

CONCLUSION

The course Congress and the President chose in enacting the Antiterrorism and Effective Death Penalty Act was not of a nation of strong, free, secure people but of insecure and frightened people. The response was similar to the early 1900s, when communism was a threat. Due process issues arose from the enactment of the Antiterrorism and Effective Death Penalty Act in 1996. After September 11, 2001, the cry went out again. Congress passed sweeping antiterrorism legislation that again weakens the due process clause of the United States Constitution. Only time will tell if these changes will be effective.

REFERENCES

Annin, Peter, & Morgantthanau, Tom. (1997) The Verdict: Death. *Newsweek,* 40–42.
Antiterrorism and Effective Death Penalty Act of 1996, Public Law No. 104–132.
Barclay v. Florida 463 U.S. 939 (1983).

Barefoot v. Estelle 463 U.S. 880 (1983).

Beall, Jennifer A. (1998). Are We Only Burning Witches? The Antiterrorism and Effective Death Penalty of 1996s Answer to Terror. 73 *Indiana Law Journal,* Spring.

Bigel, Alan. (1997). *Justices William J. Brennan Jr. and Thurgood Marshall on Capital Punishment: Its Constitutionality, Morality, Deterrent Effect and Interpretation by the Court.* New York: University Press of America.

Burbach, Max J. (1991). Prior Criminal Activity and Death Penalty Sentencing: State v. Reeves. *Creighton Law Review,* 24:547.

Clark v. Collins 19 F.3d 959 (5th Cir. 1994).

Cocker v. Georgia 433 U.S. 583 (1977).

Communist Party v. Subversive Activities Control Board 367 U.S. 1 (1961).

Comprehensive Terrorism Prevention Act of 1995. Senate Bill 735, 104th Congress.

DeMelo v. Cobb 936 F. Supp. 30 (D. Mass 1996).

Dennis v. United States 341 U.S. 495 (1951).

Devier v. Zant 3 F.3d 1445 (11th Cir. 1993).

Donahoe, Joel F. (1999) "The Changing Role of Victim Impact Evidence in Capital Cases." Western Criminology Review. Vol. 2 No. 1, pp. 1–35.

Eddings v. Oklahoma 455 U.S. 104 (1982).

18 U.S.C. Section 794.

18 U.S.C. Section 2381.

18 U.S.C. Section 3663 (a)(2).

Eldridge v. Matthews 424 U.S. 319 (1976).

Elias, Robert. (1986). *The Politics of Victimology: Victims, Victimology and Rights.* New York: Oxford University Press.

Espionage Act of 1917. Public Law No.24, ch. 30, 40 Stat. 217.

Federal Death Penalty Act of 1994. Public Law No. 103-322, 60002 (a), 108 Stat. 1796, 1959–82 (1994) Codified as 18 U.S.C. 3591–99.

Friendly, Henry J. (1977). Some Kind of Hearing. *University of Pennsylvania Law Review* 1267.

Furman v. Georgia 408 U.S. 238 (1972).

Gardner, Thomas J. (1989). *Criminal Law Principles and Cases* (4th ed.). New York: West Publishing.

Goldberg, Arthur J. (1973). The Death Penalty and the Supreme Court. *Arizona Law Review,* 15:355.

Gray, Keisha A. (1994). Note, Congressional Proposals to Revive Guilt by Association: An Ineffective Plan to Stop Terrorism. *Georgetown Immigration Law Journal,* 8:227.

Gray v. Thompson 58 F.3d 59 (4th Cir. 1995).

Gregg v Georgia, 428 U.S. 153 (1976).

Hatch v. Oklahoma 58 F.3d 1447 (10th Cir. 1995).

Illegal Immigration Reform and Immigrant Responsibility Act of 1996, Public Law 104–208 Div. C, 1996 U.S.C.C.A.N (110 Stat.) 3009 [1570]. September 30, 1996.

Immigration and Nationality Act of 1952 (McCarran Act) Public Law No. 82–414, June 27, 1952, c. 477, 66 Stat. 163, Title 8 U.S.C. 1101 et. seq. (as amended).

Immigration Reform and Control Act. Public Law 99–603, November 6, 1986, 100 Stat. 3359.

In re Kemmler 136 U.S. 436 (1890).

Kwong Hai Chew v. Colding 344 U.S. 590 (1953).

Landon v. Plasencia 459 U.S. 21 (1982).

Lesko v. Owens 881 F.2d 44 (3rd Cir. 1989).

Long, Katie. (1995). Community Input at Sentencing: Victim's Right or Victim's Revenge? *Boston University Law Review,* 45:1027.

Martin, Thomas C. (1996). Note, The Comprehensive Terrorism Prevention Act of 1995. *Seton Hall Legislative Journal,* 20:201.

Maryland Declaration of Rights Article 16.

Maryland Declaration of Rights Article 25.

McDowell v. Calderon 107 F.3d 1351 (9th Cir. 1997).

Montero v. Cobb 937 F. Supp 88 (D. Mass 1996).

Note. (1996). Blown Away? The Bill of Rights After Oklahoma City. *Harvard Law Review,* 109:2074.

O'Loughlin, Melissa A. (1996). Note, Terrorism: The Problem and the Solution—The Comprehensive Terrorism Prevention Act of 1995. *Journal of Legislation,* 22:103.

Omnibus Counter Terrorism Act of 1995, Senate Bill 390, 104th Congress 1995.

O'Neill v. Vermont 144 U.S. 324 (1892).

Payne v. Tennessee 501 U.S. 808 (1991).

Pulley v. Harris 465 U.S. 37 (1984).

Rohr, Marc. (1991). Communists and the First Amendment: The Shaping of Freedom of Advocacy in the Cold War Era. *San Diego Law Review,* 28:2.

Rosenfeld, Jim. (1995). Note, Deportation Proceedings and Due Process of Law. *Columbia Human Rights Law Review,* 26:713.

Scales v. United States 367 U.S. 203 (1960).

Scaperlanda, Michael. (1996). Are We That Far Gone? Due Process and Secret Deportation Proceedings *Stanford Law & Policy Review,* 7:23.

Schenck v. United States 249 U.S. 47 (1919).

Sedition Act of 1918 Public Law 65-150 Sect. 3.

Simmons v. South Carolina 512 U.S. 154 (1994).

Testimony of James X. Dempsey, Deputy Director, Center of Nation Security Studies before the Senate Judiciary Committee on Terrorism.

Title 21 U.S.C. Section 848(e)–(r).

Trop v. Dulles 356 U.S. 86 (1958).

United States v. McVeigh 153 F.3d 1166 (10th Cir. 1998).

Violent Crime Control and Law Enforcement Act of 1994 (Public Law No. 103–322).

Weems v. United States 217 U.S. 349 (1910).

Wilkerson v. Utah 99 U.S. 130 (1878).

Williams v. Lynaugh 814 F.2d 205 (5th Cir. 1987).

Woodson v. North Carolina 420 U.S. 280 (1976).

Zant v. Stephens 462 U.S. 862 (1983).

part V

Summing Up

chapter 23

Conclusions

Roslyn Muraskin

The former governor of Illinois, George Ryan, ended capital punishment in his state. In the year 2000, Ryan halted all executions after evidence had been discovered that 13 death row inmates had been wrongfully convicted since the resumption of the death penalty in 1973. The power of clemency should be broad enough to allow those in power to look to the sense of justice while reviewing those convicted to die.

According to an article in the *New York Times* (December 29, 2002),

Six years ago this month, it looked as if Eddie Brown would not see another New Year. "It's a miracle I'm still here," he said. . . .

In the early morning of December 17, 1996, Mr. Brown was one of five people ordered to the floor of a Brooklyn social club by a man who announced a robbery. By the time it was over, the robber, Darrel K. Harris, had shot Mr. Brown and two other men in the head and stabbed a woman. Only Mr. Brown survived his wounds. Another man fled without injury.

Mr. Harris, a former New York City jail guard, was convicted of first-degree murder for the three deaths and became the first person in the state sentenced to death since New York reinstated capital punishment in 1995. The jury rejected his lawyers' argument that he should be spared execution because severe psychological problems and cocaine and alcohol abuse had fueled his rampage.

But in July, the state's highest court overturned the death sentence and ordered that Mr. Harris serve life in prison without possible parole. The court found that the law at the time of his 1998 conviction was constitutionally flawed because it threatened a defendant with capital punishment for exercising his right to a trial.

Mr. Brown, now 54, who had been a patron at the social club, *Club Happiness* in Bedford-Stuyvesant [Brooklyn, N.Y.] spoke in recent conversations of the physical, psychological and financial repercussions he struggled with since that horrific morning of shots, screams and carnage.

359

"I still get headaches and I have high blood pressure I didn't have before," he said. "Sometimes I can't walk because of a lot of pain in my leg," which he attributes to his head wound. He has not been able to work since the shooting, he said, and has scraped by on payments from a federal program for the disabled and destitute. Mr. Brown known to his friends as *Shirt Man* had been managing a clothing store when he was shot.

"I used to break down and cry when I heard music on the radio that reminded me of the people who got killed," he said. "Sometimes I'd be driving and have to pull over to the side." Therapy now helps him stave off such bouts of despondency.

As for Mr. Harris, he is a "cold killer," who merits no pity and deserves his punishment, Mr. Brown says. But whether that punishment should have been death is "not my call," he said. "God, the supreme being, judges that" (Fried, 2002, p. 29).

Is justice been served?

And then there are states such as California that have cut their budgets: State subsidies for limbs will no longer be provided for impoverished amputees; welfare payments to the blind are being cut. College students have to pay higher fees. But what emerges untouched is the correctional budget; in fact, in California the correctional budget has seen an increase of $40 million in its $5.3 billion budget, with $220 million allocated for a new death row in San Quentin (NY Times Dec. 29, 2002).

"At a time when two-thirds of the states are facing budget shortfalls, governors are struggling to maintain their costly and overcrowded prisons, a legacy of the get-tough-on-crime climate of the past 25 years. There are over two million inmates, each costing on average more than $22,000.00 a year" (Broder, 2003, p. 5).

Is justice being served?

Prisons are busting state budgets nationwide, but not one governor wants to appear to be soft on crime. Benjamin D. deHaan, "the interim director of the Oregon Department of Corrections, asked the Legislature to close five prisons and release 3,000 prisoners to meet spending targets for the next budget cycle. Oregon's prisons are bursting at the seams because voters in 1994 approved a stiff sentencing system that lengthened the average prison stay to 40 months from 16 months. The state now houses 12,000 prisoners at a cost of $500 million a year" (Broder, 2003, p. 6).

Prisons are being built as quickly as they can be, but the experts state that they cannot keep up with the needs. Critics have stated that governors are neglecting social programs for political reasons and not caring enough about what goes on their respective states.

"'It's outrageous,' said Gloria Romero, a California state senator and the Democratic chairwoman of a new legislative committee on prisons. 'It's easy to slash those program that serve the poor, the elderly, the disabled, children on welfare. They don't have politically powerful lobbyists walking the halls of Sacramento. Why should corrections be the only department that gets and increase, and a significant one at that?'" (Broder, 2003, p. P5).

Total spending on corrections has grown more than 50 percent in the past eight years, as tougher drug laws and mandatory sentencing for repeat offenders have swelled the number of criminals behind bars (see Figure 23–01).

The federal courts have mandated an "end to triple-bunking and ordered the establishment of prison educational and recreational programs in some states. Health care expenses are spiraling, in part because the prison population is growing older. Elsewhere,

States Feel the Pinch of More Prisoners

Total spending on corrections has grown more than 50 percent in the past eight years, as tougher drug laws and mandatory sentencing for repeat offenders have swelled the number of criminals behind bars.

ESTIMATED PERCENTAGE OF STATES GENERAL FUNDS SPENT ON CORRECTIONS FOR 2002 FISCAL YEAR.

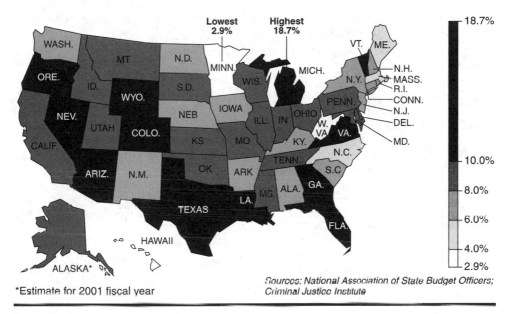

*Estimate for 2001 fiscal year

Sources: National Association of State Budget Officers; Criminal Justice Institute

Figure 23–1

governors are looking for cuts that don't imperil public safety or their political futures. About half the states have cut spending on prisons over the past year and expect further cuts for the coming year" (Broder, 2003, pp. 5–6).

Throughout the country there are other states attempting to revise the tough sentencing laws like mandatory minimums. These laws, which commenced in the 1970s, have seen a sixfold increase in the prison population of today.

"'The state ought not to change criminal penalties or release people early solely out of a concern for cost savings,' said Todd F. Gaziano, director of the Center for Legal and Justice Studies at the Heritage Foundation. 'Laws which unfairly or unjustly incarcerate people ought to be repealed regardless of the budgetary impact. But laws that the citizens demanded to protect them and that justly incarcerate criminals ought not to be touched'" (Broder, 2003, pp. 5–6).

Where, then, does the solution lie: political expedience or questions of justice and safety? In reviewing the chapters in this book, we find that there remain critical issues in the field of corrections today. Are we to imprison all those who are convicted of crimes? How do we treat the offender—do we rehabilitate or incarcerate? What about the sick, the infirm, the disabled who are in prison—what do we do with these inmates? Do we need more religion in correctional settings? How do we use the technology of the twenty-first century to oversee the running of correctional facilities? What are the alternatives to corrections, if any? How do we design correctional facilities and to what purposes? If we review the needs of the females and minorities, in what ways are we treating them or are we? Is justice being served to these inmates on a par with the majority of the prisoners? What about the death sentence? Is it a fair means of punishment? Does the execution of inmates young and old accomplish anything beyond fueling more debate?

How far do we go in the name of justice? Another case points to this very issue:

> Dr. Charles T. Sell, a St. Louis dentist, once spat in the face of a federal magistrate who was deciding whether to revoke his bail on charges of Medicaid fraud. That helped to land him behind bars, and five years later, facing more charges and after a diagnosis of mental illness, Dr. Sell is still locked up awaiting trial.
>
> His situation has posed a question that the Supreme Court has agreed to answer: Can the government forcibly medicate a person charged with a nonviolent crime to make him mentally competent to stand trial?
>
> Psychiatrists say Dr. Sell, who is 53, suffers from a "delusional disorder of the persecutory type." The government wants to give him anti-psychotic medicine so it can prosecute him. Dr. Sell and his lawyers contend that medicating him by force would violate his fundamental right to bodily integrity.
>
> The case of Dr. Sell first came to national attention in early 2001 when John Ashcroft, formerly a senator from Missouri, was seeking confirmation as attorney general and there were reports that as senator, he had once met briefly with Thomas S. Bugel, a friend of Dr. Sell, who was asking the Missouri Congressional delegation to look into accusations Dr. Sell had been abused in prison.
>
> Mr. Bugel contented that Dr. Sell was brutally shackled in a concrete slab for nearly two days in 1999 and deliberately scalded by guards a few months later.
>
> A psychiatrist who was treating Dr. Sell reported that the dentist was staying up night after night, expecting the F.B.I. to "come busting through the door" and that his mental condition was deteriorating. The psychiatrist recommended anti-psychotic medicines, and Dr. Sell was ordered detained (Thomas, 2002, p. A35).

The appeals court has stated that a "mentally incompetent individual will lose his right to refuse medication based solely on the government's unproven assertion that the individual is guilty of a nonviolent crime" (Thomas, 2002, p. A35). Dr. Sell's attorneys have argued that if this decision is allowed to stand, their defendant (and all others) will have lost his right to refuse to be medicated.

Incarceration as stated at the outset has as its purpose to punish the guilty, but at what price? Much criticism has been levied against correctional facilities, as noted throughout this book, but much of what is said is positive and is necessary for us to have the capability to punish where necessary. One question has been around since our system of justice began: Who is best to decide the course of punishment (i.e., incarceration, alternatives, death, or other means)? The expansive growth of today's correctional facilities exemplifies the overwhelming number of individuals being incarcerated (see the appendices). Crime is a large threat to society. While terrorism is a word feared as much as the act itself, but how do we conclude about corrections?

The criminal justice system continues to be in a quandary of being fair and just, meting out fairness, and still punishing the guilty. As noted in this text, corrections as an integral part of the criminal justice system continues to be problematic. If prisons are to rehabilitate, why do we continue to have recidivism? Our sentencing process, complex as it is, does not sentence all those committing crimes on an equal basis. A stereotype exists about inmates and the facilities in which they serve their time. Traditionally, corrections is closed to the outside world. Through this text, it is hoped that a better understanding of the workings of the system emerges. Corrections is a complex component of the justice system. We need to understand the philosophy of punishment and whether the punishment fits the crime.

What happens to inmates who return to the community? Are we concerned about public safety, or has prison time served a purpose? Ever since prisons were built, prisoners have returned to their communities. But as Travis points out in his chapter (see Chapter 6), the idea of returning to a crime-free life was never a realistic prospect. Should we worry about the safety of prisoners inside (i.e., those who commit suicide)? Do prisoners suffer from "pains of imprisonment"? With the sharp decline in the monies devoted to rehabilitation, is it time to turn to the practice of religion in these facilities? Is there an expectation that the reform of an offender includes a change in the spirit? We do not know if religion in correctional facilities is effective. If it does work, then perhaps society on the outside is benefited.

What of those inmates who suffer from mental illness? What does corrections do for them? As indicated, offenders who suffer from mental disorders engage in criminal activities in order to cope with their own conflicts.

What about technocorrections? We are now able to control what occurs inside the correctional facilities through the use of biometric scanning. According to Chapter 10, biometric technology seems tailor-made for the correctional system, which is based on the control of people's movements. But does our system become depersonalized because of the use of such technology?

Are we concerned with prisoners' rights? Judges have been made aware, through litigation, that there are rights that need protection with regard to prison conditions and inmate treatment. But with overcrowding in the facilities, with health concerns, and with aging inmates, how do we afford these inmates the rights to which they are entitled but still maintain the health and security of all involved?

Are there alternatives to imprisonment? Historically, we examine shaming as a punishment imposed on criminal offenders. Today shaming includes stigmatizing publicity, literal stigmatization, self-debasement, and contrition. Is shaming a plausible alternative to incarceration? For some the threat of public rebuke carries little significance, yet should offenders be given the choice of traditional punishment or a shame penalty (see Chapter 12)?

If most Americans fear going to jail, then why do so many commit crimes? Is imprisonment society's worst nightmare or the offender's worst nightmare? Correctional facilities fulfill a purpose: They lock people up and remove them from society. Are there standards that need to be followed in order to have a well-run facility? Is the test whether or not the average citizen could spend any amount of time, even a night, imprisoned and feel safe? Do we really care about the health and well-being of the offenders? Standards are important; correctional facilities cannot be nor should they be dumping grounds.

We have examined the design of correctional facilities. Does the design impact recidivism? Does the design allow for the education of inmates? Is correctional education important to the inmate who will probably return to society? Evaluations of these facilities must be ongoing in order to understand how the inmates cope and how the facilities work.

Specific states appear to treat/punish their inmates more severely than others. Is that good or bad? Women and minorities are imprisoned, and they have special needs. Issues facing these inmates are often overlooked because their numbers are not equal to those of the male prisoners; however, their concerns are legitimate. We are obligated to provide proper services to those who are incarcerated, and to do so takes funding. If we provide the necessary services to those on the inside, perhaps they will not recidivate and will become the citizens they should be. Special needs prisoners, such as those who are deaf, provide other problems not necessarily dealt with in the facilities. When the numbers are small for those needing special services, we tend to look the other way.

And then we have the questions of the death penalty. If it is not a deterrent to crime, why then do we use it? What of those who are exonerated years later? Serious reversible error permeates our death penalty system (see Chapter 21), yet there are over 3500 inmates on death row today. We live in a different world today in the twenty-first century. On September 11, we came under direct attack. There are all kinds of alerts, and there is a place, or so it seems, for the death penalty, when dealing with terrorist acts on our home soil. The Federal Death Penalty Act is based on fear and fright.

Do we lock up all criminals and throw away the key, or is there some other element that we should be examining? The key to correctional issues is understanding that corrections is a fluctuating situation, with no easy answers. No matter what our focus will be, corrections will continue to grow as it has over the decades, but only we can decide the proper direction.

REFERENCES

Broder, J. M. (2003). No Hard Time for Prison Budgets. *New York Times,* January 19, p. 5.

Fried, J. P. (2002). 6 Years After Shootings, a Victim's Pain Persists. *New York Times*, December 29, p. A35.

Thomas, J. (2002). Jailed Man Fights Efforts to Medicate Him for Trial. *New York Times*, December 26, p. A35.

Epilogue

Corrections in the Twenty-First Century: The Numbers

Roslyn Muraskin

The expansive growth of today's correctional facilities exemplifies the overwhelming number of individuals being incarcerated. According to a government report from Washington (2002), "[o]ne in every 32 adults in the United States was behind bars or on probation or parole by the end of 2001. . . . The number of adults under supervision by the criminal justice system rose by 147,000, or 2.3 percent, between 2000 and 2001. . . . In 1990 almost 4.4 million adults were incarcerated or being supervised (U.S. Department of Justice, Bureau of Justice Statistics, "Prisoners in 2001, 07/02 NCJ 195189, www.ojp.usdoj.gov/bjs).

Marc Mauer, assistant director of the Sentencing Project, an advocacy and research group based in Washington, D.C., favors alternatives to incarceration. "Almost 4 million people were on probation, 2.8 percent more than in 2000, while the number of people in prison grew by 1.1 percent to 1.3 million, the smallest annual increase in nearly three decades. More than half of those on probation, 53 percent had been convicted of felonies" (Bureau of Justice Statistics [BJS], Report, 2000). "The report showed a total of 355,400 people in New York State alone under supervision, with 101,800 incarcerated and the rest on probation or parole" (BJS). Some states have begun to eliminate mandatory minimum sentences for certain crimes. The government has found that 46 percent of those individuals who were discharged from parole in 2001 had met the conditions of supervision, while 40 percent were reincarcerated.

We house close to 6 million inmates in both federal and state facilities. In our attempt to control the lives of those incarcerated, people who are guilty of committing from the smallest of offenses to heinous crimes, our correctional system has become a reflection of the moral and political makeup of society in this day and age. The question is, How much control over one's lives do we have and should we have?

Crime is a major threat to our society as a whole. We live in a world where crime is no longer what it was in the twentieth century (i.e., burglaries, rapes, robberies, crimes of arson, homicides, etc., though none of these has disappeared). We are faced with international crimes, crimes of terrorism that affect larger numbers of people than ever before; witness September 11, 2001. This was a day that has affected more lives than any one act of terrorism. Crime affects our lives on a daily basis. Correctional facilities, as quickly as they are being built, are overcrowded and overloaded. Jails, prisons, probation, parole, and alternative programs are part of the larger component of the criminal justice system.

We face a dilemma between being fair and just and meting out fairness, the true meaning of *justice,* in criminal justice and the dilemma of locking them all up and throwing away the key forever or using capital punishment as the end all of punishment.

Corrections is designed both to control and punish offenders. The controlling of offenders satisfies the public, while punishment is acceptable in our present-day society. If we do not use capital punishment for all offenders (and we are the only Western civilization that uses it), then there lies somewhere between control and punishment room for rehabilitation. In the minds of many the latter is not acceptable, while there are those who support a system that does aim to reform offenders. The field of corrections becomes a dichotomy of ideas for both the public at large and those who work within the field of criminal justice.

Corrections in and of itself has become a dynamic and ever-changing field. Crime rates fluctuate depending on the day, the month, the year, and the population, but facilities continue to be overloaded. Alternatives have been suggested but not necessarily with a full heart. The following statistics from the Bureau of Justice are presented to provide a feel of the kind of activity found in today's correctional facilities. These statistics demonstrate the changes found in the field of corrections as the public has brought pressure to bear upon the lawmakers to do something; what this something is becomes debatable. With so many changes in policy, courts continue to be congested, prisons are filled beyond their capacities, with probation and parole officers having a backlog of cases—all this while the cost of corrections has more than tripled in the last decade.

Let us review some trends in the United States so that we might better understand corrections and our criminal justice system.

According to the U.S. Department of Justice, Bureau of Justice Statistics (October 24, 2001),

- The lifetime likelihood of going to state or federal prisons, if recent incarceration rates remain static; an estimated 1 out of every 20 persons (5.1 percent) will serve time in a prison during their lifetime.

- Lifetime chances of a person going to prison are higher for
    Men (9 percent) than for women (1.1 percent)
    Blacks (16.2 percent) and Hispanics (9.4 percent) than for whites (2.5 percent).

- Based on current rates of first incarceration, an estimated 28% of black inmates will enter state or federal prisons during their lifetime, compared to 16 percent of Hispanic males and 4.4 percent of white males.

- With regard to characteristics of state prison inmates,
    Women comprised 5 percent of the state prison inmates in 1991, up from 4% in 1986.

> Sixty-five percent of prison inmates belonged to racial or ethnic minorities in 1991, up from 60 percent in 1986.

- Sixty-eight percent of inmates were under the age of 35 in 1991, down from 73 percent in 1986.

- About 4 percent of state prison inmates were not U.S. citizens.

- Altogether 59 percent of inmates had a high school diploma or its equivalent.

- Two-thirds of inmates were employed during the month before they were arrested for their current offense; over half were employed full time.

- Among the state prison inmates in 1991,
  Fewer than half were sentenced for a violent crime.
  A fourth were sentenced for a property crime.
  About a fifth were sentenced for a drug crime.

By looking at the characteristics of jail inmates, we find the following:

- Women comprised 10 percent of the local jail inmates in 1996, unchanged from 1989.

- Forty-eight percent of jailed women reported having been physically or sexually abused prior to admission; 27 percent had been raped.

- Sixty-three percent of jail inmates belonged to racial or ethnic minorities in 1996, up slightly from 61 percent in 1989.

- Twenty-four percent of jail inmates were between the ages of 35 and 44 in 1996, up from 17 percent in 1989.

- Over a third of all inmates reported some physical or mental disability.

- About 8 percent of local jail inmates were not U.S. citizens.

- Altogether, 59 percent of inmates had a high school diploma or its equivalent.

- Two-thirds of inmates were employed during the month before they were arrested for their current offense; over half were employed full time.

- Among the state prison inmates in 1991,
  Fewer than half were sentenced for a violent crime.
  A fourth were sentenced for a property crime.
  About a fifth were sentenced for a drug crime.

By looking at the characteristics of jail inmates, we find the following to be typical:

- Women comprised 10 percent of the local jail inmates in 1996, unchanged from 1989.

- Forty-eight percent of jailed women reported having been physically or sexually abused prior to admission; 27 percent had been raped.

- Sixty-three percent of jail inmates belonged to racial or ethnic minorities in 1996, up slightly from 61 percent in 1989.

- Twenty-four percent of jail inmates were between the ages of 35 and 44 in 1996, up from 17 percent in 1989.

- Over a third of all inmates reported some physical or mental disability.

- About 8 percent of local jail inmates were not U.S. citizens.

- Altogether, 54 percent had a high school diploma or its equivalent.

- Thirty-six percent of all inmates were not employed during the month before they were arrested for their current offense—20 percent were looking for work; 16 percent were not looking.

- Among the local jail inmates in 1996,
  - A fourth were held for a violent crime.
  - A fourth were held for property crime.
  - About a fifth were held for a drug crime.

- More than 7 of every 10 jail inmates had prior sentences to probation or incarceration.

- A quarter of the jail inmates said they had been treated at some time for a mental or emotional problem.

If we compare federal and state prison inmates, the following is found:

- In 1991, federal inmates were more likely than state inmates to be
  - Women (9 percent vs. 5 percent)
  - Hispanic (28 percent vs. 17 percent)
  - Age 45 or older (22 percent vs. 10 percent)
  - College educated (28 percent vs. 12 percent)
  - Noncitizens (18 percent vs. 4 percent)
  - Employed prior to their arrest (74 percent vs. 67 percent)

- An estimated 58 percent of federal inmates in 1991 and 21 percent of state inmates were serving a sentence for a drug offense; about 17 percent of federal inmates and 47 percent of state inmates were in prison for a violent crime.

- On average, federal inmates were expected to serve almost 6½ year on a sentence of almost 10½ years, and state inmates, 5½ years on a sentence of 12½ years.

Regarding the point of recidivism,

- Of the estimated 108,580 persons released from prisons in 11 states in 1983, an estimated 62.5 percent were rearrested for a felony or a serious misdemeanor within 3 years, while 46.8 percent were reconvicted, and 41.4 percent returned to prison or jail.

Regarding the topic of sex offenders,

- On any given day in 1994 (used as an example), there were approximately 234,000 offenders convicted of rape or sexual assaults under the care, custody, or control of corrections agencies; nearly 60 percent of these sex offenders are under conditional supervision in the community.

- The median age of the victims of imprisoned sexual assaulters was less than 13 years old; the median age of rape victims was about 22 years.

- The median age of the victims of imprisoned sexual assaulters was less than 13 years old; the median age of rape victims was about 22 years.

- An estimated 24 percent of those serving time for rape and 19 percent of those serving time for sexual assault had been on probation or parole at the time of the offense for which they were in state prison in 1991.

Regarding child victimizers,

- Offenders who had been victimized as a child were on average 5 years older than the violent offenders who had committed their crimes against adults. Nearly 25 percent of child victimizers were age 40 or older, but about 10 percent of the inmates with child victims fell into that age group.

Regarding intimate victimizers,

- About 4 in 10 inmates serving time in jail for intimate violence had a criminal justice status (i.e., on probation or parole or under a restraining order) at the time of the violent attack on an intimate.

- About 1 in 4 convicted violent offenders confined in local jails had committed their crime against an intimate; about 7 percent of state prisoners serving time for violence had an intimate victim.

- About half of all offenders convicted of intimate violence and confined in a local jail or a state prison had been drinking at the time of the offense. Jail inmates who had been drinking prior to the intimate violence consumed an average amount of ethanol equivalent to 10 beers.

- About 8 in 10 inmates serving time in state prison for intimate violence had injured or killed their victim.

Concerning use of alcohol by convicted offenders,

- Among the 5.3 million convicted offenders under the jurisdiction of corrections agencies in 1996, nearly 2 million, or about 36 percent, were estimated to have been drinking at the time of the offense. The vast majority, about 1.5 million, of these alcohol-involved offenders were sentenced on supervision in the community: 1.3 million on probation and more than 200,000 on parole.

Regarding women offenders,

- Female prisoner population more than doubled since 1990.

- In 1998, there were an estimated 3.2 million arrests of women, accounting for 22 percent of all arrests that year.

- Based on self-reports of violence, women account for 14 percent of violent offenders, an annual average of about 2.1 million female offenders.

- Women accounted for about 16 percent of all felons convicted in state courts in 1996; 8 percent of convicted violent felons, 23 percent of property felons; and 17 percent of drug felons.

- In 1998 more than 950 women were under correctional supervision, about 1 percent of the U.S. female population (http://www.ojp.usdoj.gov/bjs/crimoff.htm, pp. 1–4, 10/24/01).

Based on a report compiled by the U.S. Department of Justice, Bureau of Justice Statistics in November 2000, it was estimated that 5.7 million adult residents within the United States were under some form of supervision by the Department of Corrections or about 2.8 percent of all adult residents residing in America. Now we are close to 6.6 million. Approximately 7 in 10 were supervised in the community, through probation or parole. About 9.0 percent of black adults, 2.0 percent of white adults, and 1.3 percent of adults of other races were under the supervision of correctional officials.

In statistics from the year 2000, the United States had incarcerated 2,071,686 persons. The federal and state facilities housed 1,312,354 prisoners (excluding state and federal prisoners in local jails). The local jails held an estimated 621,149 adults. Men comprised about 89 percent of adult jail inmates while white non-Hispanic inmates comprised 41 percent of the total jail population; black non-Hispanics, 42 percent; and Hispanics, 16 percent. The rate of incarceration at the end of the year 2000 was 478 inmates sentenced at a rate per 100,000 U.S. residents. About 1 in every 109 men and 1 in every 1695 women were sentenced prisoners under the jurisdiction of state or federal prisons (Beck, BJS, August 2001, p. 1).

As of December 2000, there were 1,312,354 inmates under the custody of state and federal prison authorities. Since the end of 1999 the total incarcerated population has increased by 40,388. This number includes inmates in public and privately operated facilities, as well as the number of inmates in state prisons, which has increased 1.5 percent during 2000; the number in federal prisons, 6.6 percent; and in local jails, 2.5 percent. During the year 2000, the total incarcerated populated grew by 2.1 percent—less than half the annual average (5.3 percent) since 1990 (Beck, 2001, p. 2).

During the year 2000, the United States prison population rose 1.3 percent, which was the smallest amount of annual growth rate since 1972.

As a comparison, approximately 3.3 million adults were on probation at the end of 1997. Probationers made up 57 percent of all adults under correctional supervision in 1997. Twenty-one percent of the probationers were women, a larger proportion than for any other correctional population. About 64 percent of these individuals were white, while 34 percent were black.

Between 1996 and the end of 1997, we find that the number of adults on probation increased by 101,841 (3.2 percent). During the early years of the 1990s, the population of individuals on probation grew by nearly 600,000 people, which is an average of 2.9% annually. About 62 percent of all adults discharged from probation in 1997 had successfully completed their sentences. Nearly 20 percent were incarcerated, with 5 percent under a new sentence and 14 percent serving the save sentence.

Nearly 1.2 million men and women have found themselves in custody. Approximately 94 percent of those incarcerated are males, 48 percent are white; 49 percent are black; while 3 percent includes others (i.e., American Indian, Alaska Native, Asian, or Pacific Islander).

The number of sentenced prisoners under state or federal jurisdictions per a population of 100,000 U.S. residents has increased from the early part of the 1990s to the latter part from 297 to 444 and still rising. Between the years 1990 and 1997, the imprisonment rate of white inmates rose 36 percent from 129 to 189 per 100,000; the rate for blacks increased from 1067 to 1743; while the rate for Hispanics rose 35 percent from 548 to 738 per 100,000.

Among white prisoners, those between the ages of 30 and 34 had the highest incarceration rate at the end of the 1990s: 476 per 100,000 residents. Among blacks, prisoners between the ages of 25 and 29 had the highest rate: 4565 per 100,000. Approximately 62 percent of sentenced inmates entering prison in the latter part of the twentieth century were new court commitments. Just over a third were parole or other conditional release violators, a figure up from 29 percent in the 1990s.

As of December 31, 2000, the number of sentenced prisoners per 100,000 U.S. residents was 478.

> Of the 13 states with rates greater than that for the Nation, 9 were in the South, 2 were in the West and 2 were in the Midwest. Three states—Minnesota (128), Maine (129), and North Dakota (158)—had rates that were less than a third the national rate. The District of Columbia, wholly urban jurisdiction held 971 sentenced prisoners per 100,000 residents. The number of sentenced inmates in the District of Columbia dropped 26% during 2000, as a result of an ongoing transfer of responsibility for sentenced felons to the Federal system.

Between January 1 and December 31 (2000), Idaho and North Dakota experienced the largest increase (up 14.1%) followed by Mississippi (10.9%), Vermont (10.5%), and Iowa (10.0%). Thirteen states and the District of Columbia [for reasons listed above] had the largest decline (down 13.7%), and Texas down (3.2%). Since 1990 the sentenced inmate population in state prisons has grown 72%. During this period 10 states more than doubled their sentenced inmate populations, led by Idaho (up 182%), Texas (up 164%), and West Virginia (up 142%). Between 1990 and 2000 the Federal system reported an increase of 148%—74,641 additional inmates with sentences of more than one year.

> During 2000 the number of women under the jurisdiction of State or Federal prison authorities increased 1.2%, slightly below the increase in the number of men (up 1.2%). At year's end 91,612 women and 1,290,280 men were in State or Federal prisons.
> Since 1990 the annual rate of growth of the female inmate population has averaged 7.6%, higher than the 45.9% average increase in the number of male inmates. While the number of male prisoners has grown 77% since 1990, the number of female prisoners has increased 108%. By year end 2000 women accounted for 6.6% of all prisoners nationwide, up from 5.7% in 1990.
> Relative to their number in the U.S. resident population, men were about 15 times more likely than women to be incarcerated in a State or Federal prison. At year end 2000 there were 59 sentenced female inmates per 100,000 women in the United States compared to 915 sentenced male inmates per 100,000.
> Over a third of all female prisoners were held in the 3 largest jurisdictions: Texas (12,245); California (11,161); and, the Federal system (10,245). Oklahoma (with 138 sentenced female inmates per 100,000 female state residents), Mississippi (105), and Texas and Louisiana (both with 100) had the highest female incarceration rates. Massachusetts (with 7 sentenced female prisoners per 100,000 female residents), Maine (10) and Rhode Island (12) had the lowest incarceration rates.
> Since 1990 the female prisoner population has grown at an annual average rate of at least 10% in 17 States. Texas reported the highest average annual increase in female prisoners (18.7%), followed by Idaho (15.2%), Montana (14.9%), and West Virginia (14.8%). The District of Columbia which transports responsibility of its sentenced felons to the Federal system, was the only jurisdiction to report fewer female prisoners since 1990. However, in 2000 the District of Columbia recorded a 29% increase in the number of female inmates, primarily unsentenced or with sentences of 1 year or less (Beck, 2001, pp. 4–5).

Approximately 334,500 sentenced offenders were admitted as new court commitments to state prisons during the end of the 1990s. As a point of comparison, between the years 1990 and 1997, the number of persons entering state prisons for violent offences increased by 16%. Admissions for public-order offenses were up by 37 percent, while property offenses decreased by 9 percent. The largest number of admissions to state facilities were for drug offenses. There were approximately 39,500 sentenced offenders who were admitted to federal prison; with 46 percent being drug offenders, 27 percent public-order offenders, 20 percent property offenders, and 7 percent being violent offenders.

There were an estimated 690,800 adults on parole by the end of 1997, and among persons released from prison there were about 83 percent who were placed on probation, parole, or some other type of conditional release.

The number of persons who left state facilities based on parole board decisions declined to 28% by year's end. During the same period of time, the number exiting by mandatory release grew from 29 percent to 40 percent of all releases and the number who sentence expired increased from 13 percent to 17 percent. Fewer than 9 in 10 parolees were male. An estimated 54 percent of persons on parole were white; 44 percent black; and 2 percent consisted of other races.

Approximately 334,500 sentenced offenders were admitted as new court commitments to State prisons during the end of the 1990s. As a point of comparison, between the years 1990 and 1997, the number of persons entering State prisons for violent offences increased by 16%. Admissions for pubic-order offenses were up by 37%, while property offenses decreased by 9%. The largest number of admissions to State facilities were for drug offenses. There were approximately 39,500 sentenced offenders who were admitted to Federal prison; with 46 percent being drug offenders, 27% public-order offenders, 20% property offenders, and 7% being violent offenders.

There was an estimated 690,800 adults on parole by the end of 1997 and among persons released from prison there were about 83% who were placed on probation, parole, or some other type of conditional release.

The number of persons who left State facilities based on parole board decisions declined to 28% by year's end. During the same period of time, the number exiting by mandatory release grew from 29% to 40% of all releases and the number whose sentence expired increased from 13% to 17%. Fewer than 9 in 10 parolees were male. An estimated 54% of persons on parole were white; 44% black; and 2% consisted of other races.

By end of 2002, there were 2, 033,333 prisoners held in Federal or State prisons or in local years—the total increased 3.7% from yearend 2001, less than the average annual growth of 3.6% since yearend 1995. In the year 2002, 71 inmates were executed, 5 more than were executed in the year 2001. Of persons under the sentence of death as of 2001, there were 1, 969 white inmates; 1,538 black; 28 American Indian; 33 Asian; and 13 are of unknown race . . .

States executed 69 male prisoners and 2 female prisoners.

Jails, Prisons and a "Potpourri"

To understand who those persons are held in jail facilities, we know that such persons are confined in a facility owned by a county or city. They are confined to a facility that holds the accused for approximately 72 hours or more as opposed to a temporary lockup. If sentenced, or serving a sentence of a year or less, or waiting for transfer to a prison facility or for disposition of charges of a violation, they will be held in the jail.

Persons held in jail facilities are confined in a facility owned by a county or city. They are confined to a facility that holds the accused for approximately 72 hours or more as opposed to a temporary lockup. If sentenced, or serving a sentence of a year or less, or waiting for transfer to a prison facility or for disposition of charges of a violation, they will be held in the jail.

Persons confined to a prison facility are usually confined by the state or by the federal government and are serving a sentence of more than a year except in those states that combine jail and prisons (Alaska, Connecticut, Delaware, Hawaii, Rhode Island, and Vermont).

Those accused of a crime who are on parole or postrelease supervision of some type are released on parole by an executive authority (i.e., Parole Board) or received a sentence initially to postrelease supervision from a judicial authority after serving time in a correctional facility. Such individuals will live unconfined in the community under certain stipulations, and most must fulfill conditional requirements such as holding a job, abstinence from drug use, and keeping away from known criminals while regularly reporting to a parole officer.

If we review those facilities that are privately operated, we find that such facilities held over 87,000 state and federal inmates in 2000. Within these private facilities we saw a population of 5.8 percent of all state prisoners and 10.7% of federal prisoners (Beck, 2001, p. 6).

"Among states, Texas (with 13,985 state inmates housed in private facilities), and Oklahoma (with 6,931) reported the largest number in 2000. Five states—New Mexico (40%), Alaska (33%), Montana (32%), Oklahoma (30%), Hawaii (24%), and Wisconsin (21%)— had at least 20% of their prison population housed in private facilities. Overall 8.3% of state inmates and the South and 5.9% in the West were in privately operated facilities at the end of 2000" (Beck, 2001, p. 6).

Correctional facilities require that there be reserve capacity in order to operate in an efficient manner. "Dormitories and cells need to be maintained and repaired periodically, special housing is needed for protective custody and disciplinary cases, and space may be needed to cope with emergencies" (Beck, 2001, p. 9).

> At year's end 2000, 27 States and the District of Columbia reported that they were operating at or below 99% of their highest capacity. Twenty-one States and the Federal prison system reported operating at 100% or more of their highest capacity. Florida, which is operating at 81% of its highest capacity, reported the lowest percent of capacity occupied. California, operating at 94% over its lowest reported capacity, had the highest percent of capacity occupied.

Based on the *Census of State and Federal Adult Correctional Facilities,* by June 30, 2000, there were 1558 public and private adult correctional facilities housing state prisoners. Additionally, there were 84 federal facilities and 26 private facilities that housed inmates primarily for federal authorities. The census for correctional facilities has increased by 351, up from 1207 in 1990.

The greatest construction of prisons has taken place in Texas. Through the overall construction of new facilities the states have added an additional 528,274 beds. Texas has added 109,975 beds, with California not far behind with an addition of 73,005 beds, Florida with 28,550, and Georgia, 25,812. Together these four states have accounted for nearly 45 percent of the added capacity of state prisons nationwide (Beck, 2001, p. 9).

> Two States, Colorado and Texas, more than tripled their rated capacities. Colorado with the addition of 33 public and private facilities, and Texas, with construction of the State jail system and 84 new facilities, led the Nation in the expansion of capacity. Thirteen other States experienced at least a doubling of their pubic and private prison capacities. Two States—Maine (up 18%) and New York (up 22%)—had increases in rated capacity of less than 25% (Beck, 2001, p. 9).

There were more black males than white males among the state and federal inmates by the end of the year 2000 (see Table E1). According to Beck, "At yearend 2000 black inmates represented an estimated 46% of all inmates with sentences of more than 1 year, while white inmates accounted for 36% and Hispanic inmates, 16%." Furthermore, "Although the total number of sentenced inmates rose sharply (up 77% between 1990 and 2000) there were only small changes in the racial and Hispanic composition of the inmate

Table E1   NUMBER OF BLACK MALES VERSUS WHITE MALES
(STATE AND FEDERAL INMATES)

Percent of Prisoners under State or Federal jurisdiction*

	1990	2000
White	35.6	35.7
Black	44.5	46.2
Hispanic	17.4	16.4
Other	2.5	1.7

*Based on inmates with sentences of more than 1 year. Yearend 2000 counts were based on custody counts of NPS-1A and updated from sentenced jurisdiction counts by gender (Beck, 2001, p. 11).

population. At yearend 2000, black males (572,000) outnumbered white males (436,000) and Hispanic males (206,900) among inmates with sentences of more than 1 year. More than 46% of all sentenced inmates were black inmates" (Beck, 2001, p. 11).

By the year 2000, nearly 10 percent of all black males between the ages of 25 and 29 were incarcerated.

When incarceration rates are estimated separately by age group, black males in their twenties and thirties are found to have high rates relative to other groups. Expressed in terms of percentages, 9.7% of black non-Hispanic males ages 25–29 were in prison in 2000, compared to 2.9% of Hispanic males and about 1.1% of white males in the same age group. Although incarceration rates drop with age, the percentage of black males ages 45 to 54 in prison in 2000 was still nearly 2.7%—only slightly lower than the highest rate (2.9%) among Hispanic males (ages 25 to 29) and more than twice the highest rate (1.2%) among white males (ages 30–34).

Female incarceration rates, though substantially lower than male incarceration rates at every age, reveal similar racial and ethnic disparities. Black non-Hispanics females (with an incarceration rate of 205 per 100,000) were more than 3 times as likely as Hispanic females (60 per 100,000) and 6 times more likely than white non-Hispanic females (34 per 100,000) to be in prison in 2000. These differences among white, black and Hispanic females were consistent across all age groups.

Between 1990 and 1999 the distribution of the four major offense categories—violent, property, drug, and public-order offenses—changed slightly among State prisoners. The percent held for property and drug offenses dropped while the percent held for pubic-order offenses rose. [See Table E2.]

In absolute numbers, an estimated 570,000 inmates in State prison at yearend 1999 were held for violent offense: 161,800 for robbery; 141,400 for murder; 115,100 for assault; and, 109,000 for rape and other sexual assaults. In addition, 245,000 inmates were held for property offenses, 251,200 for drug offenses, and 120,600 for public-order offenses.

Overall, the largest growth in State inmates between 1990 and 1999 was among violent offenders. During the 9 year period, the number of violent offenders grew 254,100.

Table E2	MAJOR OFFENSE CATEGORY	
	Percent of Sentenced State Inmates	
	1990	*1999*
Violent	46	48
Property	25	21
Drug	22	21
Public-order	7	10

As a percentage of the total growth violent offenders accounted for 51% of the growth; drug offenders 20%; property offenders 14%; and, public order offenders 15%.

SOURCES OF GROWTH DIFFER AMONG MEN AND WOMEN AND AMONG WHITE, BLACK AND HISPANIC INMATES

The increasing number of violent offenders accounted for 53% of the total growth among male inmates and 28% among female inmates. Drug offenders accounted for the largest source of the total growth among female inmates (35%), compared to 19% among male inmates. The increasing number of property offenses accounted for a slightly higher percent of the growth among female offenders (21%) than male inmates (13%). Although the number of public-order offenders rose sharply, they accounted for only 15% of the total growth among male inmates and 16% of the growth among female inmates.

The sources of population growth also differed among white, black, and Hispanic prisoners. Overall, the increasing number of drug offenses accounted for 27% of the total growth among black inmates, 15% of the total growth among Hispanic inmates, and 14% of the growth among white inmates. Violent offenders accounted for the largest growth for all groups—among white State inmates (47%), black inmates (50%), and Hispanic inmates (58%) (Beck, 2001, p. 11).

REFERENCES

Beck, U.S. Department of Justice, Bureau of Justice Statistics, October 24, 2001.

Mauer, M. (1999). Race to incarcerate. W.W. Norton & Co. as well as can be found Testimony of Marc Mauer, Assistant Director The Sentencing project Before the Constitution Subcommittee, House Judiciary Committee on *Felony Voter Disenfranchisement,* October 21, 1999.

U.S. Department of Justice, Bureau of Justice Statistics, "Capital Punishment Statistics". (January 8, 2003). *www.ojp.usdoj.gov/bjs/cp.htm.*

U.S. Department of Justice, Bureau of Justice Statistics, "Prison Statistics". August 24, 2003. *www.ojp.usdoj.gob/bjs/prisons.htm.*

U.S. Department of Justice, Bureau of Justice Statistics, "Prisoners in 2001" July 2, 2002, NCJ 195189. *www.ojp.usdoj.gov/bjs.*